TEX_TXET

Studies in Comparative Literature 73

Series Editors
C.C. Barfoot and Theo D'haen

Language Learner Narrative

An Exploration of *Mündigkeit* in Intercultural Literature

Helen O'Sullivan

Amsterdam - New York, NY 2014

Cover picture: Ian Willey

The paper on which this book is printed meets the requirements of 'ISO 9706: 1994, Information and documentation - Paper for documents - Requirements for permanence'.

ISBN: 978-90-420-3785-4
E-Book ISBN: 978-94-012-1034-8
© Editions Rodopi B.V., Amsterdam - New York, NY 2014
Printed in The Netherlands

Contents

Acknowledgements	vii
Chapter One *Mündigkeit* in the Contemporary Context: A Prolegomenon	1
Chapter Two On Language Memoir? A Review of the Secondary Literature	23
Chapter Three Conceptualizing the Language Learner	59
Chapter Four Linguistics and Literature: Methodological Considerations	85
Chapter Five *Mündigkeit* and the Linguistic Construction of the Subject	111
Chapter Six Loss of *Mündigkeit* in Emine Sevgi Özdamar's *Mutter Zunge*	139
Chapter Seven The Use of Language in *Mutter Zunge*	157
Chapter Eight Autonomy Abroad: Metaphors of *Mündigkeit* in Language Learner Narrative	183
Chapter Nine Language Play and *Metamündigkeit* in Language Learner Narrative	211

Chapter Ten
Concluding Thoughts   247

Appendices   257

Bibliography   269

Index   293

Acknowledgements

I would like to thank the Irish Research Council for the Humanities and Social Sciences for giving me the opportunity to complete this research. Deepest thanks to Moray McGowan for enlightening and invigorating discussions, which provoked bursts of inspiration throughout the course of the project. For their words of encouragement and incisive questions at presentations of parts of this thesis, warmest thanks to everyone in the German department. My particular thanks to Sinéad Crowe for moral support in the research process and for very helpful critical advice. Many thanks also to everyone in the Dublin Adult Learning Centre for their interested questions along the way; to many other colleagues and friends who showed critical interest and suggested various useful sources; and to the people at various conferences, workshops and seminars who said with surprise that the project sounded interesting and who offered their own reflections on language learning. Your connection with the issues made the project seem worthwhile. For his painstaking and extremely thorough proof-reading of this manuscript many thanks to Cedric Barfoot. Heartfelt thanks to both Brian and Ann Willey for all your support during the course of this project, and for introducing me to all the wit, wisdom and language play of my mother/father-tongue. A big thank you to Ian Willey for producing several interesting cover designs to fit with this project, including the one used here. Besides welcoming this work as an occasionally difficult guest into our household and giving it a room of its own, my deepest heartfelt thanks to my husband, Conor O'Sullivan, for his invaluable and unwavering belief in this project. This book is dedicated to my son, Austin, who occupied my mind as much as this project while it was being written. He arrived just in time to be acknowledged here and now sets out to develop his own capacity for *Mündigkeit*.

CHAPTER ONE

MÜNDIGKEIT IN THE CONTEMPORARY CONTEXT:
A PROLEGOMENON

Words and thoughts do not emerge out of a vacuum, but are informed by the cultural and linguistic context in which they are produced. This is evident in the language learner narratives explored here, just as it is relevant to the production of this book itself. Nonetheless, there are very often considerable conceptual, thematic and textual similarities between accounts of language learning deriving from very different sociocultural contexts. Here, it is proposed that underlying issues of *Mündigkeit* can be seen as one such commonality. On this basis a version of Kant's Enlightenment use of *Mündigkeit* has been consciously set as a framework within which a variety of stories of language acquisition are examined. This self-conscious positioning of the term at the centre of the following discussion acts as a locus for exploring the tensions arising out of the poststructuralist contestation of the Enlightenment project.

The discourse presented here is shaped to some extent by poststructuralist arguments even as it seeks to find ways in which a variety of language learner narratives might universally permit a reading in terms of *Mündigkeit*. This preliminary chapter sets the discursive context in more detail and introduces interpretations of some of the key concepts and debates that have a bearing on the exploration of *Mündigkeit* in contemporary language learner narrative.

Mündigkeit in the age of postmodernism

"The point of departure must be the text, the whole text, and nothing but the text":[1] this quotation playfully alludes to a shift of focus in the humanities away from the conception of truth and reality as something external to language to be explored and verified through this medium and towards a conception of truth as something which is changeable and changing, embedded in discourse. The quotation parodies the poststructuralist challenge to the Enlightenment search for universal truths. As we have already observed, this text is situated within the context of the discourses that represent this challenge. In examining the experiences of language learners as represented in specific texts hailing from diverse sociohistorical circumstances through the lens of a re-reading of the German concept of *Mündigkeit*, a coincidental effect of the discussion is the exploration of certain issues surrounding the possibility of Enlightenment. In his essay, "Beantwortung der Frage: Was ist Aufklärung?" (1784), Kant declares that possession of *Mündigkeit* constitutes the acquisition of Enlightenment. As Outram emphasizes, this is not, however, to be seen as an end state, but as a process.[2]

This project takes up Kant's use of the term and through careful reanalysis and redefinition argues for a close association between the Kantian concept and linguistic competence, thereby highlighting the relevance of deploying this concept in the analysis of language learner narratives in which the protagonist is struggling to gain linguistic competence in a language first experienced later in life.[3] This interpretive scheme is justified by a thematic and linguistic analysis of the narratives. Furthermore, in these autobiographical texts, distinctions between narrator and author blur, so that the interpretations also potentially lend themselves as evidence in debates surrounding the possibility of *Mündigkeit* in the extra-textual context, particularly where issues concerning how authors make use of language are considered. An examination of authors' linguistic

---
[1] Leon S. Roudiez, Introduction, in Julia Kristeva, *Revolution in Poetic Language*, New York: Columbia University Press, 1974, 8.
[2] Dorinda Outram, *The Enlightenment*, Cambridge: Cambridge University Press, 2005, 2.
[3] Henceforth referred to as a "later experienced language". The use of this phrase is further justified in Chapter Two.

construction of the language learning situation thereby also provides a modest contribution to debates about the possibility of universal concepts.

Another motivation for examining language learners in language learner narratives against the backdrop of *Mündigkeit* stems from perceptions within the primary and secondary literature that language learners in such texts are representatives of poststructuralism who are directly engaging with problems of truth and meaning as they attempt secondary socialization into a new language and culture.[4] This process is considered to necessitate developing the comprehension of a new conceptual framework for interpreting one's environment, as well as a revaluation of self, identity and the other. In the next section, I consider some of the key issues in poststructuralist discourse that contribute to this context of analysis for language learner narratives.

Poststructuralism and the pursuit of meaning
Structuralist ideas about language which had first been developed around the beginning of the twentieth century reached their zenith, as David Macey suggests, at the time of the Johns Hopkins' Conference on *The Languages of Criticism and the Sciences of Man* in October 1966. This was also the time at which Derrida presented a paper entitled "Structure, Sign and Play in the Discourse of the Human Sciences"[5] which may be viewed as marking the beginnings of poststructuralism.[6] In this paper Derrida deconstructs the idea of the centre or transcendental signified, metaphorically described at different times as God or rationality or the unconscious, structuring a system of knowledge. Derrida attributes the beginnings of consciousness of structuration and the development of destructive and deconstructive discourses to the work of Nietzsche, Freud and Heidegger. Within this theory, meaning is not seen as present in the linguistic sign, but as constantly deferred in an endless chain of

---

[4] Cf. Aneta Pavlenko, "Language Learning Memoirs as a Gendered Genre", *Applied Linguistics*, XXII/2 (June 2001), 216.
[5] Jacques Derrida, "La structure, le Signe et le Jeu dans le Discours des Sciences Humaines" in Jacques Derrida, *L'Ecriture et la Différence*, Paris: Editions du Seuil, 1967, 409-428.
[6] David Macey, *The Penguin Dictionary of Critical Theory*, London: Penguin, 2000, 309, 65.

definitions.[7] Consequently, the possibility of discovering certain knowledge about a world external to language is found to be problematic. The linear view of knowledge as represented in the thinking of Kant in which knowledge is considered to progress steadily towards truth is problematized. Within this epistemology, there cannot be one ideology that takes precedence, having proven itself to warrant a greater claim to truth, but only continuous interpretation and reinterpretation in an endless play of difference.

As already mentioned, this project analyses language learner narratives against the background of the discourses of the Enlightenment and poststructuralism. The discourse of Enlightenment is represented in the analysis of the narratives through discussion of the potential for loss and gain of *Mündigkeit* that may be reflected in the narratives. The term is employed as an interpretive tool for analysing both theme and language, making use of insights into how language may structure human subjectivity, as well as being produced by human subjects, and exploring the extent to which linguistic competence, or the lack of it, as well as the confrontation with another culture, may be said to have a bearing on *Mündigkeit*. The justification for viewing language learner narratives through this lens will be provided in detail later on. For the time being, we will consider the extent to which the discourses of poststructuralism and postmodernism are pertinent to the situation of migrants and correspondingly to the analysis of language learner narratives.

In an archetypal language learner narrative by Eva Hoffman, the narrator cites herself as an "avatar of structuralist wisdom".[8] Azade Seyhan in *Writing Outside the Nation* (2001) further notes that "the contemporary tales of migration, exile, and displacement are often seen as mirroring the fragmented consciousness of postmodern culture itself".[9] The term "postmodern" seems to lend itself less to definition than to a range of connotations. In other words, "postmodernism" is associated with a certain eclecticism and mixing of values which lead to the application of the term itself being somewhat fuzzy. In general,

---

[7] Terry Eagleton, *Literary Theory: An Introduction*, Malden: Blackwell, 1996, 111.
[8] Eva Hoffman, *Lost in Translation*, London: Vintage, 1989, 107.
[9] Azade Seyhan, *Writing Outside the Nation*, Princeton and Oxford: Princeton University Press, 2001, 4.

it may be associated with a playful, at times irreverent or ironic, mixing of traditions, styles and genres in art and literature, but a more stable definition can perhaps be found in difference, or in what the term is not. Jean-François Lyotard in *The Postmodern Condition* (1979) describes the postmodern as the passing of belief in grand narratives that may be used to legitimate particular theories of knowledge. Instead, these grand narratives are replaced by "clouds of narrative language elements" each with specific pragmatic valencies:

> Each of us lives at the intersection of many of these. However, we do not necessarily establish stable language combinations, and the properties of the ones we do establish are not necessarily communicable.[10]

Those living in an unfamiliar culture and using a foreign language find themselves dealing with a greater range of ways of making meaning, both in terms of the signs used and how they are used (that is, their specific pragmatic valencies) than monolinguals, and so we may view migrants as key embodiments of postmodern theory and consider the current vast literature on migration and cultural/linguistic displacement to be reflective of postmodern consciousness.

Azade Seyhan, however, makes the point that in fact the very concept of postmodernism arose within a specific sociohistorical context, that of the late twentieth-century Western world, and as such can only lead to insights from within that one particular framework – a framework which may not be relevant to all types of cultural displacement. She argues that it "would be impossible to contain the culturally and temporally diverse articulations of diasporic experience in the postmodern syntax".[11]

However, by discounting postmodernism through citing it as a sociohistorically grounded framework, Seyhan is implicitly acknowledging the dissolution of an absolute perspective from which to conduct enquiry and is in fact (almost inevitably) dismissing postmodernist approaches to migrant literature using the very syntax

---

[10] Jean-François Lyotard, *The Postmodern Condition: A Report on Knowledge*, Manchester: Manchester University Press, 1979, xxiv.
[11] Seyhan, *Writing Outside the Nation*, 4.

she proposes should be dismissed. Given the nature of postmodernism, it is difficult to hold such theories of migration and cultural displacement to apply only to a proportion of cross-cultural experiences, since the theory allows no alternative to the infinite array of alternatives it describes: whether or not postmodernist thought developed within Western Culture, it is a theory that claims to acknowledge all the possible perspectives which may be adopted by any culture under any circumstance. Under this articulation postmodernism appears to instantiate itself as another "grand narrative"; however, the postmodernist perspective is itself necessarily just one perspective within the field it describes. Postmodernism as a set of ideas is part of the discursive system as well as acting as its descriptor: postmodern thought appears both to argue for the decentering of discourses in the human sciences at the same time as placing itself as a discourse at their centre, thereby, necessarily caught up in the metaphysics it seeks to deny. Derrida sets this out as a key problem for a critique of metaphysics in "La Structure, le Signe et le Jeu dans le Discours des Sciences Humaines" (1967):

> *Il n'y a aucun sens* à se passer des concepts de la métaphysique pour ébranler la métaphysique; nous ne disposons d'aucun langage – d'aucune syntaxe et d'aucun lexique – qui soit étranger à cette histoire ; nous ne pouvons énoncer aucune proposition destructrice qui n'ait déjà dû se glisser dans la forme, dans la logique et les postulations implicites de cela même qu'elle voudrait contester.[12]

The following discussion is situated within postmodern discourse and as such, I acknowledge the claim to validity of a variety of perspectives within different sociohistorical traditions. However, this book also proposes to offer contribution to debates about the

---

[12] Derrida, *L'Ecriture et la Différence*, 1967, 412. For the English translation, see "Structure, Sign and Play in the Discourse of the Human Sciences" in *Writing and Difference*, trans. Alan Bass, London: Routledge, 1978, 278-94 (http://hydra.humanities.uci.edu/derrida/sign-play.html): "There is no sense in doing without the concepts of metaphysics in order to attack metaphysics. We have no language – no syntax and no lexicon – which is alien to this history; we cannot utter a single destructive proposition which has not already slipped into the form, the logic and the implicit postulations of precisely what it seeks to contest."

possibility of universal truth and meaning through exploring the ways in which commonalities of experience and understanding may be articulated across apparently diverse texts arising out of different sociohistorical traditions. The following section further explores the interrelationships between text and truth that have a bearing on the approach to the texts taken within this project. The debate about truth is relevant to *Mündigkeit* insofar as its attainment is representative of being an Enlightened human being, possessing the critical reasoning which facilitates the discovery of truth. Problems arise for *Mündigkeit* when problems arise for conceptions of truth, since it is the possibility of discovering truth that justifies and supports reasoning itself. If the possibility of universal truth is questioned, then so is the purpose of reason, and if reason comes under attack, then so does the possibility of *Mündigkeit*.[13]

"The truth, finally, is who can tell it"

Now we turn to consider versions of the truth about "truth" which are relevant to the analysis of language learner narratives, insofar as the proposal of "truth" can be seen as a force or principle against which narrative defines itself – that is as in traditional logocentrism, it is seen as the stable centre around which all other meaning may be said to revolve. This section examines the implications of an understanding of truth as contingent for the fluctuations of *Mündigkeit* suggested to be at work in language learner narratives.

Since the beginning of the search for absolute truths, the very possibility of their discovery has been at issue, since in undertaking rational enquiry there comes a point at which we require criticism of rational thought itself.[14] Postmodernist thought has heightened the sense that the search for absolute truth must be abandoned and must give way to an understanding that truth is contingent. This view of truth is echoed in a comment by the narrator in Chang-Rae Lee's novel, *Native Speaker* (1995), who states "the truth, finally, is who

---

[13] Cultural relativism in which truth is seen as contingent is logically absurd since it allows for A to believe that *p is true* and B to believe that *p is not true* and for there to be no contradiction.

[14] Frederick Beiser, "The Context and Problematic of Post-Kantian Philosophy", in Simon Critchley and William R. Schroeder, *A Companion to Continental Philosophy*, Oxford and Malden, MA: Blackwell, 1999, 23.

can tell it".[15] This statement implies that in fact "truth" is not something which can be objectively determined but is linked to human opinions and human beliefs about who is telling the truth. In this vision, the truth is an oral phenomenon, not written down, but spoken by a particular individual in a particular context. It may be argued that the idea of "absolute truth" could only arise within literate society since it requires an abstraction that does not occur in oral thought.

In his analysis of the differences between "chirographic" cultures and oral cultures Walter J. Ong notes that in oral cultures, "the integrity of the past [is] subordinate to the integrity of the present".[16] He notes how Claude-Lévi Strauss, among others, suggests that orally transmitted myths reflect a society's present cultural values rather than "idle curiosity about the past": genealogies and myths are not fixed, but adapt themselves to the present needs of their society. In oral culture, then, the truth is a narrative told in a particular time and place. Unlike the scientific knowledge that develops in literate societies knowledge contained within oral narrative is legitimated in the fact and circumstance of its utterance not through the factual status of its content. In Lyotard's words: "narrative knowledge does not give priority to the question of its own legitimation ... it certifies itself in the pragmatics of its own transmission without having recourse to argumentation and proof." [17]

The status of oral narrative with regard to truth is exemplified in several language learner narratives. In her collection of essays, *Something to Declare* (1998), Spanish speaker, Julia Alvarez comments on the oral histories that have developed within her family who originated from the Dominican Republic in the Caribbean:

> And so, I grew up hearing that my grandmother was the most beautiful woman on the Island, that my grandfather was so good he peed holy water, that my mother and uncle had a British nanny who

---

[15] Chang-Rae Lee, *Native Speaker*, London: Granta/Penguin, 1995, 6.
[16] Walter J. Ong, *Orality and Literacy: The Technologizing of the World*, London and New York: Routledge, 1996, 48. "Chirographic" is Ong's preferred term for literate societies.
[17] Lyotard, *The Postmodern Condition*, 27.

turned out to have a police record with the Scotland Yard, and so on. In my familia [*sic*], fiction is a form of fact.[18]

A passage from Patrick Chamoiseau's account of his childhood on the Caribbean island of Martinique, part of the French West Indies, suggests even more outrageous possibilities for truth in oral culture. Not only is fiction held to be a form of fact, but the more elaborate and interesting the fiction, the more likely it is to be accepted as fact. Chamoiseau grew up speaking creole and learnt French at school. In the following passage he describes his mother's reaction to him lying to her:

> Mentir à Man Ninotte n'était pas vice possible. Il fallait juste déployer un grand arroi imaginaire pour chatouiller son admiration. Voir son petit se bien débattre avec les artifices de son cerveau était plaisir pour elle: en cas de réussite, elle ne lui reprochait pièce mensonge. Finale de compte: on ne ment que quand on raconte mal.[19]

Ong's account of the development of literacy suggests that it has a profound effect on human thinking which has implications for the concept of "truth". He notes, for example, that formal logic was invented by the Greeks after alphabetic writing had been interiorized. Writing frees up the memory load of the brain and facilitates abstract thought. In this light, it is possible to see the concept of absolute truth as a structuring principle for the processes of rational thought. This means that the concept of truth as something which evolves in the telling of it – the idea, or perhaps more accurately, the ready acceptance of contingent truth that relates to the moment of its enunciation is likely to be less familiar to the writers of language learner narrative. They are, to use Ong's terminology, "chirographic

---

[18] Julia Alvarez, *Something to Declare*, New York: Penguin, 1998, 124.
[19] Patrick Chamoiseau, *Une Enfance Créole: Chemin-d'Ecole*, Barcelona: Editions Gallimard, 1996, 149. For the English translation, see Patrick Chamoiseau, *School Days*, London: Granta, 1998, 106: "Fibbing to Mam Ninotte wasn't considered outright lying. All you had to do was give your imagination enough of a workout to excite her admiration. Seeing her little one putting his very own brain through its paces pleased her no end, and she never reproached him for a tall tale when he managed to bring it off. The bottom line: a story is a lie only if you tell it badly."

folk". As Ong elaborates in his text, this predisposes certain patterns of thinking and attitudes towards language that are uncommon in those who are used to oral culture. In particular, they will be comfortable with interpreting the world according to words and not according to experience.

Ong gives several examples taken from a study by Alexander Romanovich Luria that show how this is not the case in oral culture. When asked to define a tree, a typical response from a non-literate person being interviewed would be: "Why should I? Everyone knows what a tree is, they don't need me telling them."

The presentation of abstract syllogisms unsurprisingly brings further problems. One of Luria's interviewees, a forty-five-year-old manager of a collective farm, who is quoted in Ong, is told that where there is snow, all bears are white and that in Novaya Zembla there is always snow. He is then asked what colour the bears are there, but can only respond concretely, based on his own experience, stating that he does not know, that he has seen black bears but not white ones and that each region has its own animals. He would have to see them in order to know. When he is given the syllogism for a second time, his limited literacy allows him eventually to concede that "to go by your words" they would be white, but for this farmer practical experience still takes precedence in the construction of knowledge.[20]

This distinction between oral and chirographic conceptions of truth suggests that absolute truth can be viewed as a concept engendered by a particular mode of thinking, developed through literacy. The possibility of discovering absolute truth may be viewed as the motivating force behind abstract reasoning, but as Derrida argues, it is not something that can ever be determined.

This proposed instability of truth and meaning also has repercussions for textual analysis. In recent years it has been emphasized that the meaning of written narratives cannot be reduced to the author's intention since we cannot know precisely what an author intended. It may not even be useful to know his/her intentions, since the words themselves may give rise to interesting interpretations the author did not originally anticipate. We are left with an unceasing

---

[20] Ong, *Orality and Literacy*, 52.

vista of possible interpretations and truths about the text. The words as they are written on the page may be fixed and permanent, but their meanings are shifting, not only in relation to one another in an etymological sense, but in relation to their performance at the level of discourse. Each successive generation of readers brings their own context to what they read. The idea of absolute truth may be seen as an illusion arising out of the perceived permanence of the written word. The meaning of a text can only be permanent – in the sense of having an absolute meaning – in the abstract: as soon as it becomes a tool in the action of reading, the unstable nature of the text is revealed and we see that interpretations are potentially limitless. It is worth noting again that this is a poststructuralist analysis of truth, in which "truth" is held to be a linguistic construction not grounded by anything external to language. This conception of language and its relationship to reality is controversial and will be debated further in Chapter Three.

To summarize the discussion so far: firstly, rational thought appears to be something that arises out of chirographic culture and is thus not inherent to language or to human thought, but forms one possible function of these. Secondly, it has been suggested that absolute truth may be an illusion arising out of the apparent fixity of the written word. In oral culture, narratives allow for their changing audience and truth is a function of "who tells it" as well as of the degree of authority to speak attributed to the teller. This authority is not assigned on the basis of capacity for rational argument but on contextual grounds that have to do with relationships between interactants as shown in the example of Chamoiseau gaining his authority through exciting the imagination of his mother. This conception of narrative allows for the meaning of a narrative to evolve along with its readership. It relays a truth that is more narrowly context-bound, one which acknowledges that its truth is not so much an objective fact, as dependent upon the willingness of its hearers to acknowledge its status as truth.

This brief sketch of complex current debates provides a portrait of language as a purveyor of illusory truth or if we accept that some material truths might indeed exist outside of language (as will be discussed in Chapter Three) then at the very least as an inadequate medium for representing truth or truths. Therefore it is suggested that narrative as a purveyor of truth or truths is inherently unreliable, whether or not that narrative is conveyed orally or as a written record. Even if the written record appears to have a fixed meaning, it cannot anticipate all of the interpretations brought to bear upon it by its many readers – it is instable in its reception. However, the oral narrative may shift its meaning both in production and in reception. This instability is inherent to all communication because of the gap between production and reception that allows for a range of other psychological, sociohistorical and immediate technical factors to intrude on the original message.

These problems of communicating meaning are exacerbated in a context where the interlocutors speak different languages. Here the contexts brought to bear upon a received text, whether written or spoken, differ far more widely. What could reasonably be held to be true in one context, appears absurd or unreasonable in another. "Unreasonable" in so far as it does not conform to the conventional logic – and conventional beliefs about truth – of the culture in which that language is spoken. The problem, however, is not simply one of culture, but also of language. Language as a descriptive tool for the environment allows for the formation of an infinite number of concepts. These concepts may be combined in an infinite number of ways. The concepts and the acoustic images applied to them from language to language are largely arbitrary, even if the signs are defined by their relationships to one another within a given language.[21] So they cannot be relied upon to represent reality precisely as it is. As Ong points out: "Nature states no 'facts': these come only within statements devised by human beings to refer to the seamless web of actuality around them."[22]

Instead of representing reality exactly, language can only give a representation of reality founded upon an agreed perception of that same reality which holds in a particular linguistic community. The perception of reality given in the language does not need to accord with the perceptions of every single individual (with his/her individual sense organs) in order for it to function as a convention. In fact, it is this conventional nature of language which gives rise to tensions

---

[21] See Ferdinand de Saussure, *Cours de Linguistique Générale* (1916), Paris: Payot, 2005, 100.
[22] Ong, *Orality and Literacy*, 68.

between the individual and society. Subjective perceptions are subordinated to the labels permitted within a given society for their expression. In accommodating subjective perceptions to the labels provided by society, the speaking subject gains an identity. When confronted with the language and culture of a different society, this identity is destabilized – it must now re-accommodate itself to the labels appropriate within the new context.

Here we will examine this situation through investigating language learner narratives presented in cross-cultural autobiography. The discussion will seek to show how assumed truths about reality and more especially social reality, exist as a function of cultural discourse and may dissolve or explode when different discourses of reality collide. It also seeks to show how the writers have negotiated and interpreted the alternative reality presented by the later experienced language, in the way that they deploy particular linguistic resources and through the narrative presentation of themselves as protagonists in a language learning situation. In particular, it will show how linguistic and poetic devices are used in the representation of language learning experience and what these representations may reveal, at a more fundamental level, about processes of meaning-making. Through the analysis of metaphor the possibility that these texts also reflect common, potentially universal, underlying perceptions of the language learning situation, which do in fact go beyond particular sociolinguistic contexts, will also be explored. However, this exploration of potential universals must be undertaken with the caveat that the suggested text-type examined is limited in its form by the particular sociohistorical contexts in which it has developed. The following paragraphs outline some of the features of language learner narrative which mark it out as distinct.

In examining "language learners" as a general category through the medium of language learner narrative, it must be borne in mind that the many language learners examined in this book are all literate. Furthermore, they are necessarily highly literate, since they are writing literary texts in a foreign language. This cannot be ignored in the analysis: firstly, because it means that all of the writers are at least aware if not necessarily accepting of the idea of meaning or truth as something which is stable and which can be recorded and potentially preserved in written text. Even if the authors may be aware of the concept of truth within oral culture, as shown earlier, this concept is presented as one worthy of comment and in some sense alien to the author.

Another feature of the literate mindset that is distinct from that of members of oral culture is the facility to engage in reflection on the self. Along with difficulties in deriving abstract concepts from concrete life experience, the subjects of Luria's study also presented difficulties in articulate self-analysis. When asked about positive and negative aspects of personal character, one of the people interviewed responds by talking about being married, having children, where he is from and responds to questions about possible areas for self-improvement by discussing material improvements to his farm. Another refuses to talk about his own character, saying that that is something for other people to judge, not him.

The capacity for self-analysis and self-judgement is an implicit assumption underlying all the language learner narratives analysed here. Introspectiveness and the development of the self-conscious mind appear to be associated with the development of literate culture.[23] It is, however, also notable that the peasants in Luria's study were more comfortable talking about "we" than about "I", which suggests that in addition to issues of literacy, there are issues about the collectivist versus individualist conceptions of identity. It is therefore perhaps unsurprising, firstly, that language learner narratives have arisen in a highly literate, more individualistic late twentieth-century Western context, and secondly, that when these authors of language learner narratives were presented with a conflict of cultures that destabilizes the truth assumptions, including truths about themselves, embedded in their first literate culture, they sought a means of re-establishing personal truth and identity through writing. The self of which they were conscious in the first language must be rewritten in the second language. Seyhan, considering a similar set of texts, interprets the writing as providing an alternative space, a third geography, for writers feeling displaced from both their original homeland and their host country.[24]

---

[23] *Ibid.*, 52-54.
[24] Seyhan, *Writing Outside the Nation*, 15.

Leslie Adelson criticizes Seyhan's concept of writers requiring a third geography since it implies that there are necessarily two discrete cultures which are in conflict and in which the migrant is suspended between two worlds. Adelson introduces the trope of "touching tales" as a means to describe the interaction of cultures evidenced in the work of Turkish writers within German culture. It is a concept that allows for the sharing of culture as an "ongoing imaginative project" and stresses "a broad range of common ground, which can be thicker or thinner at some junctures".[25]

Her conception of the relationship between cultures thus moves away from a fetishization of alterity. It is possible that this fetishization is a phenomenon that can be attributed to a Western antithetical mode of thinking. A concern to discover differences as opposed to commonalities is cited by Ong as a key trait of Western rational thought. In discussing oratory and the development of rhetoric, Ong notes how there is a tendency "among the Greeks and their cultural epigoni to maximize oppositions, in the mental as in the extramental world: this by contrast with Indians and Chinese, who programmatically minimized them".[26]

Along the same lines, it could furthermore be argued that some of the modern problems experienced in relation to language and identity are tied to an emphasis on concepts of nationhood and that, at least within a western context, problems of alterity or otherness are exacerbated through a tendency to "maximize oppositions".[27] It is also possible that the problem of selfhood encountered in the foreign culture is not so much a result of having to adapt oneself to a new culture, but of having possessed a more highly conscious sense of self in the first culture to begin with, engendered to a large extent by literacy.

Furthermore, the possibility must be entertained that the crises surrounding identity expressed through interest in issues of language

---

[25] Leslie Adelson, *The Turkish Turn in Contemporary German Literature*, New York: Palgrave MacMillan, 2005, 20. Reproduced with permission of Palgrave Macmillan.
[26] Ong, *Orality and Literacy*, 111.
[27] See Aneta Pavlenko, "The Making of an American: Negotiation of Identities at the Turn of the Twentieth Century", in Aneta Pavlenko and Adrian Blackledge, *Negotiation of Identities in Multilingual Contexts*, Clevedon: Multilingual Matters, 2004, 34-67.

is a product of individualistic thought in which differences between individuals and cultures are emphasized rather than minimized. As part of this process of differentiation, language is seen to be the key medium for identifying oneself, especially since the development of the nation state that has, to a large extent, tied linguistic identity to cultural identity. In such a context learning a different language is more strongly associated with a requirement to adopt a different cultural identity with all the issues of language and other apparent psychological ramifications of this to which the language learner narratives under discussion provide testimony.

Evidence for this comes from Pavlenko's analysis of early twentieth-century immigrant autobiography that arose out of a wave of migration to the United States. Pavlenko discovers that whereas the earlier migrants quickly learned English (most often described as taking a matter of months) and assimilated to the requisite "All-American" image, more recent migrants find that the transition takes much longer and produces greater anxiety. This, in itself, cannot be taken as evidence that linguistic anxiety did not exist for early twentieth-century immigrants to the US. It may be a question of what constituted appropriate discourse at the time and which aspects of the self were felt to be permissible to present in writing. At the same time, the concerns about language expressed in contemporary language learner narratives themselves may come to be exaggerated on the basis of prevailing discourses of the individual which lay down expectations as to the experience of being a language learner in an unfamiliar culture. In both situations we are confronted with a chicken and egg scenario arising out of the complexities surrounding the extent to which language shapes both social and individual reality. Is the early twentieth-century discourse evidence of a lack of linguistic anxiety or a mask with which to hide these concerns? Does the supposed anxiety disappear if no one talks about it? Is it a phenomenon external to language upon which discourse can have no influence, or is it perhaps a phenomenon influenced by discourse but by which it is nonetheless never fully supplanted? These complex connections between reality, the social construction of reality, the construction of social realities through the medium of language and the impact of this on individual subjectivity reverberates throughout this book.

In the following chapters, the possibility that the textual phenomenon of linguistic anxiety evident in many of these narratives might be interpreted on the basis of a loss of *Mündigkeit* will be explored. Through this trope of "loss of *Mündigkeit*", the experiences of language learners documented in these texts are viewed as a microcosm of contemporary postmodern discourse in which the Enlightenment project is subject to question. As a counter discourse to this postmodern framework, the texts are also analysed for the commonalities that appear to extend across diverse sociohistorical contexts. Already, the grouping of these texts within a genre would appear to belie the theme of alienation and Otherness which forms the implicit basis of many of these narratives, since the texts appear in fact to be united to each other in their recounting of common human passions and experiences, both in the narrator's relationships with others and in the narrator's relationship with language and the world through language.

Overview of chapters
The next chapter of this book provides an overview of current research into texts variously called language biography, language learner memoir and cross-cultural autobiography (among other appellations) that overlap with the proposed genre of language learner narrative. In the main, the chapter re-examines Alice Kaplan's proposal of "language memoir" as a genre and considers possible criteria for distinguishing texts that fit into the proposed genre. The discussion of the plethora of genre labels that have sprung up to describe similar texts is used as a basis for dispensing with genre in this context. Using Derrida's essay "The Law of Genre" (1980) as a springboard, "language learner narrative" is proposed as an alternative designation not restricted by the traditional conception of what constitutes a text. The category of language learner narrative differs somewhat from the previous genres with which the texts have been associated, in that it is an overarching term not just for complete published texts but also for sections of texts. These texts are grouped according to the specific situations and themes to which the signifiers in those texts make reference.

The third and fourth chapters present both a theoretical contextualization of the following study as well as the semiotic and stylistic methods of textual analysis employed. The third chapter reviews some of the key ideas about the relationship between language and reality that are presented in social semiotics as exemplified in the work of M.A.K. Halliday, Robert Hodge, Gunther Kress and Jay Lemke on which Fowler's work partially builds but which also permits an understanding of the complex relationships between text, context and society particularly pertinent to a reading of language learner narratives. This debate is also pursued in a brief overview of current thinking about the relationship between language and thought as well as the structure of concepts in the bilingual mind. This brief outline of objective research into bilingualism is not comprehensive, but aims to provide some background to how the subjective perceptions of the protagonists in language learner narratives may be understood.

Following this, the fourth chapter presents the methodological approach to the text predominantly grounded in the work of Roger Fowler's *Linguistic Criticism* (1986). In line with Fowler's thinking, the aim is not to present a systematic textual analysis machine which feeds in a text at one end and comes out with an interpretation at the other. Rather, the subjective input of the critic is kept in awareness, and the linguistic tools are employed as appears relevant to the text in question. This avoids the problem of trying to make the analysis fit the linguistic theory rather than allowing the relationship between text and reader to take precedence. This chapter presents some of the key ideas from linguistics that have been applied to the analysis of literary texts and describes the work of some of the literary and linguistic schools which have developed these ideas, insofar as these are relevant to the analysis of language learner narratives. The subsequent section of this chapter further justifies the use of a linguistic critical analysis through refuting some of the common arguments made against semiotic approaches to textual criticism as summarized by Daniel Chandler. The final section of Chapter Four outlines how the role of the critic is to be conceived of within the linguistic critical analysis of language learner narratives through introducing the concept of "interscription".

The fifth chapter of the book forms a discussion of the framework for critical analysis and interpretation that will be applied to the texts. In particular, it focuses on a redefinition of Kant's concept of

Mündigkeit as it is to be employed for the purposes of this literary analysis. Firstly, it is argued that *Mündigkeit* can be defined in relation to linguistic competence and furthermore shows how the problematic issue of expressing *Mündigkeit* may be productively interpreted in relation to Pierre Bourdieu's concepts of linguistic capital and symbolic power. This analysis makes *Mündigkeit* a highly relevant conceptual tool in the examination of the processes of language acquisition represented in language learner narratives. The first section of this chapter shows that *Mündigkeit* may be defined as a decision to use critical reason independently and that critical reason is inherently bound up with linguistic competence. The second section argues that independent critical reason is problematic given the fact that language, which forms the basis for this linguistic competence, is a social phenomenon. The final section argues that living in an unfamiliar culture can be shown to destabilize *Mündigkeit* because of several interrelated factors, including the loss of linguistic capital in the foreign context; the fact that those who experienced the language early may act as *Vormund* and may in some cases also infantilize the speaker who has experienced the language later in life for the first time; and the fact that using the foreign language involves the deployment of a different conceptual framework in critical reasoning.

Chapters Six and Seven apply the reworked concept of *Mündigkeit* within the analysis of a text by Emine Sevgi Özdamar, *Mutter Zunge* (1998), and shows how Özdamar's text provides an almost archetypal example of *loss* of *Mündigkeit* within the foreign culture. This is exemplified both in the theme of the text, which concerns a love affair that develops between the protagonist and her teacher of Arabic, leading to the protagonist's loss of reason, and in the language of the text in which the coupling of signifiers reflects an increasingly ambiguous sense of identity. Following Haines and Littler's suggestion that "the elemental imagery points to the legacy of Ottoman literature in Özdamar's work",[28] the analysis also engages with the recurrent symbols used in the text such as "death", "the soul", "love", "the rose" and "the nightingale", which can also be found in

---

[28] Brigid Haines and Margaret Littler, *Contemporary Women's Writing in German: Changing the Subject*, Oxford and New York: Oxford University Press, 2004, 128, 133.

Ottoman Divan poetry and further suggests what this might reveal about *Mündigkeit*.

Chapter Six analyses the general plot and themes of the narrative without focusing in great detail on the language used. This analysis shows how the themes of the narrative can be shown to reflect the narrator's loss of *Mündigkeit*, in particular through the narrator's voluntary imprisonment in the *Schriftzimmer* and in the love affair that develops between the protagonist and her teacher of Arabic script. The second section provides evidence from the language of the text in order to show that the textual form also reflects a loss of *Mündigkeit*, in particular through lack of linguistic competence and through the degradation of language in which meanings are increasingly shifting and not fixed.

The eighth chapter argues that an analysis of the metaphors used in language learner narratives reveals that a subjective experience of "loss of *Mündigkeit*" can be identified in a wide range of texts hailing from diverse sociohistorical contexts. The metaphors are grouped according to underlying conceptual metaphors for which the theory was developed by George Lakoff and Mark Johnson. A loss of *Mündigkeit* is said to be reflected in metaphors that articulate a loss of the sense of self, a loss of independence and the subjective experience of being infantilized. It is furthermore debated whether or not these common metaphors can be said to function to create an abstract society of language learners in which the language learners, apparently engaged in lonely individualistic struggles, in fact inhabit the discourse of language learner narrative. This is not at the level of linguistic form (that is, the exponents of this discourse may vary), but at a more fundamental and potentially universal conceptual level.

In this chapter the various metaphors used in language learner narratives are analysed and it is suggested that some of these metaphors are based on an underlying conceptual metaphor that can be seen to be relevant to more than one of the texts. In particular, this chapter considers metaphors relating to three key themes concerned with the self, language and society. The first consideration is how the self is perceived through metaphors relating to the body and to clothing. The second consideration is how the relationship to the foreign language and the possibility of making meaning in the foreign culture is perceived and the third involves metaphors of infantilization and entrapment that relate to the loss of social and symbolic capital. The proposed underlying conceptual metaphors which relate to these themes are: THE FOREIGN LANGUAGE IS A HUMAN BEING; THE FOREIGN CULTURE IS A TRAP; THE FOREIGN CULTURE IS A PLAY; THE FOREIGN LANGUAGE IS A COSTUME AND THE NON-FLUENT SPEAKER IS A CHILD.[29]

Chapter Nine presents two alternative arguments. Firstly, it questions the classic view that learning a foreign language necessarily always broadens the mind and places speakers in an advantageous position from which they can maintain a productive external perspective upon two cultures, a kind of *Hypermündigkeit* in which a person can fit into more than one culture. It is proposed as an alternative that contact with the foreign language and culture may result in a destabilized relationship to language, which is exemplified by increased focus on the signifier over the signified in a variety of forms of language play. This language play may function in two ways. Firstly, it may reveal a dissolution of the power to create meaning which could be described as *Untermündigkeit* or *Mündligkeit* (from *Mündel*). This language play involves an irrational logic by association and a tolerance for ambiguity that may be considered to represent a diminution of reason. Secondly, this chapter proposes that language play may alternatively represent, not a demonstration of loss of *Mündigkeit*, but a conscious strategy aiming to redress the balance of power between *Mündel* and *Vormund* by, for example, defamiliarizing the language for speakers well versed in the standard forms. In this analysis language play can be seen as a demonstration of linguistic competence that aims at development into or the generation of novel linguistic capital. However, in a paradoxical fashion, regaining *Mündigkeit* in this way frequently involves the same process as losing *Mündigkeit*, that is a descent into semiosis where meanings are shifting and not fixed, where the distinction between conscious manipulation and unwilled eruption of semiotic resources into the symbolic may not always be clear. This semi-controlled manipulation of language can be seen as a process of *Metamündigkeit*, which involves a refusal of resocialization into a new

---

[29] Small block capitals is the convention used by Lakoff and Johnson to indicate conceptual metaphor.

language and culture exemplified by the creation of meanings that transcend existing languages and cultures. *Metamündigkeit* is held to be an alternative to loss of *Mündigkeit*, which can reveal a process of novel integration of the semiotic resources of more than one culture.

The final chapter presents a variety of suggestions for future research into related topics. In addition to this, the key discussions are summarized and a conclusion is offered about the extent to which Kant's term *Mündigkeit* may be productively re-read and used as a critical tool for the analysis of texts that represent the experience of language learners and how this analysis of language learner narratives can reciprocally tell us something about *Mündigkeit*.

CHAPTER TWO

ON LANGUAGE MEMOIR?
A REVIEW OF THE SECONDARY LITERATURE

> ... as soon as genre announces itself, one must respect a norm, one must not cross a line of demarcation, one must not risk impurity, anomaly, or monstrosity.[1]

In her 1994 essay "On language memoir" Alice Kaplan describes a genre of texts she uncovered while seeking to find out more about the subjective experience of learning a foreign tongue. Disappointed by the accounts she found in research from the fields of linguistics, sociology and education she turned to fiction and discovered "an entire genre of twentieth-century autobiographical writing which is in essence about language learning. But it has never been categorized or named as such, either because it is discussed in terms of the history of a specific ethnic or national literature, or because language is understood in these books as mere décor in a drama of upward mobility or exile." In her article, she then suggests that these texts constitute a genre of their own which she labels "language memoir".

Under Kaplan's original somewhat problematic definition of the genre, the second language was not only foreign but could include discourses within the mother tongue such as "a new dialect, a language of upward mobility, a language of power or expressivity within the native language".[2] In SLA research[3] the genre label refers, however, primarily to texts dealing with the development of competence in a second or foreign language. Furthermore, while it cannot be disputed there are many texts that fit the criteria relevant to

---

[1] Jacques Derrida and Avital Ronell, "The Law of Genre", *Critical Inquiry*, VII/1 (Autumn 1980), 57.
[2] Alice Kaplan, "On Language Memoir", in *Displacements: Cultural Identities in Question*, ed. Angelika Bammer, Bloomington: Indiana University Press, 1994, 59.
[3] Henceforth the standard abbreviation SLA will be used for Second Language Acquisition.

this classification, there are too many commonalities between these texts and other quite dissimilar genres and text types. A more workable approach to the texts Kaplan describes, along with the related texts discovered by other researchers, is to make broad reference to "language learner narrative". This designation may be applied to whole texts or sections of texts and has the advantage that it may easily be further qualified. One can then refer, for example, to semi-fictional or semi-autobiographical language learner narrative and to language learner narrative in poetry, travel writing or SLA research. Additionally, the term is not restricted to autobiographical texts.

This chapter therefore acts as a review of the current literature on texts fitting Kaplan's proposed genre, but given its comparative newness and the lack of research pertaining to it, the chapter also engages critically with existing secondary literature to redefine the category in a more clear and consistent way. The chapter begins by re-evaluating "language memoir" and its supporting criteria, before describing texts suggested to be exponents of the genre and setting these within their sociohistorical contexts.

Deconstructing language memoir

While the term "language memoir" appears convenient – there must, after all, have been some textual similarities motivating the initial use of the term – it is unsatisfactory in several ways as reflected in the plethora of genre labels used in the secondary literature to refer to the same or similar texts. For convenience of reference, these labels are also tabulated in Appendix I.

Firstly, as previously noted, the texts mooted for inclusion are very diverse. In the disciplines of literary studies and SLA very often different labels are applied to the same or similar texts or the same or similar labels are applied to texts that much differ, both stylistically and as objects of research. These labels include: language (learning) memoir, language learner narrative, language biography, language (learning) autobiography, migrant autobiography and cross-cultural autobiography.

We begin by discussing terms used in SLA. Following this, we look in more detail at Kaplan's definition of language memoir and terms used by other researchers such as Mary Besemeres who has written on a range of cross-cultural autobiographies from a literary theoretical perspective. Unless specifically wishing to refer to a genre label employed in a particular researcher's work, where possible the discussion will refer more neutrally and more broadly to "accounts of learning a foreign language". This refers to texts of any style or genre, containing content specifically describing the subjective experience of acquiring a foreign language. The main focus is nonetheless on autobiographical and semi-autobiographical texts that thematize language learning experiences and not on what Steven Kellman terms "translingual texts" (texts written in a language learnt after childhood), though there are certainly texts that represent both categories.[4]

Over the latter half of the twentieth century there has been a rising interest in qualitative studies of second language learning processes. Beginning in the 1970s, SLA began making use of learner diaries. These offered a means to understand the affective side of language learning, the strategies that students employed and their perceptions about their acquisition. Phil Benson and David Nunan point out that this kind of research is usually limited to a short period of time, perhaps a year or less, during which the subjects record their acquisition process. Benson and Nunan cite the limited duration of these studies as the reason attention has shifted in recent years to recollection as a means of exploring longer-term experiences in more authentic settings. Particular interest has been shown in memoirs from beyond the SLA literature.[5]

As data for sociological research these texts remain controversial since many of them are literary constructions and cannot be considered objective accounts of language learning processes. This point is also emphasized by Daniela Fritz in her 2001 unpublished dissertation in which she considers the fictional representation of three language learners in literary texts by Franz Kafka (*Ein Bericht für eine Akademie*, 1919), Peter Handke (*Kaspar*, 1967) and Christa Wolf

---

[4] Steven Kellman, *The Translingual Imagination*, Lincoln and London: University of Nebraska Press, 2000. Kellman provides a highly comprehensive overview of the broader phenomenon of "translingual" texts. Along with Eva Hoffman's *Lost in Translation* (1989) and Richard Rodriguez' *Hunger of Memory* (1982), he is concerned with literary and philosophical texts of all kind by authors such as Rosa Ausländer, Joseph Conrad, Samuel Beckett, Ursula Hegi, Catherine the Great, Seneca, Anton Shammas and George Steiner – just eight of the names featuring in Kellman's roster of just over two hundred translingual authors from a variety of epochs and locations. His list is by no means definitive.

[5] *Learners' Stories: Difference and Diversity in Language Learning*, eds Phil Benson and David Nunan, Cambridge: Cambridge University Press, 2004, 12-13.

(*Kassandra*, 1983).[6] Fritz is concerned with texts which happen to contain accounts of language learning, rather than with a designated genre.

Even those texts not ostensibly literary must still be examined as textual constructions subject to the vagaries of memory and desired self-representation.[7] Aneta Pavlenko argues specifically against the simplistic use of language memoirs as ethnographic data in an article from 2001. There, she makes the case for sociohistoric, sociocultural and rhetorical analyses of these texts, on the basis that sociohistorical contexts shape the narratives produced by the learners. She argues that such memoirs must be approached "as discursive constructions, rather than as factual statements".[8] Pavlenko, along with Benson and Nunan, refers to these texts as "language learning memoirs", though again Pavlenko's terminology shifts between this descriptor and those of "language memoir" and "second language learning memoirs" among others.[9] It is also worth noting that Pavlenko describes the category of language learning memoir in terms of a genre of American cross-cultural autobiography, thereby restricting it to a narrowly defined geographical context.

Even if the literary accounts of language learning are considered inappropriate sociological research data, interest in them within SLA has prompted moves to use autobiographical material in foreign language pedagogy and to have students themselves write "learning histories". These are used for discussion in the classroom and to

---

[6] Daniela Fritz, "Language Socialization, Communicative Competence and Identity: Literary Representations of the Language Learner in Twentieth-Century German Literature", Berkeley, University of California, 2001 (unpublished dissertation). The important distinction between the literary text and ethnographic data for the purposes of social science research is also emphasized by the chair of Fritz's doctoral committee, Claire Kramsch in *The Multilingual Subject*, Oxford: Oxford University Press, 2009, 73.

[7] Cf. Jerome Bruner, *Acts of Meaning*, Cambridge, MA: Harvard University Press, 1990.

[8] Pavlenko, "Language Learning Memoirs as a Gendered Genre", 214 (Pavlenko takes the term "language memoir" from Kaplan, "On Language Memoir").

[9] In her article Aneta Pavlenko provides a very detailed list of "language learning memoirs" in which are included some of the "language memoirs" of Kaplan. Frequently cited texts are Eva Hoffman's *Lost in Translation* (1989) and Richard Rodriguez' *Hunger of Memory* (1982).

introduce students to successful models of language learning.[10] Benson and Nunan also cite a number of other uses for these accounts including use in research concerned with learning strategies, second language literacy, motivation, autonomy, self-directed learning, bilingual parenting, and the experiences of "newcoming" speakers[11] as learners and teachers. To add a further complication to the terminology, these "learning histories" are referred to by Benson and Nunan as "language-learning autobiographies" and in other research as "language biographies".[12]

The latter term is one also used in the European Language Portfolio (ELP), a record of individual linguistic skills developed between 1998 and 2000 by the Language Policy Division of the Council of Europe in Strasbourg. It aims to promote the development of plurilingualism and pluriculturalism.[13] In the ELP the term "language biography" more specifically refers not to learner reports gathered for the purpose of research into SLA, but to reflective reports created by learners in order to further their own linguistic and intercultural competence. The term is used in a generally consistent way, translated into French as *biographie langagière* and into German as *Sprachbiographie*.[14]

From this discussion it would seem that there is a reasonable divide between "language memoirs" conceived of as literary accounts, usually written by published authors of other literary fiction and non-fiction and "language biographies" conceived of as informal reports

---

[10] See *Learners' Stories*, for a list of relevant studies. See also Kramsch, *The Multilingual Subject*.

[11] See the section "Native/non-native and the intercultural speaker" in the next chapter for discussion of this term.

[12] Britta Korth, "Analyzing Language Biographies: Concepts of Language and Language Learning", University of Basel, Unpublished Report, 2001 (www.eric.ed.gov:80/PDFS/ED462000.pdf); Jiří Nekvapil, "Language Biographies and the Analysis of Language Situations: On the Life of the German Community in the Czech Republic", *International Journal of the Sociology of Language*, CLXII (July 2003), 63-83.

[13] For further details, see David Little and Radka Perclová, *European Language Portfolio Guide for Teachers and Teacher Trainers*, Strasbourg: Council of Europe, 2001 and http://www.coe.int/portfolio.

[14] See, for example, *Leben mit Mehreren Sprachen – Vivre avec Plusieurs Langues: Sprachbiographien – Biographies Langagières*, eds Rita Franceschini and Johanna Miecznikowski, Bern: Peter Lang, 2004.

written by non-professional writers, primarily used as ethnographic data in SLA research.[15]

This convenient dichotomous typology is, however, again complicated by the existence of alternative descriptions. In a doctoral dissertation from 2004, Linda Steinman cites the following variant names for accounts of learning a foreign language: language autobiographies, language narratives, life histories, autoethnographies, life narratives and testimonios. Many of these could also refer to a range of literary autobiographies that have nothing to do with narrating the experience of learning a foreign language. Steinman herself also refers to "autobiographical accounts of acculturation" and "language learner accounts" but prefers the term, "language learner narrative", which she defines as "published accounts authored by those who have lived and learned in a new language and a new culture".[16] She is not concerned with justifying the use of the more literary accounts as ethnographic data, but is willing to accept her subjective experience of the verisimilitude of the accounts for the purposes of her research.[17]

Furthermore it must be noted that Steinman's term "language learner narrative" is broader than that of "language memoir" since she uses it to refer both to longer more literary accounts of language learning and also to shorter published essays such as the anthology by Karen Ogulnick, *Language Crossings* (2000). The longer literary accounts she refers to include Eva Hoffman's *Lost in Translation* (1989), which is also included in Kaplan's definition of "language memoir", whereas the essays in *Language Crossings* are of a quite different nature and might more readily be categorized as a form of "language biography". By using the term "language learner narrative" Steinman can refer to a range of texts treating the theme of learning a foreign language though stylistically quite different. However, even with Steinman's professed awareness of the distinction between

---

[15] Texts are naturally not always approached from one position or the other. Alison Phipps in *Learning the Arts of Linguistic Survival: Languaging, Tourism, Life* (2007) uses extracts from her own reflections on learning languages as a tourist as a counterpoint to a theoretical discussion of the topic of tourist language learners. These extracts are also unique for their focus on the language learning context of tourists rather than on migrants.

[16] Linda Steinman, "Language Learner Narratives: Bridges to SLA Literature and SLA Pedagogy", University of Toronto, 2004 (unpublished doctoral dissertation), 2.

[17] *Ibid.*, 10.

personal narratives and observational research,[18] the risk remains that the texts are used uncritically, without awareness of their literary construction.

If the use of these texts in SLA research has provoked a degree of controversy,[19] such literary accounts of language learning are of more uncontroversial and evident interest to those outside of linguistics. Besides Alice Kaplan, who is a Professor of Romance Studies, Literature and History at Duke University, Mary Besemeres writes from a literary theoretical perspective about texts dealing with highly similar issues, including two Kaplan has categorized as language memoir.[20] Besemeres, however, refers to her subject of interest as "cross-cultural autobiography".[21] This term, while applicable in many cases to texts Kaplan refers to with "language memoir",[22] allows for the potential inclusion of a broader spectrum of texts. This potential is made clear in Pavlenko, who cites cross-cultural autobiography as a coverall term for immigrant autobiographies – "memoirs written by first generation immigrants who arrived to the target language country as teenagers or as adults and who discuss both the country of their birth and their new culture", ethnic autobiographies – "immigrant memoirs as well as narratives of those who arrived to the New World as children or were born and grew up in ethnic neighbourhoods" and "any other narrative exploring transitions and interactions between cultures, whether written by a member of both cultures or not, such as narratives written by temporary expatriates and visitors".[23] We see here how the distinctions between text genres start to hinge on complex definitions of nationality and strained similarities drawn between different childhood experiences and accounts of those experiences.[24] This arguably works in favour of using a broader term

---

[18] *Ibid.*, 6.
[19] Cf. Claire Kramsch, "The Multilingual Experience: Insights from Language Memoirs", *Transit*, I/1 (2005), 2 (http://escholarship.org/uc/item/9h79g172).
[20] These are the texts by Eva Hoffman (1989) and Richard Rodriguez (1982).
[21] In Mary Besemeres, *Translating One's Self: Language and Selfhood in Cross Cultural Autobiography*, Oxford: Peter Lang, 2002, Besemeres illustrates precisely Aneta Pavlenko's comments in "Language Learning Memoirs as a Gendered Genre", 216, about the postmodern concern with language as "the main site of world and identity construction".
[22] *Ibid.*, 64: in fact Besemeres cites Kaplan's use of this term.
[23] Pavlenko, "Language Learning Memoirs as a Gendered Genre", 215.
[24] See Gérard Genette, "Genres, 'Types', Modes" in *Poétique*, XXXII (November 1977), 408: "L'histoire de la théorie des genres est toute marquée de ces schémas

like "cross-cultural autobiography" as Besemeres herself does. However, for our own purposes, this term does not emphasize experiences of language learning.

In an article published three years later, Besemeres uses a different terminology. In this article she makes a subtle distinction between "memoirs of language immersion" (implying a brief stay abroad) and "memoirs of language migration" (implying an extended stay abroad). The latter term she uses with reference to Eva Hoffman's *Lost in Translation*, the text cited most frequently as an example of the genre of language memoir.[25] Besemeres states that she considers "memoirs of language immersion" to be related to "memoirs of language migration" though she argues in her article for the former's inclusion as a subgenre of travel writing. The difference between these two types of memoir is otherwise weakly articulated, since both are concerned with what Besemeres describes as "focus on the experience of learning another language as a foreigner and cultural outsider – and translating the self in the process".[26] It is also unclear whether through stating that memoirs of language immersion are "related to" memoirs of language migration Besemeres views these texts (comparable to language memoirs) and memoirs of language immersion as two subcategories of the genre travel writing (see figure 1) or if only memoirs of language immersion belong to the category of travel writing with memoirs of language migration forming a genre of their own (see figure 2):

---

fascinants qui informent et déforment la réalité souvent hétéroclite du champ littéraire et prétendent découvrir un 'système' naturel là où ils construisent une symétrie factice à grand renfort de fausses fenêtres." This is also cited in a translation of Derrida's article "The Law of Genre" as follows "The history of genre-theory is strewn with these fascinating outlines that *inform and deform reality*, a reality often heterogenous to the literary field, and that claim to discover a natural 'system' wherein they construct a factitious symmetry heavily reinforced by fake windows" (Jacques Derrida and Avital Ronell, "The Law of Genre", *Critical Enquiry*, VII/1 [Autumn 1980], 55-81). What this brief quotation does not show is that Genette goes on to assert the utility of such temporary schemas.

[25] See, for example, Kaplan, "On Language Memoir"; Pavlenko, "Language Learning Memoirs as Gendered Genre"; Kramsch, "The Multilingual Experience: Insights from Language Memoirs".

[26] Mary Besemeres, "Anglos Abroad: Memoirs of Immersion in a Foreign Language", *Biography*, XXVIII/1 (Winter 2005), 28.

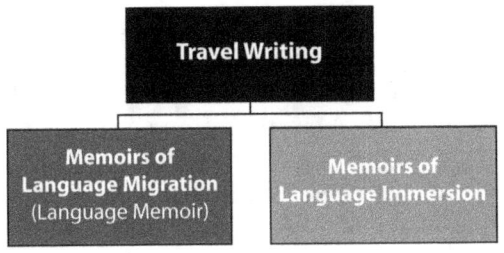

Figure 1

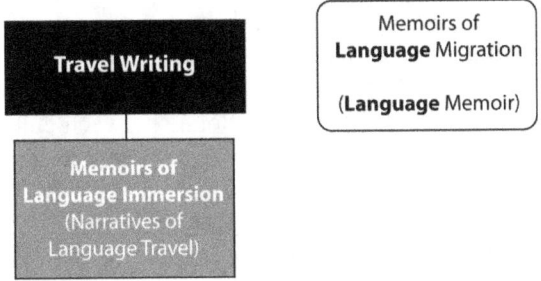

Figure 2

Again, this lack of clarity results in a somewhat fluid terminology for these types of texts further heightened by the use of stylistic variants: later in the article Besemeres refers to "narratives of language immersion", "narratives of linguistic and cultural immersion" and "narratives of language travel" the first two of which could clearly apply to Hoffman's text as well as other texts that would fall into the category of language memoir as previously described. Furthermore, in Besemeres' article all of the terms she uses refer to extended literary texts such as those described in Kaplan's article, rather than shorter essays and published texts resembling rather the learner diaries used in second language acquisition research, such as Ogulnick's anthology, *Language Crossings* (2000) and Ogulnick's own account of learning Japanese, *Onna Rashiku: Like a Woman* (1998).

The following discussion considers the possibility of defining language memoir in relation to a protagonist's level of engagement with the foreign culture and will serve to highlight the difficulties of assigning a genre classification to these texts.

Besemeres begins by stating that much travel writing is written by monolingual outsiders visiting a foreign culture, who do not necessarily learn the foreign language, but report back on the culture to their compatriots with an outsider's perspective in one of their first languages. In this sense, she suggests that traditional travel writing might be viewed as more "monologic" in structure and that the monolingual perspective is "likely to limit cross-cultural vision in some significant ways".[27] Even where a dialogue between the two cultures emerges in the text, as Besemeres states, "the dialogue can be an unequal one, with the authority of the author's cultural assumptions exposed briefly to question before being firmly reasserted over those of the speakers of the other language".[28] Besemeres uses her discussion of three texts to argue against an extreme cultural and linguistic determinism and to highlight that dialogue between cultures is possible within a monolingual text. She aims to show that writers such as Sarah Turnbull in *Almost French* (2005) and Peter Hessler in *River Town* (2001) manage to write against the discourses of their own culture and succeed in articulating the perspective of the culture they are immersed in. The emphasis on cultural immersion is one factor that links these "travel writing" texts with so-called "language memoir". Following Besemeres, a higher level of engagement with the foreign culture is supposedly seen in both text types, thus contrasting these with the monologic travel writing Besemeres deplores.

If language memoirs might distinguish themselves through a higher level of engagement with the foreign culture, this must be more narrowly defined. If, for instance, the fact of a narrative being written in the foreign language rather than the mother tongue can be said to constitute high engagement, then not all of the texts discussed by Kaplan show engagement to this degree. Kaplan's own memoir *French Lessons* is written in her first tongue, English.[29] This does not therefore constitute a useful criterion for distinguishing narratives of language travel/immersion from narratives of language migration. Perhaps language memoirs can alternatively be identified through *integration* into the foreign culture. In most cases the learner is staying

---

[27] *Ibid.*, 29.
[28] *Ibid.*, 30.
[29] Alice Kaplan, *French Lessons*, Chicago and London: University of Chicago Press, 1993.

in the foreign country either by force or by choice for an indefinite period of time, whereas in narratives of language travel the period of stay is for the most part temporary – this is at least the case with the Hessler text that Besemeres analyses.

One might also expect a greater degree of introspection about the process of self-development within the foreign culture in language memoir than in travel writing. In this sense language memoirs are, as Kaplan suggests, perhaps closer to the genre of *Bildungsroman* whereas travel writing may resemble more of a report about external events and people rather than focussing on the development of one narrative protagonist.[30] However, this again does not in the end help to distinguish language memoir from Besemeres' "narratives of language travel" since the criticism of one's own cultural assumptions that she considers vital to this genre necessarily implies a higher level of introspection than is found in traditional travel writing. The problems with distinguishing narratives of language immersion/travel from traditional travel writing on the one hand and from language memoirs (narratives of language migration) on the other will now be demonstrated on the basis of examples from the two texts Besemeres discusses.

Besemeres begins by analysing an account written by Sarah Turnbull, *Almost French* (2005), in her first language, English, that describes her encounters with French culture. In this text, the relationship between the author and her French partner allows for a dialogue to emerge between the cultures in which the couple are both enlightened about their own cultures through each other's alternative perspectives. There are aspects of this text that relate it more closely to language memoir despite it having been written in the native language: the protagonist lives in the foreign culture for an indefinite period of time, attempting to integrate and relating her introspections about that experience in a dialogic way.

One aspect of the text that might go against this analysis is that Turnbull's introspections concern culture more so than language. Nevertheless, she at times produces a vivid and down-to-earth description of her sense of invisibility in the foreign culture and the lack of cultural and linguistic capital on her part that contribute to this.[31] Even if she does not write a great deal about problems of

---

[30] Cf. Kaplan, "On Language Memoir", 69.
[31] See Chapter Five for further discussion of Bourdieu.

language and translation, there are many examples in the text, some quoted by Besemeres, in which she openly reveals her lack of pragmatic and cultural competence. Turnbull says the wrong thing at the wrong time,[32] finds herself ignored for unknown reasons,[33] and, as her partner points out to her, is about to cause unwitting offence to the baker by entering the shop in a tracksuit.[34] Besemeres also cites Turnbull's description of a cocktail party in which she valiantly but unsuccessfully attempts to break the ice with a French couple by "filling the silences with embarrassingly inane remarks".[35] Besemeres considers that this passage captures the "diversity of social worlds" in a dialogic way: "The comically one-sided conversation reveals to Turnbull gradually not only that 'the rules' for conversation might be different in the new context, but that getting to know others at a party is not, for the couple she approaches, the self-evident good that it is for her."[36]

However, despite these more reflective passages, there are other passages which, as Besemeres highlights, read as generalizations and broad-brush stereotypes from an ethnocentric perspective. This often involves a poorly veiled derision of French culture:

> Althought toilet humour is considered poor taste in France, sex-related witticisms are acceptable in virtually any social setting. Sustaining linguistic volleys of naughty innuendo is a national sport. Sometimes these word games are subtle and sophisticated. But often the banter is ribald and silly ...[37]

> But as everyone knows from Proust's legendary page-long sentences, the French language doesn't lend itself to concision. Its beauty lies in the fluid rhythms of musical, meandering passages which express a multitude of possibilities and doubts before reaching any conclusion. Oblique messages are revered as subtle and sophisticated whereas direct language is considered too blunt – an appropriate writing style for a robot but not for an erudite human being.[38]

---

[32] Sarah Turnbull, *Almost French: A New Life in Paris*, London and Boston: Nicholas Brealey, 2005, 63.
[33] *Ibid.*, 68.
[34] *Ibid.*, 130.
[35] *Ibid.*, 63.
[36] Besemeres, "Anglos Abroad", 31.
[37] Turnbull, *Almost French*, 53.
[38] *Ibid.*, 84.

Turnbull's text wavers between monologic travel writing and a more dialogical approach to the implicated cultures that might validate the text for inclusion in a subgenre of language memoir including texts that deal with more brief periods of cultural and linguistic immersion in adulthood. If the criterion of "level of engagement" is set up for determining language memoir then the assignment of this text to the category hinges on the extent to which Turnbull can be deemed to engage self-critically with French culture. Besemeres acknowledges the essentialism of some of Turnbull's descriptions which she likens to "the style and spirit of satirical travel guide-books like the 'Xenophobe' series".[39] Yet Besemeres also considers the retrospective accounts of some of the "critical incidents" in intercultural communication that Turnbull describes as being more evidently dialogical in nature, involving a greater insight into both Australian and French perspectives on the same situation. On this basis it would be very difficult to determine if Turnbull truly does engage with the foreign culture in a non-ethnocentric way. It suggests that the text may in fact represent a transition or interplay of cultural values and assumptions that is at times monologic and at others dialogic.

The second text that Besemeres considers is *River Town: Two Years on the Yangtze* (2001), by Peter Hessler, in which the American author describes his experience of working in Fuling in the province of Sichuan in China, teaching English literature as a Peace Corps volunteer. Again, this text is potentially a prime candidate for a subgenre of language memoir, since it deals not with an indefinite period of stay but a briefer period of linguistic immersion. Although the text is written in English, the author makes an effort to learn Mandarin and there is evidence of critiquing his own cultural assumptions. For example, his own perspective on Chinese culture is defamiliarized by the reports of his students on how he and his American colleague appear to them. Besemeres quotes the following example of an essay written by a student entitled "Why Americans are so Casual":

> I'm a Chinese. As we all know, the Chinese nation is a rather conservative nation. So many of us have conservative thinking in some degree. I don't know whether it is bad or good.

---

[39] Besemeres, "Anglos Abroad", 30.

> Our foreign language teachers – Peter and Adam – came to teach us this term. It provides a good opportunity of understanding the American way of life. In my opinion, they are more casual than us Chinese people. Why do I think so? I'll give you some facts to explain this.
>
> For example, when Mr. Hessler is having class, he can scratch himself casually without paying attention to what others may say. He dresses up casually, usually with his belt dropping and dangling. But, to tell you the truth, it isn't considered a good manner in China, especially in old people's eyes. In my opinion, I think it is very natural.[40]

This short description by the Chinese student is reminiscent of descriptions in Swift's *Gulliver's Travels* (2001) cited by Fowler as an example of defamiliarization:

> At last I beheld several Animals in a Field, and one or two of the same kind sitting in Trees. Their Shape was very singular, and deformed, which a little discomposed me, so that I lay down behind a Thicket to observe them better .... Their Heads and Breasts were covered with a thick Hair, some frizzled and others lank; they had Beards like Goats, and a long ridge of Hair down their Backs, and the fore-parts of their Legs and Feet, but the rest of their Bodies were bare, so that I might see their Skins, which were of a brown buff Colour. They had no Tails, nor any Hair at all on their Buttocks, except about the *Anus*; which, I presume Nature has placed there to defend them as they sat on the Ground; for this Posture they used, as well as lying down, and often stood on their hind Feet .... The Hair of both Sexes was of several Colours, brown, red, black, yellow. Upon the whole, I never beheld in all my Travels so disagreeable an Animal, or one against which I naturally conceived so strong an Antipathy.[41]

That the teacher can "scratch himself casually", has his belt "dropping and dangling" and this is all seen as "very natural" suggests indirectly that the American appears to the Chinese as some kind of uncivilized animal or ape. At the very least the two teachers are presented as if they were animals being observed in a zoo, thus the inclusion of this

---

[40] Peter Hessler, *River Town: Two Years on the Yangtze*, New York: HarperCollins, 2001, 36. This lengthier excerpt than that given in Fowler is taken from Jonathan Swift, *Gulliver's Travels*, London: Penguin, 2001, 205.
[41] Roger Fowler, *Linguistic Criticism*, Oxford: Oxford University Press, 1986, 43.

extract might suggest that the author is willing to set up his own culture for criticism by members of the foreign culture.

Much later in the text, Hessler also appears to unashamedly caricature himself and how he might appear to the Chinese by describing an imaginary Chinese self called "Ho Wei", the name Hessler has been given by his Chinese friends and acquaintances:

> Ho Wei was completely different from my American self: he was friendlier, he was eager to talk with anybody, and he took great pleasure in even the most inane conversations. In a simple way he was funny; by saying a few words in the local dialect he could be endlessly entertaining to the people in Fuling. Also Ho Wei was stupid, which was what I liked the most about him. He spoke with an accent; he had lousy grammar; and he laughed at the simple mistakes that he made. People were comfortable with somebody that stupid, and they found it easy to talk with Ho Wei, even though they often had to say things twice or write new words in his notebook.[42]

Here we are confronted with a description that might be interpreted in one of two ways. Firstly, it could be interpreted as a self-ironizing description which attempts to view the author through the eyes of the Other; secondly, in parodying this version of himself and suggesting that this foolish oriental persona had appeal for other Chinese people, an alternative reading is hinted at, in which there is a subtle mockery of the Chinese Other.

The examples from these texts suggest that more so than a willingness to engage self-critically with the foreign culture they reveal the difficulty of engaging with a foreign culture in a manner that involves a genuine leap out of an ethnocentric perspective. Variation between excerpts also highlights that such a willingness may not be absolute but may either develop in the course of the narrative or be subject to the general fluctuations of daily social contacts in which a desire to open up and engage with the Other can vary from context to context.

The difficulty with evaluating the level of critical engagement with the foreign culture also problematizes defining genre in terms of a criterion that focuses on the protagonist's cultural perspective, which in this brief analysis is revealed to be exceedingly slippery. The

---

[42] Hessler, *River Town*, 238-39.

following section evaluates whether or not language memoir could be more accurately defined through considering the type of language learning experience described in the texts. Following this, the proposed genre of "language memoir" is subject to further question within the context of Jacques Derrida's problematization of the concept of genre as a whole.

Questioning the genre
In an article written in 2005 entitled "The Multilingual Subject", Claire Kramsch first wrote about language memoir and cited some texts commonly included within this genre such as those by Hoffman, Rodriguez, Dorfman and Huston as well as less commonly cited texts such as Jacques Derrida's *Le Monolinguisme de l'autre* (1996) and Elias Canetti's *Die Gerettete Zunge* (1989). Furthermore, without clearly defining how she differentiates these texts from language memoir Kramsch also cites a few texts as examples of "reflective accounts of multiple language use". These include Yoko Tawada's *Überseezungen* (2006) and *Talisman* (1996) and Christine Brooke-Rose's *Between* (1968). The inclusion of these less commonly cited texts within the category further troubles the validity of the term language memoir. Canetti's *Die Gerettete Zunge* (1989) is by no means widely known and/or read specifically as a "language memoir" but as an autobiography.[43] The text becomes a language memoir in retrospect and we see its genre classification changed in response to a new historical context.[44]

---

[43] Richard H. Lawson, *Understanding Elias Canetti*, Columbia: University of South Carolina, 1991; Walter H. Sokel, "The Love Affair with the Mother Tongue: On the Relation Between Autobiography and Novel in Elias Canetti", *Germanic Review*, LXXVIII/1 (Winter 2003), 39-48; Waltraud Wietholter, "Sprechen-Lesen-Schreiben: Zur Funktion von Sprache und Schrift in Canettis Autobiographie", *Deutsche Vierteljahrsschrift für Literaturwissenschaft und Geistesgeschichte*, LXIV/1 (March 1990), 149-71.

[44] Boris Tomashevsky, "Literary Genres", in *Russian Poetics in Translation* 5, eds Lawrence O'Toole and Ann Shukman, Colchester: Department of Language and Linguistics, University of Essex, 1978, 55, is cited on this in David Bordwell, *Making Meaning: Inference and Rhetoric on the Interpretation of Cinema*, Cambridge, MA and London: Harvard University Press, 1989, 147: "no firm logical classification of genres is possible. Their demarcation is always historical, that is to say, it is correct only for a specific moment of history; apart from this they are demarcated by many features at once, and the markers of one genre may be quite different in kind from the markers of another genre and logically they may not exclude one another, only being

The genre label "language memoir", rather than being a useful categorization for a collection of texts which previously did not fit under any other adequate description, appears to broaden itself in various directions until it encompasses such a huge diversity of texts that it becomes effectively meaningless. In addition, setting up the genre term risks a perceptual bias in the analysis of texts, thus predisposing the discovery of such memoirs wherever we choose to look for them. This argument is lent further weight by the fact that Kaplan herself invented the designation after purposefully searching for texts that contained narratives about learning a language. She admits herself that the more she looked the more texts she found, so that nearly every text appeared in the end in some way to be about learning language.[45]

Beyond the slippery criterion of "level of engagement" with the foreign culture dealt with in the earlier analysis of Besemere's article, are there then any necessary and sufficient criteria that could mark a text as being a language memoir? Could the genre be determined, for example, on the basis of more concrete criteria, such as the following? Firstly, the text contains passages relating the experience of learning a foreign language; secondly, the protagonist is identified to a large extent with the author of the text (that is, the text is in some sense autobiographical); thirdly, the protagonist lives in the foreign country for an indefinite period of time; fourthly, the protagonist is fully immersed in the foreign culture and comes to criticize his/her own cultural assumptions because of it.

In her doctoral dissertation Steinman includes the qualification that at least 20% of any given text must be narrative about learning a foreign language. It would be very satisfying to be able to test the texts against these criteria and include or exclude them from the genre on this basis, but what of the marginal cases? With other more qualitative criteria it is also extremely difficult to determine whether or not they have been fulfilled, that is how do we know if the protagonist has come to criticize his/her own cultural assumptions – on what criteria do we deem this criterion itself to be covered? The arbitrary designation of language memoir in cases where the learner is in the foreign culture for an indefinite period of time is also to a large

---

cultivated in different genres because of the natural connection of compositional devices."
[45] Kaplan, "On Language Memoir", 64.

extent nonsensical: even if a person has been in a foreign country for many years, we can never know for certain that s/he will not return home. One might as well ask, how many years constitute an indefinite period of time? Again, this is a nonsensical categorization, since the number of years a learner has been in a country is no absolute marker of the level of integration that has taken place. It is perfectly possible for him or her to have been entirely living in a linguistic and cultural ghetto and not learnt a single foreign word.

The inadequacy of set criteria for defining language memoir highlights the general arbitrariness of genre categorizations. As previously indicated, a genre might best be seen as a non-natural category that at a particular moment in history appears useful. In an era when postmodern theories call into question the nature of human subjectivity "language memoir" now appears historically useful and we find the neophyte genre universalizing itself as it reaches out from the texts of our time to encompass texts of the past and to suggest texts of the future. Pavlenko has called Eva Hoffman's autobiography a response "par excellence" to the postmodernist call and so the text has taken its place at the head of a postmodern genre.[46] With this new found category in mind Kramsch is able to appropriate *Die Gerettete Zunge* (1989) as a "language memoir" in retrospect, Kaplan is able to situate her own memoir within a family of texts, and researchers in SLA are able to turn to a set of texts for qualitative analysis. The genre label "language memoir" is perhaps both useful and meaningless. It is useful as a rough data-gathering framework; it is meaningless insofar as it can appropriate texts previously assigned to other genres. There are indeed so many texts that sit uncomfortably on the margins of this genre and in fact very few that sit neatly within it. The following brief examination of the contexts of language learner narratives give an idea of the diverse, at times highly idiosyncratic, acquisition contexts within which these narratives are produced.

The contexts of language learner narratives
The conditions in which further languages are acquired naturally prove to be as complex and varied as the life histories of the individuals acquiring them. In the case of bilinguals and multilinguals, it may not even be clear which language was the first spoken. In the introduction to his autobiography *Out of Place* (1999), Edward Said

---

[46] Pavlenko, "Language Learning Memoirs as Gendered Genre", 217.

describes Arabic as his first language and English as that of his education.[47] This may be correct in socio-political terms, but Said's personal relationship to these tongues is somewhat different:

> I have never known what language I spoke first, Arabic or English, or which one was really mine beyond any doubt. What I do know, however, is that the two have always been together in my life, one resonating in the other, sometimes ironically, sometimes nostalgically, most often each correcting, and commenting on, the other. Each can seem like my absolutely first language, but neither is. I trace this primal instability back to my mother, whom I remember speaking to me in both English and Arabic ...[48]

Kellman also notes that both Vladimir Nabokov and George Steiner claim to have been reared equally in three different languages.[49]

This suggests that if the criteria for selecting texts is too heavily guarded, being restricted only to texts written in a foreign language, describing the acquisition of an unfamiliar tongue in a foreign country in adulthood, then not only might there be very few exponents of this context, but also a good many insightful discussions of processes of language learning may be unduly excluded from the analysis.

Possible texts have been found variously through references in secondary literature on language memoir and cross-cultural autobiography, recommendations by friends and colleagues and through serendipity. The most extensive lists of texts are provided by Alice Kaplan, who cites both French and English texts, and Aneta Pavlenko, who cites the texts as language learning memoirs and autobiographic essays and provides examples in English only. A full list of all the texts discovered that are potentially relevant to this category is included in Appendix II, listed by date of publication. This listing by date shows that autobiographical publications revealing a more deliberate focus on issues of language acquisition are more common from the 1990s up to the present moment, with the most explicit focus, in the form of thematically edited collections, revealed in the most recent publications such as Wendy Lesser's *The Genius of*

---

[47] Edward Said, *Out of Place: A Memoir*, London: Granta Books, 1999, xv.
[48] *Ibid.*, 4.
[49] Kellman, *The Translingual Imagination*, 3.

Language and Mary Besemeres' and Anna Wierzbicka's *Translating Lives: Living with Two Languages and Cultures.*[50]

The current list is by no means comprehensive, but, quite on the contrary, is continually expanding. It must also be noted that in grouping together this great variety of texts of varying degrees of literary quality and ambition, there is no intention, from a literary perspective, to treat these texts as somehow second-rate. As far as possible, value judgements have been suspended in grouping together these texts – they are there for the presence of language learner narrative and are examined for the way in which the language learning situation has been textually conveyed, no matter how expressively or matter-of-factly language has been used in doing so.

The contexts for these texts can be divided into subgroups according to a wide variety of types of migration, including both temporary and more extended visits to a foreign country. A variety of social contexts of language acquisition are also represented. These can be divided into roughly four categories: first, narratives written in a foreign language about permanent immigration into a foreign culture; second, narratives of growing up with more than one language, particularly making a distinction between a family language and a second official language that might be spoken at school; third, narratives written in a first experienced language (or in the foreign language) about a brief period of time spent abroad; fourth, narratives written in the first language about acquiring a particular discourse of that language, such as literary discourse.

The French language in colonial contexts

At times, the contexts of migration and language learning in which the protagonists have participated can be related to wider societal patterns of migration and economic forces, such as the relationship of former French and British colonies to France and Britain or the vast migration of individuals to the USA during the twentieth-century. Patrick Chamoiseau's *Une Enfance Créole: Chemin d'école* (1996) fits into the French colonial context as does Jacques Derrida's *Le Monolinguisme de l'autre*. The latter text is a partly philosophical and partly autobiographical text. Derrida describes not only the issue of

---

[50] Mary Besemeres and Anna Wierzbicka, *Translating Lives: Living with Two Languages and Cultures*, Queensland: University of Queensland Press, 2007. *The Genius of Language*, ed. Wendy Lesser, New York: Anchor Books, 2004.

learning the language of a foreign nation, but also the problems that arise when the language possessing greatest currency within one's own nation is not that which one has spoken since birth. Derrida describes the colonized nation's idealization of the colonizing language and nation and points out that this idealization also extends to some extent to minorities within that same nation. In the case of France, this would describe speakers of Breton:

> Pour le petit Provençal ou le petit Breton, il y a bien sûr un phénomène analogue. Paris peut toujours assurer ce rôle de metropolis et occuper cette place pour un provincial, comme les beaux quartiers pour une certaine banlieue. Paris, c'est aussi la capitale de la littérature. Mais l'autre n'a plus dans ce cas la même transcendance du là-bas, l'éloignement de l'être-ailleurs, l'autorité inaccessible d'un maître qui habite outre-mer. Il y manque une mer.[51]

In fact, the perceived position of the French departments "d'outre-mer" with respect to the capital might not be as dissimilar to the situation of French nationals who speak only Breton, or Francophone speakers from Switzerland, as Derrida suggests. The psychological distance may be equally great, even if the geographical distance is somewhat diminished. Meizoz documents the struggles of Swiss writers such as Rousseau, Töpffer and Ramuz to gain acknowledgement in Paris. Even into the twentieth century these writers have been accused of "regionalisms". Meizoz notes the following quotation from Ramuz: "Nous avions ici deux langues, une qui passait pour 'la bonne', mais dont nous nous servions mal parce qu'elle n'était pas à nous, l'autre qui était soi-disant pleine de fautes, mais dont nous nous servions bien parce qu'elle était à nous."[52]

---

[51] Jacques Derrida, *Le Monolinguisme de l'Autre ou la Prothèse d'Origine*, Paris: Editions Galilée, 1996, 73-74: "For the little Provencalian or the little Breton, there is, of course, a comparable phenomenon. Paris can always provide that role of *metropolis* and occupy that position for a provincial, just as the well-off districts do for certain suburbs. Paris is also the capital of literature. But in this case the other no longer has the same transcendence of being *over there*, the distance of *being elsewhere*, the inaccessible authority of a master who lives *overseas*. There is no sea." (Unless otherwise indicated, translations from the French are my own.)
[52] Jérôme Meizoz, *Le Droit de "Mal Ecrire" Quand les Auteurs Romands Déjouent le "Français de Paris"*, Geneva: Editions Zoé, 1998, 71: "Here we had two languages, one that was 'the good one', but which we used poorly, because it didn't belong to us,

Meizoz's characterization of the "periphery" must surely apply as equally to the situation of writers from Algeria as it does to writers from Switzerland:

> Une des propriétés de la périphérie d'un champ (ou de ce qu'on appelle couramment une "province") serait donc la suivante: l'impuissance, non à créér [sic] des formes, mais à les diffuser et les imposer à l'ensemble par ses propres moyens. Le miracle des capitales, s'il en est, c'est donc de rendre visible et lisible – respectivement invisible et illisible – le labeur des coulisses.[53]

The influence of the capital extends not only across colonized countries and countries speaking the same tongue, but also to provinces speaking entirely different languages. There are accounts made by speakers of Breton dating from the nineteenth century who have only come to learn the official French of "their" country late on in life: politically it belongs to them, but in reality they have little or no connection to it. Two well-known examples of Bretons who have adopted French as a literary language are Jean-Marie Déguignet author of the *Mémoires d'un paysan du bas-Breton* (1998)[54] and Pierre-Jakez Helias author and translator of *Le Cheval d'Orgueil* (1975).[55] In an extract from the latter text provided in the edited collection *Entre deux langues: Bilinguisme et autobiographie* (2004), Helias describes how French was promoted by teachers and parents alike, whether it was seen as a means to gain servants for the rich bourgeois of Paris who would be able to understand the orders being given to them or as a means to gain access to better life conditions than those provided in the native Breton-speaking environment.[56]

---

the other that was, as it were, full of faults, but which we used because it belonged to us."

[53] *Ibid.*, 77: "One of the properties of the periphery of a field (or what is commonly called a 'province') would therefore be the following: the impossibility, not of creating forms, but of disseminating them and imposing them on everyone by one's own means. The miracle of capital cities, if such there is, is to render visible and legible – respectively invisible and illegible – the work that goes on behind the scenes."

[54] Jean-Marie Déguignet, *Mémoires d'un paysan du bas-Breton*, Ergué-Gabéric: An Here, 1998.

[55] Pierre-Jakez Helias, *Le Cheval d'Orgueil*, Paris: Plon, 1975.

[56] *Entre Deux Langues: Autobiographie et Bilinguisme*, eds Micheline Cellier-Gelly, Claire Torreilles and Marie-Jeanne Verny, Paris: Adapt Editions, 2004, 71.

The language of the "melting-pot"

The texts relating experiences of migration to North America during the latter half of the twentieth century include Eva Hoffman's *Lost in Translation* (1989) and Kyoko Mori's *Polite Lies: On Being a Woman Caught Between Cultures* (1997). Kyoko Mori is a Japanese woman who moved to the USA at the age of twenty to go to college and who now, when in Japan, finds it "exhausting to speak Japanese all day, every day".[57] Her text forms a series of essays, rather than a memoir in the manner of Eva Hoffman's narrative. Julia Alvarez' *Something to Declare* (1998) is also a series of essays written in English, a later experienced language, although she began learning the language as a child, at about the age of nine, after her family emigrated to the USA from the Dominican Republic. Ilan Stavans' *On Borrowed Words* (2001), which subtitles itself "a memoir of language", is an account of relationships with his multiple languages many of which have been spoken and/or read since childhood: Yiddish, Hebrew, Spanish and on later immigration to the USA, English.[58]

Voluntary visits to a foreign tongue

These migratory patterns can also be distinguished on the basis of how long the protagonist remained in the unfamiliar culture and whether or not, to any great extent, they learnt the foreign language. There are many texts that recount more brief periods of stay in a foreign culture. These are generally written in the first language and would include the two texts by Turnbull and Hessler already discussed as well as Alice Kaplan's own *French Lessons* (1993), in which she recounts among other things, her experiences of learning French during brief trips to France. Further examples include Richard Watson's *The Philosopher's Demise: Learning French* (1995), an English-language account written by an American scholar of Descartes about his experiences learning French in Paris, which he has read and translated for over thirty years, but never learnt to speak.[59] Karen Ogulnick's *Onna Rashiku (Like a Woman)* (1998) has also been written in the first language, but the text forms a detailed non-literary commentary about

---

[57] Kyoko Mori, *Polite Lies: On Being a Woman Caught Between Cultures*, New York: Henry Holt, 1997, 10.
[58] Ilan Stavans, *On Borrowed Words*, New York: Penguin, 2001.
[59] Richard Watson's *The Philosopher's Demise: Learning French*, Columbia, MO and London: University of Missouri Press, 1995.

a learner diary written while the author was living in Japan and learning Japanese.[60] The text includes some excerpts from the diary. *Turning Japanese* (1991) by David Mura is also written by a US citizen visiting Japan, but differs in that David Mura is, as he describes himself, a "third-generation Japanese-American" whose parents have raised him as an American citizen. The only difference he notes between himself and other Americans is that his family ate Japanese food.[61] For Mura, travelling to Japan involves a confrontation with another culture, but one that is intimately bound up with his own ethnic and family heritage.

Where the protagonist has spent a brief period of time in the foreign culture, the visit to the foreign language and culture has usually been a voluntary choice rather than driven by particular social or economic forces. Many of the narratives in which the protagonist moves permanently to a foreign culture are also accounts of voluntary migration made for quite personal, if not necessarily economic, reasons. There are many texts that fall into this category. Where the stay is longer, the text is also more likely to have been written in the foreign language. Examples include Wladimir Kaminer who was born in Moscow in 1967 and has been living in Berlin since 1990, where he writes and contributes regularly to newspapers and magazines. He has included writings about language in his collection of essays *Schönhauser Allee* (2001).[62] There are other authors who optionally live in Germany and write in German. These include, for example, Yoko Tawada, who moved from Japan to Germany to study for a master's degree at the University of Hamburg. Many of her texts are short snapshots of particular moments in the author's experience of German life, culture and language, some of which provide a highly defamiliarizing take on German from the perspective of a Japanese learner.[63] In the French context voluntary transition between two national languages and cultures is also exemplified by Nancy

---

[60] Karen Ogulnick, *Onna Rashiku (Like a Woman)*, Albany, NY: SUNY Press 1998.
[61] David Mura, *Turning Japanese*, New York: Anchor Books, 1991, 7.
[62] Wladimir Kaminer, *Schönhauser Allee*, Munich: Wilhelm Goldmann, 2001.
[63] Yoko Tawada, *Ein Gast*, Tübingen: Konkursbuchverlag, 1993; *Talisman*, Tübingen: Konkursbuchverlag, 1996; *Überseezungen*, Tübingen: Konkursbuch Verlag Claudia Gehrke, 2006; *Sprachpolizei und Spielpolyglotte*, Tübingen: Konkursbuch Verlag Claudia Gehrke, 2007.

Huston's *Nord perdu* (1999),[64] Andreï Makine's *Le Testament Français* (1997)[65] and Vassilis Alexakis' *Paris-Athènes* (2006).[66] Nancy Huston migrates from Canada to France after spending time studying in Paris. Vassilis Alexakis' move from Greece to Paris is also motivated initially by study – at the age of eighteen he obtains a bursary to study journalism in Lille for three years. Andreï Makine was born in Siberia in 1957 with Russian as a mother tongue, but acquires a taste for French language and literature as child from a French grandmother with whom he would spend his summers. In 1987 he moves to France and begins writing in French.[67]

Economic migration to a foreign tongue
In the German context many of the texts have not been written by voluntary expatriates but by authors who may have initially migrated for economic reasons before subsequently staying. There are many pieces written in the German context relating back to the call for *Gastarbeiter* that originally considered the workers to be visitors and not permanent immigrants until the Immigration Act of 2005. Prior to this date non-native residency was interpreted in terms of the return of ethnic Germans or the temporary hosting of migrant workers, asylum seekers or civil war refugees.[68] There are several anthologies of *Gastarbeiter* writing such as those put together by Irmgard Ackermann that contain a few select passages reflecting on learning and using German.

The Turkish-German author, Emine Sevgi Özdamar, also initially came to Germany as a temporary *Gastarbeiter* or "guest worker" in 1965 and again in 1976 as an actress. Within the German context of reception there was an earlier tendency to refer to *Gastarbeiterliteratur* and then later to *Migrantenliteratur*, both terms that are rather problematic in their exoticizing of the texts and for their suggested exclusion of texts written by migrants from an implied mainstream or more canonical German literature. The terms connote a

---

[64] Nancy Huston, *Nord Perdu: Suivi de Douze France*, Montréal Leméac: Actes Sud, 1999.
[65] Andreï Makine, *Le Testament Français*, London: Sceptre, 1997.
[66] Vassilis Alexakis, *Paris-Athènes*, Paris: Stock, 2006.
[67] *Entre Deux Langues*, 71.
[68] Norbert Cyrus and Dita Vogel, "Germany", in *European Immigration: A Sourcebook*, eds Anna Triandafyllidou and Ruby Gropas, Aldershot and Burlington, VT: Ashgate, 2007, 127.

certain condescension towards this literature, suggesting something about its quality, nonetheless on a non-literary basis. In mentioning the circumstances in which many of Germany's great translingual writers, such as Özdamar, first came to Germany, it must therefore be emphasized that this is not an attempt once more to reduce these texts to the terms of *Gastarbeiterliteratur*, but simply to note the sociohistorical context within which these language learner narratives were written.[69]

The multilingual childhood
There are several texts that recount multilingual experiences in childhood. Written in English we find Richard Rodriguez' *Hunger of Memory* (1982), an account of Rodriguez' Spanish-English bilingual upbringing in the US written in his language of education, English.[70] Ariel Dorfman's *Heading South, Looking North: A Bilingual Journey* (1998) recounts a life moving between Argentina, the US and Chile and his changing relationships to Spanish and English, both learnt in childhood.[71] In the German context we find an account of multilingual upbringing that is also one of the texts most commonly included in the category of "language memoir" – Elias Canetti's *Die Gerettete Zunge* (1989), referred to earlier. This text is a literary autobiography that recounts the narrator's acquisition of a variety of languages throughout childhood and adolescence including Bulgarian, Ladino, Spanish, English and French, but gives particular focus to his acquisition of German. Having been born in the port of Rustschuk (Russe) on the lower Danube into a Sephardic Jewish family, then having moved to England briefly, and learnt French in school, Canetti finally learnt German after his father's death when he moved with his mother and brother to Vienna. His mother drilled the language into him at the age of eight and Canetti describes it as his "mother tongue".

---

[69] See Moray McGowan, "Turkish-German Fiction Since the Mid 1990s", in *Contemporary German Fiction: Writing in the Berlin Republic*, ed. Stuart Taberner, Cambridge: Cambridge University Press, 2007, 212: "Turkish-German writing, which would not exist in its contemporary variety and aesthetic sophistication without the history of labour migration, has moved well beyond these origins: ... there is no excuse for hearing only the dull throb of a *Gastarbeiter* beating on a cardboard suitcase in the rich polyphony of contemporary Turkish-German writing."
[70] Richard Rodriguez, *Hunger of Memory*, New York: Bantam Dell, 1982.
[71] Ariel Dorfman, *Heading South, Looking North: A Bilingual Journey*, London: Hodder and Stoughton, 1998.

It is the language in which he later wrote his many books for which he gained a Nobel Prize.[72]

Intralingual migration
One final subgroup of texts that can be identified is that of texts describing the acquisition of new discourses or new regional varieties of the mother tongue, which I am calling "intralingual migration" to distinguish it from "translingual migration" between two different languages. Belonging to this category we find Annie Ernaux's *La Place* (1983) in which the author describes her acquisition of educated discourse and how this changes her relationship with her father.[73] We also find Jean-Paul Sartre's *Les Mots* (1964), an autobiographical account reflecting upon Sartre's childhood acquisition of standard French and his relationship with French literature.[74] In the English context we find an autobiography that relates the experience of adapting to a different culture in the mother-tongue as well as occasionally referring to issues of speaking a different regional variety: *The Winter Sparrows: Growing up in Scotland and Australia* (1980) by Mary Rose Liverani.[75]

This brief outline of some of the contexts in which language learner narratives have been produced shows that while there are frequently certain social and economic factors which shape the overall patterns of migration, the course this takes at an individual level for narrators of language learner narratives is unique, and not only in those cases where the migration has been voluntary. The many texts going under the rubric of "language memoir" are texts of diverse styles, by authors of diverse origins, writing about diverse experiences. The only certain commonality is that at some point in the text an experience of learning language is narrated, an experience common to all but the most utterly deprived of human beings.[76] The definition of language memoir – as may well be the case for other genres, but in

---

[72] Elias Canetti, *Die Gerettete Zunge*, Munich: Carl Hanser Verlag, 1977.
[73] Annie Ernaux, *La Place*, Paris: Gallimard, 1983.
[74] Jean-Paul Sartre, *Les Mots*, Paris: Gallimard, 1964.
[75] Mary Rose Liverani, *The Winter Sparrows: Growing Up in Scotland and Australia*, Melbourne: Sphere, 1980.
[76] One frequently cited case is that of "Genie", a girl who was found at the age of thirteen having been severely abused and having up to that point experienced next to no linguistic input. See Susan Curtiss, *Genie: A Psycholinguistic Study of a Modern-Day "Wild Child"*, New York: Academic Press, 1977.

this case even more so – therefore arises not so much out of the content or style of these texts but out of the critical discourse using the term "language memoir" and circulating the names of texts considered worthy of inclusion within the genre.

Despite this diversity, as the following discussion will show, the narratives that construct the language learning situation can be shown at a fundamental level to reveal certain recurrent patterns of engagement with later experienced languages and unfamiliar cultures that shape a wide range of discourses across English, French and German texts in similar ways. Light is shed upon these patterns through deployment of the concept of *Mündigkeit*. Firstly, however, we will consider an alternative means of categorizing these texts that avoids a reductivist genre designation.

On language learner narrative

Daniel Chandler summarizes some of the key debates surrounding the problem of assigning genre to a corpus of texts, relating to contemporary interest in the constructed nature of genre, including problems of who is constructing the genre category and on the basis of what and for what purpose. These debates are particularly pertinent in the case of genres that have traditionally been perceived as relatively stable categories such as the novel, but in the case of language memoir, it is worth giving serious consideration to whether or not a genre label is relevant at all in this context. It is proposed here, that in terms of language memoir it may be equally fruitful to do away with an analysis on the basis of genre. Literary criticism is concerned with texts deemed "literary" (the nature of "literariness" is a debate in itself), and the study of such texts involves groupings according to author, sociohistorical period and literary style. Within comparative literature, texts may also be grouped according to the treatment of particular themes across a range of texts from different cultures and sociohistorical contexts. However, it is fair to say that in most cases, the criticism is concerned with the entirety of a text – the concrete object as it is found from first paragraph to last paragraph or perhaps even more concretely from front cover to back cover. Thus, when a text is assigned to a genre, it may be assumed that we are concerned with the entirety of a text, so defined. Even this definition is problematic, since texts have ways of exceeding their apparently concrete limits.

In "The Law of Genre" Jacques Derrida discusses the problem of genre with an example of a text citing its own boundary thereby disrupting the boundary that constitutes genre by making that boundary a part of the text it is meant to delimit. The text he uses is by Maurice Blanchot in which the first line of the text is repeated at the beginning of the last three paragraphs of the text, thereby creating a text that is unbounded or perhaps only boundary.[77] The text problematizes its own genre definition through simultaneously citing and questioning its own genre boundary, at once narrating and talking about the narrative: proclaiming the commencement of an account at the same time as the impossibility of giving an account:

> The "account" which he claims is beginning at the end and, by legal requisition, is none other than the one that has begun from the beginning of *La Folie du jour* and in which, therefore, he gets around to saying that he begins, etc. And it is without beginning or end, without content and without edge. There is only content without edge – without boundary or frame – and there is only edge without content.[78]

What has the reader read? Is it an account? Is it the account of an account? Was there even an account to begin with given the proclaimed impossibility of giving an account and the reluctance of the narrator to be situated as a subject of the narrative? Derrida's essay raises various problems for the easy classification of texts within particular genre taxonomies.

It might, however, only seem appropriate in an age of electronic text and apparently limitless hyper- and intertextuality that we dispense with the concept of text as a bound and bounded concrete entity assignable in its entirety to one particular genre. These apparent textual limits have been constructed by the author, the editor and the publisher; as readers and critics of text, we are not restricted to them. The format of reading in online contexts does not create this freedom, but it does emphatically suggest and highlight the possibility of non-linear reading. For this reason, it is proposed here not to look at entire texts as representatives of particular genres, but to delimit portions of those extended texts that can be isolated as language learner narratives.

---

[77] James Joyce's *Finnegans Wake* (1939) similarly has a last line that continues with the first line.
[78] Derrida and Ronell, "The Law of Genre", 70.

This delimitation will attempt to ground itself in particular recurrent signifiers of the text that may be associatively linked with the situation of being an individual learning a foreign language in a foreign culture as demonstrated in the following diagrams. In this way the identification of language learner narratives becomes a more certain game. The recurrence of these signifiers will also extend to any text dealing with language learning situations, regardless of length, style, or other content. If we view genre identity as an artificial construct, then we may consider language learner narratives as a kind of genre identity performed in various texts to differing degrees, without necessitating the strained classification of the entire text as a "language memoir". The key signifiers are understood as being "hyperlinked" to each other across a range of texts.

In general, language learner narratives will exhibit certain characteristics that relate to these signifiers, such as a prevalence of metalinguistic reflection within the context of language learning. This will be determined by concrete surface features of the text that relate to this theme and may be flagged by commentary on particular languages or use of language as well as reference to speech, silence, writing, written characters, sounds, the learning situation and so on. Rather than following a merely intuitive categorization of textual passages as language learner narratives, we may make explicit at least some of the intuitive criteria, drawing on quotations from the range of primary texts chosen for this project.

The most obvious feature of such narrative is that there is explicit reference either to "language" or "languages" in the abstract or to a specifically named language, as in the following passages:

> j'avais cru trouver un équilibre entre deux pays et deux langues[79]

> it would benefit his Japanese[80]

> I would also forsake my closeness to the Polish language[81]

---

[79] Alexakis, *Paris-Athènes*, 21: "I thought I had found a balance between two countries and two languages."
[80] John David Morley, *Pictures from the Water Trade: An Englishman in Japan*, London: Deutsch, 1985, 29.
[81] Elizabeth Dykman, "The Vagabond Years", in *Language Crossings*, ed. Karen Ogulnick, New York: Teachers College Press, 2000, 31.

In other cases, the reference is not made to the language as a whole, but to its constitution. This type of discussion may include metalinguistic references in which words from the foreign language are included in quotation marks:

> ... pitched him into the magic circle where words and sentences became palpable events[82]

> I am unable to use the word "I" I do not go as far as the schizophrenic "she" – but I am driven, as by a compulsion, to the double, the Siamese-twin "you".[83]

The following passage from Nancy Huston includes reflection on the metalinguistic reflection of others:

> On entraperçoit le vrai vous que recouvrait le masque et l'on saute dessus: Non, mais...vous avez dit "une peignoire"? "un baignoire"? "la diapason"? "le guérison"? J'ai bien entendu, vous vous êtes trompé? C'est que vous êtes un alien!" [84]

Elsewhere, the concern is not with the language or its constitution but with linguistic behaviour, the production of the later experienced language and how it comes across to those who experienced it early in life:

> ... le fait de parler le français avec un accent[85]

> I have to form entire sentences before uttering them; otherwise, I too easily get lost in the middle. My speech, I sense, sounds monotonous, deliberate, heavy[86]

> J'ai d'ailleurs du mal à trouver le ton juste[87]

---

[82] Morley, *Pictures from the Water Trade*, 29-30.
[83] Hoffman, *Lost in Translation*, 121.
[84] Huston, *Nord Perdu*, 33: "People see the *real you* that the mask was hiding and they jump on it: No, but...you said '*une* peignoire'? '*un* baignoire'? '*la* diapason'? '*le* guérison'? I heard you right enough, you made a mistake? It's because you're a foreigner!"
[85] *Ibid.*: "... the fact of speaking French with an accent."
[86] Hoffman, *Lost in Translation*, 118.
[87] Alexakis, *Paris-Athènes*, 11: "Besides this, I have trouble finding the right tone."

Es kamen aus meinem Mund die Buchstaben raus.[88]

These statements can all be further grouped according to the features of the language learning situation to which reference is being made. At the most fundamental level we can assume that in the foreign context this involves a language learner, an unfamiliar language, a group of people who speak it as a first language and a culture with which it is associated. The underlying description of the event of "language learning abroad" may be conceptualized in terms of the agent (the language learner), the object (the unfamiliar language), the process (language learning) and the context consisting of those first language speakers, and the physical and cultural spaces in which the learning takes place, including a whole host of other events that do not directly have to do with language learning. Using these key concepts we can propose a conceptual network made up of other concepts connected to these key concepts (at any level) that arise in language learner narratives along with their metaphorical correlates in any particular text. Identifying a language learner narrative thereby involves identifying in a text the recurrence of particular signifiers fitting into the conceptual network suggested overleaf.

On this diagram the key concepts are unformatted, the textual signifiers appear in bold and their metaphorical counterparts in bold italics. The bulleted outline following this diagram offers a more complete set of concepts at the expense of making explicit the conceptual links to the same degree. An example is given in English only; the signifiers would be slightly different for French and German but arguably retain a similar underlying core of key concepts. The presented signifiers are all headwords intended to subsume any grammatical variants such as plural forms or verb forms marked for tense, person or aspect.

---

[88] Özdamar, *Mutter Zunge*, 18.

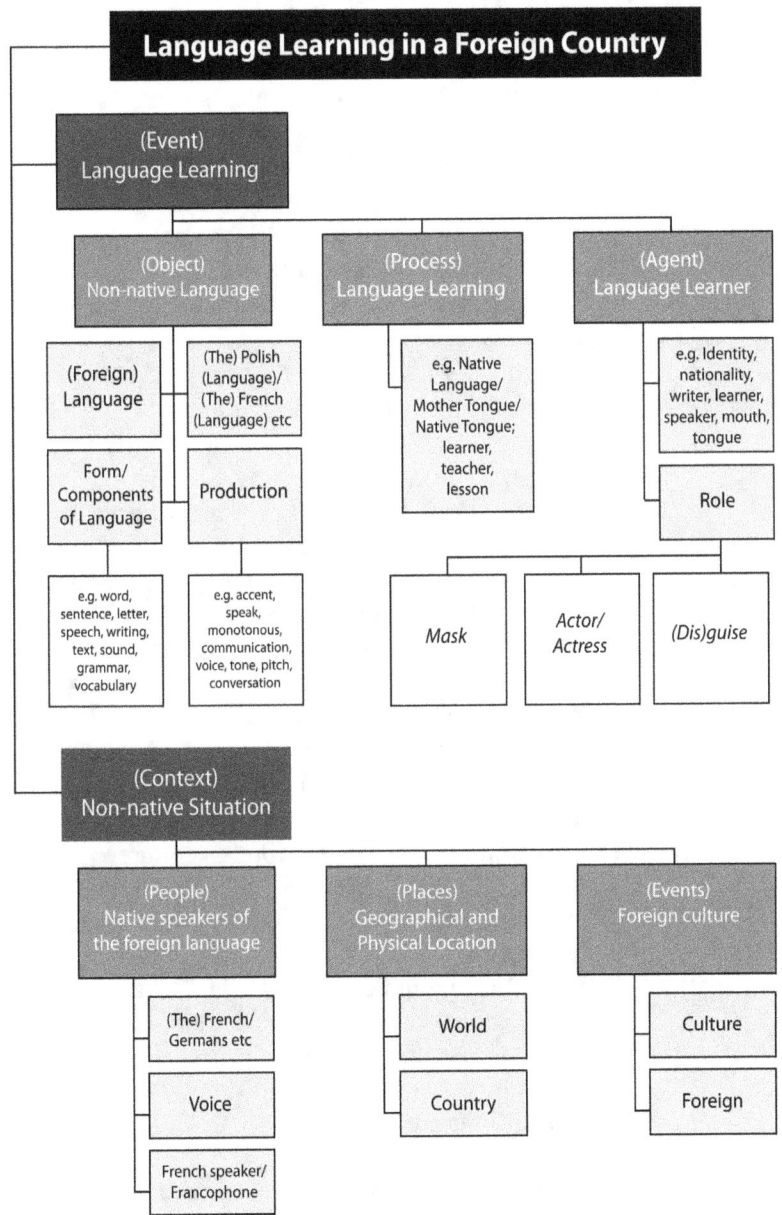

Figure 3

Language Learning in a Foreign Country
- (Event) **Language** Learning
  - (Object) Unfamiliar **language**: **foreign language, (the) X (language)**
    - Form/Components of **language**
      - Components: **word, sound, letter, sentence** etc.
      - Structure: **grammar, vocabulary** etc.
    - Production: **communication, speak** etc.
      - Instrument of production: **voice, pen, hand** etc.
      - Features of production: **tone, pitch** etc.
      - Quality of production: **accent, monotonous, breathy** etc.
      - Type of production: **speech, conversation, monologue, dialogue, writing, text** etc.
  - (Process) **Language** learning: **learn, learning, speaking, teacher, lesson** etc.
  - (Agent) **Language** learner: **learner, speaker, self, identity, role, nationality, native tongue** etc.
- (Context) Unfamiliar situation in a foreign culture
  - (People) Native speakers of the foreign **language**: **teacher, (the) French, other people** etc.
  - (Places) Geographical and physical locations: **world, country, land, place, terrain, city** etc.
  - (Events) Foreign culture: **culture, foreign, behaviour, customs, traditions, values, assumptions** etc.

Determining whether or not the text we are dealing with is an example of language learner narrative is facilitated with reference to this conceptual map. It does not provide means for an absolute determination of language learner narrative but operates as a useful evaluative framework. Presence or absence of the proposed signifiers will already include or exclude a range of texts from the category. This might then be further refined through examining the concepts on a qualitative and quantitative basis, that is, are there a greater or lesser number of these signifiers present in the text? Are these signifiers strongly or weakly linked to the main node in the map – how far from the main node is the relevant signifier? In this way, taking an idealized version of language learner narrative the constellation of texts clustering around this ideal can be modelled and the key hyperlinks that unite the texts and that all lead back to the homepage of language learner narrative might be more easily determined.

Summary and conclusions
This chapter has given an overview of the current secondary literature within the disciplines of SLA and literary studies on texts describing the process of acquiring a second language. We have seen that up until now there has been no consistent terminology to describe these texts variously known as "language biographies", "language autobiographies", "language learning memoir", "language memoir" and "language learner narrative". Similar and sometimes the very same texts have also been studied under the heading of migrant autobiography or cross-cultural autobiography. The most commonly used term to describe them is "language memoir". However, the classification of texts as "language memoir" proves extremely problematic, firstly because not all texts refer solely to the language learning process and, secondly, because the criteria used for determining language memoir are to a large extent quite arbitrary and may not account adequately for the vast range of types of language learning experience described in these texts. As an alternative, this study appropriates the suggested descriptor "language learner narrative" and provides a model for the determination of this text type based on the concrete presence of particular signifiers associated with the target language learning situation within the text. This term does not encompass the entirety of a text but may be restricted to particular textual passages and quotations. The proposed category furthermore crosses common boundaries so as to include a diverse range of textual

styles and traditional genres including the fictional, the non-fictional, the autobiographical, the semi-autobiographical, the poetic and the prosaic, thereby enabling a textual analysis focussing on the treatment of a particular theme across text types.

Chapter Three

Conceptualizing the Language Learner

As shown in the preceding chapter with regards to the question of "language learner narrative" finding terminology that captures and describes a phenomenon without distorting it can be significantly problematic. The concept of language learner narrative assumes that what is understood by "language learner" and what counts as a process of "language learning" is quite clear. These, however, warrant further explication, at the very least to develop an understanding "language learners" that will serve us well for the following chapters.

Native/non-native and the intercultural speaker
Issues of power and control frequently arise with regard to how language learners position themselves in their own texts and how they are discursively positioned by the new language and culture they are encountering. These issues are further explored in Chapter Five, which looks at how a capacity for *Mündigkeit* may be interpreted in relation to Bourdieu's concepts of linguistic capital and symbolic power. For the time being, it must be noted that conceptions of the relationship between the language learner and those commonly designated "native speakers" of the language they are acquiring have recently been altered within foreign language pedagogy and second language acquisition in response to an awareness that descriptions in terms of native and non-native speakers are somewhat reductive. That is to say that the terms risk ignoring the diversity of communicative skills and capacities possessed by speakers of a particular language, native and non-native alike. Talk of "non-native" speakers is seen to highlight the language learner's "inadequacy" in speaking the non-native language, thereby placing the language learner in a weak position with regard to native speakers, who are set up as the gold standard of linguistic performance. Following on from Michael

Byram's proposition of the "intercultural speaker" in his book *Teaching and Assessing Intercultural Communicative Competence*,[1] Kramsch also indicates that there can be no stable description of what constitutes native competence.[2] This section considers the problematization of the term "native speaker", before describing and evaluating Byram's alternative model of the "intercultural speaker". In what follows is included discussion of the ways in which the concepts developed by Byram and Kramsch connect with the dynamics of *Mündigkeit* in intercultural interaction proposed here.

As highlighted by Alan Davies, the concept of the "native speaker" is both a reality and a myth. From a common-sense point of view, the concept of the "native speaker" is very much alive in the minds of language-users, and more so particularly for those who are learning a foreign language and seeking some model of linguistic competence to strive for. Even if this myth must be theoretically dismissed once we investigate the true complexity of native language use and see that a "non-native" may have greater linguistic competence than a native in terms of grammatical understanding or level of education in the language, it is still regarded as being of practical importance.[3]

There is at times a problematic confusion between the conditions in which a person acquired a language ("at their mother's knee") and assignation of native linguistic competence, designating itself a somewhat indeterminate conception of higher level performance (grammaticality, pronunciation) in a particular language, or simply autochthonous authenticity – their competence is native by birthright, no matter how inadequately they have mastered the language.[4]

Performance in a language necessarily varies from person to person and from skill to skill, so that a non-native speaker (that is, one who did not learn the language from birth) may be more greatly proficient in writing the language than many native speakers. In terms of language education, seeking out the opinions of native speakers on

---

[1] See Michael Byram, *Teaching and Assessing Intercultural Communicative Competence*, Clevedon: Multilingual Matters, 1997, 32.
[2] Claire Kramsch, "The Privilege of the Intercultural Speaker", in *Language Learning in Intercultural Perspective: Approaches through Drama and Ethnography*, eds Michael Byram and Michael Fleming, Cambridge: Cambridge University Press, 1998, 20-23.
[3] Alan Davies, *The Native Speaker: Myth and Reality*, Clevedon: Multilingual Matters, 2003, 6-7.
[4] Cf. Kramsch in *Language Learning in Intercultural Perspective*, 16.

grammaticality is in fact frequently problematic, since most spoken language is not particularly grammatical and a native speaker cannot be relied upon to reproduce the grammatical forms codified in grammar books for "non-native" language learners to acquire. On this point Kramsch cites a survey by Valdman in which French speakers are found to use the informal "Tu vas oú?" and the even less standardized "Oú tu vas?" as much as 80% of the time.[5]

As an alternative to the reductivist dichotomy of native/non-native speaker Byram proposes instead a model of the "intercultural speaker" that indicates competencies going beyond the linguistic to include all of the ways in which an individual relates to other languages, cultures and people. As Byram points out, the idea of the "intercultural speaker" will include many of the attitudes, knowledge and skills that are also required for intracultural communication; however, Byram argues that there is nonetheless an extra psychological dimension to intercultural communication.

Firstly, there is a greater awareness of otherness that leads to the attribution of national identities and characteristics to the interlocutor (in addition to factors such as gender, ethnicity, age, social class etc.) and that can affect communication. As suggested in Chapter One, an exacerbated psychological experience of intercultural difference might also be heightened by discourses that very much tie linguistic identity to cultural and national identity and vice versa. Secondly, Byram suggests that:

> The FL [Foreign Language] speaker may experience a degree of powerlessness vis à vis a native speaker. They may sense the constraints of insufficient knowledge and skill in linguistic competence to meet the specific requirements of the interaction.[6]

In this work it is proposed that this sense of powerlessness forms part of the loss of *Mündigkeit* being described. As Byram further indicates in a footnote, these power dynamics of communication are not only found in intercultural communication, though in an intracultural situation of communication speakers are less likely to be aware of the dynamics that structure their interaction. Methodologies such as critical discourse analysis developed in the work of Norman

---

[5] Kramsch, "The Privilege of the Intercultural Speaker", 25.
[6] Byram, *Teaching and Assessing Intercultural Communicative Competence*, 41.

Fairclough, Ruth Wodak, Teun van Dijk and others aim at uncovering these and bringing them to consciousness.[7]

In agreement with Byram's suggestion that a sense of powerlessness is frequently heightened in situations of intercultural communication, Chapter Eight reveals many metaphors across a range of texts articulating a loss of *Mündigkeit*. The concept of *Mündigkeit* developed in Chapter Five ties this sense of powerlessness not only to a lack of linguistic competence but also to a lack of linguistic capital in the foreign situation and to the repercussions that the loss of these has on the individual's sense of selfhood and identity.

Having established the increased psychological dimension to intercultural communication, in addition to the social issues inherent in all communication, Byram outlines his model of the "intercultural speaker". The concept of the intercultural speaker places the capacities of the language learner and speakers of the foreign language on the same footing, since irrespective of linguistic competence all are deemed to require similar attitudes, knowledge and skills when interacting with each other. These attributes are bracketed together as "intercultural communicative competence". Byram outlines five factors that contribute to intercultural competence, also known as the five *savoirs*. These are excerpted as:

Attitudes [savoir être]*: Curiosity and openness, readiness to suspend disbelief about other cultures and belief about one's own ...*

Knowledge [savoirs]*: of social groups and their products and practices in one's own and in one's interlocutor's country, and of the general processes of societal and individual interaction ...*

Skills of interpreting and relating [savoir comprendre]*: Ability to interpret a document or event from another culture, to explain it and relate it to documents from one's own ...*

Skills of discovery and interaction [savoir apprendre/faire]*: Ability to acquire new knowledge of a culture and cultural practices and the ability to operate knowledge, attitudes and skills under the constraints of real-time communication and interaction ...*

Critical cultural awareness/political education [savoir s'engager]*: An ability to evaluate critically and on the basis of explicit criteria*

---

[7] Byram, *Teaching and Assessing Intercultural Competence*, 55, n.5. See also *Methods of Critical Discourse Analysis*, eds Ruth Wodak and Michael Meyer, London: SAGE Publications, 2009.

perspectives, practices and products in one's own and other cultures and countries.[8]

Interestingly, Lies Sercu felt that a sixth factor of *savoir communiquer* should be included in the list, though it is perhaps arguably intended under *savoir comprendre* and *savoir faire*.[9] Nonetheless, in contrasting the concept of the intercultural speaker with that of the native speaker, the native speaker is a concept usually defined in terms of linguistic competence, a factor that is explicitly absent from Byram's list. Even with the inclusion of *savoir communiquer*, this factor is not satisfactorily covered, since linguistic ability and communicative ability, understood as an ability to use language appropriately in interaction, do not necessarily go hand in hand.

The concept of the "intercultural speaker" as a model of competence for language education is particularly productive and democratic; indeed many of the language learners writing language learner narratives already exhibit a high level of intercultural communicative competence that permits the articulation of their experiences with new ways of being, behaving and speaking about the world. However, the very fact of writing such accounts frequently presupposes the myth of the native/non-native dichotomy and a perception of difference that underlies the experiences and creates meaning for the encounters described. Until the concept of native/non-native is dispensed with in our common-sense conceptions of language and culture learning, the psychological reality of the myth remains and structures how unfamiliar languages and cultures are implicitly perceived and therefore written about in language learner narrative.[10]

---

[8] Byram, *Teaching and Assessing Intercultural Competence*, 50-53. For ease of reference the name of the relevant *savoir* has been inserted into the description in square brackets.
[9] Inma Álvarez, "Foreign Language Education at the Crossroads: Whose Model of Competence?", *Language, Culture and Curriculum*, XX/2, 2007, 127.
[10] The *Mündigkeit* concept presented in Chapter Five retains some of this implied linear movement from lack to possession, rejection to acceptance, which is then counter-balanced by the idea of *Metamündigkeit* presented in Chapter Nine. There is also arguably a case for validating the common-sense conception of "foreign" languages and non-native speakers. In a similar vein Anna Wierzbicka argues in a recent article for the acknowledgement of common-sense notions of culture and the psychosocial experience of difference that this gives rise to: Anna Wierzbicka, "In Defense of 'Culture'", *Theory and Psychology*, XV/4 (August 2005), 575-97.

Byram's model represents a political shift away from linguistic competence issues perhaps instigated by the at times problematic power relations engendered by focus on linguistic performance in language teaching. In many ways, this project supports Byram's alternative conception of the "intercultural speaker" as a pedagogic goal, insofar as it explores power relations engendered by the native/non-native dichotomy that rely upon notions of available linguistic competence and linguistic capital. *Mündigkeit* is perceived as a factor in negotiating the power relations inherent in any linguistic interaction that are particularly brought to the fore in the acquisition of a language later in life. Thus, rather than entirely dispense with conceptions of native versus non-native in favour of referring to the language learners in these texts as moving towards or performing competence as intercultural speakers, it is proposed instead to refer to first experienced or early experienced languages and later experienced languages as well as more or less familiar cultures. These terms avoid imputing levels of competence, authenticity or birthright to the speaker/writer and instead define their relationship to different languages in terms of initial point of exposure – what is subsequently made of that exposure is a different matter entirely.[11] However, it may be assumed that a greater level of exposure has some correlation to a greater level of competence, defined in terms of grammaticality, appropriate use of vocabulary and communicative success, and also that at the point of initial exposure, the foreign language and culture was perceived as "other"/"unfamiliar"/"different" and thus as a challenge to early acquired modes of speaking, behaving and evaluating. The use of the verb "experience" rather than "acquire" also aims to highlight that a language or a culture is dynamic and not something that can be possessed like a material object. Where the texts themselves express a construction of power relations in terms of native/non-native speakers, then these terms will be retained in inverted commas.

Reference will also be made to "newcoming" rather than to "non-native" speakers, suggesting a freshness of perception but also an unfamiliarity with the language, as well as a sense of "becoming" and changing within a new intercultural mode of being. This idea of

---

[11] It also bypasses thorny debates about the possibility of a critical period for language acquisition, since it makes no correlation between time since initial exposure and end-level competence.

becoming also aims to reflect Alison Phipps' concept of "languaging", that is, the learning and use of languages viewed as an active embodied process, rather than as the acquisition of a detached skillset or set of competencies.[12]

"The multilingual subject"

Since completing research for this text, Claire Kramsch's initial article on language memoir has been developed and published as a full-length study of "the multilingual subject", which includes examination of literary texts as well as student accounts of language learning. This fascinating and wide-ranging work considers the construction of the self in and through language from a variety of angles. It aims to draw out some of the qualitative aspects missing from traditional SLA research by focusing on how "language constructs the historical sedimentation of meanings that we call our 'selves'".[13] The focus is on the lived experiences of language learners and so exhibits some parallels with and differences from the current work that it would be worthwhile responding to before proceeding.

In *The Multilingual Subject* Kramsch focuses on aspects of learning foreign languages that cannot be quite fully grasped by traditional psycholinguistic or sociolinguistic research methodologies, because they are vague and fluid phenomena such as feelings, perceptions, bodily awareness and emotions that accompany language learning experiences. Kramsch is interested in accounts of language learning from the applied linguistics perspective, including an examination of the benefits of using accounts of language learning for teaching in the foreign language classroom. She examines three types of data: (1) published testimonies and "language memoirs". These accounts are viewed as reconstructions of past lived experiences that may not be fully representative of those experiences. They are also expressed within a variety of genres, including the literary. The potentially fictitious, occasionally literary nature of the texts Kramsch proposes to examine, leads her to espouse "modes of inquiry that take into account their metaphoric and literary nature", however, they are still construed at some level as "data" about language learning,

---

[12] Cf. Alison Phipps, *Learning the Arts of Linguistic Survival*, Clevedon: Channel View Publications, 2007, 3.
[13] Kramsch, *The Multilingual Subject*, 2.

revealing truths, though they be subjective;[14] (2) a variety of spoken and written data elicited in foreign language learning classroom contexts analysed from a sociolinguistic perspective; (3) online data from chat rooms, telecollaboration projects and text message exchanges.

The variety of data being used in the study already highlights the interdisciplinary nature of any kind of language study. *The Multilingual Subject*, by necessity, interweaves concepts and theories from applied linguistics, cultural studies, foreign language pedagogy, literary studies (including literary theoretical approaches) and second language acquisition. This makes the work difficult to place within a specific disciplinary field, a problem of identification that in itself echoes comments about the multilingual subject's fluid boundaries contained within the study.[15] This is nowhere more apparent than in the conceptualization of subjectivity, for which Kramsch states that it is the boundary which creates the subject.

Given the necessity of defining clear boundaries if only for the sake of maintaining secure language and continuing conversation, the differences between the concepts of selfhood, identity and subjectivity in Kramsch and the way in which these concepts are used here, will be explicitly articulated in the following paragraphs.

For Kramsch, the subject is a symbolic entity that is constituted and maintained through language.[16] The self is a psychological entity – it is not specified what form this entity takes, whether linguistic or non-verbal, emotional or otherwise. Kramsch also makes further distinctions between the "individual" as distinct from the collective community (a sociological or political entity with a particular identity), the "person" as a moral, quasi-metaphysical entity, the "self" as a psychological entity and the "subject" as a symbolic entity constituted and maintained through language. The terms are briefly defined and leave room for overlapping semantic ground: however, this is not necessarily a problem. It is perhaps again more useful not to view the categories as mutually exclusive, but instead as representing different aspects of the phenomenon in question, grouped together in various ways. Here it is conceptual rather than disciplinary boundaries that are being tested. The literature on conceptions of the self, identity, ego,

---

[14] Kramsch, *The Multilingual Subject*, 5.
[15] *Ibid.*, 184-85.
[16] *Ibid.*, 17.

consciousness and similar is in itself vast, with approaches to these key terms being made from a variety of disciplinary standpoints. The most that can be hoped for, by any individual researcher, is to set a pin in the ground somewhere within the shifting terrain to mark an initial navigation point.

In what follows, these concepts are explored a little further by contrast with Kramsch's formulation. Full justice to them would only be served by a far longer treatment than can be presented here.[17] The following aims merely to set a preliminary workable foundation for describing these abstract concepts, which can be viewed as coming into being in the act of their being described, by which understanding it is all the more important to identify how they are to be interpreted within this particular work.

Kramsch's notion of the "subject" and the conception of "self" used here resemble each other, insofar as the "self" in this work, is considered to involve maintenance through language or linguistic chatter. Since it is debatable to what extent there can be any kind of psychological awareness of self without language, the differentiation between self and subject is not adopted here. "Self" would then encompass Kramsch's conception of "self" and "subject". As described elsewhere, the understanding of it here, is something akin to consciousness.

Identity, Kramsch describes as "identification with a social or cultural group" but does not describe in what manner that identification is performed.[18] Here, it is understood that identity arises out of a projection of aspects of self towards the other and the response of the other towards that projection. The projection itself may be performed through language or other social codes, along the lines of Pierre Bourdieu's concept of *habitus*. On this understanding, identity could be described as the internalization of modes of being and behaving acceptable to a wider collectivity. It is reflected in response to the question "who are you?". It implies a certain social accountability about representation of the self.

The "individual" as a concept would by contrast emphasize difference from the collectivity, whether physical or psychological. It might be viewed as the suffusion of identity with selfhood – selfhood

---

[17] Indeed the topic is so vast and unresolved that the concepts have their own journal: *Self and Identity* published by Psychology Press.
[18] Kramsch, *The Multilingual Subject*, 25, n.9.

being that aspect of being that can differ from wider societal norms and expectations, whether these concern language or other social codes.[19]

Kramsch does not make explicit whether or not the concept of "person" as a metaphysical conception of the individual might not at some level also include the transcendence of individual personhood and involve the collective, in which case the sense of a separate person might be irrelevant. Nonetheless, "person" as a signifier, may be useful for indicating moral and metaphysical aspects of being. Again, precise distinctions between concepts referencing aspects of human being prove problematic as definitional aspects of the terms and contextual usage frequently reveal slippage. This movement between freedom and constraint by boundaries is one of the paradoxes of language both articulated by Kramsch and also here in slightly different form in the concept of *Metamündigkeit* presented in Chapter Nine. In that chapter, Julia Kristeva's idea of the semiotic, a pre-verbal realm in which bodily rhythms instantiate the beginnings of signification, is used to explore how authors of multilingual texts use creative use of multiple languages to disrupt the normal boundaries between sense and nonsense and between languages and cultures. It is particularly interesting for the way in which it emphasizes the role of the body within subjectivity. Kramsch takes up Kristeva's theory in a different way from Chapter Nine here when she details the concepts of "symbolic [1]" and "symbolic [2]". The former, which Kramsch compares with Kristeva's notion of the "symbolic",[20] describes symbolic forms as a mode of representation, the latter describes them as a mode of construction, constructing perceptions, emotions, attitudes and values.[21]

As Houxiang Li points out in his review of *The Multilingual Subject*,[22] there are a wide range of theories invoked in Kramsch's valuable work, not all of which are perhaps given the space and

---

[19] The idea of "society" or "collectivity" with a homogeneous set of norms values and expectations is in itself a reification of actual diverse social behaviours, values and assumptions. Such groupings and stereotypes are nonetheless psychologically real means of reducing cognitive complexity, as first indicated by Walter Lippman in *Public Opinion*, 1922 (http://www.gutenberg.org/ebooks/6456).
[20] Kramsch, *The Multilingual Subject*, 96.
[21] Cf. *Ibid.*, 7.
[22] Houxiang Li, "Claire Kramsch: The Multilingual Subject", *Applied Linguistics*, XXXII/1 (February 2011), 113-26.

elaboration they deserve. With some of the discussion above and the further discussion in Chapter Nine I hope to contribute in a modest way to their further exploration. What is certain is that the field of study concerned with subjective accounts of language learning experiences finds itself somewhat in flux – situated between disciplines and drawing on diverse concepts. Tentative steps are being made towards crystallizing some kind of "symbolic ordering",[23] as particular theories, theorists and concepts prove most valuable in application to these texts. Nonetheless, as the subject in question itself teaches us, while the bounding of such a study to a particular mode of analysis or discipline, such as applied linguistics or literary linguistics, or indeed the symbolic construction of a new field entirely, is necessary to even begin a discussion, this constraint risks the reduction and reification of the richness of human symbolic creativity and how we conceptualize our relationship to it.

Critical framework
Having established the approach taken here to some of the key terms relating to "language learners", this part of the chapter moves on to consider aspects of the relationship between text, society/culture and the individual that are relevant to how language learners construct their experiences in narrative.

Firstly, it examines how text may be related to "context" on the basis of the theoretical approach taken in social semiotics, a theory that has contributed to the development of the linguistic criticism outlined by Roger Fowler upon which the close reading of language learner narratives will be based. Within this discussion, the relationship between the individual, language, thought and reality is explored, since the conception of this relationship has direct implications for arguments about *Mündigkeit* in this process.

The social semiotic approach
To paraphrase Shakespeare: would "that which we call a rose / By any other name ... smell as sweet"?[24] Both the way in which a text is produced and the way in which it is received are dependent on cultural contexts for the attribution of significance. Social semiotics is

---

[23] On this concept, see further in Chapter Nine.
[24] See William Shakespeare, *Romeo and Juliet*, II.ii.45-46, in *The Portable Shakespeare*, New York: Penguin, 1977, 239.

a discipline that attempts to account for the processes of "meaning-making" or *semiosis* that give rise to the production and reception of texts within any given social and/or historical cultural context. In this section the merits of social semiotics as a theoretical approach will be evaluated.

Hodge and Kress provide the following definition for the discipline:

> Social semiotics is primarily concerned with human semiosis as an inherently social phenomenon in its sources, functions, contexts and effects. It is also concerned with the social meanings constructed through the full range of semiotic forms, through semiotic texts and semiotic practices, in all kinds of human society at all periods in human history.[25]

The scope of this book means that social semiotic methods are discussed in relation only to texts. It is therefore primarily concerned with language as a form of semiosis. However, social semiotics also provides tools for the analysis of culture in a broader sense including analysis of the composition of visual images, styles of dress, magazines, rites, ceremonies etc., what Hodge and Kress call the "multiplicity of visual, aural, behavioural and other codes".[26] In its concern with how human beings construct meaning out of their environment, social semiotics investigates cultural practices as a whole. This makes it particularly useful as a framework within which to examine texts concerned with cultural differences, since it facilitates a discussion of both culture and language as signifying practices. Language learner narratives can be described as accounts of individuals attempting to make meaning out of an unfamiliar language and culture. We may expect that in many cases the language learner's use of the later experienced language retains some of the semiotic practice common both to the first language and culture, depending to a greater or lesser degree, on the extent to which the author has assimilated the conceptual framework belonging to the later experienced culture. One of the interests in these texts is in the way in which semiotic practices and conceptual frameworks originating in the first culture interact with those originating in the second culture and in

---

[25] Robert Hodge and Günther Kress, *Social Semiotics*, Cambridge: Polity, 1988, 261.
[26] *Ibid.*, vii.

how this process is signified through employing the semiotic resources of the language associated with the second culture.

Social semiotics allows a consideration of language learner narratives both in terms of a process of "meaning-making" and in terms of semiotic practices as a whole. In the study of the texts presented here, language is accepted as a privileged system of signification in any culture over and above other semiotic practices such as visual arts, dance, kinship systems etc. If we accept that language is the predominant medium through which we conceptualize our environment, then it is reasonable to suppose that these other semiotic codes are subordinate to language and can be understood through it. The language and/or languages belonging to a particular culture are therefore likely to reflect and represent the social relations and concepts embedded in other media. It is perhaps also in this alternative sense that we may understand Claude Lévi-Strauss' description of language as the "semiotic system *par excellence*".[27] Where a non-linguistic semiotic code reflects a different reality to that presented by the language used within the same culture, for example, one in which gender relations are inverted, this is marked and is likely to serve a particular artistic purpose of subversion. In general, the fact that other semiotic codes within a culture frequently communicate the same value systems as language and may be easily described through this medium lends weight to the assumption that language is the primary medium through which we construct signification and develop cultural codes of all kinds.

The complex relationships between language, thought and reality hinted at in the above paragraph will now be explored in more detail, since the interpretation of this interrelationship has a direct bearing on the feasibility of employing *Mündigkeit* as a universal frame of reference for describing and explaining the experiences articulated in narratives of language learning.

In their own articulation of social semiotics, Robert Hodge and Gunther Kress draw on the work of Wittgenstein in order to suggest that the smallest unit of signification should be interpreted not as one linguistic element, such as the signifier for "cat", but as a combination

---

[27] The full quotation, which is cited in Daniel Chandler, *Semiotics: The Basics*, London: Routledge, 2002, 9, in fact reads "language is the semiotic system *par excellence*; it cannot but signify, and exists only through signification" (Claude Lévi-Strauss, *Structural Anthropology*, Harmondsworth: Penguin, 1972, 48).

of elements, together forming a proposition. A word is thereby no longer the primary example of a verbal sign. One of the problems with the concept of the "word" as verbal sign is that there are many words such as "the", "a", "quite", "so", "why", "because" that have no direct referent in reality. If instead a proposition is taken to be the smallest unit of meaning, we will always be able to picture the reality that the proposition signifies on what Hodge and Kress call the "mimetic plane", that is, the referential dimension of a semiotic phenomenon.[28] The distinction between the two propositions "a cat sat on the mat" and "the cat sat on the mat" therefore no longer needs to be discovered through the impossible task of knowing what "the" refers to, but can be explained through understanding "the" only in its relationship to other words within the relevant syntagm. However, since both propositions evoke the same picture of the world,[29] the distinction between the two propositions does not occur on the mimetic plane but on the "semiosic plane" concerned with the social dimension of semiotic phenomena, that is, how producers and receivers are linked to each other and to signifiers and signifieds. In the case of "the cat sat on the mat" and "a cat sat on the mat" the distinction marks a difference in how much knowledge of the cat the speaker wishes to imply is held by both speaker and addressee.[30] In using propositions as the smallest unit of signification any analysis of meaning necessarily draws on additional social and cultural knowledge. This is the starting basis for Hodge and Kress' social semiotic analysis of texts and other semiotic phenomena.

In Hodge and Kress' analysis we see how language is considered to be constitutive of social reality, that is, the relations that hold between individuals within a society. This is what Hodge and Kress term the "semiosic plane". In Chapter Five, entitled "Social

---

[28] Hodge and Kress, *Social Semiotics*, 261-62. In referring to the "mimetic plane" it does not seem that Hodge and Kress wish to suggest a direct correlation between a real extra-linguistic world and the language used to describe it, but rather to suggest that language creates a conceptual version of reality that can be mentally pictured.

[29] Here, it is understood that where Hodge and Kress state that the two propositions do not evoke the same "picture of the world", the inverted commas that they use around "picture of the world" serve to indicate that they mean a picture of the world on the semiosic and not the mimetic plane, since on the mimetic plane the propositions "a cat sat on the mat" and "the cat sat on the mat" clearly evoke the same picture of the world.

[30] *Ibid.*, 25.

Definitions of the Real" they outline their interpretation of the concepts of "truth" and "reality" in terms of the semiosic and mimetic planes as follows:

> "Truth" is ... a description of the state when social participants in the semiosis process accept the system of classifications of the mimetic plane. "Truth" is the state of affairs when the terms in the classificatory system, and the system itself, appear as "secure", ... to the participants in the semiosis process. "Truth" therefore describes a relation of participants in the semiosic process towards the system of classification which is at play in the process. "Reality" is the description by the participants of that part of the system of classification which is held to be "secure" and which is at play in the interaction. At the time when participants are prepared to invoke the term "truth", there seems to them a perfect fit between the system of classification and the objects which that system describes: a relation which seems at once transparent, natural, and inevitable.[31]

It can be seen here how in Hodge and Kress' interpretation reality is posited as "a description". The view that reality is a "description" is absurd within a realist metaphysics which accepts there is a world that exists independently of our own thoughts and beliefs. In a realist metaphysics, the term "reality" has a clear referent outside of human subjectivity that is more than a linguistic fabrication. Within a constructivist epistemology, however, "reality" appears as an idea within human subjectivity. In other words, reality appears to be interpreted as having no material existence outside of language that could ground the use of language and determine the truth of propositions. In these terms, Hodge and Kress' suggestion might appear extreme. But it is one that is also presented in poststructuralist discourse and in the writings of other social semioticians. In his *Language as Social Semiotic* (1978), Halliday has the following to say about the relationship between language and reality:

> ... as language becomes a metaphor of reality, so by the same process reality becomes a metaphor of language. Since reality is a social

---

[31] *Ibid.*, 122.

construct, it can be constructed only through an exchange of meanings. Hence meanings are seen as constitutive of reality.[32]

Either phrases such as "reality is a description" or "meanings are seen as constitutive of reality" are themselves being used in a metaphoric sense, so that the reality referred to is not a material reality but an abstract reality as it exists in the minds of individuals, or these phrases must be interpreted as espousing an extreme idealism or even a solipsistic constructivism in which matter is denied and the only proposition deemed to contain any truth of which we can be certain is that anything we hold to be real is in fact a linguistic construction. Taken to its logical extremes this statement seems to imply that there can be no reality without language since "meanings are seen as constitutive of reality". If these authors really are arguing for reality as a linguistic construction, one would have to wonder how, for example, babies and animals are able to interact with their environment at all, since for them, it would not exist.[33]

One of the key texts that articulates the viewpoint of social constructivism articulated here and that seems to have influenced the conception of reality found in Hodge and Kress as well as in Halliday, is Berger and Luckmann's *The Social Construction of Reality* (1966):

> We have seen how language objectifies the world, transforming the *panta rhei* of experience into a cohesive order. In the establishment of this order language realises a world, in the double sense of apprehending and producing it.[34]

In this description there is a clear contradiction between the proposition that language produces reality, thereby suggesting that there is no reality independent of language, and the proposition that language apprehends reality, thereby suggesting that there is a reality ontologically independent of language, that can be captured in language.

---

[32] Michael A. K. Halliday, *Language as Social Semiotic: The Social Interpretation of Language Meaning*, London: Edward Arnold, 1978, 191.
[33] This is not a problem if "babies" and "animals" are themselves considered to be products of the human mind rather than entities with independent existence.
[34] Peter Berger and Thomas Luckmann, *The Social Construction of Reality: A Treatise in the Sociology of Knowledge*, London: Penguin, 1966, 169.

In some articulations of social semiotics the decisive role that language plays in constituting subjective and social reality is at times presented as constituting reality as a whole, to the extent that material reality is rejected, instead being described as a discursive construction. The distinction between social reality and material reality is often somewhat muddied over in the texts, so that a discussion of "social reality" glides into a discussion of "reality" thus ignoring the crucial force of the modifier in the former phrase.

Berger and Luckmann, upon whom Hodge and Kress as well as M.A.K. Halliday draw, switch readily from a discussion of the function of conversation in "reality-maintenance" to a discussion of the way in which conversation maintains "subjective reality", to the assertion that "At the same time that the conversational apparatus ongoingly maintains reality, it ongoingly modifies it".[35] Shortly afterwards Berger and Luckmann concede that "subjective reality is never totally socialised …. At the very least the … individual will have the same body and live in the same physical universe",[36] but the problem that this raises for the thesis that reality is "socially constructed" is not entered into in great detail. In the philosophical prolegomena to their treatise, Berger and Luckmann articulate a view of reality that considers reality to be located in consciousness. The reality of everyday life they describe as

> … already objectified, that is, constituted by an order of objects that have been designated as objects before my appearance on the scene. The language used in everyday life continuously provides me with the necessary objectifications and posits the order within which these make sense and within which everyday life has meaning for me.[37]

The social construction of reality, for Berger and Luckmann, comes into being along with consciousness. In their thinking, the reality of everyday life as it is expressed in language is paramount. Any experience that cannot be mediated through language is considered somehow to pertain to a different reality:

> The theoretical physicist tells us that his concept of space cannot be conveyed linguistically, just as the artist does with regard to the

---

[35] *Ibid.*, 173.
[36] *Ibid.*, 176.
[37] *Ibid.*, 37.

> meaning of his creations and the mystic with regard to his encounters with the divine. Yet all these – dreamer, physicist, artist and mystic – also live in the reality of everyday life. Indeed, one of their important problems is to interpret the coexistence of this reality with the reality enclaves into which they have ventured.[38]

While acknowledging non-linguistic "realities", Berger and Luckmann privilege "everyday" reality that is mediated by language. In doing so, they are privileging social reality in their understanding of reality since without language there would be no consensus objectification of reality among groups of human beings. This social constructivist view of reality is both anthropocentric and linguacentric. In other words, it privileges a language-mediated discovery of reality.

The recurrent tension between a constructivist standpoint and the assumption of ontological reality that appears in much social semiotic discourse, also appears in Jay Lemke's *Textual Politics: Discourse and Social Dynamics*. Although Lemke's discussion is situated within the context of social constructivism, he also acknowledges a material reality that exists outside of discourse. He makes the point that our understanding of reality is socially and culturally distorted through the way in which our language abstracts away from the dynamic continuity of physical and biological life.[39] For Lemke, social control is furthermore not just discursive but also occurs through threat of bodily pain. This supports the proposition of a concrete material reality external to language:

> Our bodies are vulnerable to pain, and the deliberate inflicting of pain on bodies, is, I believe, the primary and fundamental mode of social control. Those of us who come from middle and upper-middle class subcultures, who identify with intellectual values, tend to resist thinking about socialization and social control in terms of bodies at all, and certainly in terms of pain [sic]. We would rather focus on verbal modes of control, on belief systems and value systems, on ideologies and discourses, on the purely textual politics of our society, but in an ecosocial system actions lead to change through linkages to other processes, linkages that are both semiotic and material.[40]

---

[38] *Ibid.*, 40.
[39] Jay Lemke, *Textual Politics: Discourse and Social Dynamics*, London: Taylor and Francis, 1995, 84.
[40] *Ibid.*, 133.

Lemke's acknowledgement of both the semiotic and the material is a starting point for the conception of reality that will be espoused in this study.

Here, a distinction is drawn between social reality within a particular cultural context and material reality. Taking a realist standpoint, natural non-human phenomena are considered to be asocial in and of themselves. Human beings can attribute meanings to these phenomena but without us being there they remain real.[41] It is therefore maintained that a material reality exists that precedes human perception. Language does not produce reality, rather reality precedes language. But language does shape our perception of that reality. It is, however, predominantly constitutive of aspects of the world pertaining to human culture and to social relations and institutions. This appears to be the "reality" that social semioticians are primarily concerned with, so that they are often seemingly caught in a tautology in which it is claimed that social reality is socially constructed. The emphasis on the social within their theory of reality might itself be viewed as a proof that their theory is indeed applicable to social reality, insofar as this emphasis can be viewed as an inclination deriving from their own standpoint as sociologists. In other words, their own intellectual and discursive inclinations shape their stance towards "reality" so that social reality takes precedence in their understanding of the concept. Material reality is thereby sidelined in these discussions. This sidelining is particularly clear in the following statement from Lemke: "If we set aside as unproductive in this context various realist and positivist certitudes about the form of external realities, we can ask how our perceptions are shaped by both our own and others' habitual culture-specific uses of language, visual imagery and other semiotic resources."[42]

In the discussion presented here, social and material realities are given equal weighting. It is assumed that there is a material world that exists outside of discourse, but that language extensively shapes our social relationships and our culture and creates the social reality

---

[41] Cf. the quotation at the beginning of the chapter which actually reads: "That which we call a rose / By any other name would smell as sweet" (Shakespeare, *Romeo and Juliet*, II.ii.45-46. The realist views espoused here are also most convincingly defended in John R. Searle's *The Construction of Social Reality*, London: Penguin, 1995, which nicely inverts Berger and Luckmann's own title as well as their arguments.

[42] Lemke, *Textual Politics*, 96.

within which we operate, as well as steering our perception of material reality. Material reality is posited as one dynamic reality, whether or not that reality is differentially perceived in different cultures. Social reality is constituted as a variety of versions and/or perceptions of reality within the minds of language-users; as such it is diverse and pluralistic. For the purposes of this project it is understood that there exists both an objective reality, outside of the minds of individuals, and a subjective reality, which is socially constructed. The difficulty is that language rarely manages the task of objectively describing reality. Our understanding of reality is bound up with the cultural significance we attribute to different aspects of it, so that complete epistemic objectivity is frequently difficult and often impossible. How the material world might be translated into language is explored further in Chapter Eight, which examines George Lakoff and Mark Johnson's theory of conceptual metaphor and applies it to the analysis of language learner narrative.

Having now discussed how language is key in shaping our perceptions of reality and our interactions with it, if not actually shaping material reality itself, we turn to consider how this socially constructed reality may be represented in the minds of individual bilinguals.

Language, the individual and the world

This section presents some of the conceptual issues that might arise for language learners living in a foreign tongue, so as to consider some of the implications this might have for how the language learners make use of their translingualism in their writing.

Aneta Pavlenko criticizes Steven Pinker's claim that he has "never heard a foreign emotion word whose meaning was not instantly recognizable"[43] on the grounds that what he recognizes is an English translation and not the concept as it is expressed in the foreign language. Pavlenko makes a distinction between semantic and conceptual representations in the mind, on the basis of which it is possible to understand the meaning of a word without grasping the concept that underlies it. An understanding of the specific concept requires considerable experience of situations, ideas and events for

---

[43] Steven Pinker, *How the Mind Works*, New York and London: W.W. Norton, 1997, 367, quoted in Aneta Pavlenko, *Emotions and Multilingualism*, Cambridge: Cambridge University Press, 2005, 85.

which the word in question is relevant. Thus, while it may be possible to understand the definition of the Japanese term *amae* as a feeling of dependence on someone, it would be difficult for an English-speaker to say whether or not *amae* was relevant to a particular situation. There is furthermore the problem that a person from another culture will more than likely evaluate the concept from their own standpoint. As Pavlenko states, "One also wonders to what degree they would be able to inhibit the appraisal dimensions of particular concepts acquired in the first language, and see the dependence encoded in *amae* as desirable, rather than a type of relationship that, in the Western view, adults should grow out of (Morsbach & Tyler, 1986)".[44]

In terms of language learner narratives, Pavlenko's distinction between meaning and concept implies, among other things, that without experience of the relevant culture, one can acquire the meaning of foreign words in the form of a translation into one's own conceptual framework, but that an understanding of the concepts belonging to a particular culture can only be developed through living in a foreign culture. However, the separation between meanings and concepts is not unproblematic. As René Appel points out, if meanings are what linguistic signs point to and concepts are external to language, grounded in non-linguistic multi-modal information,[45] then a concept cannot "belong" to a language, yet this is what Pavlenko at times implicitly suggests, when she talks, for example, about conceptual transfer between languages.[46] It seems that attempting to divorce concepts entirely from their linguistic encoding is somewhat doomed to failure since we constantly use language to articulate concepts, indeed this is the only means by which we can express them, though our experiences might be quite different.

If we consider the non-linguistic multi-modal information as something that occurs within a particular cultural context, then this seems to flag up the close connection between language and culture. It is possible that a concept appears to be tied closely to a language, because it tends to be formed from non-linguistic multi-modal

---

[44] Pavlenko, *Emotions and Multilingualism*, 85.
[45] Pavlenko describes this information as taking the form of "imagery, schemas, motor programs, auditory, tactile and somatosensory representations, based on experiential world knowledge" (Aneta Pavlenko "New Approaches to Concepts in Bilingual Memory", *Bilingualism: Language and Cognition*, III/1 [September 2000], 2).
[46] René Appel, "Language, Concepts and Culture: Old Wine in New Bottles?", *Bilingualism: Language and Cognition*, III/1 (September 2000), 5.

information that is received in one particular cultural context and the linguistic label applied to it is one taken from a language that is frequently used in that context. It seems likely that this close connection between a concept and a specific linguistic label is mutually reinforcing, so that they are eventually almost indissociably linked in the mind. It is important to highlight this point because it is easy to forget, particularly in a European context with a typically and traditionally "one language, one nation" official form of geographical and cultural division that the two are not in fact indissociable: different cultures may be encoded in the same language and different languages might encode similar experiences, values and accepted modes of behaviour.

As the discussion of language, thought and reality above has shown, in this study it is held that language has a vital shaping impact on thinking, though it is accepted that some concepts may be non-linguistic. Thus, rather than considering that those who have first experienced a language later in life have acquired the meaning of a word without the relevant concept to go with it, one might suggest that they have misapplied their own concept of a word to the unfamiliar term. The concept of "bread" would therefore be applied to the French word *pain* and the English school pupil learning French for the first time, when speaking French will perhaps visualize a loaf of sliced bread rather than a baguette, because he retains his conception of bread from his earlier experience. However, we are not restricted to using *pain* to refer to a baguette and "bread" to refer to a loaf because the similarity of the concepts in the two languages allows for reference to one or the other according to the situation, so a bilingual in French and English might speak to his English son in French asking him to pass the *pain* that is in fact a loaf of sliced bread.[47]

Language learners living abroad thus face the problems both of acquiring the unfamiliar concepts that underlie foreign words, and also of being able to determine when they might have misapplied their own early experienced concept to a word from the new culture. If they

---

[47] Another argument against the conflation of conceptual and semantic representations is that some aphasic patients who have lost their linguistic capabilities have still been able to carry out tasks which require conceptual knowledge. However, it is worth considering whether or not such patients would have been able to carry out these tasks if they had never possessed language. See François Grosjean, *Life with Two Languages: An Introduction to Bilingualism*, Cambridge, MA and London: Harvard University Press, 1982, 247.

wish to understand and be accepted into the unfamiliar culture, they will furthermore also need to be able to accept that the early experienced concepts they are familiar with inhibit their use of the new language and are thereby compromised. The distinction also suggests that it is perfectly possible to use another language through, in large part, applying one's own early experienced concepts without ever gaining real insight into the other culture. Instead, as suggested in the analysis of the texts in the preceding chapter, one's own ethnocentric perspective may be retained. This makes the distinction between an ethnocentric and a non-ethnocentric stance appear very clear-cut. In reality, it is likely that language learners will be willing to challenge their early experienced conceptualizations to varying degrees. At the one extreme we find a visitor to another culture with no knowledge of the foreign culture who writes a travelogue about his/her experiences abroad from the perspective of his/her own culture. At the other extreme we find a language learner who has lived in the culture for an extended period of time, who has assimilated enough experiences within that culture to understand the conceptual basis for keywords[48] of the non-native language and who writes about the foreign culture on the basis of a far-reaching assimilation of his own early experienced conceptual framework to the framework of the later experienced culture.

The recent publication in the English language by Daniel Everett about the Pirahã tribe who live along the Amazon in Brazil potentially fits into this category. The author deeply admires aspects of Pirahã culture and his experiences go so far as to lead to renunciation of his Christian faith and to reconsider his relationship to any kind of "truth" that is not based on reason and immediate experience.[49] However, even with this admiration for the Pirahãs cultural value of immediacy, certain cultural practices, that the author attributes to a strongly Darwinist perspective on life, are not so easily accepted by an outsider. Everett's mentor Steve Sheldon reports an incident in which a woman can be heard on a nearby beach screaming in pain with a breech birth

---

[48] For a fascinating study of how commonly used lexical items can index core cultural concepts, see Anna Wierzbicka, *Understanding Cultures through their Key Words: English, Russian, Polish, German and Japanese*, Oxford: Oxford University Press, 1997.

[49] Daniel Everett, *Don't Sleep, There are Snakes: Life and Language in the Amazonian Jungle*, London: Profile Books, 2008, 270-73.

where she is left to struggle alone and eventually to die.⁵⁰ In another example, Everett and his wife have a adopted a sick baby whose mother has died, only to discover on returning one day from going jogging that some of the Pirahãs have force-fed the baby strong alcohol and killed it. They have done so in the belief that no Western medicine could make up for being nursed by a Pirahã woman and because they know that no Pirahã woman would nurse a sick baby in place of her own child. They also believed that the baby was already near death and that its suffering was simply being prolonged.⁵¹

Literature on the effectiveness of intercultural training has also shown that while an individual may come to have a good cognitive grasp of the perspective of another culture, emotional responses frequently continue to operate according to the norms of the earlier experienced culture.⁵² Thus, although Everett has come to respect the Pirahãs evolutionist approach to life, he still feels great distress and lack of understanding about the baby's death. This is not to say that the Pirahãs did not feel some level of discomfort and sorrow at the suffering of the woman in labour and at the death of the child, but that this suffering was more easily accepted within the culture as a necessary part of the group's survival. The example of Everett's experiences shows how difficult, if not impossible, is the wholesale adoption of alternative values, beliefs and assumptions. Although they may be modified, early experienced cultural values resist being re-written in their entirety.⁵³

For the authors of language learner narratives, it can never be a clear-cut case of adopting a later experienced culture and language and becoming "American" or "German", for example, since that understanding of the unfamiliar culture will always be in dialogue or in tension with an early experienced conceptual framework. The language learner cannot eradicate their past experiences of similar events, situations and phenomena that they had previously encoded

---

⁵⁰ *Ibid.*, 90.
⁵¹ *Ibid.*, 96.
⁵² Eva Kinast, "Interkulturelles Training", in *Handbuch Interkulturelle Kommunikation und Kooperation*, eds Eva Kinast, Alexander Thomas and Sylvia Schroll-Machl, Göttingen: Vandenhoeck and Ruprecht, 211-12.
⁵³ For further discussion of potential for cross-cultural assimilation in the context of literature and biography about missionary work, see Frampton Fox, "Reducing Intercultural Friction through Fiction", *International Journal of Intercultural Relations*, XXVII/1 (February 2003), 99-123.

differently. In fact, the language learner is unlikely ever to achieve the same conceptual understanding of a language as a speaker who experienced the language early in life, in a similar way to the fact that no two early speakers of a language will ever achieve precisely the same understanding as each other, though in the case of the language learner the understanding is likely to diverge more widely.[54]

As the language learner uses the less familiar language s/he can play with both cultural contexts, so that rather than using the language in a way that more closely resembles the understanding of those concepts as experienced by a majority of speakers native to that population, s/he is in a position, either intentionally or unintentionally, to broaden the signification of that concept by allowing it to reverberate with echoes of a different cultural experience to the one in which it evolved. To return to the "bread" example, for a bilingual who speaks English and French, the French *pain* can be translated as "bread" but it is not the same as "bread", just as the German *Brot* is not the same as *pain*. As the Frenchman writes about "bread", the possibility of *pain* will, arguably, always remain as an echo or possibility in his conceptualization of "bread", no matter how many times he has opened a packet of pre-sliced bread. The writing that emerges out of such conceptualizations, as exemplified in language learner narratives, has the potential to resemble more closely the conceptualizations embedded in the early experienced language, in the later experienced language or to reverberate with echoes of both. That is, a speaker with early experienced French, writing in German, can use the word *Brot* but use it with a certain ambiguity of reference so that it simultaneously connotes, for example, perhaps both a slice of rye bread and a baguette.[55] For this reason, although a text may clearly

---

[54] See Annette De Groot, "On the Source and Nature of Semantic and Conceptual Knowledge", *Bilingualism: Language and Cognition*, III/1 (September 2000), 7.

[55] François Grosjean outlines in more detail research into conceptual relationships in the bilingual mind between lexical items from different languages which have similar referents. In particular this research has considered the existence of a co-ordinate model of bilingualism in which concepts from the two languages are kept entirely separate and compound bilingualism in which the concepts exhibit greater overlap. These two models are now known in the literature as the "separate-concept model" and the "shared-concept, concept-association model". See also Wendy Francis, "Clarifying the Cognitive Experimental Approach to Bilingual Research", *Bilingualism: Language and Cognition*, III/1 (September 2000), 14-15. The degree of overlap is considered to be determined largely by the extent to which the languages were learned in different cultural settings. However, rather than making a clearcut

take the form of "German" the cultural resonances and pragmatics of language use are such that it situates itself in an ambiguous zone in which it might be, for example, neither "French" nor quite fully "German".

This section has outlined the view of the organization of concepts in the bilingual mind that is adopted in this book. In particular it has suggested that concepts, though separate from language, cannot always easily be divorced from the language in which they are encoded. Where there is convergence in some aspects of a concept the translation between languages will be relatively easy. One question that still remains is whether or not *Mündigkeit* is a term that can translate across languages and cultures so as to reveal universal applicability. In order to determine this, it would be necessary to pinpoint elements of its definition grounded in the non-linguistic and then proceed to apply the term to a variety of situations in a variety of linguistic and cultural contexts. In Chapter Eight of this book it is suggested that recurrent conceptual metaphors deriving from common non-linguistic aspects of human experience that are used in language learner narratives can be interpreted in relation to *Mündigkeit*. Without wishing to reduce every language learning situation to such terms, the other following chapters also aim to show that the concept of *Mündigkeit*, as developed here, exhibits wide-ranging, if not universal potential as a productive tool in the interpretation of the process of language learning as constructed in these texts. However, without the possibility of examining texts from a broader range of cultures and from non-European cultures in particular, the validity of *Mündigkeit* as a universal concept must remain beyond the scope of this study.

---

distinction in this way, it is now more generally accepted that a bilingual's conceptual system will be more or less co-ordinate/compound in different contexts and at different stages of acquisition or life experience (Grosjean, *Life with Two Languages*, 240-44).

Chapter Four

Linguistics and Literature:
Methodological Considerations

The linguistic approach to literature is not a new one. Given that linguistics provides a toolkit for the rigorous analysis of the medium of literature, it is in many ways remarkable that the disciplines of linguistics and literature have not already been subsumed into an overarching discipline within universities.[1] Nonetheless, within literary study that is not explicitly linguistic in methodology, some of the stylistic and more scientific and/or theoretical approaches to texts involving close reading developed after the publication of Ferdinand de Saussure's *Cours de Linguistique Générale* in 1916 have now become engrained to such an extent that some contemporary critics refer to nineteenth century discussions of literature that did not pay attention to the language of the text in very scathing terms indeed. In his introduction to literary theory Terry Eagleton speaks of the "aestheticist chit-chat" and "literary talk which would ramble comfortably from the texture of Tennyson's language to the length of his beard".[2] This chapter describes the methodological approach of this study, setting it briefly within its historical context and presenting some of the linguistic critical tools employed in the textual analysis.

Following on from Saussure's structuralism, the work of the Russian Formalists was some of the first to apply the methodology of linguistics to the study of literature. This movement is particularly associated with the writings of Roman Jakobson, Boris Eikhenbaum,

---

[1] For an interesting plea for diversity of methodologies in respect of literature and a caution against over-extension of scientific principles into this domain, see Deborah Cameron, "Evolution, Science and the Study of Literature: A Critical Response", *Language and Literature*, XX/1 (February 2011), 67-71.
[2] Eagleton, *Literary Theory*, 38.

Victor Shklovsky and Yury Tynanov.[3] Their work attempted to give literary criticism a more objective and scientific basis. As Macey argues, a similar close reading of texts developed in Britain as the Practical Criticism of I.A. Richards at Cambridge University in the 1920s and in the US in the 1930s to 50s as New Criticism certainly helped to contribute to English literature becoming a serious academic discipline, more concerned with the style of the text itself, "rather than a body of untheorized and subjective value-judgements".[4]

In *Literature as Social Discourse* (1981), Roger Fowler cites three key schools of thought that he considers to have contributed largely to the development of the later twentieth-century stylistics. These are Anglo-American literary criticism using verbal analysis such as the Practical and New Criticisms just mentioned; modern American and contemporary European linguistics; and French Structuralism. Aspects of these are considered briefly in the section below, more or less chronologically. The aim of this section is not to present a comprehensive survey but to highlight some of the key ideas that have contributed to Fowler's ideas about Linguistic Criticism.

Ferdinand de Saussure's *Cours de Linguistique Générale* (1916)

The work of the Swiss linguist, Ferdinand de Saussure (1857-1913), published posthumously in 1916, was to exert a great influence over the development of descriptive linguistics in the twentieth century. He is considered to be one of the founding figures of modern linguistics.[5] He is commonly known for three key ideas, or rather, the proposition of three dichotomies relevant to language that have been influential ever since the publication of the *Cours de Linguistique Générale*.

Firstly, Saussure makes a clear distinction between diachronic (historical) and synchronic (descriptive) approaches to the analysis of language. In the former, changes in linguistic state are analysed through time and in the latter, each stage of a language at a particular point in history is viewed as a self-contained system. This is not to say that languages are not constantly changing, but that in any given act of

---

[3] Macey, *The Penguin Dictionary of Critical Theory*, 336.
[4] *Ibid.*, 331.
[5] See, for example, Robert H. Robins, *A Short History of Linguistics*, London: Longman, 1997, 225.

communication the speaker makes use of language as it stands without reference to the syntactic and semantic changes of the past. At the beginning of the twenty-first century an English speaker can use the word "chair" without knowing that etymologically it derives from the Greek *kathedra* (lit. *kata*-down + *hedra*-seat) via the Latin *cathedra* and the Old French *chaiere*, whereas in diachronic analysis the linguist is interested in precisely this history. A synchronic analysis, considers the state of the language not just as perceived by an individual speaker but as it exists abstractly across all members of a speech community.

In his *Cours de Linguistique Générale* Saussure acknowledges that language is intrinsically social,[6] however, for the purposes of linguistic study, he chose deliberately to exclude the concretely social from his analysis of language. Instead, he refers in his study of language to *langue*: a suprapersonal abstraction from language as it is used across a particular society. Language as it is actually spoken by individual members of a speech community is labelled *parole*. This second dichotomy of Saussure's, *langue-parole* is problematic almost from its inception, as Robins suggests: "Much influenced by the sociological theory of Emile Durkheim, de Saussure perhaps exaggerated the suprapersonal reality of langue over and above the individual, more especially as he recognised that changes in langue proceed from changes made by individuals in their parole, while he yet declared that langue is not subject to the individual's power of change."[7] During the latter half of the twentieth century models of language ignoring the social function of language were increasingly outmoded in favour of models that take account of language in use in particular social contexts. The linguistic discipline of sociolinguistics investigates regional and social variation within languages[8] and the

---

[6] Saussure, *Cours de Linguistique Générale*, 21.
[7] Robins, *A Short History of Linguistics*, 225.
[8] Ronald Wardhaugh, *An Introduction to Sociolinguistics*, Oxford: Blackwell, 1998, 5: "while many linguists would like to view any language as a homogeneous entity and each speaker of that language as controlling only a single style, so that they can make the strongest possible theoretical generalizations, in actual fact that language will exhibit considerable internal variation, and single-style speakers will not be found ...."

discipline of pragmatics emphasizes the difficulty of developing context-independent grammar.[9]

Besides the dichotomy *synchronic-diachronic* and the more problematic distinction between *langue* and *parole* Saussure is also known for defining units of language in relative and not absolute terms. It is important in Saussure's theory that linguistic units are defined by their function with respect to other units of the linguistic structure, in particular through syntagmatic and paradigmatic relations. "Syntagmatic" relations are those in which linguistic elements relate to one another in a linear sequence whereas "paradigmatic" relations are those in which signs may be substituted one for another. The relationship between a noun and a verb is syntagmatic and may be marked by agreements for grammatical features such as person, number and gender. The relationship between nouns is paradigmatic – one noun may be substituted for another within a grammatical sequence. A unit's function within the linguistic system is determined by both its syntagmatic and its paradigmatic relations to other units in the system. Systematicity of description is characteristic of the vast contribution of Saussure's work to the development of the study of language on a scientific basis. His influence is found, for example, in the work of the Russian Formalists through Roman Jakobson[10] and in the work of the anthropologist Claude Lévi-Strauss [11] whose application of structuralism to the human sciences went on to influence French Structuralism of the 1950s and 1960s.[12] We will now consider some of the concepts and approaches deriving from these theories particularly relevant to the analysis of language learner narratives.

Russian Formalism
As Macey notes, Roman Jakobson dismissed more subjective discussions of literature as "a form of *causerie* which happily slipped from lyrical effusions on the elegance of poetic forms to anecdotes

---

[9] Stephen Levinson, *Pragmatics*, Cambridge: Cambridge University Press, 8.
[10] Richard Bradford, *Roman Jakobson: Life, Language, Art*, London: Routledge, 1994, 59.
[11] *Ibid.*, 3.
[12] Nigel Fabb, *Linguistics and Literature: Language in the Verbal Arts of the World*, Oxford: Blackwell, 1997, 3.

about the artist's life".[13] The Formalists' approach aims to be scientific, taking as its object of study the intrinsic qualities of the literary text. Each individual author's own style is to be studied as a linguistic system within itself. The text is abstracted from external reality and viewed as a linguistic object governed by intrinsic rather than extrinsic laws. Jakobson argued that literary study should be concerned not with literature but with *literaturnost* or "literariness" – those qualities that make a work a *literary* work. One of the devices considered to be intrinsic to literature was described by the Russian literary theorist, Viktor Shklovsky (1893-1984), in "Art as Technique" (1917) as *ostranenie* or "defamiliarization", in which habitual perception is disrupted and made conscious. Habitual perception is the mode of interpreting the world that is highly automatic and unconscious: "Habitualization devours work, clothes, furniture, one's wife, and the fear of war."

Habitualization makes us perceive the world according to common categories and stereotypes and prevents us seeing things as they are. Shklovsky considers that art is there to dehabitualize the everyday, "to impart the sensation of things as they are perceived and not as they are known" and to "make the stone *stony*" again.[14] Poetic language, which Shklovsky describes as "a difficult, roughened, impeded language", serves this purpose of defamiliarization.[15] Shklovsky furthermore notes that in many cultures poetic language has in fact been written in a foreign language, which suggests that a text's poetic quality may be quite literally induced by the unfamiliarity of the language in which the text is written, whereby it impedes immediate comprehension.

The concept of defamiliarization is picked up again in Jan Mukařovsky's (1891-1975) idea of "foregrounding" (*actualisace*)[16] in which maximum focus is given to the utterance itself, so that it is

---

[13] Macey, *The Penguin Dictionary of Critical Theory*, 336. Cf. Eagleton's comments above.
[14] Viktor Shklovsky, "Art as Technique", in *Literary Theory: An Anthology*, eds Julie Rivkin and Michael Ryan, Malden, MA: Blackwell, 2004, 16.
[15] *Ibid.*, 19.
[16] Terence Hawkes, *Structuralism and Semiotics*, London: Routledge, 2003, 58.

"deautomatized" and becomes conscious.[17] Mukařovsky considers this to be a key feature of poetic language in contrast to standard language. This view of poetry is also found in Jakobson, who considers the poetic function of language to be one in which focus is given to the message itself and not to what the message is communicating.[18] The Formalists were not concerned with the social context of the text's production, a feature also common to I.A. Richard's Practical Criticism, developed at the University of Cambridge in the 1920s.

I.A. Richards' *Practical Criticism*

As in the Formalist approach, Richards aimed at a close verbal analysis of texts in isolation from the context of their production. In his *Practical Criticism* (1929), I.A. Richards details the results of an informal experiment he conducted primarily with undergraduates reading English at Cambridge University, in which he distributed anonymous poems to people and collected their comments, upon which he would lecture the following week. In conducting his experiment he had three aims. The first of which was to provide, "a new kind of documentation to those who are interested in the contemporary state of culture whether as critics, as philosophers, as teachers, as psychologists, or merely as curious persons".[19]

The second of his aims, clearly stated in the introductory remarks to the book is "not only to present an instructive collection of contemporary opinions, presuppositions, theories, beliefs, responses and the rest, but also to make some suggestions towards a better control of these tricksy components of our lives".[20] In making some "suggestions towards a better control of these tricksy components of our lives" Richards appears to be aiming at developing subjective

---

[17] Jan Mukařovsky, "Standard and Poetic Language", in *The Routledge Language and Cultural Theory Reader*, eds Lucy Burke and Tony Crowley, London and New York: Routledge, 2000, 226.
[18] The Formalists' distinction between literary language and ordinary language is not uncontroversial: however, the politics of "literariness" is a debate which must be reserved for another occasion. See, for example, Roger Fowler, *Literature as Social Discourse: The Practice of Linguistic Criticism*, London: Batsford Academic and Educational, 1981, 20.
[19] Ivor A. Richards, *Practical Criticism*, London: Routledge and Kegan Paul, 1966, 3.
[20] *Ibid.*, 6.

opinions (subjective hence "tricksy"), in this case about poetry, on a more objective basis ("better controlled" hence objective). This objectivity derives from placing the text as an object of study at the centre of the analysis, but in doing so risks denying extra-textual factors that contribute both to its structure and its interpretation. As Eagleton notes: "It was the beginnings of a 'reification' of the literary work, the treatment of it as an object in itself, which was to be triumphantly consummated in the American New Criticism."[21]

New Criticism

As in Richards' Practical Criticism the primary focus of New Criticism is on poetry. The New Critics were based in the southern United States of America and included Cleanth Brooks, John Crowe Ransom, Allen Tate and Robert Penn Warren. These critics study the text as a linguistic artefact in abstraction not only from the social conditions of its production but also without major reference to the author. René Wellek and Austin Warren in their *Theory of Literature* (1949) vigorously condemn approaches to literature which focus on the author's biography.[22] Not only do New Critics condemn the idea that the biographical and social conditions of a text's production might in any way be relevant to an interpretation of the text, they also do not consider the text to have any influence on the world around it.[23] The text is to be interpreted in complete isolation.

The verbal analysis presented in the texts of New Criticism such as Cleanth Brooks and Robert Penn Warren's *Understanding Poetry* (1938), and René Wellek and Austin Warren's *Theory of Literature* (1949), investigates the effect of various textual characteristics but not through the application of linguistic theories and use of linguistic terminology. The effects considered include phonological effects such as onomatopoeia; rhythmic effects displayed in different metres; choice of lexis; tone; metaphor; symbol; use of rhetorical devices such as hyperbole and litotes and deviations in word order. The analysis

---

[21] Eagleton, *Literary Theory*, 38.
[22] René Wellek and Austin Warren, "Literature and Biography", in *Theory of Literature* (1949), eds René Wellek and Austin Warren, Harmondsworth: Penguin Books, 1978, 75-80.
[23] Fowler, *Literature as Social Discourse*, 12.

thereby followed on from the tradition of literary criticism to a large degree, but is significant for Linguistic Criticism in its focus on use of language.

As Fowler notes, this form of literary criticism gives impetus to the development of stylistics as a discipline. This impetus is also provided by the application of more sophisticated linguistic theories developed in the mid-twentieth century and beyond.[24] The following section presents some of the key linguistic concepts arising out of these theories, some of which will be applied, where appropriate, in the analysis of language learner narrative, particularly in the analysis of Özdamar's *Mutter Zunge* (1998). The main inspiration for Linguistic Criticism is taken from Roger Fowler. However, where there is an occasional lack of clarity in Fowler's presentation, concepts are drawn directly from the work of M.A.K. Halliday.

Reading the text: the tools of Linguistic Criticism
Fowler refers to his approach to literature as "Linguistic Criticism" in contrast to "stylistics" in order to emphasize that the approach to literary language is one that derives its terminology and approach from the discipline of linguistics in a more systematic and sophisticated way, rather than engaging in a close reading and borrowing or inventing terms as the critic deems appropriate.[25] This section outlines in detail Fowler's framework for analysis of language and argues for the increased methodological rigour of a form of literary criticism deriving its terminology from the discipline of linguistics.

Fowler's methodology examines language at all levels of structure and moves beyond what has traditionally been the highest unit of analysis in linguistics, the sentence, to examine text structure. In this, he additionally aims to take account of the pre-existing social, economic, political, and ideological discourses that shape texts.

---

[24] *Ibid.*, 14.
[25] Fowler, *Linguistic Criticism*, 1986, 2. Fowler cites the following as an example of this: David Lodge, *The Language of Fiction: Essays in Criticism and Verbal Analysis of the English Novel*, London: Routledge, 2002.

Branches of linguistics which examine units of language higher than the sentence, such as text linguistics[26] that were, at most, in gestation in 1977 when Fowler published *Linguistics and the Novel* have, since then, become more firmly established.[27] Furthermore, Saussurian and Chomskyan models of linguistics disregarding the social function of language have become more controversial. In examining how sentences are understood, it very quickly becomes necessary to consider issues such as speaker knowledge of how language functions within its social context. This new focus for linguistics is also reflected in the development of sociolinguistics and pragmatics. Sociolinguistics had its tentative beginnings in the middle decades of the twentieth century and became more firmly grounded in the 1970s with the work of Bernstein and Labov. As for pragmatics, Dan Sperber and Deirdre Wilson pinpoint the real catalyst for the development of this discipline to 1967 when the philosopher Paul Grice gave a series of lectures at Harvard, in which one of the key concepts was that of "implicature" or how we come to understand what is meant by what is said, rather than simply what is said.[28] Pragmatics thereby takes account of the social context of an utterance, rather than considering language in isolation from the situation of its production. We may place Fowler's approach to literary texts within the context of this broadening of linguistic study from language to the social situatedness of language. Although Fowler's Linguistic Criticism pays close attention to the text itself, it also aims to situate the text within its social context.[29] The following provides a brief explanation of some of the linguistic concepts relevant to this approach.

---

[26] For example, Robert-Alain de Beaugrande and Wolfgang Dressler, *Introduction to Text Linguistics*, London: Longman, 1981.
[27] Roger Fowler, *Linguistics and the Novel*, London: Methuen, 1977.
[28] Daniel Sperber and Deirdre Wilson, "Pragmatics", in *Oxford Handbook of Contemporary Philosophy*, eds Frank Jackson and Michael Smith, Oxford: Oxford University Press, 2005, 468-501.
[29] This contextual approach to the study of language was further developed by Fowler along with Robert Hodge, Günther Kress and Tony Trew at the University of East Anglia as "Critical Discourse Analysis". See Katie Wales, "In Memory of Roger Fowler (1938-99)", *Language and Literature*, IX/1 (February 2000), 6.

In traditional linguistic analysis, meaningful language is divided into several levels beginning with the study of minimal distinctive units of sound in phonology, up to the level of the sentence in syntax. Alongside phonology and syntax are included morphology, which involves study of word formation, in particular the description of morphemes (the minimal distinctive unit of grammar), and semantics, that considers word meaning. As previously mentioned, in the analysis of literary texts, study of the form of language is insufficient. A close reading of texts is far more productive if it involves an understanding of how language is used and this is where concepts from text linguistics, pragmatics and discourse analysis become relevant. Critical Discourse Analysis (also known as Critical Discourse Studies) in particular draws on a variety of disciplines such as rhetoric, text linguistics, anthropology, philosophy, sociopsychology, cognitive science, literary studies and sociolinguistics in order to critique language use and the way in which particular discourses may contribute to the constitution and reproduction of particular power relations within society.[30] In many respects, the following methodology fits within the eclectic paradigm of CDA, particularly given Fowler's involvement with the development of CDA at the University of East Anglia, however, it differs in the critical attitude taken towards the texts. One of the commonalities that unites different approaches, methodologies and terminologies within CDA is the critique of social power relations within macro-level discourse through the examination of specific instances of discourse strands within texts.[31] The aim of investigating language learner narrative is not to examine the texts as instances of wider discourses (re)producing power relations predominant within one particular society, but to consider the texts as individual creative acts that may make use of discourses in unique and unusual ways, particularly given the possibility that the texts may draw on discourses from more than one society. The examination of language learner narrative does not aim at uncovering power relations on societal level, but partly considers how these may operate on an

---

[30] *Methods of Critical Discourse Analysis*, eds Ruth Wodak and Michael Meyer, London: SAGE Publications, 2009, 3.
[31] A text may in fact contain within it several discourse strands that relate to different discourses (see *ibid.*, 46-47).

individual level, as language learners engage with the discourses that surround them. This differs from the general conception of the purpose of CDA.[32]

Fowler's Linguistic Criticism is therefore used as a model for Linguistic Criticism of the text without ideological or social critique. The aim remains a literary interpretation. This interpretation nonetheless aims to some extent at uncovering why the text might be structured in the way that it is. Employing the descriptive apparatus of traditional linguistics is not an end in itself. In other words, it is not enough to say that a particular poem involves alliteration on the basis of the phoneme /p/, but to explain the literary function of such alliteration.

The description of Fowler's methodology provided below is a summary based on three of his key texts *Linguistics and the Novel* (1977), *Literature as Social Discourse: The Practice of Linguistic Criticism* (1981) and *Linguistic Criticism* (1986).

For the analysis of textual structure Fowler suggests three key concepts. These are "thematization", "progression" and "cohesion". Thematization refers to the highlighting of key topics and themes in a text through linguistic manipulations such as word order changes, noticeable phonology or unusual use of vocabulary. Progression refers to the expectation that propositions in a cohesive text will form a logically or chronologically related sequence of ideas.[33] Fowler's

---

[32] I would disagree, for example, with van Dijk's assertion that "Power, power abuse, dominance and their reproduction typically involve collectivities, such as groups, social movements, organizations and institutions" (Teun van Dijk, "Critical Discourse Studies: A Sociocognitive Approach", in *ibid.*, 78). Power relations exist between individuals as much as between groups and not all of this individual power is derived from institutionalized social discourse, but may involve unique norms and rules, as in a variety of well-known kidnappings such as the Josef Fritzl case. In such a case, power is both materially and discursively constructed through physical imprisonment as well as verbal threats of being gassed or receiving an electric shock. In this case, wider social norms are transgressed through behaviours which include incest and imprisoning one's family. As shown particularly in Chapter Nine, transgression of social norms does not, however, have to include behaviour which society views as "criminal", but may involve other forms of individual creativity, which nonetheless take part in a powerplay between the individual and the discourses of the other contained in the language of which they make use.

[33] Fowler, *Linguistic Criticism*, 61.

concept of "cohesion" is taken from Halliday and Hasan who suggest five kinds of cohesive relationship between sentences. These are: "Reference", "substitution", "ellipsis", "lexical cohesion" and "conjunction". The following provides an outline of these concepts as far as they will be relevant to the analysis of language learner narrative – further details and subcategorizations with examples can be found in Halliday and Hasan's *Cohesion in English* (1978).

"Reference" occurs where a word in a subsequent sentence refers to a word elsewhere in the text. Use of personal pronouns (*he*, *she*) to substitute for a proper noun falls into this category, as does the use of demonstrative pronouns (*this*, *that*). Halliday and Hasan make further distinctions between reference to something outside the text ("exophoric" reference), and reference to something within the text ("endophoric" reference), subdivided into "anaphoric" reference (reference to preceding text) and "cataphoric" reference (reference to following text). These distinctions are useful in analysing a sentence such as: "That must have cost a lot of money." As Halliday indicates, it is not clear whether the word "that" refers to a preceding statement (that is, anaphoric reference) such as "I've just been on holiday in Tahiti" or to something outside the text, within the context of the utterance (that is, exophoric reference) such as a collection of silverware.[34] Exophoric reference is particularly relevant to language that is highly context bound and that assumes a high level of convergent knowledge between speaker and addressee. As such, exophoric reference will be less relevant to language learner narrative.

The type of substitution occurring in the cohesive relationship of reference as opposed to that of substitution itself is semantic rather than grammatical, though the distinction is not always clear-cut. The referent is the same in both cases, whether one refers to it as "that" or as "the holiday in Tahiti". The use of "that" in the preceding sentence, which substitutes for "the cohesive relationship", would be an example of such reference. On the other hand, substitution is a kind of grammatical shorthand. The referent will be similar but not the same. The substitute has the same grammatical function within the sentence as the item it replaces, but does not necessarily refer to precisely the

---

[34] Michael A. K. Halliday and Ruqaiya Hasan, *Cohesion in English*, London: Longman, 1976, 33.

same item. In the statement, "My axe is too blunt. I must get a sharper one", "one" refers not to the same axe but to a different axe. The identity is at the grammatical level where "axe" and "one" are both Head in the nominal group. Halliday suggests that substitution might be:

> ... the most strictly cohesive relation .... Substitution is a purely textual relation, with no other function than that of cohering one piece of text to another. The substitute, or elliptical structure signals in effect "supply the appropriate word or words already available"; it is a grammatical relation, one which holds between the words and structures themselves rather than relating them through their meanings.[35]

"Ellipsis" is a kind of substitution in which the item in question is replaced with nothing. Halliday alternatively calls ellipsis "substitution by zero".[36] He provides the following example of ellipsis: "Joan brought some carnations, Catherine some sweet peas." In this instance we assume that Catherine also "brought" some sweet peas rather than doing something else with them. Fowler makes the point that ellipsis is a cohesive device commonly found in dialogue. It provides evidence that speakers are focused on the same topic as well as sharing the same background knowledge. An example in French is provided in the passage below taken from Vassilis Alexakis' *Paris-Athènes* (1989): "J'avais décidé d'assumer mes deux identités, d'utiliser à tour de rôle les deux langues, de partager ma vie entre Paris et Athènes."[37] In this example, Alexakis puts the verbal phrase "J'avais décidé" to work three times (as indicated by the three infinitives) but only explicitly states the phrase once.

"Lexical cohesion" is an overarching term for the textual processes of "lexical reiteration", and "collocation". "Lexical reiteration", as the name suggests, involves, at its most specific, the repetition of a lexical item later in the same piece of text. Halliday, however, posits a scale of reiteration beginning with repetition of precisely the same lexical

---

[35] *Ibid.*, 226.
[36] *Ibid.*, 142.
[37] Alexakis, *Paris-Athènes*, 246: "I decided to adopt my two identities, to use each language in turn, to share my life between Paris and Athens."

item and moving through the alternative use of synonyms (for example "ascent" for "climb"), near-synonyms ("volume" for "book") and superordinate terms ("seat" for "chair"). Emine Sevgi Özdamar's *Mutter Zunge* (1998) exhibits extremely high lexical cohesion on the basis of lexical reiteration, as will be shown in the discussion of her work in Chapters Six and Seven.

"Collocation" is the natural co-occurrence of words all relating to the topic of a text within that text, thus if the text is about the weather, we might expect words such as *frost, snow, shower, rain, lightning* or *sunshine* to occur. We would be surprised to find words such as *negotiations, defeat, reparations* or *treaty*. As seen in the preceding chapter, in identifying a text as a language learner narrative, looking for collocation is a particularly useful tool. In such texts we would expect references to *conversation, country, culture, foreign language* (including references to specific languages such as *German, French, Spanish, English, Japanese* etc.); *mother-tongue, native, native-tongue, origin, script, sounds, tongue, translate, translation, verbal, voice, vowels, word, writing*.[38]

The final textual device taken from Halliday and Hasan that Fowler discusses is that of "conjunction". Conjunction indicates the semantic relationships between elements of the text that are not necessarily found in immediate sequence. As summarized by Fowler, conjunctive relations may be additive, adversative or causal. Additive conjunction occurs where a following sentence supplies additional information about a topic.[39] Fowler does not explicate the linguistic features that are characteristic of such conjunction; however Halliday and Hasan signal the key linguistic marker as "and" in its conjunctive function as opposed to its paratactic function where it coordinates two structural elements of equal status (for example, men, women *and* children; here *and* there etc.). In its conjunctive function *and* links a following clause to a preceding clause as an independent fact. Adversative conjunction occurs where the second sentence expresses a contrast or conflict with the first and may be, though is not always, marked by grammatical elements such as "yet", "nevertheless", "but", "despite", "though",

---

[38] This list is taken from a brief glance at selected citations from eight of the language learner narratives mentioned in this book.
[39] Fowler, *Linguistic Criticism*, 66.

"however" etc. Causal conjunction is present when the implicit or explicit relationships between clauses involve, for example, conditions, reasons and consequences.

The definition of terms provided here has not been intended as an encyclopaedic overview of all the possible linguistic concepts that may be deployed in the analysis of language learner narrative; however, it does suggest ways in which Linguistic Criticism can provide a more incisive approach to textual analysis. This will also be borne out in the textual criticism to be practised in the following chapters. Firstly, however, the next section will further justify the proposed methodology by defending semiotic analysis against common criticisms.

Apologia for a semiotic criticism

In presenting the following arguments it is understood that Linguistic Criticism, in its systematic analysis of language as a signifying practice (just one of many semiotic codes), may be considered a form of semiotic criticism, subject to the same objections as other forms of semiotic criticism. This section begins by summarizing some of the main arguments against a semiotic approach to literature, as presented by Daniel Chandler, before presenting the case for a modified semiotic approach to the texts as well as by suggesting in what ways this can be productive. It will be argued that the criticisms levied at semiotics are not so much of quality as of degree. In other words, the semiotic approach has its failings and perhaps the greatest has been to overestimate its analytic power and scientific validity. However, that does not mean that this approach should be entirely discarded. It will be argued that the quasi-scientific or objective methods of social semiotics can lend greater explanatory power to a subjective textual interpretation.[40] They enable the literary critic to analyse textual effects and to argue for a particular interpretation in a manner that keeps the language of the text and the social discourse this may reflect as a guiding principle for interpretation.

---

[40] Eagleton, *Literary Theory*, 90: "What semiotics represents, in fact, is literary criticism transfigured by structural linguistics, rendered a more disciplined and less impressionistic enterprise which, as Lotman's work testifies, is *more* rather than less alive to the wealth of form and language than most traditional criticism."

Daniel Chandler usefully summarizes some of the key criticisms levied at the semiotic approach:

> 1. Sometimes semioticians present their analyses as if they were purely objective "scientific" accounts rather than subjective interpretations. Yet few semioticians seem to feel much need to provide empirical evidence for particular interpretations, and much semiotic analysis is loosely impressionistic and highly unsystematic (or alternatively, generates elaborate taxonomies with little evident practical application).
> 2. Semiotics is often criticized as "imperialistic", since some semioticians appear to regard it as concerned with, and applicable to, anything and everything, trespassing on almost every academic discipline.
> 3. Semioticians do not always make explicit the limitations of their techniques, and semiotics is sometimes uncritically presented as a general-purpose tool. Saussurean semiotics is based on a linguistic model but not everyone agrees that it is productive to treat photography and film, for instance, as "languages".
> 4. Some semiotic analysis has been criticized as nothing more than an abstract and "arid formalism" which is preoccupied with classification .... Susan Hayward declares that structuralist semiotics can lead to "a crushing of the aesthetic response through the weight of the theoretical framework"
> 5. In structuralist semiotics the focus is on *langue* rather than *parole* (Saussure's terms), on formal *systems* rather than on *processes* of use and production.
> 6. Feminist theorists have suggested that despite its usefulness to feminists in some respects, structuralist semiotics "has often obscured the significance of power relations in the constitution of difference, such as patriarchal forms of domination and subordination".
> 7. Insofar as semiotics tends to focus on synchronic rather than diachronic analysis (as it does in Saussurean semiotics), it underplays the dynamic nature of media conventions .... It can also underplay dynamic changes in the cultural myths which signification both alludes to and helps to shape. Purely structuralist semiotics ignores process and historicity ....[41]

---

[41] I have inserted the paragraph numbers here. The extracts are not necessarily given in the original order. The points are taken from Chandler's extended online version of

The first criticism suggests that semiotics misrepresents and disguises itself; it is presented as an objective approach to the texts, when in fact its procedures and methods are no less subjective than other approaches. Sections of texts are selected to fit the argument being presented rather than a random sample being subjected to analysis. That semiotics may present itself as an objective approach, when its methods can in fact be highly subjective, is a problem that primarily derives from language in which semiotic criticism is coded raising the expectation of an absolute interpretation for a particular text. Semiotics risks disappointing the expectation of complete scientificity that its terminology performs. This is particularly the case, when that terminology is developed to such a degree that it forms an almost impenetrable elitist jargon. This jargon may be wielded as symbolic power over non-semiotic critics, thereby rendering very difficult any counter-criticism and any productive dialogue of alternative approaches to the text. In cases where the skill of the interpreter is low, the terminology may be used as a cover for lack of critical substance in the analysis. This is compounded by the fact that, as Chandler says:

> ... few semioticians make their analytical strategy sufficiently explicit for others to apply it either to the examples used or to others. Structuralist semioticians tend to make no allowance for alternative readings, assuming either that their own interpretations reflect a general consensus or that "their text interpretations are immanent in the sign structure and need no cross-validation".

Precisely for this reason, this project employs a Fowlerian approach that requires no more than a basic understanding of linguistic terminology in common use.

In his Introduction to *Linguistic Criticism* (1986) Fowler further emphasizes that while the techniques of Linguistic Criticism are highly productive in the interpretation of texts and a good deal more objective than many subjective analyses in the literary tradition,

---

Semiotics: The Basics (2002) which can be found at http://www.aber.ac.uk/media/Documents/S4B/sem11.html.

> ... linguistics is not a discovery procedure: not an automatic machine which, fed a text at one end, delivers at the other some significant generalizations about the character of the text. To pursue the mechanical metaphor, it is easy to envisage a machine which would run through a text and count, say, instances of nominalizations, or abstract words, or prepositional phrases, or whatever. But that would be mechanized numerical analysis, not linguistics (which is concerned with the nature of nominalization as part of a speaker's knowledge); and it is certainly not criticism.[42]

With the development and use of ever more sophisticated text analysis software in the last two decades, the type of machine Fowler describes is now a reality and enjoys widespread use in corpus linguistics. Text analysis software can help to back up or refute intuitions about a text. Through using word frequency counts with the help of a concordance programme one might, for example, be able to discover as yet undocumented themes in a text that may or may not be more significant than themes intuited to be significant. Along these lines, the computer application could provide more evidence for a line of argument, refute a particular argument or open up productive new lines of research.

In *Electronic Texts in the Humanities* (2000), Susan Hockey summarizes several other applications of text analysis software for literary analysis.[43] These include: 1. Researching the influence of one author upon another through matching exact and partially matching sequences of words; 2. Examining "phrasal repetends" or common collocates of particular words across an author's entire body of work; 3. Genre identification – Burrows (1992) has been able to identify texts as novels based on the high frequencies of *I, you, he, she* and the verb *said*; 4. Examination of the relationship between narrative and dialogue, and examination of characters, in particular with reference to grammatical words which are not normally examined in conventional criticism;[44] 5. Thematic analysis can be undertaken, though there is

---

[42] Fowler, *Linguistic Criticism*, 6.
[43] Susan Hockey, *Electronic Texts in the Humanities: Principles and Practice*, Oxford: Oxford University Press, 2000, 66.
[44] Hockey (*ibid.*, 70) cites the following quotation from John Burrows', founder of computational stylistics, *Computation into Criticism: A Study of Jane Austen's Novels*

necessarily a good deal more subjective input required in such studies. Here, the researcher must decide in advance in what ways the theme of violence, for example, is likely to be expressed in the text – which words can be deemed to be associated with this theme, for example. For this, relevant word lists and phrases would need to be compiled.

The examples above illustrate just some of the many issues in literary criticism into which text analysis software can generate insights. However, the software is only ever as judicious as the person who is using it. It is ultimately, as Hockey points out, for the individual researcher to ask themselves if the computer can help them with a problem they have already determined to solve rather than asking in a more vague way, what the computer might be able to do for them with no specific goal in mind.[45] It is up to the researcher to decide what they require the software to look for and why they consider it worthy of investigation in the first place. The apparent mechanical objectivity of computer software obscures the need for this subjective input to some degree.

Furthermore, the user of the software is limited by the subjective considerations of the software designers as to what is useful material to extract from a text and these may not correspond to the original project the researcher was undertaking, but in fact serve to distort the research process. Beyond considerations of time and energy and the dangers of obfuscating the subjective input into an interpretation, there exists the further problem that the researcher needs to be competent both in literary analysis and to a basic degree in computational linguistics, at least to the extent that s/he can productively use text analysis software. These investigations, while interesting and highly likely to become more significant in time, go far beyond the scope of this particular research project and beyond the current skill-set of this researcher. It is therefore partly for pragmatic reasons and partly because the methodology of computational linguistics in its application to literary texts is still being developed, that it is

---

and an Experiment in Method, Oxford: Clarendon Press, 1987, 1: "It is a truth not generally acknowledged that, in most discussions of works of English fiction, we proceed as if a third, two-fifths, a half of our material were not really there."
[45] Hockey, *Electronic Texts in the Humanities*, 67.

considered preferable in this project to keep to a linguistic analysis, making some use of common spreadsheet software.

In the linguistic critical analysis undertaken here, rather than viewing the lack of total objectivity as a disadvantage, it would be far more accurate to view the inclusion of a measure of objectivity as a distinct benefit. As Fowler and many other contemporary critics indicate, close analysis of a text limits the level of wild speculation and impressionism a critic can engage in and keeps the focus of the criticism on the text itself.[46]

This approach also provides a response to Daniel Chandler's fourth criticism. If we go beyond the scientific veneer of semiotics and the sense that it is somehow in opposition to "literary" criticism, we can instead use semiotics as an interpretive tool within an aesthetic and subjective response to the text. The understanding of sign systems and the construction of meaning within discourse that semiotics attempts to develop is as applicable to literature as it is to any other form of language and may be used to elucidate the ways in which the discourse of the text interacts with the value systems that shape our own identities in order to produce a particular aesthetic and emotional response. Fowler makes the point that although a text in itself is an objective fact, in that the language of the text pre-exists any reading of it, the significance of the signs present in the text, in terms of the discourses they represent, requires a semiotic analysis that extends beyond the text to the culture in which it was produced.[47]

Therefore, in response to the fifth criticism set out by Chandler, Roger Fowler's approach to literary texts uses the benefits of objective descriptions of linguistic structures while not being blinded to the fact that the text also functions as a social discourse and derives much of its meaning from the context of its production and reception. Fowler is

---

[46] See, for example, Eagleton's comments about "aestheticist chit-chat" (*Literary Theory*, 72).

[47] Fowler, *Linguistic Criticism*, 168-69: "a literary text, like any other text, is primarily the realization of a mode of discourse (more usually, more than one mode). That is to say, its basis is a way of writing that precedes it and is found more widely than in just the individual work .... although linguistic structures as such are objective (thus linguistic analysis is tremendously valuable in criticism), their significances in discourse cannot be read off automatically from the text: a semiotic assessment in relation to cultural factors is required."

not concerned solely with the structure of the language but with the ways in which the structures reflect the particular social meanings that appear to be embedded in the text. Chandler cites David Buxton on a similar point:

> David Buxton ... argues that structuralist approaches "deny ... social determination" and he insists that "the text must be related to something other than its own structure: in other words, we must explain how it comes to be *structured*" (Buxton, 1990, 13). We must consider not only *how* signs signify (structurally) but also *why* (socially); structures are not causes. The relationships between signifiers and their signifieds may be ontologically arbitrary but they are not socially arbitrary.[48]

Correspondingly, within Fowler's framework it is not considered sufficient only to examine the orthography, phonology, prosody, syntax and morphology of a text, since the text interacts with the culture(s) within which it is produced and this "Non-linguistic knowledge is required for a full reading of the text".[49] Furthermore, in response to the criticism that semiotics abstracts a text from its sociohistorical context and ignores the dynamic nature of meaning, Fowler's approach, drawing on social semiotics, views the text not as an object, but as a social discourse with an interactional dimension:

> To treat literature as discourse is to see the text as mediating relationships between language-users: not only relationships of speech, but also of consciousness, ideology, role and class. The text ceases to be an object and becomes an action or process.[50]

Fowler's view of the text not as an object, but as an action or process also offers a counter-stance to the seventh criticism, that asserts that structuralist semiotics may "underplay dynamic changes in the cultural myths that signification both alludes to and helps to shape". The criticism preceding this one that, "structuralist semiotics" has

---

[48] Chandler, "Criticisms of Semiotic Analysis", in *Semiotics for Beginners* (see n.41 for online address).
[49] Fowler, *Linguistic Criticism*, 169.
[50] Fowler, *Literature as Social Discourse*, 80.

often obscured the significance of power relations in the constitution of difference, such as patriarchal forms of domination and subordination, is partially countered in this book through the examination of the texts in terms of a struggle with *Mündigkeit*, which, as Chapter Five suggests, can be shown to be intimately related to societal power relations by expanding the description of this struggle with *Mündigkeit* by making use of Bourdieu's concept of linguistic capital.

To conclude, the semiotic approach espoused here allows for the fact that the critic can never expect to arrive at a final interpretation for the text, however objective and scientific the criticism purports to be. This acknowledges that if the critic is to make any statement at all about the text, s/he cannot avoid speaking from within his or her own interpretive framework no matter how reflexively and self-critically s/he proposes to do so. It is also acknowledged that the critic will also, to a greater or lesser extent, be swayed by his or her aesthetic and emotional responses, themselves engendered by the critic's primary enculturation.

The role of the critic: on interscription
In this study of language learner narrative, the aim is not to find a definitive interpretation for the text. Nonetheless the social semiotic approach proposed above is considered to offer a means to gain as much information as possible about the text and its sociohistorical context as well as a means to engage self-critically with the sociohistorical context of the critic, thus allowing for the detailed presentation of the context for interpretation as well as sufficient detail to argue for the validity of the interpretation within the proposed context. In this way, it is hoped to be able to provide a greater degree of evidence for the origins of the text and a better indication of the networks of signification and connotation in which the text is situated.

Where cultural differences exist between the contexts of production and reception, a social semiotic approach is even more useful, and makes the work of the critic even more valuable, since through setting the text within its cultural context, illuminating the construction of signification in both, and as far as possible clarifying the relationship between the two, the critic's description or interpretation can extend the meanings yielded by the text for the reader. It is proposed here that what the critic produces is neither a description (a re-representation of the text in his or her own words) nor an interpretation (with its suggestion of a greater degree of personal input in the description) but an "interscription". This new concept aims to suggest a piece of writing that mediates between the cultural context out of which the text was born (mediated by the author's own consciousness), the text itself, and the critic's own consciousness, shaped as it is by his own cultural context. The critic as interscriptor would be aiming ultimately at uniting other readers to the text in a relationship where there is greater understanding, even if this can never be perfectly achieved. The metaphor of "relationship" is deliberate since the role of interscriptor is to be understood as a kind of intercultural mediator between the conceptual framework of the text and the conceptual framework of the reader. The success or failure of an interpretation therefore hinges on the extent to which the critic is able to read a text with the greatest awareness of the conceptual meanings of the signs present, based on the fullest possible understanding of the contextual, cultural and individual factors that have informed the production of that text and on the critic's ability to communicate these meanings to the reader.[51]

This is admittedly a tall order, requiring facility to engage with concepts that do not accord with the critic's own conceptual framework on their own terms. It will furthermore be easier for the critic to communicate the significance of a particular text if s/he has a similar cultural background to the reader of the criticism. To take a simple example, if a text is written in Arabic and commented on in Arabic, then a reader, with no competence in Arabic, will have access neither to the text nor its criticism. For this reader, the signs of the text will point to nothing, remaining for him or her linguistically if not

---

[51] Cf. *ibid.*, 66: "The reader in a sense constructs a text – a version of a text – out of his own cultural knowledge, including his linguistic knowledge .... the version he constructs is adequate to the extent that his competence is adequate, and (as every critic and teacher of literature knows) readers' versions vary considerably because readers vary substantially in the degree to which they are attuned to the cultural systems which ideally relate to the text. This cultural relativity produces, for the writer, an awkward obstacle to communication: for the student of literature, a suspicion that reliable, agreed interpretation may not be possible."

culturally insignificant.[52] If the text is written in Arabic and commented on in English, then the reader is able to glean meaning from the text by way of the critic, without reading it, though that understanding is necessarily a reinscription of the text mediated by the critic. In a game of Chinese whispers significations are altered as the message passes from context to text to critic to reader.

This criticism aims to deepen the understanding of the culture presented by the original text by focusing on its linguistic structure. This does not mean viewing the meaning as being embedded in author intention or the author's biography, and thus, as Barthes argues in the "Death of the Author", limiting possibilities of interpretation,[53] but it does mean considering the signification of the text in relation to the cultural context of its production, since this is crucial in understanding not just probable meanings of the text but the specific cultural values, beliefs and assumptions communicated within the text.

Perfect interscription would pay equal attention to both the text and its context, with an awareness of the way in which the discourses of the text, and the cultural contexts of the text and the critic interact at a given moment in the process of making meaning. At its most comprehensive such a criticism could potentially demand the referencing of wide-ranging cultural material; however any danger of superficiality is made up for by the integrity of the methodology. When viewing literature as a form of communication between the writer and her/his imagined audience, then in analysing that communication, it is relevant as with any other form of communication to consider the producer of the message, the message itself and the recipient of the message, in this case the author, the text and the reader or interscriptor. The interpretation of any communication is possible only with reference to the conventionally accepted definitions for particular signs and these will be broadly similar within one language and cultural context, varying in connotation according to the social discourse within which they are embedded. An understanding of the social discourses represented in

---

[52] That is, the text could conceivably take on non-linguistic cultural significance as an artwork or as a sacred artefact.
[53] Roland Barthes, "The Death of the Author", in *Image-Music-Text: Essays Selected and Translated by Stephen Heath*, London: Fontana, 1977, 142-48.

the author's background, in the text's background and in the critic's background is not only vital to the most productive interpretations of a text, it arguably is definitive of a productive interpretation. However, it is worth reiterating that this is not intended to suggest that there is only one possible meaning for the text. The author is viewed not as the sole site of meaning for the text, but as a node in a network of discourses, a subject position upon which a number of discourses converge from some or all of which a text is derived that then forms its own node or site of discursive convergence. It may be possible to delimit a text by way of the discourses that it immediately excludes, though, ultimately the difficulty remains that every discourse to which it ostensibly does refer will also refer to other discourses, even those excluded in the text being read, in an infinite web of intertextuality. In reading, the reader constructs the limits of interpretation.

CHAPTER FIVE

MÜNDIGKEIT AND THE LINGUISTIC CONSTRUCTION
OF THE SUBJECT

Ich ... verlor meine Mündigkeit.[1]

It is argued here that the term *Mündigkeit* as it is used in Kant's essay "Beantwortung der Frage: Was ist Aufklärung?" may be productively reliteralized through examining its relationship to linguistic capital as described in the essays of Bourdieu contained in *Language and Symbolic Power*. It is shown that through reconnecting the term with its formal connotations of linguistic competence, it may be productively extended as a metaphor for the analysis of texts describing and using multilingualism. The German lexical item is considered to evoke a more useful conceptual paradigm for the criticism of such texts than the common English translations of "maturity", "majority" or "responsibility". The following discussion begins by examining the definition of *Mündigkeit* provided in Kant's essay, then considers how *Mündigkeit* may be linked to Bourdieu's concept of symbolic power before considering the relevance of *Mündigkeit* to the situation of foreign language learners in an unfamiliar social context abroad.

Within the context of Kant's essay two key definitions emerge for *Mündigkeit*. The first of these is to be found in one of the most cited passages:

---

[1] Abdellatif Belfellah, "Deutsche Sprache: Gnade, Erfahrung und Prüfung in einem fremden Idiom", *Lettre International*, XX (Spring, 1993), 60, cited in Simone Hein-Khatib, *Sprachmigration und Literarische Kreativität: Erfahrungen Mehrsprachiger Schriftstellerinnen und Schriftsteller bei ihren Sprachlichen Grenzüberschreitungen*, Frankfurt am Main: Peter Lang, 1998, 56.

> Aufklärung ist der Ausgang des Menschen aus seiner selbstverschuldeten Unmündigkeit. Unmündigkeit ist das Unvermögen sich seines eigenen Verstandes ohne Leitung eines anderen zu bedienen.[2]

The second sentence here implies also its opposite, and the definition for our term *Mündigkeit*, namely: "*Mündigkeit* ist das Vermögen sich seines eigenen Verstandes ohne Leitung eines anderen zu bedienen."[3] In other words, *Mündigkeit* is the ability to use one's reason without being led by another, and the possession of *Mündigkeit* implies Enlightenment. One key aspect of *Mündigkeit* that arises out of this primary definition is its status as a competence or ability. Another aspect of *Mündigkeit* is that of *independent* reason. Kant makes clear that it is not enough to have the ability to reason independently, *Mündigkeit* also requires an underlying courage and decisiveness that promote the actual use of independent reason. Prerequisites for *Mündigkeit* are therefore the ability to reason independently and the courage to do so. Without courage to use one's independent reason, according to Kant's somewhat controversial suggestion, one may be considered guilty of "selbstverschuldete Unmündigkeit":[4] "*Selbstverschuldet* ist diese *Unmündigkeit*, wenn die Ursache derselben nicht am Mangel des Verstandes, sondern der Entschließung und des Mutes liegt, sich seiner ohne Leitung eines andern zu bedienen."[5]

These two prerequisites for *Mündigkeit* are summarized in Kant's Enlightenment motto: "Habe Mut, dich deines *eigenen* Verstandes zu bedienen!" ("Have the courage to use your reason independently!

---

[2] Immanuel Kant, "Beantwortung der Frage: Was ist Aufklärung?" (1784), in Ehrhard Bahr, *Was ist Aufklärung?*, Stuttgart: Philipp Reclam, 1974, 9: "Enlightenment is man's emergence from his self-inflicted immaturity. Immaturity is the inability to use one's own reason without being led by another" (my translation).
[3] Cf. Theodor Adorno, *Erziehung zur Mündigkeit*, Frankfurt am Main: Suhrkamp Verlag, 1970, 133.
[4] Cf. James Schmidt, "What Enlightenment Was: How Moses Mendelssohn and Immanuel Kant Answered the *Berlinische Monatsschrift*", *Journal of the History of Philosophy*, XXX/1 (January 1992), 89, n.63.
[5] Kant, "Beantwortung der Frage: Was ist Aufklärung?", 9: "This *immaturity* is *self-inflicted*, when the cause of it is not due to a lack of understanding, but the lack of courage and resolution to use it without guidance from another" (my translation; emphases in the original).

Dare to be wise!") A person who is *mündig*, according to Kant's definition, is someone who is daring to use their reason and doing so independently. This involves the assumption of personal responsibility: "Having attained *Mündigkeit* is said to enable man to pursue ends that are not determined *for* him but *by* him."[6] To follow Barnard, *Mündigkeit* is a moral capacity, founded on a conception of the individual as an agent of decisions.[7] The primordial choice is that of deciding to use one's own reason, rather than relying on the reason of another. *Mündigkeit* in this interpretation is therefore about the ability to make decisions and give reasons for those decisions. The moral quality that forms the basis for *Mündigkeit* is common to all. It is assumed that every human being has the ability to make a decision – informed or uninformed. However, we cannot speak of *Mündigkeit*, according to Kant's definition, unless we are certain that the decisions being made derive from independent critical reason and do not blindly follow the reasoning of another. At this point, we turn to consider what is to be understood by critical reason and furthermore by independent critical reason.

The issue of independent critical reason

The definition of *Mündigkeit* given so far, might read as follows. *Mündigkeit* is the ability and willingness/courage to use independent critical reason. In the following discussion, we examine what is to be understood by critical reason and examine the possibility of its independence as well as its relationship to language.

Thomson gives the following broad-brush definition for critical reasoning:

> Critical reasoning is centrally concerned with giving reasons for one's beliefs and actions, analysing and evaluating one's own and other people's reasoning, devising and constructing better reasoning. Common to these activities are certain distinct skills, for example, recognising reasons and conclusions, recognising unstated assumptions, drawing conclusions, appraising evidence and evaluating

---

[6] Frederick Barnard, "Aufklärung und Mündigkeit – Thomasius, Kant, Herder and The Enlightenment", *Deutsche Vierteljahrsschrift für Literaturwissenschaft und Geistesgeschichte*, LVII/2 (1983), 278.
[7] *Ibid.*, 289.

statements, judging whether conclusions are warranted; and underlying all of these skills is the ability to use language with clarity and discrimination.[8]

One might also say that critical reason involves setting forward hypotheses about our perception of the world; checking for underlying beliefs and assumptions and testing them against experience. Reason is uncritical when it is based on intuition, rather than analysis and when a person follows the reasoning of another, rather than coming to his/her own conclusions. Thomson suggests that linguistic competence underlies critical reasoning ability, but does not further explicate whether language is considered to be the medium of critical reason or merely serves to facilitate or augment reason.[9] The issue of whether or not language is a facilitator for critical reason or a necessary condition for it is linked to the debate surrounding the relationship between language and thought. The stance taken towards this debate within this book is outlined below.

In *Language and Thought* (1998), Carruthers and Boucher collate the latest thinking with regard to language and thought from an interdisciplinary standpoint and propose two main models of relationship. The first is the communicative conception of language, which regards language as an adjunct to thought. The second is the cognitive conception of language, which regards language as crucially implicated in thinking. They make a distinction between two types of cognitive conception: the first is the requirement thesis – that language is a necessary condition for thought, or certain kinds of thought; and the second is the constitution thesis – that language is the medium of thought. The constitution thesis is represented in the work of Wittgenstein, as in the passage below, where he suggests that the process of thinking is disguised in language and that it is language that gives us our picture of reality: "Die Sprache verkleidet den Gedanken. Und zwar so, daß man nach der äußeren Form des Kleides, nicht auf die Form des bekleideten Gedankens schließen kann; weil die äußere

---

[8] Anne Thomson, *Critical Reasoning: A Practical Introduction*, London: Routledge, 2002, 195.

[9] Cf. *Language and Thought: Interdisciplinary Themes*, eds Peter Carruthers and Jill Boucher, Cambridge: Cambridge University Press, 1998, 8.

Form des Kleides nach ganz anderen Zwecken gebildet ist, als danach, die Form des Körpers erkennen zu lassen ...."[10]

Carruthers and Boucher argue against such a thesis on the grounds that "it is perfectly possible that non-language-using creatures may have fully determinate thoughts, but thoughts that *we* cannot have knowledge of",[11] however, they readily admit that the requirement thesis

> ... has at least a degree of limited applicability, since it is plain that children rely upon language to acquire many of their beliefs and concepts. It seems obvious indeed, that a languageless person could never entertain thoughts about electrons or neutrinos, genes or cell-division, for example, since it is only through language that we can learn of these things.[12]

Wittgenstein's view of language is somewhat extreme if he intends, as Carruthers and Boucher suggest, that all thought involves language.[13] They further argue, that in fact "it seems most unlikely that language should be necessary for all forms of thought" and highlight cases such as Williams Syndrome, in which generally normal to high linguistic competence occurs with low cognitive ability, and Specific Language Impairment in which there is impaired grammatical competence along with normal non-verbal intelligence.

As an alternative to Wittgenstein's view, they argue that

> [the] cognitive conception of language need not involve any commitment to extreme claims of these sorts. First, it need only maintain that language is involved in (and is partly constitutive of) *some* kinds of thinking. It can thus allow that spatial reasoning, for example, can be conducted independently of language, while claiming

---

[10] Ludwig Wittgenstein, *Tractatus Logico-Philosophicus / Logisch-philosophische Abhandlung*, Frankfurt am Main: Suhrkamp, 2003, 30: "Language disguises thought. And indeed in such a way that one cannot make out the form of the thought thus vested from the external shape of the dress; because the external shape of the dress is fashioned for quite different reasons than to allow the shape of the body to be identified" (my translation). See also Thomas Mautner, *Dictionary of Philosophy*, London: Penguin, 2005, 657.
[11] *Language and Thought*, 4.
[12] *Ibid.*, 1-2.
[13] *Ibid.*, 3.

> that many other types of reasoning – such as reasoning about unseen causes, thinking about the thoughts of another person, or reasoning about which train to catch to be in London for a 3pm appointment – are crucially conducted in language.[14]

This view allows for the influence of language on perception without suggesting, along the lines of the Whorfian linguistic relativity hypothesis, that the structure of the human mind itself is experienced along with a language and culture.[15] Carruthers and Boucher offer the following weaker reading of the Whorfian Hypothesis.

> ... there remains the possibility that differences of a conceptual and grammatical sort between different natural languages might influence the *perceptions* of those brought up to speak those languages. Indeed there is mounting evidence that this is in fact the case .... Such a view is relatively weak, however, since consistently with it, we can allow that the *thoughts* and *thought-processes* of all human beings remain fundamentally the same (though whether this is because of the universal structures present in all natural languages, as the cognitive conception of language would maintain, can be left open).[16]

On the basis of this, it will be sufficient, for the purposes of this project, to accept as a reasonable assumption that the language one speaks has a shaping influence on perception, and is used in many reasoning processes, without constituting the whole of cognitive capability. This is an acceptable proposition whether or not one argues that language acts to augment human reason (communicative conception) or is the basis of human reason (constitution thesis). In either case, language is considered to have some significant role in everyday reasoning processes and perception.

Applying this understanding of thought within this book is furthermore justified by the fact that the contention that thought has a linguistic form accords with the subjective perceptions of the language learners presented in the literary texts, where they describe their awareness of thinking in one language or another:

---

[14] *Ibid.*, 12 (emphasis in the original).
[15] *Ibid.*, 6.
[16] *Ibid.*, 13 (emphases in the original).

> Ich bin entzweigerissen. Ich war schon immer entzweigerissen. Aber diesmal geht es nicht um Einheit und Widersprüchlichkeit eines Konzepts. Der Widerspruch ist die Sprache, in der ich denke. Ich finde nicht die Sprache, die das Erlebte ausdrücken kann. (Carmen-Francesca Banciu)[17]

> The thought that there are parts of the language I'm missing can induce a small panic in me, as if such gaps were missing parts of the world or my mind – as if the totality of the world and mind were coeval with the totality of language. (Eva Hoffmann)[18]

> In der Muttersprache sind die Worte den Menschen angeheftet, so daß man selten spielerische Freude an der Sprache empfinden kann. Dort klammern sich die Gedanken so fest an die Worte, daß weder die ersteren noch die letzteren frei fliegen können. (Yoko Tawada)[19]

These examples show that the concept of language as the medium of our thoughts is a common intuition, whether or not it is an objectively verifiable fact. Given this, it indeed seems reasonable to suggest, as Thomson does, that linguistic skill furthermore has a facilitating effect on the use of rational thought and critical reason, particularly of the kind that Kant had in mind. In his own essay Kant himself makes clear that reason may be expressed in writing or in speech. He speaks of the cleric's unlimited freedom "sich seiner eigenen Vernunft zu bedienen und in seiner eigenen Person zu sprechen" ("to make use of his own reason and to speak as his own person"), and of a scholar, "der sich an ein Publikum im eigentlichen Verstande durch Schriften wendet" ("who addresses, a public as such, in his writings").[20] If reason is expressed in language it suggests that

---

[17] Carmen-Francesca Banciu, *Berlin ist mein Paris: Geschichte aus der Hauptstadt*, Berlin: Ullstein, 2002, 44: "I am torn in two. I have always been torn in two. But this time it is not about the unity and contradictions of a concept. The contradiction is the language I think in. I cannot find a language to express what I have experienced" (my translation).
[18] Hoffman, *Lost in Translation*, 217.
[19] Yoko Tawada, *Talisman*, 15: "In your mother tongue words are attached to people, so that you rarely experience playful pleasure in the language. Thoughts cling so tightly to the words that neither the first nor the second can fly freely" (my translation).
[20] Kant, "Eine Beantwortung der Frage: Was ist Aufklärung?", 13.

this is also the form that reason takes in the mind. However, it must be borne in mind that linguistic competence does not automatically entail rationality. Language may be a medium of both reason and unreason as will be discussed in more detail in Chapter Nine.

Mündigkeit, Mund and the voice of reason

If critical reason is facilitated through linguistic competence, it remains to examine how linguistic competence relates to *Mündigkeit*. The form of the lexical item *Mündigkeit* itself implies a close connection with speech, since it apparently contains as its root morpheme, *Mund*. However, the etymological derivation of this word is somewhat more complicated. The Grimms' dictionary of 1885 cites the root of *Mündigkeit* as the feminine form of *mund*, a word that is not now commonly known in German:

> MÜNDIG, adj. gewalt habend; im alter sich selbst zu vertreten; ***ableitung vom fem. mund*** sp.2683. ein zunächst im mittelniederdeutschen als *mundich* (SCHILLER-LÜBBEN 3, 134ᵃ) erscheinendes, hier nicht auf die rechtssprache beschränktes wort, da es neben mündig auch vernünftig, bei verstande, und bevollmächtigt bedeutet ... [21]

According to Kluges' etymological dictionary of 1934 *Die Mund*, is in fact likely to be cognate with the Latin *manus* meaning "hand". The term appears in Old High German and Middle High German with the meaning of *Schutz* or "protection" along with the Old High German verb form *muntōn* meaning "to protect". The term *mündig* is a development from Middle High German *mündec*, which derives from this feminine form of *mund*.[22] *Mündigkeit* originally refers to the age at which a person can take legal responsibility for themselves. Previous to this age, they would have been a *Mündel* or *Mündlein*

---

[21] Jakob und Wilhelm Grimm, *Deutsches Wörterbuch, Bd. 1. Lief 1* (1885), Leipzig: Verlag von S. Hirzel, 1962, XII/1, Col. 2688-92: "MÜNDIG, adj. having power; of the age to represent oneself; ***derivation from fem. mund*** sp.2683. a word appearing in Middle Low German at first as *mundich* (SCHILLER-LÜBBEN 3, 134), here not restricted to legal language, since it also means sensible, sane and having authority..." (my translation and italics, bold italics in the original).
[22] Friedrich Kluge, *Etymologisches Wörterbuch der Deutschen Sprache*, Berlin: Walter de Gruyter, 1934, 402-403.

under the guardianship of a *Vormund*. The use of the term *mündig* is widespread in legal documents in this sense before Kant's use of it in his essay.

One of the many examples available in the Deutsches Rechtswörterbuch (DRW) is the following: "wenne eyn kint czwelff iar alt wirt, so ist is mundig unde man mag obir is richten."[23] However, as the Grimms show, citing a quotation from Lessing among others, the term *Mündigkeit* later develops an association with the cognate of its feminine root, the masculine *Mund* in the writings of various writers and translators, so that it develops the sense of "speaking for oneself" rather than remaining silent:

> wenn der neure dichter übrigens eine vermehrung der personen vorzunehmen für nöthig befände, so würde er, vielleicht nicht ohne glück eines von den beiden kindern des Herkules, welche seine beiden vorgänger nur stumm aufführen, **mündig machen können**. LESSING 4, 254

> mündig sei, wer spricht vor allen; wird ers nie, so sprech er nie. PLATEN 253

The association between *Mündigkeit* and speech precedes these two authors, as the Grimms further indicate, in Luther: "denn die weisheit öffnete der stummen mund, und machet der unmündigen zungen beredt. weish. Sal. 10, 21; aus dem munde der unmündigen und seuglingen ... hastu lob zugericht. Matth. 21, 16."[24]

Even if it is based on a false etymology, the connection between assuming legal responsibility for one's own actions – for what one

---

[23] From the online edition of the Deutsches Rechtswörterbuch: http://www.rzuser.uni-heidelberg.de/~cd2/drw/e/mu/ndig/mundig.htm. This text dates from around 1400: "When a child reaches the age of twelve, it is of age and may be judged."

[24] Grimm, *Deutsches Wörterbuch*, Col. 2688: "If the novel poet held a multiplication of characters to be necessary, so might he, perhaps not without success, make one of Hercules' two children speak whom his two predecessors only presented as mute. LESSING 4, 254; He be 'mündig' who speaks before all; if he never becomes it, let him not speak"; "For wisdom opened the mouth of the dumb, and made the tongues of them that cannot speak eloquent" (*The Holy Bible*, King James Version, Wisdom of Solomon, 10: 21); "Out of the mouth of babes and sucklings thou hast perfected praise" (*The Holy Bible*, King James Version, Matthew, 21: 16).

does by one's own hand – and speaking on one's own behalf – assuming responsibility for one's own words – is evidently one that has commonly been drawn. It is in fact questionable to what extent the two may be reasonably distinguished. Assuming legal responsibility for oneself includes both words and actions, and so it would appear that the two etymologies, if such were not philologically invalid, warrant unification in the word *Mündigkeit* from the very outset. Whether or not *Mündigkeit* derives etymologically from *der Mund* meaning "mouth" or its feminine cognate relating to the age of legal responsibility, the term *Mündigkeit* itself encompasses the notion of speaking for oneself and by formal association (if not etymological or semantic) links itself to the concept of *Mund* within German culture.

Metaphorically, *Mund* may be used to denote speech, language, or the voice. However, in making this association between *Mündigkeit* and *Mund* it must still be borne in mind that Kant's original definition does not include linguistic competence as a necessary condition of *Mündigkeit* – rather he refers to the moral capacity to make decisions for oneself based on independent critical reason, though admittedly it would appear from the above discussion that language is implicated both in the reasoning process and certainly in Kant's essay in the expression of that reason. However, the basis for declaring a person *mündig* is not their linguistic competence, but their ability and willingness to use critical reason independently. Given this moral aspect to *Mündigkeit*, a person who is *mündig* may or may not possess great linguistic competence and critical reasoning ability. It is the decision to use whatever reason is available, and to do so independently, that is the constitutive basis for *Mündigkeit*. However, it would seem fair to suggest that greater critical reasoning ability increases the likelihood of independent use of critical reason, since the critical subject in question will possess a greater number of concepts at his/her disposal, thus increasing the probability that he/she may combine these in an independent way. Furthermore, greater critical ability can reasonably be assumed in most cases to produce a greater degree of critical confidence, which itself may facilitate the moral decision or even desire to use one's reason independently. Thus, while linguistic competence may enhance critical reasoning ability,[25] it does

---

[25] Further evidence for this is given below.

not automatically entail *Mündigkeit*, even if it may be said to increase the likelihood of its occurrence.

Adorno makes a similar connection between reason and linguistic competence in his discussion with Becker, when he suggests that learning a foreign language might resolve problems of mental rigidity that contribute to *Unmündigkeit* in the case of those who have completed apprenticeships in a specialized area now needing to retrain: "Dazu wäre es dann z.B. nötig, daß er möglicherweise eine Fremdsprache lernt, obwohl er sie gar nicht braucht, weil ihm dadurch ein anderer Erfahrungshorizont entsteht."[26] Following on from the previous argument, it appears fair to suggest that there is a good correlation between linguistic competence and *Mündigkeit*, even if it is an indirect one. One could argue that such a correlation is assumed implicitly within cultures, such that migrant workers may be treated as citizens who are *unmündig* because of an assumed lack of linguistic competence. The simplified use of German with migrants in Germany (for example, verb forms being used only in the infinitive), commonly known as "Foreigner Talk", implies not only an expectation that migrants will not be able to comprehend full grammatical sentences in German, but at another level that a form of "baby talk" is all that would be appropriate to their general level of understanding. The following poem by the migrant author Kumar provides an entertaining example of such Foreigner Talk:

> ERSTAUNEN
> An der Haltestelle gestern
> kam ein Junge auf mich zu
> und fragte mich:
> Entschuldigen Sie
> Wie früh haben wir es jetzt?
> – "Fünf vor halb!" –
> Der Junge dankte
> Und ging weiter,
> Seinen Basketball dribbelnd.

---

[26] Adorno, *Erziehung zur Mündigkeit*, 142: "To this end, it would then be, for example, necessary, that he perhaps learn a foreign language, even though he does not need it at all, because a different horizon of experience arises for him through this" (my translation).

> In der Wilhelm-Busch-Strasse heute,
> Hielt neben mir ein Wagen an,
> Und ein nervöses Gesicht fragte mich:
> "Hallo! Du! Deutsch verstehen?"
> Ich blieb stehen und staunte
> Mein Staunen war zu [sic] vielleicht zu lang.
> Und seine Zeit vielleicht zu knapp.
> Daher zischte der BMW-Fahrer ein
> "Ach!"
> Und fuhr weiter.
> Ich stand noch da
> Und staunte weiter.[27]

Thus far we have seen that *Mündigkeit* involves a decision to use critical reason independently. That critical reason may or may not be well developed, but if it is, then this may facilitate its independent use. However, the question of how critical reason is to be independent has not yet been discussed. If the type of reason under discussion here is primarily linguistic then we must take into account the social nature of language and the linguistic construction of the thinking subject. If *Mündigkeit* requires independent critical reason, it will be useful to gauge to what extent such independent reason is possible, given its basis in language. For these purposes we will require an analysis of how *Mündigkeit* might be said to operate within specific social contexts. In order to do this, the concept will be examined in relation to Bourdieu's concepts of "linguistic capital" and "symbolic power". This discussion will form the basis for examining how the term *Mündigkeit* can usefully be applied to themes arising in language learner narratives. It will be argued that for the individual language learner any level of *Mündigkeit* (beyond that of a babbling infant), that

---

[27] From Anant Kumar, *Kasseler Texte*, Schweinfurt: Wiesenburg Verlag, 1998 cited in Marilya Veteto-Conrad, "German Minority Literature: Tongues Set Free and Pointed Tongues", *The International Fiction Review*, XXVIII/1 and 2 (2001), 81-82: "ASTONISHMENT / At the bus-stop yesterday / a boy came up to me / and asked: / Excuse me / How late is it now? / – 'Twenty-five past!'– / The boy thanked me / And went on, / Dribbling his basketball. / In Wilhelm-Busch-Strasse today, / A car stops next to me, / A nervous face asks me: / 'Hello! You there! Speaky German?' / I stopped still in astonishment / My astonishment was too perhaps too long. / And his time perhaps too short. / So the BMW-driver hissed a / 'Pf!' / And drove on. / I was left standing / Still astonished" (my translation).

has been facilitated through linguistic competence in the early experienced language, is destabilized on encountering a foreign language and culture. Through this encounter there is a loss of personal linguistic agency and symbolic power within the foreign context and a troubling of *Mündigkeit* induced through the challenge presented to the representation of critical reasoning in the foreign language and through the undermining of personal courage and sense of self in the foreign context. The discussion of the texts examines how this troubling of *Mündigkeit* is represented and in addition the thematic and textual strategies used for regaining *Mündigkeit*. Finally, it is suggested that in certain circumstances it might be reasonable to suggest that the language learners display not only the reassertion of *Mündigkeit*, but what might be termed *Hypermündigkeit* – based on heightened personal courage, independence and critical reason deriving from encountering another language and culture and the facility to understand alternative interpretive frameworks.

The linguistic construction of the thinking subject
As suggested earlier, there are cognitive abilities that operate without language, but we are specifically interested in that form of thought that is linguistic and developed through language. The correlation between linguistic competence and critical reason is accepted as a common belief for which there is a good degree of evidence. In considering the possibility of independent critical reason it must therefore be borne in mind that language itself is a social phenomenon, in which the signs and their related signifieds are determined by convention.[28] Consequently a person's linguistic reasoning can never be independent of another individual's, in an absolute sense, since the very concepts with which one is thinking and reasoning have their basis in social conventions.

This tension is explored in Peter Handke's play *Kaspar* (1968). The basic premise of the play is that language acts both as a means of offering a person a subject position and identity through language and also as a means of socializing and alienating that subject from itself and its environment, so that it can never truly speak independently. The way in which the constitution of the human subject is inextricably

---

[28] Cf. Saussure, *Cours de Linguistique Générale*.

intertwined with human culture external to the subject is also strongly articulated in Jerome Bruner's *Acts of Meaning* (1990):

> It is man's participation *in* culture and the realisation of his mental powers *through* culture that make it impossible to construct a human psychology on the basis of the individual alone .... Our culturally adapted way of life depends upon shared meanings and shared concepts and depends as well upon shared modes of discourse for negotiating differences in meaning and interpretation.[29]

If we accept this premise, then we must accept that absolutely independent reason cannot exist – no reason can ever be wholly independent of other ideas either preceding it or contemporaneous with it. If it were to be independent, it would be a reason, which, from the standpoint of society was in fact unreasonable. In actuality, such a situation is unlikely to occur, since, as the tragic cases of feral and neglected children show, highly developed language and corresponding linguistic reason, in most cases, do not evolve at all without input from society.

The acquisition of language provides not only a means of developing critical reason, but also offers a place in the symbolic order[30] and the production of an identity for the thinking subject. Here we will make a distinction between "self" and "identity" similar to the one made by Besemeres. The term "self" is used to refer to the subjective perception of independent being. It is akin to consciousness. This consciousness is brought about through linguistic interaction with the environment and the awareness of self and "other" that develops out of this interaction. It is a being or consciousness that has the potential for *Mündigkeit*. Besemeres, in more general terms, relates the concept to the idea of "an inner life". It could perhaps be described as the linguistic chatter of the mind when it is not engaged in conversation. It emerges for the first time through the early experienced language(s) and is characterized to a large extent by conceptions of individual being (or person) that are available in the early experienced culture. The type of culture (for example,

---

[29] Bruner, *Acts of Meaning*, 12-13 (emphasis in the original).
[30] This refers to the whole of culture, not just language (cf. Macey, *The Penguin Dictionary of Critical Theory*, 373-74).

individualist or collectivist) will be reflected in the individual's conception of self. Their consciousness of selfhood may be correspondingly inward or outward-looking.[31]

"Identity" is a narrower conception of self that emerges from the interaction of that "self" within the social situation. Besemeres describes "identity" as follows:

> A person's 'identity' is their answer to someone else's question 'who are you?', or to the question that they are obliged to ask themselves in front of others. It is a response to a kind of pervasive societal census.[32]

Thus, identity takes the form of various statements that the self perceives to be true according to the expectations of society. In English, common statements would be: "I am young/middle-aged/old; I am a mother/daughter/brother/father; I work as a..." etc. Such identity statements form the basis for a range of expected behaviours and modes of expression. It is the "self" which can imagine identifications that differ from the social norm. The extent to which the creation of alternative identifications is tolerated differs from culture to culture. In this interpretation both self and identity are linguistic constructions; the main difference is that the self is a moral agent who can make decisions about himself/herself as an individual, whereas identity is a socially sanctioned conception of that individual. Thus in terms of the migrant moving from one culture to another, both identity and selfhood must be renegotiated in the foreign language, but it is the confrontation of selfhood with the foreign language that has the greatest repercussions for morale, for reason and consequently for *Mündigkeit*. The learner's most intimate sphere, the "linguistic chatter" of the mind, is threatened as the concepts they took for granted in their mother tongue are challenged by the alternatives presented in the foreign language. Not only does the learner find himself/herself assigned a new social role (in many cases of lower status) and a new identity in the foreign culture, the very basis for how they perceive and organize their world is challenged. In the following

---

[31] Cf. Besemeres, *Translating One's Self*, 22 The definition for "self" here, invokes the concept of person in order, it is hoped, to alleviate Besemeres' justifiable concern that "self" is an anglocentric term.
[32] *Ibid.*, 21.

section, it is argued that this confrontation leads to the unsettling of *Mündigkeit* and that perceptions of the self within society and the consequent degree of *Mündigkeit* possessed by an individual within any one context are related to the possession of different forms of capital, as outlined by Bourdieu. In particular, we are interested in the acquisition of linguistic capital and its relationship to the development of symbolic power.

Mündigkeit and symbolic power

As we have seen, *Mündigkeit* is expressed through language. It was suggested that heightened linguistic competence might increase the likelihood of *Mündigkeit* and its corresponding expression in writing or speech. However, to be *mündig* does not necessitate linguistic expression and as will be shown in the following discussion, it is not so much the fact of possessing linguistic competence, as the fact of possessing linguistic capital within a given social situation that facilitates the expression of *Mündigkeit*.

The term "linguistic capital" is taken from Bourdieu and refers not simply to linguistic competence but rather to a specific kind of linguistic competence – one that is sanctioned by the most powerful members of society:

> Linguistic utterances or expressions are always produced in particular contexts or markets, and the properties of these markets endow linguistic products with a certain 'value'. On a given linguistic market, some products are valued more highly than others; and part of the practical competence of speakers is to know how, and to be able, to produce expressions which are highly valued on the markets concerned.[33]

In an absolute sense, one might be highly linguistically competent, but in relative terms that competence might be of no value within one's social context. In that sense, it is possible to possess a high level of linguistic competence but no linguistic capital.[34] Conversely, if one is

---

[33] John Thompson, "Translator's Introduction", in Pierre Bourdieu, *Language and Symbolic Power: The Economics of Linguistic Exchanges*, Cambridge: Polity in Association with Basil Blackwell, 1991, 18.
[34] Cf. Thompson, "Translator's Introduction", 21-22.

proficient only in the most prestigious form of language used in a society, one might possess more linguistic capital than another person who is fluent in several languages, none of which have prestige in that particular society. Those in possession of linguistic capital are also more likely to wield symbolic power – they will have higher status within the social hierarchy.

Their position is, however, dependent upon a tacit convention within that particular social context accepting that power as legitimate:

> ... in the routine flow of day-to-day life, power is seldom exercised as overt physical force: instead, it is transmuted into a symbolic form, and thereby endowed with a kind of *legitimacy* that it would not otherwise have. Bourdieu expresses this point by saying that symbolic power is an 'invisible' power which is 'misrecognised' as such and thereby 'recognised' as legitimate. The terms 'recognition' (*reconnaissance*) and 'misrecognition' (*méconnaissance*) play an important role here: they underscore the fact that the exercise of power through symbolic exchange always rests on a foundation of shared belief. That is, the efficacy of symbolic power presupposes certain forms of cognition or belief, in such a way that even those who benefit least from the exercise of power participate, to some extent, in their own subjection.[35]

In order for a person's critical reason to be validated within a particular social context, it is dependent on the authority that derives from the possession of symbolic power. So it is that Kant's scholars are in a position that allows them to freely express *Mündigkeit*. As Bourdieu states: "For the philosopher's language to be granted the importance it claims, there has to be a convergence of the social conditions which enable it to secure from others a recognition of the importance which it attributes to itself."[36]

It may therefore be the case that a particular person who is in all other respects *mündig*, is unable to express that *Mündigkeit* because of the prevailing social conditions, regardless of their level of linguistic competence and critical reasoning ability:

---

[35] *Ibid.*, 23 (emphasis in the original).
[36] Bourdieu, *Language and Symbolic Power*, 72.

> The competence adequate to produce sentences that are likely to be understood may be quite inadequate to produce sentences that are likely to be *listened to*, likely to be recognised as *acceptable* in all the situations in which there is occasion to speak. Here again, social acceptability is not reducible to mere grammaticality. Speakers lacking the legitimate competence are *de facto* excluded from the social domains in which this competence is required, or are condemned to silence.[37]

Mündigkeit cannot be an end state of reason to be achieved, since it is subject to the vagaries of social context. If a person is inhibited in expressing and therefore in exercising Mündigkeit within a particular context, this has repercussions for Mündigkeit itself. Not only does the doubt provoked by social censure inhibit Mündigkeit, but social censure may also affect the very development of Mündigkeit in the first place, given the pressure for the individual to make his/her reason conform to the reasoning of wider society.

Other members of society may censor the unacceptable voice, or the speaker possessing linguistic competence but lacking linguistic capital may censor himself/herself. At the social level we find suppression of the production of disfavoured forms of language through denying individuals the right to speak in a public arena, or in after-the-fact book burnings or other forms of censorship. At an individual level, the internalization of this censorship potentially results in silencing oneself, not speaking and not writing, but effacing the self. Relating linguistic competence to its value on a particular linguistic market, allows for the possibility that a person who possesses very little linguistic capital, in Bourdieu's terms, in one "linguistic market" or society, may find that they possess a great deal within another domain or society. At this point we turn to consider the situation of language learners living in a foreign language and culture with respect to the concepts of Mündigkeit, linguistic capital and symbolic power.

---

[37] *Ibid.*, 55 (emphases in the original).

Mündigkeit and the situation of foreign language learners

Thus far we have defined *Mündigkeit* as the ability and willingness to make decisions for oneself based on critical reason. This ability is facilitated and encouraged by linguistic competence; however a person does not need to be expressing their reason through language in order to be considered *mündig*. *Mündigkeit* is about the moral decision to use one's reason, whether or not one then expresses that reason through speech or writing. It was previously suggested that linguistic competence supports and encourages the independent use of critical reason, since it provides for a greater degree of individuality in the combining and even development of concepts. However, to re-examine the relationship between *Mündigkeit* and linguistic competence in a social context, it is more reasonable to expect that a person possessing the right kind of linguistic capital, not simply linguistic competence, would have more confidence in their own reason, since it will be validated by the symbolic power accruing to such capital. Symbolic power is grounded in the beliefs and values of one particular society, so we might expect that for one individual possessing a stable level of linguistic competence, he/she will possess different levels of linguistic capital and symbolic power in different societies. To consider this from the perspective of one language only, as shown in the studies made by sociolinguists such as William Labov, a particular accent or dialect will have different values depending upon the context in which it is being used and the way in which the power relations are structured in the speech community as a whole.

When it comes to the use of several languages, the relative prestige of different codes is somewhat more complicated, particularly because each language will represent a different set of beliefs and values and determinants for symbolic power. The conceptual foundation upon which critical reason was built in the first language is challenged, along with concepts of the self and others that allow the thinking subject to relate to their environment. The hypothesis that will be tested in the examination of language learner narratives conducted here is that the language learner living in a foreign culture is faced with several issues serving to trouble their basis for *Mündigkeit*. Firstly, by definition, as language learners, they automatically have limited ability in the form of linguistic competence valued in the later experienced culture. Their means of expressing themselves is devalued and they are automatically devoid of linguistic capital. Secondly, the challenge to their own cultural beliefs and values that the foreign language culture presents may undermine their sense of self as a thinking subject and further trouble their moral capacity to make decisions for themselves, as they come to question inherent assumptions in their own interpretive framework. Furthermore, in lacking linguistic and cultural competence, the language learner is reliant on speakers with earlier exposure to the language to provide a guide for the interpretation of their new society. If they follow their own reason, the learner is less likely to see the foreign culture from the alternative perspective necessary for its deeper understanding. Thus, both in terms of the loss of linguistic capital and the challenge to their sense of self as an autonomous critical subject, the language learner may in a literal sense, be demoralized, leaving them less able "sich seines Verstandes ohne Leitung eines anderen zu bedienen" ("to use one's reason without being led by another"). Their *Mündigkeit* is under threat.

In considering how a threat to *Mündigkeit* may be represented in these texts, it is important to be clear about who we are describing as the language learner. If we take as our language learner, the author of the account, then very often, the idea of apparent threat is immediately challenged, since each text, written in a foreign language first experienced after childhood, represents a supreme feat of linguistic competence on the part of the author. Given such levels of verbal expression, is it fair to suggest that the authors might in any way be *unmündig*? This depends on three issues. Firstly, whether or not the linguistic competence these authors exhibit holds the status of linguistic capital in the foreign culture; secondly, one needs to consider what is being said in the text, but furthermore, *how* it is being said, and the function which that form of verbal expression is intended to perform. In general, the discussion here focuses on the textual construction of the language learner and is not so much concerned with whether the language learner portrayed has the author as its referent or a fictionalized idea of the author, or a fictional character *per se*.

Even if the author can be shown to exhibit a high level of linguistic competence, this linguistic competence does not necessarily entail the rationality that is a further prerequisite for *Mündigkeit*. It is now worth turning to a consideration of unreason and its connection to language. The following presents a preliminary discussion of this issue that will be pursued further in Chapter Nine.

It is a truism that if one is speaking or writing, one is not necessarily speaking or writing rationally, in the sense of reason outlined above. It is possible to express thoughts that are disconnected from one another and contain free association not guided by any sense of logic. In *The Language and Thought of the Child* (1959), Piaget makes a distinction between syncretistic perception and deductive, analytic thought. He considers analytic thought to derive out of the ability to "adapt information" that is developed in dialogue with others. It is the product of successful linguistic socialization. Syncretistic perception on the other hand is, according to Piaget, to be found in egocentric logic – which he considers to be the initial mode of language for the child, before it begins to understand that other people have thoughts different from its own. In such logic a person jumps to conclusions, does not seek justifications, reasons by analogy, uses visual schemas and value judgements. Piaget compares syncretistic thought to the symbolism of dreams and suggests that processes of condensation and displacement as outlined by Freud are syncretistic operations:

> Like the dream, [syncretism] 'condenses' objectively disparate elements into a whole. Like the dream, it 'transfers,' in obedience to the association of ideas, to purely external resemblance or to punning assonance, qualities which seem rightly to apply only to one definite object. But this condensation and transference are not so absurd nor so deeply affective in character as in dreams or autistic imagination. It may therefore be assumed that they form a transition between the pre-logical and the logical mechanisms of thought.[38]

He goes on to suggest, on the basis of a text by Hans Larsson *La logique de la poésie* (1919) that the artistic imagination (which he considers to be one of the forms of autism) consists primarily in seeing objects not analytically as does intelligence, but syncretistically – it sees how the parts make up the whole, rather than how the whole

---

[38] Jean Piaget, *Language and Thought of the Child*, London: Routledge, 1959, 158-59.

may be divided into parts. This has implications for how we understand the metaphorical and formal associations many of the writers make within and across languages in our later analysis, particularly when it comes to the issue of understanding language play in Chapter Nine, where it would appear that Piaget's distinction between syncretistic and analytic thought is somewhat overdetermined.

When one has a greater range of linguistic forms at one's disposal one has greater ability to converge with the forms being used by one's interlocutor and appropriately adapt language to that person in a rational manner, but a person also has greater ability to use forms unknown by that person and to deliberately diverge. Potentially, depending on the languages or language varieties a person speaks or writes and the linguistic competence they possess, they could diverge from speech that is spoken anywhere in the world and speak an idiom that is an absolute idiolect, in that it could be understood in its entirety by no one but the speaker.[39]

The knowledge of more than one language gives the writer an extended range of stylistic possibilities in the production of their text. They may code-switch – alternating between two or more different language varieties in order to arouse different associations in the mind of the reader, or they may choose to write only in the foreign language, perhaps in order to circumvent the associations bound up with the words of the first language. This latter possibility is suggested by Leonard Forster commenting on Rilke's work in French:

> The use of a foreign language affords a further possibility: the words are not burdened with irrelevant associations for the poet, they are

---

[39] An absolute idiolect is rarely found, however, every representation of language articulated by an individual is but an imperfect copy of an idealized original or very often constitutes a blend of the various languages and discourses they have encountered. In her memoir *Chernobyl Strawberries*, Vesna Goldsworthy speaks about her grandmother's highly individual speech: "Surrounded by Hungarian, German and Romanian workers, she picked up words from their languages and for the rest of her life spoke 'Granny', a unique Montenegrin-Central European dialect in which Ottoman and Austro-Hungarian layers of vocabulary blended into a singular concoction. No one else in the world spoke this language." Here we see that within her family this idiolect has even been given the affectionate name of "Granny" (Vesna Goldsworthy, *Chernobyl Strawberries: A Memoir*, London: Atlantic Books, 2006, 186-87).

fresh and pristine. This is their appeal, particularly for a poet who has his great work behind him, in which he has exploited the resources of his mother-tongue to the full.[40]

A further possibility is that linguistic competence in more than one language, through the self-conscious awareness of language it may produce, and most certainly has produced for the authors of language learner narratives, in fact serves to undermine *Mündigkeit* since writers no longer experience the social need, or the personal ability, to commit themselves to any one socially sanctioned representation of the world, so that this linguistic confrontation may result in an illogical, at times often highly entertaining and creative, play of linguistic associations. Interestingly, Forster notes that:

> Concrete poetry has become a world-wide movement in the last ten years, and the juggling with sounds, letters and shapes gives rein to the deep-seated play-urge which we all possess. The result is a truly international poetic idiom, and it is worth noting that many of the pioneers of concrete poetry are polyglot by upbringing or by environment.[41]

The writers may create their own language, perhaps born out of a form of egocentric logic – one that can only be truly comprehended by another person with precisely the same linguistic competence as the author him/herself.[42] The language produced out of this self-conscious awareness, may, following Jakobson's analysis of linguistic purposes, be described as poetic: "The set (*Einstellung*) toward the MESSAGE as such, focus on the message for its own sake, is the POETIC function of language."[43]

---

[40] Leonard Forster, *The Poet's Tongues: Multilingualism in Literature*, London: Cambridge University Press in association with the University of Otago Press, 1970, 66-67.
[41] Forster, *The Poet's Tongues*, 88.
[42] Cf. Larkin and Littler's comments on Özdamar's *Mutter Zunge* in Chapter Seven where Larkin suggests that only Turkish-Germans can truly understand Özdamar's prose.
[43] Roman Jakobson, "Closing Statement: Linguistics and Poetics", in *Style in Language*, ed. Thomas Sebeok, Cambridge, MA: MIT Press, 1971, 356.

The idea that the confrontation of different languages within one text may serve in itself to produce the poetic will be explored in more depth in Chapter Nine. At this stage it is taken as sufficient to note some indications of support for this hypothesis. Firstly, in Gürsel Aytaç's analysis of the language used in Emine Sevgi Özdamar's *Das Leben ist eine Karawanserei* (1994), it is suggested that the poetry of the text arises out of the German being written with "türkisches Sprachgefühl" ("a turkish feel for language"). This, Aytaç claims, gives the text a magic which is lost in the Turkish translation.[44] This idea of the multilingual text would accord with Viktor Shklovsky's description of "literariness" in "Art as Technique". The automatic perception which a person experiences on encountering their own language is challenged when that language touches on the representations of the world presented by other languages. The multilingual text literalizes Shklovsky's idea of *Verfremdung* or defamiliarization. Ordinary prose is made other, made foreign:

> A work is created 'artistically' so that its perception is impeded and the greatest possible effect is produced through the slowness of perception. As a result of this lingering, the object is perceived not in its extension in space, but, so to speak, in its continuity. Thus 'poetic language' gives satisfaction. According to Aristotle, poetic language must appear strange and wonderful; and, in fact, it is often actually foreign …[45]

In terms of *Mündigkeit*, a poetic multilingual text may express verbal independence or individuality, but it does not necessarily express reason in the traditional prosaic form just outlined. However, it is commonly intuited that learning a foreign language "broadens one's horizons", "opens the mind" and provides for the understanding of alternative perspectives that Piaget considers essential in the development of rational communication. For this reason, the current project proposes to examine the possible function of the literary

---

[44] Gürsel Aytaç, "Sprache als Spiegel der Kultur. Zu Emine Sevgi Özdamar's Roman *Das Leben ist eine Karawanserei*", in *Interkulturelle Konfigurationen: Zur deutschsprachigen Erzählliteratur von Autoren nichtdeutscher Herkunft*, ed. Mary Howard, Munich: Iudicium, 1997, 176.

[45] Shklovsky, "Art as Technique", 19.

devices used and also the function of the text itself as a linguistic product with respect to *Mündigkeit*. The possibility will be considered that the literariness of the text, perhaps born of the confrontation of multiple languages, allows for the expression of a logic that may not accord with the type of reason traditionally accepted as *mündig* but which forms a logic of its own capable of challenging the Kantian term and superseding it in order to hint at a new way of understanding or *Metamündigkeit* that operates within and around traditions.

Before concluding this chapter we cannot leave aside a consideration of some of the similarities and differences that hold between language learner narrative and the traditional literary genre most commonly associated with the documentation of a process of *Mündigkeit* – the *Bildungsroman*.

Language learner narrative and the *Bildungsroman*

The traditional *Bildungsroman* – for which Goethe's *Wilhelm Meisters Lehrjahre* (1796) is often cited as an archetypal example – describes the socialization of a young protagonist. In the classic *Bildungsroman*, the development that occurs for the protagonist could be described as a transition from a culture of youth in which value is placed on the exploration of identity, to a culture of maturity in which identity has stabilized and value is placed upon exercising ones abilities within dutiful occupation. Moretti notes the following comments of Karl Mannheim on this point:

> In 'stable communities', that is in status or 'traditional' societies, writes Karl Mannheim, '"Being Young" is a question of biological differentiation'. Here, to be young simply means not yet being an adult. Each individual's youth faithfully repeats that of his forebears, introducing him to a role that lives on unchanged: it is a 'pre-scribed' youth, which, to quote Mannheim again, knows no 'entelechy'. It has no culture that distinguishes it and emphasises its worth. It is, we might say, an 'invisible' and 'insignificant' youth.[46]

This process of education is outlined in *Wilhelm Meisters Lehrjahre* (1796) as follows:

---

[46] Franco Moretti, *The Way of the World: The Bildungsroman in European Culture*, London: Verso, 1987, 4.

> Es ist gut, daß der Mensch, der erst in die Welt tritt, viel von sich halte, daß er sich viele Vorzüge zu erwerben denke, daß er alles möglich zu machen suche; aber wenn seine Bildung auf einem gewissen Grade steht, dann ist es vorteilhaft, wenn er sich in einer größeren Masse verlieren lernt, wenn er lernt um anderer willen zu leben, und seiner selbst in einer pflichtmäßigen Tätigkeit zu vergessen. Da lernt er erst sich selbst kennen, denn das Handeln eigentlich vergleicht uns mit andern.[47]

The *Bildungsroman* as a genre, arises at a time when youth is no longer the "pre-scribed" prelude to an adult life resembling that of one's forbears, but instead it comes to represent "an uncertain exploration of social space".[48] Continuity between the generations has been destabilized by social mobility engendered in part by industrial capitalism. Youth comes to represent this new age, characterized by mobility and inner restlessness. Within *Bildungsromane*, Moretti identifies two main principles of textual organization. The first, common in the Anglo-German tradition, is that of the "classification" principle in which the narrative has a clear teleology leading to a reclassification that is stable and definitive. The second, common in the Russian and French novels, is that of the "transformation" principle in which the focus is on narrativity and an open-ended process of meaning making without end.[49] In the former, there is a conception that youth must come to an end, whereas in the latter, "youth cannot or does not want to give way to maturity: the young hero senses in fact in such a 'conclusion' a sort of betrayal, that would *deprive* his youth of its meaning rather than enrich it".[50]

---

[47] Johann Wolfgang von Goethe, *Wilhelm Meisters Lehrjahre*, Munich: Deutscher Taschenbuch Verlag, 1999, 529-30: "When a man makes his first entry into the world, it is good that he have a high opinion of himself, believes he can acquire many excellent qualities, and therefore endeavours to do everything; but when his development has reached a certain stage, it is advantageous for him to lose himself in a larger whole, learn to live for others, to forget himself in dutiful activity for others. Only then will he come to know himself, for activity makes us compare ourselves with others." Translation from *Goethe: The Collected Works – Wilhelm Meister's Apprenticeship*, ed. and trans. Eric A. Blackall in collaboration with Victor Lange, Princeton, NJ: Princeton University Press, 1995, 301.
[48] Moretti, *The Way of the World*, 4.
[49] *Ibid.*, 7.
[50] *Ibid.*, 8.

These two contradictory principles are, according to Moretti, the essence of the *Bildungsroman*, that he furthermore considers to be the "*functional principle* of a large part of modern culture". He goes on to propose that:

> The success of the Bildungsroman suggests in fact that the truly central ideologies of our world are not in the least – contrary to widespread certainties; more widespread still, incidentally, in deconstructionist thought – intolerant, normative, monologic, to be wholly submitted to or rejected. Quite the opposite: they are pliant and precarious, 'weak' and 'impure'. When we remember that the Bildungsroman – the symbolic form that more than any other has portrayed and promoted modern socialisation – is also the most contradictory of modern symbolic forms, we realise that in our world socialisation itself consists first of all in the interiorisation of contradiction. The next steps being not to 'solve' the contradiction, but rather to learn to live with it, and even transform it into a tool for survival.[51]

Moretti summarizes this situation as the conflict between "the ideal of *self-determination* and the equally imperious demands of *socialisation*", or elsewhere as the conflict between "individuality" and "normality", that can be seen as a recurrent theme of modernity. How a teleology of *Mündigkeit* as described in Kant's 1784 essay, or as implied in the "classification" principle of the *Bildungsroman*, is to be squared with alternative deconstructive narratives focused on the processes of meaning making has been pursued to some degree in the introduction.

If we follow Moretti's interpretation of the *Bildungsroman* as a genre concerned with the contradictions and problems of processes of socialization in modernity, then narratives of language learning, particularly those with a focus on developing an identity within the foreign culture, certainly resemble this genre. If the *Bildungsroman* describes issues surrounding the primary socialization of a young person into his first language and culture, it can reasonably be argued that language learner narratives examine problems of secondary or tertiary socialization (and so on) in which the conflict between self-determination and socialization within the individual's biography is

---

[51] *Ibid.*, 10.

resumed. Arguably, the possibility of such resocialization is itself one of the key characteristics of modernity that contributes to the youthful character of the contemporary era and in turn lends further support to the principle of "transformation" which conflicts with the principle of "classification". The difficulty within postmodernism is that resocialization has increasingly become a norm against which entelechy struggles to assert itself. The incredulity towards metanarratives posed by postmodern thought refuses any final position and perpetuates the exploration of potentialities which in *Wilhelm Meisters Lehrjahre* (1796) was to form the first stage of the protagonist's education. We are asked to start anew, begin again, retrain and reconsider, since only by doing so is it possible to be fully socialized within a material society that itself is evolving faster than the course of any one individual life trajectory. Not only is there a break between generations, there is also a break within the course of individual histories. In contemporary society, the ideal of socialization demands a perpetual re-socialization which, it would appear, problematizes the very possibility of socialization to begin with.[52]

The next chapter suggests that a clear struggle with *Mündigkeit* in an intercultural context can be seen in Emine Sevgi Özdamar's *Mutter Zunge* (1998). Here, not only does the unfamiliar social context deprive the narrator of a voice, but the self is devoured in a love affair that develops between the narrator and her teacher of Arabic. It is argued that the threat to *Mündigkeit* is reflected both in the themes of the text as well as in the use of language.

---

[52] See also Susan Fanetti, "Translating Self into Liminal Space: Eva Hoffman's Acculturation in/to a Postmodern World", *Women's Studies*, XXXIV/5 (July/August 2005), 417.

Chapter Six

Loss of *Mündigkeit* in Emine Sevgi Özdamar's *Mutter Zunge*

The definition of *Mündigkeit* given in the preceding chapter outlines the way in which Kantian *Mündigkeit* may be associated with reason. The following discussion of Emine Sevgi Özdamar's text *Mutter Zunge* ("Mother Tongue") explores a particular tension already marked out as problematic for the development of *Mündigkeit*, namely that of the tension between the individual and society. In particular this text is shown to portray the way in which a desire for independent self-expression may be challenged by a conflicting desire for connection with others.

Much of the secondary literature examining Emine Sevgi Özdamar's collection *Mutter Zunge* (1998) has given primary focus to the author's migrant background, the loss and recovery of identity and the function of language in this respect;[1] recurrent tropes of the

---

[1] See, for example, Adelson, *The Turkish Turn in Contemporary German Literature*, 2005; Elizabeth Boa, "Sprachenverkehr: Hybrides Schreiben in Werken von Özdamar, Özakin und Demirkan", in Mary Howard, *Interkulturelle Konfigurationen: Zur deutschsprachigen Erzählliteratur von Autoren Nichtdeutscher Herkunft*, Munich: Iudicium, 1997; Christian Begemann, "'Kanakensprache'. Schwellenphänomene in der Deutschsprachigen Literatur Ausländischer AutorInnen der Gegenwart", in *Schwellen: Germanistische Erkundungen einer Metapher*, eds Nicholas Saul, Daniel Steuer, Frank Möbus and Birgit Illner, Würzburg: Königshausen and Neumann, 1999; Bettina Brandt "Collecting Childhood Memories of the Future: Arabic as Mediator Between Turkish and German in Emine Sevgi Özdamar's Mutterzunge", *Germanic Review*, LXXIX/4 (Fall 2004), 295-316; Margaret Littler, "Diasporic Identity in Emine Sevgi Özdamar's *Mutterzunge*", in *Recasting German Identity: Culture, Politics, and Literature in the Berlin Republic*, eds Stuart Taberner and Frank Finlay, Rochester, NY: Camden House, 2002, 219-34; Frauke Matthes, "Beyond Boundaries? V.S. Naipaul's *The Enigma of Arrival* and Emine Sevgi Özdamar's *Mutter Zunge* as Creative Processes of Arrival", *eSharp: Electronic Social Sciences, Humanities, and*

criticism being, for example, "hybridity", "the Third Space", and the defamiliarization of the German audience.

Arguably, this focus leads to a pigeon-holing of the text as a "migrant" text.[2] The thematic content is seen primarily in terms of Özdamar's status as a migrant and the migrant status of the narrator in the text. Perhaps this focus is one that Özdamar herself invites, given the suggestion put forward by Breger[3] that the language she uses aims to "perform" the status of a migrant or *Ausländerin* (foreigner), an individual who deliberately and subversively aims not to fit into some concept of homogeneous German culture.[4] However, if one considers the explicit theme of the text, what is being described is a universal experience that goes beyond any one cultural tradition, even if the way in which it is played out is influenced by particular sociohistorical circumstances. It is the theme of the love story. For the most part, this is mentioned in the secondary literature in passing, as if the love affair were incidental to issues of migration and identity. Here, the theme of the love affair will be used to show how Özdamar's writing appears

---

Arts Review for Postgraduates, V (Summer 2005): (http://www.gla.ac.uk/media/media_41169_en.pdf); Annette Wierschke, "Auf den Schnittstellen Kultureller Grenzen Tanzend: Aysel Özakin und Emine Sevgi Özdamar", in *Denn du Tanzt auf einem Seil: Positionen Deutschsprachiger MigrantInnenliteratur*, eds Sabine Fischer and Moray McGowan, Tübingen: Stauffenburg, 1997, 179-94.

[2] Sabine Milz comments on Michael A. Bucknor's description of the phenomenon of "exclusion by inclusion": "On the one hand, ethnic minority writers are given much public and academic support, while, on the other hand, the very same institutions tend to reduce them to 'ethnic ghettos' by racially and ethnically marking their works" (Sabine Milz, "Ethnicity and/or Nationality Writing in Contemporary Canada and Germany: A Comparative Study of Marlene Nourbese Philip's and Emine Sevgi Özdamar's Writing of Hybridity and its Public and Critical Reception", *Zeitschrift für Anglistik und Amerikanistik: A Quarterly of Language, Literature and Culture*, XLVIII/3 [2000]. See http://docs.lib.purdue.edu/clcweb/vol2/iss2/4/).

[3] Quoted in Kader Konuk, *Identitäten im Prozess: Literatur von Autorinnen aus und in der Türkei in Deutscher, Englischer und Türkischer Sprache*, Essen: Blaue Eule, 2001, 98: "Claudia Breger ... liest den 'Akzent' in Özdamars Texten als ein Zeichen dafür, daß darin nicht eine Türkin redet, sondern eine Figur, die als 'Ausländerin' posiert" ("Claudia Breger ... reads the 'accent' in Özdamar's texts as a sign that it is not a Turkish woman who is speaking, but a character who is posing as a 'foreigner'") [my translation]).

[4] In fact, Konuk, *Identitäten im Prozess*, 90 argues that Özdamar challenges ideas of cultural purity, such as are implicit in her often being positioned as a foreigner in relation to German culture.

not so much to present problems of ethnicity as problems of transcending a particular sociohistorical background in order to discover points of contact and connection. It will further be shown how the development of the love affair is a crucial factor and potential obstacle in the narrator's quest to rediscover her mother-tongue and a sense of self that transcends any one linguistic tradition.

The following analysis of *Mutter Zunge* (1998) examines both content and form. The analysis of form provides a detailed stylistic examination of how standard German is subverted in the text to create effects of defamiliarization and to reflect a challenge to cultural homogeneity. It also examines the way in which a poetic style is used in the text in a way that arguably reflects the romantic content. Reference will also be made to a suggested literary/social context for the text that indicates how some of the linguistic features appear to derive from the tradition of Ottoman Divan poetry. It will be shown that it is these elements suffusing the text which contribute in large part to the defamiliarizing effect of the text on its reception within German culture.

The main focus of the analysis of content is the way in which the possibility of a secure identity for the narrator is shown to be troubled by three interconnected issues. Firstly, her position as a migrant; secondly, the unequal power relationship of teacher and student; and thirdly, the ensuing love affair. It is argued that these themes are united by a quest for linguistic competence as a means to regain *Mündigkeit*; an independent *Mündigkeit* which is, however, disrupted in the text by the narrator's conflicting drive for connection and rootedness.

On power, love and letters

In the semi-autobiographical text *Mutter Zunge* (1998) the short stories "Mutter Zunge" and "Großvaterzunge", or "Mother-tongue" and "Grandfather-Tongue" tell the story of a young Turkish woman living in Germany. In order to rediscover the "mother-tongue" she feels she has now lost, she travels from East to West Berlin for lessons in Arabic, in order to reconnect with the Arabic script in which her grandfather wrote Turkish, before it was banned by Mustafa Kemal (Atatürk) in favour of Latin script in 1928.[5]

In the "other" Berlin the narrator meets Ibni Abdullah, described as a "great master" of Arabic writing. From the moment of their meeting, there are indications that a love affair is imminent. The first few paragraphs of the text send the symbol of the rose on a voyage from Western symbolism to Turkish aphorism as it is stated that Abdullah's hands smell of roses[6] and where he strikes, as a master, it is there that roses will blossom.[7] This serves to indicate that Abdullah is both teacher and potential lover. However, the love affair that develops, comes as a consequence of and as a complicating factor in the unequal relationship between teacher and student, with the teacher conventionally holding authority over the student. In this language learner narrative, the desire for linguistic competence offered by the teacher comes to threaten *Mündigkeit*, as the extreme emotions provoked by this desire threaten to overwhelm reason.

The opposition of emotion versus reason is one of several binary oppositions running through the text, oppositions which are, however, challenged and counter-balanced, as will be shown further on, by a spiritual and mystical perspective that threatens to dissolve the oppositions into unity in a non-linguistic realm.[8] The inadequacy of "dichotomous paradigms" for interpreting "the cultural capital of Özdamar's literary prose" is also detailed by Leslie Adelson:

> When spiritual longing is voiced in the language of erotic desire, however, as it is in Islamic mysticism and many other mystic traditions, the indexical words and letters of the tongue story appear anything but literal …. Littler finds that Özdamar's letters of the Arabic alphabet "liberate themselves" from scriptural doctrine and

---

[5] Özdamar, *Mutter Zunge*, 14.
[6] *Ibid.*, 15: "seine Hand roch nach Rosen" ("His hand smelt of roses": this and all subsequent translations from *Mutter Zunge* are my own). Cf. Littler, "Diasporic Identity in Emine Sevgi Özdamar's *Mutterzunge*", n.26.
[7] Özdamar, *Mutter Zunge*, 15 "die Hand der schlagenden Meister stammt aus dem Paradies, wo Sie schlagen, werden dort die Rosen blühen" ("The hand of the master who strikes comes from paradise, where you strike, there roses will bloom").
[8] Adelson in *The Turkish Turn in Contemporary German Literature*, 152, speaks of the "apparent aversion to polar oppositions in Özdamar's prose".

"symbolic reference" altogether (223-225). No personal, cultural, or national identity can be fixed, according to this analytical framework.[9]

The following provides an analysis of the precise way in which the apparent dichotomous paradigms are undermined by the inadequacy of language to express the quasi-mystical experience of love presented in the text, an experience which, it is suggested, transcends the personal, cultural and national boundaries described above.

The first apparent opposition is that of emotion and reason, that aligns itself in a traditional manner with the opposition between female and male. The protagonist's desire for Ibni Abdullah is contrasted with his role as a teacher guarding against the threat of emotion so that he can remain in control as a representative of the authoritative texts from which the narrator is to learn the Arabic script. Margaret Littler suggests that:

> For the western feminist reader it is clear that the Koranic texts from which she learns represent the Law of Islam, a patriarchal symbolic system which permits no expression to the protagonist's desire: "ich habe kein Wörterbuch gefunden für die Sprache meiner Liebe."[10]

One might argue that this western feminist interpretation overstates the case made against patriarchalism in the text. An alternative view sees the statement "ich habe kein Wörterbuch gefunden für die Sprache meiner Liebe" ("I have found no dictionary for the language of my love") not as a criticism of a patriarchal symbolic system, but of symbolic systems as a whole. Language is adequate for the division of the environment into discrete concepts but struggles to express the unifying holistic experience of an emotion like love.

Faced with this experience of love, the narrator struggles to regain the secure sense of self, rooted firmly in a particular linguistic tradition from which she can speak with *Mündigkeit*. Her insecurity has left her vulnerable to *Unmündigkeit*. She longs not for independent self-expression but the unity and self-dissolution of a mystical love, as will be shown in more detail below. This desire to

---

[9] *Ibid.*, 155.
[10] Littler, "Diasporic Identity in Emine Sevgi Özdamar's *Mutterzunge*", 223.

dissolve her autonomous sense of self is expressed in nostalgia for childhood, where no one would question her *Unmündigkeit*. Naïvely, she believes that she can be reborn into her mother tongue and feel the security and comfort of a connection with "her roots" through Arabic, the written script of her grandfather.

"Ich ging den arabischen Frauen mit Kopftüchern hinterher, ihre schwangeren Töchter neben ihnen, ich will unter ihre Röcke gehen, ganz klein sein, ich will ihre Tochter sein in Neukölln."[11] Hidden beneath the skirts of the Arab women, she could be literally "insignificant", signifying nothing, expressing nothing. Yet the narrator's apparent drive for self-diminishment is in fact in tension with an impulse to rediscover a sense of her self of which this drive simultaneously forms a part. She has gone to Ibni Abdullah in order to acquire the linguistic competence that she hopes will aid her to regain her lost identity. However, the discrepancy between her own level of competence and that of her teacher provokes inexpressible desire. Ibni Abdullah presents a tantalizing suggestion of certainty and security within her position as a migrant, endowed, as he is, with knowledge of the authoritative Koranic texts that the narrator seeks to understand in order to understand her grandfather.

Through the law and authority of the Koranic texts Ibni Abdullah may also claim authority over his pupil. In acknowledgement of her subordinate position in relation to Abdullah the narrator states:

> Wenn mein Vater mich in Ihre Hände als Lehrling gebracht hätte, hätte er mich in Ihre Hände gegeben und gesagt, "Ja, Meister, ihr Fleisch gehört Ihnen, ihre Knochen mir, lehre sie, wenn sie ihre Augen und Gehör und ihr Herz nicht aufmacht zu dem, was Sie sagen, schlagen Sie, die Hand der schlagenden Meister stammt aus dem Paradies, wo Sie schlagen, werden dort die Rosen blühen".[12]

---

[11] Özdamar, *Mutter Zunge*, 21-22: "I followed behind the Arabic women wearing headscarves, their pregnant daughters next to them, I want to go beneath their skirts, be quite small, I want to be their daughter in Neukölln."

[12] *Ibid.*, 15: "If my father had delivered me to your hands as an apprentice, he would have given me over to you and said, 'Yes, master, her flesh belongs to you, her bones to me, teach her, if she does not open up her eyes and ears and heart to what you say, beat her, the hand of the master who strikes comes from paradise, where you strike, there roses will bloom'."

This passage instates symbolic connections between Turkish and German through presenting the rose both as the product of submission to authority and as the flower of love.[13] The intoxicating passion that develops between the narrator and her teacher involves, for the narrator, subjection to authority as well as loss of autonomy, both of which are to be found in the "selbstverschuldete Unmündigkeit" described by Kant. Her desire follows not the logic of reason, but of emotion. She willingly submits to her teacher. As Konuk states: "Sie begibt sich freiwillig in eine Situation der Unfreiheit im 'Schriftzimmer' um den Befreiungsakt zu vollziehen und die Muttersprache zurückzugewinnen."[14]

The pain of being metaphorically beaten by her teacher expresses itself as the pain of *Liebeskummer* or lovesickness. Where the roses of love blossom, it is there that the narrator is truly lost. She dissolves into her environment as if she did not exist:

> Ich laufe, die Liebe hat mich gefärbt ins Blut, mein Kopf ist weder bei mir, weder weg von mir, komm und sieh, was die Liebe aus mir gemacht hat, deine Liebe hat mich gesehen, hat mein Herz rausgenommen, es krank gemacht, hat Absicht, es zu töten, manchmal bin ich wie ein Wind, manchmal wie staubige Wege, manchmal schlage ich wie Wasser auf Wasser, komm und sieh mich, was die Liebe aus mir gemacht hat.[15]

She is everywhere and nowhere, her situation is unstable, her identity unclear. She is like a wind, a dusty path. She is literally neither here, nor there, taken over by the unreason of this love. This passage shows how the narrator's selfhood, already weakened through lacking her mother-tongue, quickly dissolves in the face of Ibni Abdullah's authority. Her cultural identity is in flux and she is left with the

---

[13] Within Islamic mysticism the rose is also used as a symbol of love.
[14] Konuk, *Identitäten im Prozess*, 88-89: "She deliberately places herself into a situation of imprisonment in the 'writing room' in order to complete the act of being freed and to win back her mother tongue."
[15] Özdamar, *Mutter Zunge*, 28: "I run, love has coloured my blood, my head is neither with me nor away from me, come and see what love has made of me, your love has seen me, taken out my heart, made it sick, intends to kill it, sometimes I am like a wind, sometimes like dusty paths, sometimes I beat like water on water, come and see me, what love has made of me."

linguistic chatter of a mind endlessly code-switching, rearranging and integrating features of a range of linguistic possibilities, at the heart of which lies a creativity and desire, bordering on the mystical.

As previously suggested, the hints of mysticism in the text are arguably presented as a means for overcoming the binary oppositions evident in the narrative, collapsing these in a search for the universal. Konuk notes some specific oppositions and divisions in the text, in particular, the generation gap between mother and daughter, the division between East and West Berlin, between man and woman, Arabic and Turkish, Orient and Occident. Margaret Littler presents the elements of Islamic mysticism in the text as a way of bridging the gap between the narrator and her lover: "The total identification with the beloved implied by his 'entering her body' could be construed as an echo of the Sufi desire to overcome the painful separation from God, obliterating the sense of self to experience oneness with Allah."[16] The mystic tropes of the text reflect the narrator's increased syncretism with her lover and also emphasize the universal nature of her experience of love. Even her situation as female student of a male mentor, who represents the rational discovery of God through the text, suggests the syncretism of different mystic traditions, the Islamic and the Christian; the Arabic and the German; the medieval and the contemporary. The relationship between the narrator and Ibni Abdullah may be paralleled with the relationship between the uneducated female German mystics, seeking to find the words to express the emotional experience of *unio mystica* or union with God, and their male mentors, representative of a scholastic rational discovery of God. When the narrator states that she has no dictionary for the language of her love, it is not so much the feminist criticism of a patriarchal system as the struggle of a mystic attempting to describe an emotional experience going beyond words. The female German mystics of the thirteenth century, who devoted themselves to the speculative, emotional and experiential knowledge of God, also found that their experiences went beyond words. About such experiences, the

---

[16] Littler, "Diasporic Identity in Emine Sevgi Özdamar's *Mutterzunge*", 228-29.

male mystic Meister Eckhart can only say, "daz eines, daz ich dâ meine, daz ist *wortelôs*".[17]

The narrator believes she can regain symbolic power through competence in Arabic. However, despite the script's personal value to her, as the script of her grandfather, within the wider context of German society the script has little symbolic value. Ibni Abdullah transmits the desired competence to the narrator lesson by lesson. After the first lesson, the narrator heads out into Berlin having acquired a specifically quantifiable amount of language, her first five Arabic letters.[18] However, it soon becomes clear that in the mind of the narrator the letters are not such an inanimate commodity as they might at first appear. Very soon, they are anthropomorphized and take on an active, almost threatening, human quality. Instead of the narrator acquiring their symbolic power she submits to them. Like a schoolgirl timidly entering the schoolroom, she states: "Der Diwan, auf dem ich saß, machte mich artig. Ich sah dort auf mich wartende Buchstaben."[19]

In their anthropomorphosis, the letters have taken on their own threatening quality and they act independently of the narrator, not allowing her to possess them. She passively sat as: "Es kamen aus meinem Mund die Buchstaben raus."[20] This statement reflects a disruption of her use of language both literate and oral. As the letters come out of her mouth, they are empty symbols signifying nothing, like a monotonous recitation of the Western alphabet. On the page, they take on their meaning, not only in their conventional symbolic function, but also iconographically in the imagination of the narrator, described by Littler as a "picture-language of hearts, arrows, and

---

[17] "That which I mean is without words." See Werner König and Hans-Joachim Paul, *Dtv-Atlas zur Deutschen Sprache*, Munich: Deutscher Taschenbuch Verlag, 1978, 81. König and Paul do not attribute this citation to Meister Eckhart; however a variety of internet sources do, though they do not provide exact citations. See for example: http://www.engeler.de/entdeckungen.html.
[18] Özdamar, *Mutter Zunge*, 17.
[19] *Ibid.*, 18: "The divan I was sitting upon made me well-behaved. I saw letters waiting for me there."
[20] *Ibid.*: "Letters came out of my mouth."

women's eyes".[21] The value of the letters is non-verbal, primarily aesthetic. The signifier has been distanced from its original signified.

Furthermore, as the lessons continue, it grows increasingly clear that her desire for the letters has projected their image onto Ibni Abdullah in a kind of alphabetamorphosis or reduction of his human identity to linguistic elements.[22] She sees in him the language she so desperately longs for: "Ibni Abdullahs Gesicht sah wie ein zorniger Buchstabe aus, der seine eine Augenbraue hochgezogen hatte."[23] Again later, she fantasizes a reversal of their power in which she finally commands the letters as she states: "Ibni Abdullahs Gesicht hat etwas von einem bettelnden Buchstaben, der auf Knien läuft."[24]

It is Ibni Abdullah's possession of this much desired linguistic competence that allows him to possess the narrator.[25] Her desire for language, bound up as it is with the exoticism and Otherness of Arabic, appears to lead her not to the enhanced practice of *Mündigkeit* but on a path to the unreason of love. Both in submitting to the teacher's authority and falling in love with him, she loosens her grip on independent reason and threatens any *Mündigkeit* she might previously have had. The weakening of her selfhood is further depicted in the text through the textual metaphor of Ibni Abdullah entering her body and being carried with her wherever she goes.[26] Her connection with this desired Other, who, seemingly, represents for her the lost orient of her Grandfather, happens at the cost of *Entfremdung* or alienation from her Self.

---

[21] Littler, "Diasporic Identity in Emine Sevgi Özdamar's *Mutterzunge*", 224.
[22] Cf. *Ibid.*, 225.
[23] Özdamar, *Mutter Zunge*, 19: "Ibni Abdullah's face looked like an angry letter which had raised one eyebrow."
[24] *Ibid.*, 23: "Ibni Abdullah's face had something of a letter, begging, going on its knees."
[25] Cf. Stephanie Bird, *Women Writers and National Identity: Bachmann, Duden, Özdamar*, Cambridge: Cambridge University Press, 2003, 161: "her desire to understand her identity by understanding the roots of her mother tongue translates into her desire for the man who teaches her those roots. As she admits upon leaving his room and him, 'Ich habe mich in meinem Großvater verliebt' ['I have fallen in love with my grandfather']" (my translation).
[26] Özdamar, *Mutter Zunge*, 21: "Ich lief einen Monat lang mit Ibni Abdullah in meinem Körper" ("I went about for a whole month with Ibni Abdullah in my body").

Her desire for the Other and close identification with it through love leads to a growing sense of her own Otherness as she walks the streets of Berlin. In trying to reconnect with her Grandfather-Tongue she has placed a greater distance between herself and the city. She believes a man and woman have looked at her oddly and asks two men passing by: "'Meine Herren, spielt in meinem Gesicht ein Affe?'"[27] Littler interprets this in terms of cultural identity, suggesting that, "The protagonist's identification with Ibni Abdullah sensitizes her to her own 'aping' of German culture". The closer she grows to Ibni Abdullah and the Otherness of Arabic script he represents, the greater the distance she feels between herself and German culture and the more she feels she is mimicking German identity rather than finding a reasonable place within it – rather in the way that an ape appears, from an anthropocentric point of view, to mimic human beings.

An alternative reading, taking as its point of departure the love story, would see in the strangeness that she feels, and believes people to see in her, the defamiliarizing effect of being in love; the sense that the connection between two people is somehow unique and places the lovers beyond the reaches of normal society. It is perhaps significant that it is a married couple who notice the change in her expression. They look on her with the knowing indulgence of those already initiated into the ways of love. This experience of being set apart is further represented by the lover's isolation in the *Schriftzimmer*: it is a location set apart from society that also eschews any specifiable context. The narrator expresses the sense of non-localizability engendered by love in the following passage:

> Die ganze Welt sind wir, er wird nicht in mich reinkommen, wir werden keine Kinder machen, keine Brüder werden geboren, die sich töten, S-Bahnen werden nicht mehr arbeiten, keiner kann sich vor S-Bahnen schmeißen, es werden keine Arbeiter in die Welt kommen, deren Tod nicht mal ihre Müdigkeit ihnen wegnehmen kann, es wird keine zwischen den Ländern den Tod suchenden Emigranten geben. Es gibt nur uns, wir werden unser Leben keiner Leiche verdanken, jeder Tote ist ähnlich dem Lebenden und stellt dem Lebenden die

---

[27] *Ibid.*: "Sirs, is there an ape playing across my face?"

Frage vom Tod. Palästina wird nicht gegründet und nicht getötet, die Waschbecken, die Stehlampen, die Tische werden nicht sein, alle Stifte werden wir vergessen.[28]

The first line of this passage echoes the final verse of a poem by the metaphysical poet John Donne, *The Sun Rising* (1633) which in a highly similar way to this narrative creates an image of lovers who are set apart from the rest of society in their own self-sufficient unity:

> She's all states, and all princes I;
> Nothing else is;
> Princes do but play us; compared to this,
> All honour's mimic, all wealth alchemy.
> Thou, Sun, art half as happy as we,
> In that the world's contracted thus;
> Thine age asks ease, and since thy duties be
> To warm the world, that's done in warming us.
> Shine here to us, and thou art everywhere;
> This bed thy centre is, these walls thy sphere.[29]

The comparison with John Donne is also interesting for the way in which Donne may be said to espouse the view that spiritual love may be attained through physical love[30] – a view also intimated by the narrator's descriptions of the love affair, in the following passage, for example, where she elevates the transfer of her lover's saliva into a form of spiritual ritual:

---

[28] *Ibid.*, 30-31: "We are the whole world, he will not enter me, we will make no children, no brothers will be born who kill each other, trams will no longer work, no-one can throw themselves before the tram, there will be no more workers in the world whose tiredness cannot even be relieved by death, there will be no emigrant seeking death between countries. There is only us, our life will not be owed to a corpse, every dead man is similar to the living and poses the question of death to the living. Palestine will not be founded and not be killed, the sink, the standing lamp, the table will not be, we will forget all pens."
[29] John Donne, "The Sun Rising" (1633), in *The Complete Poems of John Donne*, ed. Robin Robbins, Harlow: Pearson, 2010, 249 (I would like to thank Moray McGowan for pointing out this parallel).
[30] See Ian Mackean, "The Love Poetry of John Donne", February 2001: http://www.literature-study-online.com/essays/donne.html.

> Seine Spucke ist ein silbernes Getränk, ich trank es und betete: "Mein Allah, mit der tötenden Liebe mach mich bekannt, trenn mich nie einen Moment von der tötenden Kraft der Liebe, hilf mir genügend, hilf meinem Kummer, das heißt, mach mich abhängig von den Schmerzen der Liebe, solange ich lebendig bin, trenne mich nie vom Fluch der Liebe, ich möchte verflucht sein, weil der Fluch möchte mich."[31]

The love she experiences creates its own Otherness; its own uncivilized, playful and monkey-like "madness". In the awareness she now places on other people's perception of her we see how her physical self-image is threatened by a growing sense of syncretism between her own physicality and that of Ibni Abdullah born out of romantic love and erotic desire.

The following passage suggests that the narrator is succumbing to a quasi sado-masochistic destruction of her own image in the desire for Ibni Abdullah to wield authority over her; to the extent that she becomes a subjugated part of him, passive and unable to speak:

> Verwahrlost, Haar gelöst, fortwimmern will ich, mit einem Blick hast du meine Zunge an deine Haare gebunden. Ich bin die Sklavin deinen Antlitzes. Zerbrich nicht diese Kette, lehne mich nicht ab, Geliebter, ich bin die Sklavin deines Gesichts geworden, sag mir nur, was tue ich jetzt, was tue ich jetzt.[32]

She welcomes the chains that bind her to him, she is the slave of his countenance. With her tongue bound to his hair she cannot speak or act for herself; he must tell her what to do. Not even knowledge of the letters can help her regain the reason that has been rendered passive by

---

[31] Özdamar, *Mutter Zunge*, 31: "His spittle is a silver drink, I drank it and prayed: 'My Allah, introduce me to deathly love, never separate me a minute from the fatal power of love, help me enough, help my heartache, that is, make me depend on the pangs of love, as long as I am alive, never separate me from the curse of love, I would like to be accursed, because the curse would like me.'" As will be shown later Ibni Abdullah stands in contrast to this view of love, unable to reconcile physical love with spirituality.

[32] *Ibid.*, 31-32: "Bedraggled, hair loose, I want to whimper away, with one glance you bound my tongue to your hair. I am the slave of your countenance. Do not break this chain, do not reject me, Beloved, I have become the slave of your face, just tell me, what do I do now, what do I do now."

love and submission to authority. Her hands lie on her lap like letters without tongues.[33] Unspeaking. Unable to act.

Yet, in the face of her disruptive emotions, Ibni Abdullah maintains his authority as representative of reason: "'Du bist ungeduldig, unkonzentriert', sagte Ibni Abdullah. 'Die Schrift verzeiht es dir nicht.'"[34] His voice grows not less powerful, but gains relatively heightened power as his pupil's love for him impinges on her own ability to speak rationally. She can find no prosaic words for what she is feeling, only a medley of metaphorical images; she describes how love cannot speak with words, there is no dictionary for it, but it speaks with cries, with the sound of the nightingale:

> Ich sprach zu dem Ibni Abdullah, der in meinem Körper war:
> Mein Herz wollte fliegen, hat keine Flügel gefunden, meine Liebe ist ein Hochwasser, es schreit, wirft mein Herz vor sich her, es weint, keine Hand habe ich gefunden, die sie ihm abwischt, ich habe mich in Liebeshochwasser gehen lassen, ich habe kein Wörterbuch gefunden für die Sprache meiner Liebe. Ich sprach wie die Nachtigall, blaß geworden wie die Rosen. Das ist ein Weh, ein Geschrei, so frei, so frei.[35]

Again, we see the image of love as an unstable body of water upon which her heart is uncontrollably tossed. Yet in the face of her desire she is not concerned by the loss of her reason, instead she actively courts it – keen for her own intoxication. In her desire to be associated with Ibni Abdullah's linguistic power, she loses physical power within herself, her knees buckle.

> Weingebender, bring mir Wein, nimm meinen Verstand mit Wein weg, es hat keinen Wert diese Welt, ich will ein in deinen Händen

---

[33] *Ibid.*, 24: "meine Hände lagen wie Buchstaben ohne Zunge auf meinen Knien" ("My hands lay like letters without a tongue upon my knees").
[34] *Ibid.*, 32: "'You are impatient, unfocused', said Ibni Abdullah. 'The script does not forgive you for it.'"
[35] *Ibid.*, 32: "I spoke to Ibni Abdullah who was in my body: My heart wanted to fly, found no wings, my love is a high tide, it cries, throws my heart before it, it weeps, no hand have I found that can wipe it away from him, I have let myself go in love's high tide, I have found no dictionary for the language of my love. I spoke like the nightingale, turned as pale as the roses. It is woe, a cry, so free, so free."

spazierendes Weinglas sein, mein Schatten soll sich nur in dein Gesicht legen. Knabe, bist du aus einer Huri geboren, mein Verstand ist aus seinem Ort weggeflogen, deine Wimpern sind Pfeile, die mein Blut tranken, deine saubere Stirn ist ein verfluchtes Meer, kann die Kraft am Knie bleiben, wenn man in deine schwarzen Augen guckt, dein Mund, wenn er was sagt, das bringt die Toten ins Leben zurück.[36]

In this passage we see the close connection of the dissolution of her reason and the dissolution of her body. Ibni Abdullah is presented as a being whose physicality threatens to absorb her, body, mind and soul – her reason is intoxicated, her knees grow weak; in vampiric fashion his eyelashes drink her blood, her "shadow" rests in his face. She is the literal container for outpourings of his intoxicating desire – a wine glass travelling in his hands.

Ibni Abdullah takes on a God-like status in the narrator's imagination, becoming for her the voice of ultimate authority, able to call the dead back to life. However, the emotions she feels bring with them their own power of influence. Abdullah is soon to succumb to love himself. This is reflected in the image of Ibni Abdullah throwing his hands across his mouth when they make love. His voice of rational authority is threatened with silence. The narrator begins to possess his body as he has possessed hers: "Du hast deine Schönheit, die die Welt schmückt, mir gegeben, wankelmütig gelaufen in meinem Körper."[37]

After their physical connection through love-making we see the first extended verbal dialogue in the text. It is a dialogue that Ibni Abdullah uses to try and divorce himself from their physical communication and re-establish order. It is Ibni Abdullah who authoritatively declares the conversation open: "'Wir werden reden'" ("we will speak") before making his demands for a "holy love", one in which their souls, but not their bodies may connect. "Holy love" will

---

[36] Ibid., 28: "Wine-giver, bring me wine, take my reason with wine, this world is worthless, I want to to be a wine-glass travelling in your hands, my shadow should lay itself upon your face only. Boy, were you born of a woman in paradise, my reason has flown from its place, your eyelashes are arrows, which drank my blood, your pure brow is an accursed ocean, can the knee keep its strength when one looks into your black eyes, your mouth, when it says something, brings the dead back to life."
[37] Ibid., 39: "You have given me your beauty which adorns the world, changeably run through my body."

allow him to carry on with his work, it will allow the script to maintain its authority so that the narrator can be disciplined and learn once again – she is growing westernized, only thinking of sex. Her body distracts her mind. The narrator's response is to threaten to destroy all the pieces of script she has, so that her silenced body may speak instead. In response to this Ibni Abdullah threatens to destroy his own body so that the narrator's has none to address: "'Wenn du das machst, ich werfe mich in den ersten See. Ich will die heilige Liebe.'"[38]

In their attitudes towards their love we see two very different perspectives on the spiritual realm. For Ibni Abdullah the spiritual is something that transcends the material world including the physical body to be recaptured, interpreted and expressed through the mind, through the script. For the narrator it is also a transcendent experience, however, she instead considers the locus of expression for spirituality not to be the script but the experience of physical union that creates a synthesis of divided elements, transcending language itself. To unite with Abdullah in that way is, to her, emblematic of losing the self in unification with Allah. Abdullah, however, is aware of the concrete physicality of the union in which the self as site of experience and perception cannot be entirely dissolved. Their physical union may still be interpreted as an act of communication, a form of body language that creates a shared experience between two discrete entities.

If the narrator is to find her way back to language and back to reason, away from the body language of physical desire, she must submit to the script once more. But love and desire continue to inhibit reason. She cannot be reborn in Arabic as she had hoped. It never was her first tongue and in "der Fremdsprache haben Wörter keine Kindheit".[39] She cannot reconnect with her childhood origins through Arabic. She comes to Arabic as an adult. She communicates verbally with Ibni Abdullah through the few Arabic words borrowed into Turkish she has learnt as a child:

> Ich suchte arabische Wörter, die es noch in türkischer Sprache gibt. Ich fragte Ibni Abdullah: "Kennst du sie?"

---

[38] *Ibid.*, 42-43: "If you do that, I will throw myself into the first sea. I want holy love."
[39] *Ibid.*, 44: "[in] the foreign language words have no childhood."

Leb – Mund
Ducar – Befallen
Mazi – Vergangenheit
Medyun – verbunden
Meytap – Feuerwerkskörper
Yetim – Waise[40]

It is these borrowings which she believes to offer some means of reconnecting with her estranged roots, with her grandfather. It is these words which she can share with Ibni Abdullah, that create for her the illusion of a deeper communication. Yet where she sees similarity, Abdullah sees difference:

"Kennst du sie?"
... "Ja", sagte: Ibni Abdullah, "es hört sich ein klein bißchen anders an."[41]

The love affair with her Arabic teacher can be seen as the physical expression of a metaphorical incestuous desire for her grandfather, a projection of her own desire for him as a source of recovering her lost roots. At the very heart of all the layers of desire lies a fundamental need to connect not with Ibni Abdullah or her Grandfather, but with herself. She begins as an alienated migrant longing to rediscover her origins and reconnect with an original Turkish identity. However, through attempting to reconnect with her mother-tongue through an unknown grandfather-tongue, rather than experiencing a rebirth into her first linguistic construction of selfhood she perpetuates her longing. Her extreme desire for reconnection with her roots is conflated and confused with a desire for Arabic, and as possessor of that linguistic competence Ibni Abdullah soon becomes the mistaken object of that desire. Ironically, in order to get closer to what the narrator considers her access to linguistic competence and the possibility of a revitalized selfhood, her sense of that self is in fact dissolved in love and

---

[40] *Ibid.*, 29. I searched for Arabic words that still exist in Turkish. I asked Ibni Abdullah: "Do you know them?" *Leb* – mouth, *Ducar* – to befall, *Mazi* – past, *Medyun* – connected, *Meytap* – firework, *Yetim* – orphan.
[41] *Ibid.*, 29. "Do you know them?" ... "Yes", said: Ibni Abdullah, "it sounds a little different."

submission to her teacher's authority. Her body speaks in place of her reason and tells of her longing where she cannot express it in words. Ibni Abdullah, wishing to maintain control over sexual desire through the disciplined intelligence of reason draws away from the relationship and the lovers must part.

CHAPTER SEVEN

THE USE OF LANGUAGE IN *MUTTER ZUNGE*

In the preceding analysis of Emine Sevgi Özdamar's *Mutter Zunge* (1998) we see how the threatened dissolution of discrete identities leads to a situation in which, to quote Adelson, "no personal, cultural, or national identity can be fixed".[1] The merging of discrete identities is reflected in the language Özdamar uses as will be demonstrated in the following close analysis.

The defamiliarizing effect of Özdamar's language has been highlighted by Annette Wierschke:

> Özdamar spielt mit der deutschen Sprache, durchsetzt sie mit fremden Metaphern, fremdklingenden Wörtern und exotischen sprachlichen Konstruktionen und verstößt gegen grammatikalische Regeln .... Dadurch wird in der Sprache eine Fremdheit hergestellt, die für deutsche LeserInnen einen ganz eigenen Reiz hat und einen poetischen Klang und Rhythmus trägt.[2]

Indeed, much of the literature on the language of Özdamar's prose cites the defamiliarizing effect of the textual interplay of several languages and notes the poetic effects that this gives rise to. However, while this fact is noted, there are few, if any studies of the precise linguistic ways in which these effects are created and in particular that show how the text may have been influenced by Özdamar's own

---

[1] Adelson, *The Turkish Turn in Contemporary German Literature*, 155.
[2] Annette Wierschke, *Schreiben als Selbstbehauptung: Kulturkonflikt und Identität in den Werken von Aysel Özakin, Alev Tekinay und Emine Sevgi Özdamar*, Frankfurt am Main: IKO, 1996, 173: "Özdamar plays with the German language, suffuses it with foreign metaphors, foreign-sounding words and exotic linguistic constructions and breaks grammatical rules .... In this way a foreignness is created in the language, which has a unique charm for German readers and which bears a poetic sound and rhythm" (my translation).

native literary traditions. The following discussion aims to remedy this by providing a close linguistic reading of the text. It will furthermore show how the thematic content of the narrative is reflected in Özdamar's use of language. There are many recurrent features in this text that contribute to the defamiliarization of the German language. The following analysis examines features on several levels and suggests the effects of this use of language.

The most obvious ways in which the language differs from German are in grammatical errors that act as a marker that the narrator does not have full command of the German language or has a command of a colloquial register that reflects having learnt a non-standard form of German "on the streets" rather than in the classroom. Some of the more obvious errors (several emphasized in bold)[3] include:

1. Non-standard use of conjunctions or prepositions:

(10) "Einmal **wie** sie ihren Sohn im Gefängnis zum ersten Mal sah" ("once **how** she saw her son in prison for the first time").
(13) "Meine Stiefel knirschen wie **von** Werbefilmcowboy" ("my boots creak like those **from** a cowboy in a commercial").
(16) "Wir schauten beide auf den Teppich [als] ob dort ein Tier rückwärts gefallen war und sich nicht retten konnte" ("we both looked at the carpet [as] if an animal had fallen backwards there and could not save itself").

2. Non-standard word order:

(10) "als ich fragte, was **ist** mit meinem Sohn" ("when I asked, what with my son **has happened**").
(12) "Wenn der Zug in Köln ankam, ich **machte** immer Augen zu" ("As the train arrived in Cologne, I always eyes closed").
3. Lack of articles:
(9) "Zunge hat keine Knochen" ("tongue has no bones").
(12) "Kommunist-Freund sagte" ("communist-friend said").

---

[3] Numbers given in brackets preceding each quotation here and elsewhere in this chapter indicate page references.

4. Misuse of case endings:
(11) "Dieser Sätze" (for accusative) ("these sentences").
(19) "Als ich ... mein Hemdärmel hochzog ... " ("when I pushed up my shirtsleeve").

5. Lack of agreement in use of tense:
(9) "ich *erinnere* mich jetzt an Muttersätze, die sie in ihrer Mutterzunge *gesagt hat*, nur dann, wenn ich ihre Stimme mir *vorstelle*, die Sätze selbst **kamen** in meine Ohren ... " (My emphases.)
("I now remember mother-sentences, that she has said in her mother tongue, only then when I remember her voice, the sentences themselves came to my ears ... ").

Besides non-standard use of German, another noticeable feature of the text is the repetition of particular nouns and noun phrases, the repetition of particular verbs and verbal forms as well as the significant repetition of certain syntactic structures. These repetitions are presented below along with a consideration of the significance of such repetitions as well as the textual effects to which these repetitions give rise.

Nouns and noun phrases
In the first lines of the text the word *Zunge* is repeated three times in three subsequent sentences, four if one includes the title.

> MUTTERZUNGE
> In meiner Sprache heißt **Zunge**: Sprache.
> **Zunge** hat keine Knochen .... Ich saß mit meiner gedrehten **Zunge** in dieser Stadt Berlin.[4]

The noun *Zunge* is picked up again only a few lines on and is connected with the word Mutter that itself is repeated four times within the space of three sentences:

---

[4] Özdamar, *Mutter Zunge*, 9: "MOTHER-TONGUE: In my language tongue means language. Tongue has no bones .... I sat with my twisted tongue in this city Berlin." (Bold emphases here and in all subsequent quotations from *Mutter Zunge* are my own.)

> Wenn ich nur wüßte, wann ich meine **Mutterzunge** verloren habe. Ich und meine **Mutter** sprachen mal in unserer **Mutterzunge**. Meine **Mutter** sagte mir ...[5]

Before the end of the first page the word *Mutter* is repeated three more times in the neologism *Muttersätze* and again in *Mutterzunge* and *Mutter*. On the next page, the word *Mutter* appears in different combinations a further four times. Besides the repetition of *Zunge* and *Mutter* there are several other key lexical items that frequently recur. For example, on her meeting with Ibni Abdullah, there are highly repetitive references to *Tod* (death) and *die Seele* (soul). There are eight references to death, being dead or the dead on one page and seven references to *die Seele* within one paragraph on the subsequent page. These would seem a premonition (perhaps the most appropriate word here) for the profundity of the relationship that is to develop between them.

There are several other lexical items that occur again and again, these include *das Herz* ("heart"), *die Seele* ("the soul"), *der Tod* ("death"), *die Rose* ("rose"), *der Garten* ("garden"), *die Liebe* ("love"), *der Traum* ("dream"), *der Fuß* ("foot"), *die Augen* ("eyes"), *die Hand* ("hand"), *der Mund* ("mouth"), *der Flügel* ("wing") and *der Vogel* ("bird") among others. An examination of these as tropes is pursued in a later section on imagery and the relationship of this imagery to the social context of production that gives particular reference to Ottoman Divan poetry. For the moment, however, if we consider the above as lexical items, rather than as tropes with wider symbolic significance, the repetition of these words gives rise to several effects. Firstly, their repetition creates the appearance of a highly cohesive text in which there are strong semantic links between sentences. Secondly, they may suggest that the writer has a limited range of vocabulary due to being a newcoming speaker, so that the repetition is not so much a deliberate feature of text as one resulting from the linguistic limitations of the writer. However, we cannot determine whether the writer really is limited in that way, or has chosen to perform the identity of newcoming speaker, or is using these

---

[5] *Ibid.*: "If only I knew when I had lost my mother-tongue. My mother and I once spoke in our mother-tongue. My mother said to me ...."

repetitions to create some other effect. One of the effects created by these repetitions is arguably a kind of semantic satiation,[6] in which the sense of the words becomes lost to the reader and focus is turned instead to the formal appearance of the words. As a literary device, this would be effective in conveying the sense of being unfamiliar with German, in effect defamiliarizing the language for the native speaker.

In order to further examine the extent to which the language is characteristic of newcoming speakers, a basic corpus analysis of the short story "Mutter Zunge" has been undertaken.[7] For the purposes of this brief analysis it is assumed that features of this extract are also reasonably characteristic of the story "Großvaterzunge" ("Grandfather tongue"), though the limitations of this book mean that a comprehensive verbal analysis including this short story will not be undertaken. The key results of the analysis of verb forms used in "Mutter Zunge" are summarized in the table below. The analysis is intended to be suggestive rather than definitive since it is based on several assumptions for which it is not possible to provide evidence without considerable further research going beyond the intended focus of this chapter. The first assumption is that the way in which verbs are used by a writer may be indicative either of that writer's level of competence in the language, or of his/her ability to perform a particular level of competence for an intended effect, that is, creating a particular narrative voice, such as the narrative voice of a language learner. It is hypothesized, for example, that use of a limited range of verbs or a restriction of verb use to particular tenses may indicate newcoming competence.

Furthermore, the analysis is partly conducted on the basis of a comparison with frequency results obtained from the Leipzig/BYU

---

[6] Evidence for this from neuroscience research, at least for the verbal repetition of a word, can be found in Lee Smith and Raymond Klein, "Evidence for Semantic Satiation: Repeating a Category Slows Subsequent Semantic Processing", *Journal of Experimental Psychology*, XVI/5 (September 1990), 852-61.

[7] This was done manually using an Excel spreadsheet working from a hard copy of the text. This is partly since specialist corpus analysis software such as WordSmith Tools was not available for use, but partly also because a manual analysis provides a sufficient amount of data for the arguments proposed here and is also in some respects less time-consuming. Use of software, if available, would require, for instance, digitizing the original text either by scanning or typing it up, and then tagging the text for parts of speech.

corpus in *A Frequency Dictionary of German: Core Vocabulary for Learners* (2006) by Randall Jones and Erwin Tschirner. This comparison is partly made on the assumption that language learners are more likely to use verbs that occur frequently in the language and that knowledge of less frequent verbs indicates a higher level of linguistic competence. However, language learning does not proceed in such a structured manner – lexical items are developed on the basis of experience rather than frequency. Words for issues of immediate concern to a particular language learner will be learnt no matter what their frequency or their complexity. In "Mutter Zunge", for example, the words *bellen* ("bark"), *Gassenmoschee* ("backstreet mosque") and *Hodscha* all appear, even though they are not among the 4034 most frequent words in German contained in the dictionary. The reason for producing a frequency dictionary in the first place was to aid language learners in acquiring vocabulary that will usefully structure their linguistic input and rapidly expand their competence since it is estimated that the 4034 words of the dictionary constitute between 80% and 90% of all the words in the corpus, depending on the register.[8] However, this argument also partly works in favour of the original assumption, since more frequent verbs are more likely to be experienced than infrequent ones!

An additional factor in the analysis is that the short story is being compared to a corpus of German deriving from a variety of genres (including spoken language, literature, newspapers, academic texts and instructional texts) so the comparison could be considered inequitable; however, the authors of the frequency dictionary have taken care to indicate where a particular lexical item is over- or under-represented in one of the subcorpora with which they were working. For this reason, it is assumed that the data contained in the frequency dictionary provides a reasonable representative sample of common German language use with which "Mutter Zunge" may be compared, as long as it is taken into account that language use in the narrative may be skewed in a particular direction by text-specific factors such as text topic, the fictional nature of the text and its status as a short story, as well as the author's linguistic competence.

---

[8] *A Frequency Dictionary of German: Core Vocabulary for Learners*, eds Randall Jones and Erwin Tschirner, London: Routledge, 2006, 2.

The analysis proceeded using the following methodology. Firstly, every occurrence of a verb form found in the text (totalling 1348 words) was listed. The list was then sifted for lexical verbs, that is auxiliary verbs associated with the different tenses were removed. In total, there were 243 instances of lexical verbs belonging to 84 different lemmas (for example the lexical verb forms *gehen* ("go"), *ging* ("went"), *gegangen* ("gone") all counted as belonging to the lemma or headword "gehen"). The frequency of these verbs was compared to the 100 most frequent verbs contained in the frequency dictionary as well as to the overall Leipzig/BYU corpus of 4,200,000 words. A total of 39 lemmas in "Mutter Zunge" were also found in the table of 100 most frequent verb lemmas in German, that is 39/84 lemmas were "most frequent verbs" (46.4%). 33 additional lemmas in "Mutter Zunge" were part of the Leipzig/BYU corpus, but not in the 100 most frequent verbs. This means that a total of 72/84 lemmas, or approximately 85.7% were in the 4034 most frequent words contained in the frequency dictionary. Twelve lemmas (≈14.2%) did not occur in the frequency dictionary of 4034 entries, in other words, these were not commonly found verbs within the 4,200,000 words present in the corpus selected by Erwin and Tschirner. These were: *(he)rausholen* ("fetch"), *(he)rausspucken* ("spit out"), *aufhängen* ("hang"), *bellen* ("bark"), *knirschen* ("creak"), *pflücken* ("pluck"), *schnappen* ("grab"), *verfluchen* ("curse"), *vergießen* ("seal"), *wackeln* ("totter"), *wickeln* ("wind") and *wiedererkennen* ("recognize"). Without access to the data for the rest of the verbs from their corpus we cannot determine precisely how infrequent these verbs might be. These findings are summarized in the table overleaf:

Table 1

	Number /84	Percentage
Percentage of "Mutter Zunge" verb lemmas also found in table of 100 most common German verbs	39	46.4%
Percentage of "Mutter Zunge" verb lemmas also found among 4034 most frequent words of German.	72	85.7%
Percentage of "Mutter Zunge" verb	12	14.2%

lemmas not found among 4034 most frequent words of German		

It is also useful to consider what percentage of the text is constituted by the most frequent lemmas. Choosing those "Mutter Zunge" lemmas that are also contained in the most frequent verb list of the frequency dictionary we find that 13.79% of the "Mutter Zunge" text is made up of verbs that occur in the list of 100 most frequent verbs. These same verbs constituted 8.24% of the Leipzig/BYU corpus. This appears to represent a quite significant difference of nearly 6% that might indicate that frequent verbs are proportionally more predominant in "Mutter Zunge" than in the German language as a whole, particularly since the 100 most frequent verbs of German, that is not just those used in "Mutter Zunge", constitute just 10% of the total Leipzig/BYU corpus. This may suggest limited linguistic competence on the part of the author or alternatively the repetition of high frequency verbs may be used by the author to suggest limited linguistic competence, or be used as a stylistic device for some other purpose such as to create a repetitive rhythmic effect.

Besides the relative frequency of the verbs used in the text, another factor that might indicate competence diverging from common usage, caused by lack of early experience of the language, is the use of tenses and particular verb forms.

The 243 verbs were distributed among the tenses as shown in the tables in Appendices VI and VII. The preterite tense and present simple tense forms were by far the most frequent tenses used. The narrative regularly switches between these two tenses. For the most part, the text relates past events and so the narration of the past is occasionally being related in the present tense. The function of the present within narration about the past in this text seems to be more about giving immediacy to past events than due to any lack of competence with preterite forms for certain verbs, since, as can be seen in the table, there are ten verbs used in both past and present forms: for example, *arbeiten* ("work"), *denken* ("think"), *haben* ("have"), *kommen* ("come"), *sagen* ("say"), *sein* ("be"), *sitzen* ("sit"), *sprechen* ("speak"), *stehen* ("stand") and *warten* ("wait").

The more unusual aspects of the use of verbs that emerge from this analysis include five instances in which it is unclear whether the written verb form is to be interpreted as a first person singular present tense form with both the pronoun and final schwa omitted as in colloquial speech, or if it is in fact the second person singular imperative form with which the former would be isomorphous. The context for these forms is shown below:

> a. (13) "**Stehe** auf, **geh** zum anderen Berlin, Brecht war der erste Mensch, warum ich hierher gekommen bin, vielleicht dort kann ich mich daran erinnern, wann ich meine Mutterzunge verloren habe." ("Stand up, go to the other Berlin, Brecht was the first person, why I came here, perhaps I will be able to remember when I lost my mother-tongue.")
> b. (13) "**Steh auf**. **Geh** auf Fingerspitzen in die Türkei, in einem Diwan sitzen, Großmutter neben mir." ("Stand up. Go on finger-tips to Turkey, sit in a divan, Grandmother next to me.")
> c. (13) "Warum **steh** ich im halben Berlin? **Geh** diesen Jungen suchen?" ("Why do I stand in half Berlin? Go to seek this boy?")

From these examples it seems clear that the intended interpretation is the first person singular present simple, however, the effect of these forms, particularly in contexts (a) and (b) is quite ambiguous. At first sight, the form appears to be the second person imperative form. Arguably, this has the effect of suggesting an intimacy between the narrator and the reader in which the reader is commanded to get involved somehow with the action presented. The effect is that of a subtle invitation to the reader to migrate with the narrator across time and space from one side of Berlin to the other, to Turkey, from present to past, that is to move both into and with the narration.

The point in the narration at which we see these ambiguous forms is also the point at which we find the repetition of *sitzen* ("sit") in the infinitive where it appears to function as an unconjugated verb. The first example can be seen in (b) above "in einem Diwan sitzen". The second occurs in the sentence immediately following this as: "In Istanbul im Türkischen Bad sitzen" ("Sit in Istanbul in a Turkish bath"). The reader is left with the idea of action but no knowledge of who/when or how it was carried out – the only clue is in the preceding clause that has already been identified as ambiguous; and so the sentence "Geh auf Fingerspitzen in die Türkei, in einem Diwan sitzen,

Großmutter neben mir", almost appears to be an invitation to the reader to finger-tip their way to Turkey (turning pages?) and sit on a divan (reading?) and perhaps, finally, with the introduction of "neben mir", to imagine themselves in place of the narrator, sitting next to the narrator's grandmother.

Having examined the general tense forms used, it is interesting to consider precisely which conjugations of each tense are used, since this will also potentially tell us something about the point of view from which the narrative is related as well as the variety of verb forms in which the narrator is competent.

Along with repetition of certain nouns and verbs we see a striking amount of repetition of entire phrases and variations on the same sentence construction with the use of the same verb. Listed together as they are below, these structures are somewhat reminiscent of substitution exercises for language learners:

> (9) "die Sätze selbst kamen in meine Ohren wie eine von mir gut gelernte Fremdsprache ..." ("the sentences themselves came to my ears like a foreign language I had learnt well ...")
> (11) "Die Schriften kamen auch in meine Augen wie eine von mir gut gelernte Fremdschrift." ("The writings came to my eyes like a foreign script I had learnt well.")
> (9) "Wenn ich nur wüßte, wann ich meine Mutterzunge verloren habe." ("If only I knew when I lost my mother-tongue. ")
> (11) "Wenn ich nur wüßte, in welchem Moment ich meine Mutterzunge verloren habe." ("If only I knew at what point I lost my mother-tongue.")
> (12) "Vielleicht habe ich meine Mutterzunge im IC-Restaurant verloren." ("Perhaps I lost my mother-tongue in the Intercity Train restaurant.")
> (13) "Vielleicht habe ich dort meine Mutterzunge verloren." ("Perhaps I lost my mother-tongue there.")
> (13) "vielleicht dort kann ich mich daran erinnern, wann ich meine Mutterzunge verloren habe ..." ("perhaps I can remember there when I lost my mother-tongue ...").
> (12) "Ich erinnere mich an ein anderes Wort in meiner Mutterzunge, es war im Traum." ("I remember another word in my mother-tongue, it was in a dream.")
> (12) "Noch ein Wort in meiner Mutterzunge kam mal im Traum vorbei." ("Another word in my mother-tongue passed by in a dream.")

(17) "Ich ging aus dem Schriftzimmer mit fünf ersten arabischen Buchstaben raus zum anderen Berlin." ("I went out of the scriptorium with five first arabic letters into the other Berlin.")
(17) "Ich trat ins Schriftzimmer ein." ("I entered the scriptorium.")
(18) "Ich trat ins Schriftzimmer ein." ("I entered the scriptorium.")
(23) "Ich trat in das Schriftzimmer in Wilmersdorf ein." ("I entered the scriptorium in Wilmersdorf.")
(26) "Ich konnte aus diesem Schriftzimmer nicht mehr raus." ("I could no longer leave this scriptorium.")
(41) "Ich geh raus aus dem Zimmer." ("I am leaving the room.")
(44) "Ich ging zum ersten Mal aus diesem Zimmer raus." ("I left the room for the first time.")
(20) "ich wußte, daß in diesem Moment Ibni Abdullah in meinen Körper reingekommen war ..." ("I knew at this moment that Ibni Abdullah had entered my body .... ")
(21) "Ich lief einen Monat lang mit Ibni Abdullah in meinem Körper in beiden Berlin." ("I went about a whole month with Ibni Abdullah in my body in both Berlins.")
(21) "Einmal lief ich mit Ibni Abdullah in meinem Körper auf der Straße ..." ("Once I went with Ibni Abdullah in my body out on the street ....")
(21) "Ich stand mit Ibni Abdullah in meinem Körper vor der Grenze." ("I stood with Ibni Abdullh in my body before the border.")
(22) "Ich ging mit Ibni Abdullah in meinem Körper in Häuser rein ..." ("I went with Ibni Abdullah in my body into houses ....")
(30) "Ich sprach zu dem Ibni Abdullah, der in meinem Körper ist ..." ("I spoke to the Ibni Abdullah who is in my body ....")
(31) "Ich lernte die Schrift schlecht, weil ich immer mit dem Ibni Abdullah, der in meinem Körper war, mit anderen Wörtern sprach ..." ("I learnt the script poorly, because I always spoke to the Ibni Abdullah who was in my body with other words ....")
(32) "Ich sprach zu dem Ibni Abdullah, der in meinem Körper war ..." ("I spoke to the Ibni Abdullah who was in my body ....")
(44) "Ich ging mit Ibni Abdullah, der in meinem Körper ist, Zeitung in der Hand, in die Nähe der Autobahn." ("I went with Ibni Abdullah, who was in my body, newspaper in hand, near the motorway.")
(45) "Ich wollte Ibni Abdullah, der in mir ist, in Ohnmacht bringen." ("I wanted to render Ibni Abdullah, who is in me, unconscious.")

Again, the repetition may be viewed as deriving from learning the German language later in life and consequently having a more limited range of vocabulary and knowledge of syntactic structures at one's disposal, but it must nevertheless primarily be analysed for the textual effects this use of language creates.

We have seen how the text reveals a high degree of lexical and syntactic cohesion. This cohesion may suggest a familiarity and continuity, a sense of repetitive ease that, perhaps, by contrast, only heightens the sense of disrupted meaning created by the instances of elliptical syntax of which there are many instances in the narrative. A further effect of this repetition could be that the repeated words appear to lose their meaning entirely as in a religious chant. Certainly, in his work on Ottoman Divan poetry, Walter G. Andrews notes a similar repetition of particular tropes and co-occurring ambiguous syntactic constructions that he also considers to operate in tandem to create particular stylistic effects:

> On the one hand, limitations on vocabulary, and concomitantly on theme and context, create a predictability in the concatenation of words that frees the discourse to a certain extent from the shackles of syntax ... regularly repeated relationships between words – relationships with a definite history – create associations on a level other than that of grammar/syntax.
>
> On the other hand, where a limited vocabulary might be a disambiguating factor in the area of syntax, it also engenders a high degree of polysemy in its own right. Poetic usage has the effect of stretching and expanding the sense of words, and where words undergo this type of expansion over a long period in many contexts, they take on a broad range of meanings and an allusiveness that heighten the potential for ambiguity.[9]

On the basis of these comparable linguistic features and the use of common tropes detailed below it seems highly likely that it is this Ottoman literary tradition reflected in *Mutter Zunge* (1998) and which forms the substrate or superstrate linguistic and cultural framework that suffuses the German to create a defamiliarizing effect. However, considering the text within the German context alone, a syntax that frequently confuses and/or omits the grammatical markers of standard

---

[9] Walter Andrews, *Poetry's Voice, Society's Song: Ottoman Lyric Poetry*, Washington: University of Washington Press, 1985, 58.

German has several possible effects and functions within the text. Primarily, it can be seen as marking the narrator's social position as a migrant and speaker of German as a later experienced language. In some cases, the non-standard usages shown can be related back to the linguistic structures of Turkish, and thus form part of the "interlanguage"[10] that emerges when German is spoken as a second language by a first language speaker of Turkish. The overlaying of Turkish syntax on German lexis creates an overall effect of "defamiliarization". However, from the standpoint of the German reader each particular type of linguistic deviation from standard German creates its own particular literary effect. In what follows, it is sought to examine precisely which expectations are being challenged and in what ways.

The term "interlingual" is used here for the language contact evident in texts because terms like "creolization" and "pidginization" are too political and suggest relations of dominance and subordination between the languages in question. The term "multilingual" is also inappropriate because it is not the case that two languages are being used in a form of textual code-switching, as, for example, in Gloria Anzaldua's *Borderlands: La Frontera* (1999).[11] What presents itself in *Mutter Zunge* (1998) gives the sense that one language has been infused or suffused with another language in order to create something new. The term "interlingual" also bears out parallels with the term "interlanguage" which suggests both a developmental stage en route to competence resembling those with greater experience of the language, one in which structures from the early experienced language may be found in the later experienced language, but also suggests the creation of new structures that arise out of the movement between two languages. By speaking of interlingual German it is aimed to describe a usage of German that bears up the features of another language as well as other unique linguistic features that may arise out of language contact and language competence born of later exposure.

The syntactic features distinguishing the language used in *Mutter Zunge* (1998) from standard German may be grouped broadly into substitutions, ellipses, repetitions, word order deviations, insertions and parataxes. These devices serve in many cases to give a sense of

---

[10] Cf. Larry Selinker, "Interlanguage", *International Review of Applied Linguistics in Language Teaching*, X/3 (1972), 209-31.
[11] Gloria Anzaldua, *Borderlands/La Frontera*, San Francisco: Aunt Lute Books, 1999.

words being thrown together creating unexpected juxtapositions or emphasizing the effect of the textual meaning being elusive, not quite present. Haines and Littler similarly describe the effect of Özdamar's writing in terms of a sense of incomplete meaning: "Many passages in Özdamar's prose leave the non-Turkish-speaking reader with a sense of 'loss', not having access to all the potential meanings of the words."[12]

Nora Larkin, following Littler, similarly argues that you need an understanding of both Turkish and German traditions in order to understand Özdamar's prose:

> In order to fully comprehend her work written in her new language, the reader would need to be knowledgeable of both German and Turkish. Therefore, the reader would most likely be in a very similar situation as Özdamar and her characters, a situation of people of in-between cultures, languages and traditions.[13]

There are several problems with this suggestion. Firstly, we must interrogate the suggestion that one might be able to "fully comprehend" a piece of writing. What form does "full comprehension" take? Larkin seems to imply that it requires very similar semiotic competence to Özdamar's own – an understanding of the signs in the social context the author constructs for their usage. Perhaps it is intended to imply that a reader who fully comprehends a text will gain more value from the writing, (measured, perhaps, in terms of enlightenment or pleasure or emotional satisfaction or any other form of positive reaction). It is, however, with any text, somewhat suspect to suggest which readership might gain most value from what is written. In the case of Özdamar's writing, it has been the German public as a whole and not only those who have knowledge of both Turkish and German who have given a positive reception to her writing. This is reflected in the many literary prizes Özdamar has received.

---

[12] Haines and Littler, *Contemporary Women's Writing in German*, 123.
[13] Nora Larkin, "Changing Ethnic Identities in Post-National Germany: A Study of Turkish-German Literature, Politics and Society", University of New Hampshire, 2006, 37 (http://www.unh.edu/urc/sites/unh.edu.urc/files/media/pdfs2011/award_pdfs/2006/paper_larkin.pdf).

Secondly, since the literariness of a text arguably resides in the degree to which the reader must strain to discover meaning within it and in an engagement with the text that occurs through the reader inserting his/her own interpretation into the interstices of signification, if the reader has "full comprehension" with all possible meanings disambiguated then the text loses something of its literariness and arguably its interest. This may be compared with a point made by de Beaugrande and Dressler that one paradoxical feature of textuality is that, quite frequently, the less informative a text is, that is, the less all the meanings of a text are disambiguated, the more effective the text is likely to be.[14] Arguably, it is this feature of textuality that prevents the act of reading from becoming an event in which the reader is a passive recipient of the monologue provided by the text and allows the process to become a dialogue between author and reader in which meanings are negotiated in the process of reading. Perhaps the real thrill of literature for the reader lies in the fact that s/he has greater opportunity to "speak". In support of this argument, it is worth mentioning that the translation of *Das Leben ist eine Karawanserei* (1994) into Turkish did not receive the same positive reception as the German edition – the literary effect of the interlingual German having been lost.[15] It is another sense of "loss" in the German context, that

---

[14] They note that where information is missing, or merely implied by a statement so that the receiver is forced to supply the information him/herself, "it is as if they were making the assertion themselves". They give the example of a telephone company which warns: "Call us before you dig. You may not be able to afterwards." Robert-Alain de Beaugrande and Wolfgang Dressler, *Introduction to Text Linguistics*, 8. This is comparable to Wolfgang Iser's ideas on the interaction between text and reader presented in *The Act of Reading: A Theory of Aesthetic Response*, Baltimore and London: The Johns Hopkins University Press, 1980, especially 165-69.

[15] See Şeyda Ozil: "Die türkische Übersetzung vermag dem türkischen Leser nicht das zu bieten, was der deutsche Rezipient in dem Buch findet. Denn die aus dem Türkischen übernommenen Redewendungen, die im Deutschen okkasionelle Wortbildungen sind, werden nun in ihrer usuellen Gebrauchsweise benutzt. Von dem Außergewöhnlichen bleibt da keine Spur .... Während der Deutsche zu kreativem Spiel mit seinen Vorstellungen und Erfahrungen angeregt wird, findet der türkische Leser eine konkret umrissene Welt vor sich." "The Turkish translation cannot offer the Turkish reader what the German recipient finds in the book. Since the idioms taken from Turkish which are occasional word formations in German are only being employed in their usual way. There remains no trace of the extraordinary .... While the German is inspired to play creatively with his experience and imagination, the Turkish reader finds before him a concretely delineated world" (my translation). Şeyda Ozil,

Haines and Littler describe, which in fact enhances the text's literary character. In other words, the text gains from the lost understanding of the Turkish cultural resonances. For the German reader, the sense of loss occurs not just at the lexical level as indicated by the quotation above but perhaps more especially at the syntactic level in which, from the standpoint of a German reader, the ellipsis of particular grammatical elements vastly heightens the ambiguous nature of textual meaning.

One of the most noticeable features of the syntax is the omission of conjunctions, both co-ordinating and subordinating and also the omission of personal pronouns in subordinate clauses where the referent is the same as in the main clause:

> (10) "Sein Vater ist hingegangen, Ø kam zurück" ("His father went there, came back").
> (12) "an einem anderen saß ein Mann, Ø liest sehr gerne in einem Buch" ("at another sat a man, happily reads a book").
> (19) "sagte Ibni Abdullah, Ø schickte mich weg" ("said Ibni Abdullah, sent me away").
> (13) "Ø Steh auf, Ø geh zum anderen Berlin" ("Stand up, go to the other Berlin").
> (13) "Ja, sie laufen über mich, aber Ø laufen vorsichtig" ("Yes, they run over me, but run carefully").

This structure is usual in the Turkic languages;[16] however, its effect as a syntactic structure in German is quite the opposite. For a reader used to a West Germanic language this arguably gives a sense of the action occurring almost magically, as if from nowhere. It is not explicitly stated who is coming back, it is hinted that it is the father, but he is not specified. What we see is a "coming back" – the image created is of an action liberated from the agent, almost as if it were beyond the will of the agent. This sense most probably arises from the fact that the closest grammatical parallel in standard German to a structure that

---

"Einige Bemerkungen über den Roman, *Das Leben ist eine Karawanserei* von Emine Sevgi Özdamar", *Diyalog*, I (1994), 125-31.

[16] Turkish is a PRO-Drop language in which the pronoun as subject of a clause may be omitted. See Elvan Göçmen, Onur Şehitoğlu and Cem Bozşahin, "An Outline of Turkish Syntax", (March 1995), 3 (http://130.203.133.150/viewdoc/summary?doi=10.1.1.29.6353).

may forgo its agent is the passive. A similar effect of agentless action is created in instances where positions in the grammatical structure are filled twice, that is there is a repeated past participle. In fact this again appears to be a transference of Turkish syntax in which a clause may consist of a verb group only.[17] To the eye of someone used to a West Germanic language the repeated verb creates a distance between the action and its agent with the second verb appearing liberated or distanced from an agent. Alternatively, it could be viewed as creating the effect of indecision or a lack of fluency. Such verbal repetitions in spoken English or German are known in linguistics as "disfluency phenomena".[18]

In the examples cited from *Mutter Zunge* (1998) the second verb, from the standpoint of German syntax, introduces a new predicate within the same clause.[19] In other words it creates an ambiguity as to what is actually being said in that clause.

In many cases, in spite of their apparent optionality, the main verbs or participles are not being used as alternatives but are to be understood as a sequence in which the majority of the second clause (whether main or subordinate) has been omitted, leaving only the verb describing the action. In this case there is a further sense of the action moving forward at a rapid pace, almost as if the events do not occur in a linear sequence but simultaneously, leaving an aura of uncertainty and raising questions about what is actually happening and what is being said. Is it more important that the train is going or stopping? Is it going and stopping all at once? Is it more important that the Hodscha is standing or crying? Does he cry as he stands or after he stands?

> (10) "unser Hodscha ... ist ... gestanden, geweint" ("our Hodscha stood up, wept").
> (12) "Ein Zug fährt, hält"[20] ("A train goes, stops").

---

[17] Turkish is also a complement drop language. See the above link.
[18] Sandrine Henry, "Repeats in Spontaneous Spoken French: the Influence of the Complexity of Phrases", *Proceedings of DiSS'05, Disfluency in Spontaneous Speech Workshop*, (September 2005), 1 (http://www.up.univ-mrs.fr/delic/papiers/Henry-2005DISS.pdf).
[19] In H.P. Grice's rules for *rational* communication (based on the co-operative principle) such ambiguity flouts the maxim of manner. Levinson, *Pragmatics*, 103.
[20] Though in this instance we can more readily see the two verb forms as indicating sequential actions rather than an ambiguity as to what is happening.

(13) "Die Kantinenarbeiter rauchen, reden über Töpfe und Teller" ("The cantine workers spoke, speak over pots and plates").

The same technique is use with adjectival modifiers, here creating above all the sense that meanings are collapsing in on one another and that separate concepts indicated by separate signifiers are coupling together into unified wholes, soon to be overlaid the one on top of the other. Where the comma appears one can readily imagine a hyphen joining the two modifiers so that they be read as: *artig-schläfrig* ("well-behaved, sleepy"); *unheilig-unbarmherzig* ("unholy-unmerciful). The immediacy of their sequence brings us close to imagining concepts such as *schläfrartig* or *unbarmherzheilig*:[21]

(15) Die Kissen sitzen auf der Erde artig, schläfrig
(15) nur das Fenster zum Hof war unheilig, unbarmherzig wach[22]

These brief examples serve to show how the more explicit textual themes seem to be reflected in the language of the text itself. Just as the narrator's personal identity threatens to merge with that of Ibni Abdullah, so do linguistic concepts threaten to merge. Separate concepts and identities are coupling, taking steps towards intermingling and losing their own individual function and position within the symbolic order as meaning shifts between the two signifiers to create a new and unfamiliar range of significance.

Imagery in *Mutter Zunge*

"Mutter Zunge" and more especially, "Großvaterzunge" are both extremely rich in metaphorical devices. In the short narrative "Großvaterzunge" there are several recurrent tropes that are key to the narrative. These include *das Herz* ("heart"), *die Seele* ("soul"), *der*

---

[21] The Turkish-German poet Zehra Çirak frequently makes use of a similar device of compounding. In her collection, *Leibesübungen*, Cologne: Kiepenheuer and Witsch, 2000, she blends separate concepts into configurations such as "Erinnerungsallergie" (10) ("memory allergy"), "Sattsichschlafen" (17) ("sleep oneself sated"), "quietschgefröhlicht" (20) ("extremely cheerfulled"), and "besorgnisbewegt" (20) ("moved by unease"). Thanks to Moray McGowan for suggesting possible parallels.
[22] "The cushions sit on the floor well-behaved, sleepy"; "only the window to the courtyard was awake in an unholy, unmerciful way."

Tod ("death"), *die Rose* ("rose"), *der Garten* ("garden"), *die Liebe* ("love"), *der Traum* ("dream"), *der Fuß* ("foot"), *die Augen* ("eyes"), *die Hand* ("hand"), *der Mund* ("mouth"), *der Flügel* ("wing") and *der Vogel* ("bird") among others. These motifs recur in a variety of contexts. The number of references to the same motifs almost turns the detailing of their occurrence into a reassembling of the text in a different order. This frequent recurrence of the same motifs makes for a densely woven, highly cohesive narrative that nevertheless remains somewhat obscure to the reader because of the metaphoric nature of the textual references. Recognition of the various ways in which the motifs are employed is key to a deeper understanding of the narrative. A listing of two of these motifs in context is provided in Appendix III.

The recurrent motifs of the text are all common poetic tropes both within a European and/or Anglophone context and more especially within the context of the literary tradition of Ottoman Divan poetry. Andrews provides a detailed list of the words most frequently repeated in the *gazel*, a particular form of Ottoman divan poetry consisting of a short lyric poem in couplets, or lines made up of two half-lines. *Gazels* may be anything from four to fourteen lines in length, though are usually between five and seven.[23] The recurrent tropes of these poems cited by Andrews include many of those that are also found in *Mutter Zunge*. The table below indicates which of the *Mutter Zunge* tropes either exactly match the most frequently repeated lexical items identified by Andrews or fit into one of the broader recurrent categories of trope he has suggested.[24]

Table 2

Mutter Zunge	Ottoman Divan poetry	
	Most frequently repeated words (Turkish)	Common general category represented by most frequent words
der Tod	N/A	7. World
die Seele	*can* (soul, life)	1. Person
das Herz	*dil/gönül* (heart)	1. Person
der Fuß	N/A	1. Person

---

[23] Andrews, *Poetry's Voice, Society's Song*, 3.
[24] *Ibid.*, 41-49

das Auge	*göz* (eye)	1. Person
die Hand	*el* (hand)	1. Person
der Mund	N/A	1. Person
der Flügel	N/A	5. Garden/Nature
der Vogel	N/A	5. Garden/Nature
der Garten	N/A	5. Garden/Nature
die Rose	*gül* (rose)	5. Garden/Nature
die Liebe	*'işk* (love)	2. Love
der Traum	N/A	N/A

In order of frequency the most commonly repeated lexical items Andrews found in Ottoman Divan poetry were the following:

Table 3

1. Soul, life
2. Ruler
3. Heart (dil)
4. Love
5. Heart (gönül)
6. Face
7. World (cihan)
8. Beloved
9. Sigh
10. Eye
11. Grief
12. Moon
13. Day, sun
14. Head
15. Blood
16. Rose
17. Cypress
18. Place, ground
19. Lover
20. World ('alem)
21. Time, breath
22. Curl, lock
23. Love, sun
24. Wheel
25. Hand
26. Tear, wet

It is from this list that Andrews identifies the common categories and subcategories of:

Person (face, eye, head, body, facial features, hand, heart, hair, foot, spirit)

Love (love, lover, beloved, rival, beauty, beloved's behaviour, lover's state)

Cosmos/Fate (heavens, heavenly bodies, fate/turning of heavens, light)

Suffering (grief, sigh/plaint, weeping, trouble/torment, lover's state, wounding, burning)

Garden/Nature (plants/flowers/trees, garden, birds, water, weather/season, wind)

Authority (ruler, subject, state/rule/power, other authority, authority symbols, royal behaviour)

World (world, people, earth, geography, life/death, work, commerce, wealth, ornament, clothing, road/house, weapons, color)

Time (general time)

And upon further investigation of the poetry in order to find further lexical representatives of these categories, he discovers the additional three:

Wine gathering/entertainment (party, intoxication/drinker/drinking, poetry, tales, music, lights)

Mysticism (mystic/mystical state, symbols, separation, annihilation/union annihilation, inner/outer self, awareness, path, way)

Islam (God, holy places, persons, for instance, Muhammad)

The parallels between the recurrent categories found in Ottoman divan poetry and *Mutter Zunge* (1998) are striking. Within the context of Ottoman divan poetry these tropes are highly symbolic and are based around a "this-world/that-world" polarity with each referent to this-world also symbolizing an aspect of that-world or the world of the divine. For example, in this-world the lover symbolizes physical love and in that-world symbolic love. In this-world the beloved is a "tormentor" whereas in that-world s/he is a "healer". Thus each symbol can be interpreted on two levels.[25]

The richness of meaning this engenders for the tropes when interpreted within the Ottoman tradition is further heightened when the Western connotations of these tropes are included in the

---

[25] *Ibid.*, 72-73.

interpretation. Thus the rose, in its "that-worldly" context symbolizes God, in its "this-worldly" context the beloved and in Western European tradition evokes "love" and more particularly "romance". This example also highlights the possibility of a core of conceptual overlap in the range of connotation of each of these symbols across Western European and Ottoman contexts, despite some of the ostensible differences. Further, more precise contextualization for the interpretation of these symbols within an Ottoman context is provided in Andrews, however, in what follows we will concentrate on a consideration of how these symbols translate themselves to the secular Western European context of interpretation in which *Mutter Zunge* is generally received.

In the West several of these poetic tropes connote transcendence, in particular, death, the soul, prayer and perhaps even the image of the bird. Several others are romantic in connotation, especially the heart, fire and the rose. The associative links between the heart and fire are made quite strongly in the narrative. At one point, Ibni Abdullah stares at a candle until it finally fades, before switching on a cassette upon which a man sings a song from the Koran in which a heart is consumed by fire and melts like lead in the fire until the fire goes out.[26] Other common tropes connote issues of freedom and imprisonment; in particular, the images of the bird and the slave are frequently employed. In a scene early on in the narrative a flying bird is juxtaposed with the image of two prisoners at the prison window. One of the prisoners asks the other if he had seen "it". It is uncertain if "it" refers to the bird or the narrator who is jogging past. In any case, in relation to the prisoners, the bird and the narrator have very similar positions. They are both beings who live outside the confines of the prison and who ostensibly have freedom.[27] A later passage in the narrative directly construes the narrator as a bird: "Ich bin ein Vogel. Geflogen aus meinem Land."[28]

Interpreting a poem by Taşlıcalı Yahya Bey (d. 1582 C.E.) Andrews provides the following interpretation for the symbol of the bird in Ottoman poetry:

---

[26] Özdamar, *Mutter Zunge*, 24.
[27] *Ibid.*, 11.
[28] *Ibid.*, 27. "I am a bird. Flown out of my country."

The bird has a number of possible significations, primarily vulnerability and powerlessness, but it also has the quality of being able to fly to great heights both spiritually ... and in terms of mundane success and power, the high-flying bird being a common trope for the successful person.[29]

Ibni Abdullah refers to the narrator in different ways as a bird. Citing a song he says:

> Du lustige **Nachtigall** meines Herzens.[30]

and later:

> Wenn du mich anguckst, setzt sich
> ein **Vogel** auf meine linke Schulter und
> fliegt und setzt sich auf die andere Schulter.[31]

By the narrator the image of the bird is also to be used to express a desire for love and transcendence:

> Mein Herz wollte **fliegen**, hat keine **Flügel** gefunden ...[32]
> Mein Allah, gib mir zwei **Flügel**, oder mach mich zum **Vogel**, entweder mach mein Herz zu Stein, oder gib mir einen Geduldstein.[33]

In the middle of the narrative, in defence of her inability to learn the Arabic script, there is what appears to be a page long poetic statement of the narrator's love for Ibni Abdullah in which the many images that have been employed up until that point coalesce to form a vivid portrait of the narrator's emotions:

> Du Seele in meiner Seele, keine ist dir ähnlich, ich opfere mich für deine Schritte. Mit deinen Blicken schautest du mich an, ich gebe mich zum Opfer deinem Blicke. Verwahrlost, Haar gelöst, fortwimmern will ich, mit einem Blick hast du meine Zunge an deine

---

[29] Andrews, *Poetry's Voice, Society's Song*, 131.
[30] Özdamar, *Mutter Zunge*, 27: "You merry nightingale of my heart."
[31] *Ibid.*, 30: "When you look at me a bird lands on my left shoulder and flies and settles on my other shoulder."
[32] *Ibid.*, 32: "My heart wanted to fly, found no wings."
[33] *Ibid.*, 36: "My Allah, give me two wings or make me into a bird, either turn my heart to stone or give me a patience stone."

> Haare gebunden. Ich bin die Sklavin deines Antlitzes. Zerbrich nicht diese Kette, lehne mich nicht ab, Geliebter, ich bin die Sklavin deines Gesichts geworden, sag mir nur, was tue ich jetzt, was tue ich jetzt .... Mein Herz wollte fliegen, hat keine Flügel gefunden, meine Liebe ist ein Hochwasser, es schreit, wirft mein Herz vor sich her, es weint, keine Hand habe ich gefunden, die sie ihm abwischt, ich habe mich in Liebeshochwasser gehen lassen, ich habe kein Wörterbuch gefunden für die Sprache meiner Liebe. Ich sprach wie die Nachtigall, blaß geworden wie die Rosen. Das ist ein Weh, ein Geschrei, so frei, so frei. Dann kam noch ein Lied:
> Hab Angst, daß ich sterbe. Bevor ich sterbe, will ich ihn noch mal sehen, sein Gesicht, mein Gesicht, zwischen uns der Mond, als ich im Garten war, weinten die Äste, habt ihr meinen Geliebten gesehen, Sterne, Monde, jetzt weint er vielleicht, sagt zu oft "Ach", gebt mir einen Weg rauchender Berge, ich will zu ihm – man sagt, der Tod ist billig.[34]

The poetic images and the romantic content of the text, here as elsewhere, mutually reflect one another. A poetic style is predominantly conjured up through repetitions on phonetic, prosodic and syntactic levels as detailed here. These features are particularly evident in the following passage:

> "Ich laufe, die Liebe hat mich gefärbt ins Blut, mein Kopf ist weder bei mir, weder weg von mir, komm und sieh, was die Liebe aus mir gemacht hat, deine Liebe hat mich gesehen, hat mein Herz rausgenommen, es krank gemacht, hat Absicht, es zu töten, manchmal

---

[34] *Ibid.*, 31-32: "You soul in my soul, no-one is like you, I sacrifice myself to your steps. With your gaze you looked at me, I give myself in sacrifice to your gaze. Bedraggled, hair loose, I want to whimper away, with one glance you have tied my tongue to your hair. I am the slave of your countenance. Do not break this chain, do not reject me, Beloved, I have become the slave of your face, just tell me, what do I do now, what do I do now .... My heart wanted to fly, found no wings, my love is a high-tide, it cries, throws my heart before it, it weeps, I have found no hand to wipe it from him, I have let myself go in love's high-tide, I have found no dictionary for the language of my love. I spoke like the nightingale, turned pale as the roses. That is woe, a cry, so free so free. Then came another song: I fear I am dying. Before I die, I want to see him again, his face, my face, between us the moon, when I was in the garden, the branches wept, have you seen my beloved, stars, moons, now he weeps perhaps, says too often 'ah', give me a path of smouldering mountains, I want to go to him – it is said death is cheap."

bin ich wie ein Wind, manchmal wie staubige Wege, manchmal schlage ich wie Wasser auf Wasser, komm und sieh mich, was die Liebe aus mir gemacht hat."[35]

Here we see alliterative word groups such as: *laufe, Liebe*; *Wind, Wege, Wasser*. In the last line both phonetic and prosodic elements combine to create an onomatopoeic effect: <u>manch</u>mal <u>schl</u>age *ich wie* <u>Was</u>ser *auf* <u>Was</u>ser in which the alternating stressed and unstressed syllables and the repeated fricative sounds create the effect both of the upward and downward movement of waves as well as the rushing sound of them breaking.

Repetitions are found on other linguistic levels as well. In the following passage on the same page we see the repetition of the auxiliary verb *hat* in relation to "love": "was die Liebe aus mir gemacht hat, deine Liebe hat mich gesehen, hat mein Herz rausgenommen, es krank gemacht, hat Absicht, es zu töten." In each clause the narrator is presented as being in some way the object of love. It might also be suggested that the repetition of *hat* in this grammatical function serves to push the word out of its context, in which case the lexical meaning of the word in which something is possessed by something else would be highlighted. In this case it is the narrator who is possessed by love.

Other repeated phrases serve to repeat particular prosodic patterns and give more weight to the meaning of stressed syllables: *weder <u>bei</u> mir, weder <u>weg</u> von mir*. In this example the stress emphasizes a contradictory perception; she cannot literally be both with and without her head, but the paradoxical logic of her emotions allows her to perceive this to be the case.

In analysing the linguistic patterns and effects of Özdamar's writing in this text, we see how the events of the narrative are reflected in their linguistic representation. In the encounter between German and Turkish and Turkish and Arabic we see in *Mutter Zunge*, identities and languages blend in a way that arguably creates a kind of

---

[35] *Ibid.*, 28: "I run, love has coloured my blood, my head is neither with me nor away from me, come and see what love has made of me, your love has seen me, has taken out my heart, made it sick, intends to kill it, sometimes I am like a wind, sometimes like dusty paths, sometimes I beat like water on water, come and see me, what love has made of me."

hyperliterary text that has a heightened ability to challenge readers' usual categories of perception, through increased possibilities of defamiliarization resulting from the intermingling of different cultural and textual frameworks. This hyperliterary text promises as much signification as it withholds thereby providing the reader with both the motivation to read the text as well as the opportunity to read into it and insert their own significations into its framework thereby engaging in a satisfying intercultural dialogue.

The linguistic examples given here reveal how the more explicit themes of the text are reflected in the form of the text as it was written. Just as the narrator's personal identity threatens to merge with that of Ibni Abdullah, so do linguistic concepts threaten to merge. Separate concepts and identities are coupling, taking steps towards intermingling and losing their own individual function and position within the symbolic order as meaning shifts between the two signifiers to create a new and unfamiliar range of significance. In the encounter between German and Turkish and Turkish and Arabic we see in this text, identities and languages blend together and defamiliarize the language. However, even with this production of defamiliarization, the text can be seen as an attempt at resolution of the dissimilarities forcing alienation. Not only can this text be seen to reflect a struggle for the dissolution of self and other in a mystical sense, as shown in its suggested links to Ottoman divan poetry, but it can also be interpreted as a striving towards a transcendent unity, that will eradicate the alienation inherent in immigrant experience, through its textual integration of diverse cultural traditions and conceptual frameworks.

CHAPTER EIGHT

AUTONOMY ABROAD: METAPHORS OF *MÜNDIGKEIT* IN LANGUAGE LEARNER NARRATIVE

> Ces histoires se font écho, d'une manière émouvante, sans fard, parce qu'elles touchent à ce qu'il y a de plus profond en chacun de nous dans le savoir et dans le dire, aux origines de l'un et de l'autre.[1]

Having examined how the troubling of *Mündigkeit* is represented both linguistically and thematically in Özdamar's text *Mutter Zunge* (1998), this chapter examines how this crisis is represented in a broader spectrum of language learner narratives by focussing on three prerequisites for *Mündigkeit* and examining the key tropes that represent the unsettling of these, within the larger corpus. The analysis of these tropes of the crisis of *Mündigkeit* is undertaken with reference to George Lakoff and Mark Johnson's theory of conceptual metaphor.[2] In suggesting underlying conceptual metaphors within language learner narratives that are also proposed to be reflective of a crisis of *Mündigkeit*, it is also hoped to support the possibility of universal conceptualizations of the language learning situation that transcend the diverse sociohistorical backgrounds of the writers. At

---

[1] *Entre Deux Langues*, eds Cellier-Gelly, Torreilles and Verny, 5: "These stories echo each other in a moving way, without pretension, because they touch what is most profound in each of us in what we know and in what we say, at the origins of all of us."

[2] Lakoff and Johnson's theory of metaphor considers metaphor from a cognitive perspective and is one of many theories of metaphor which have been developed over the centuries. See Terence Hawkes, *Metaphor*, London: Methuen, 1972 or Murray Knowles and Rosamund Moon, *Introducing Metaphor*, London: Routledge, 2006. For a recent overview of metaphorology from a post-structuralist standpoint, see Anselm Haverkamp, *Metapher: Die Ästhetik in der Rhetorik: Bilanz eines Exemplarischen Begriffs*, München: Wilhelm Fink Verlag, 2007. Haverkamp explores in particular the palaeonymic qualities of the term "metaphor" with the signifier designating various concepts throughout its history.

the very least, if not ultimately universal, the striking resonances of these metaphors may be attributed to a discourse of the self and of language common to the predominantly European cultures with which the authors of these narratives have some relationship. In this more relativistic view, the metaphors of *Mündigkeit* can be seen as a use of metaphor that may derive from a common European discursive heritage.

It must also be noted, however, that in the preliminary examination of the texts, a certain level of perceptual bias must necessarily be accepted. Firstly, the assignment of metaphors from these texts to underlying conceptual metaphors itself involves a metaphorizing process of subjective comparison and interpretation that could be contested. Secondly, the linkage of these conceptual metaphors to the prerequisites for *Mündigkeit* argued for in Chapter Five, also involves a process of judicious interpretation. It is hoped, however, that the quantity of evidence presented from a quite diverse range of texts, lends these interpretations more weight. As suggested in the quotation at the start of this chapter, the texts from authors unknown to each other certainly seem to resonate in their metaphorical descriptions in a way that suggests universal experiences of language learning articulated in different, culturally and personally appropriate ways.

Once the more straightforward evidence for the interpretation of these metaphors within the framework of *Mündigkeit* has been explored, some of the more complex uses of metaphor in language learner narrative that might either expand or explode this line of reasoning will be discussed.

The first prerequisite for *Mündigkeit* is that of a sense of independent selfhood and/or identity. A crisis of this may be represented by descriptions of the language as a body or as clothing. Some of the tropes emerging from the texts relevant to this theme include images of being an actor, a traitor or a spy. The second prerequisite is the possession of language and more especially rational language. This second theme links with the first since the destabilization of meaning is often portrayed in the texts as giving rise to a destabilization of identity for the speaking subject at both verbal and non-verbal levels. The third and final prerequisite for *Mündigkeit* is the possession of social and symbolic capital. This theme is important for an understanding of how the unfamiliar social world is experienced by the narrators of language learner narratives, particularly in respect of social status in the unfamiliar culture. A crisis of this is shown to be reflected in the texts through metaphorical descriptions of entrapment and infantilization.

Metaphors we live by

The purpose in examining metaphors in language memoirs is to examine how individual authors conceptualize the linguistic and cultural differences they have encountered. There has been much debate over the latter half of the twentieth century and beyond about the connections between language and identity and/or the self, some of which have been discussed in Chapter Three. Within relativist theories which have been popular over the last few decades, it is widely acknowledged that the language a person speaks plays a large role in his or her conceptualization of the world and the way s/he conceives of his or her role within it. Following Bakhtin, the point is also commonly made that every language encodes within it a variety of world views and belief systems, such that a person's thinking is never made up of only one way of looking at the world – whether or not that person speaks any foreign languages.[3] What is interesting in encountering a foreign culture is how contrasts in world view are brought suddenly and sharply into focus. In speaking a later experienced language and living in a foreign culture an alternative world view is no longer an option from a personal stylistic repertoire to be adopted at will, it is forced upon the speaker through their use of the later experienced language. In speaking this language a person may also experience a forced reconceptualization of their own self, one which destabilizes personal meanings and behaviours constructed over many years in the early experienced language.

In *Metaphors We Live By* (1980) Lakoff and Johnson articulate a view of metaphor which suggests it to be a pervasive conceptual process in language, structuring our perception of reality, rather than simply being a stylistic embellishment which states something in a figurative way that could have been stated literally.[4] This view is one that is also found in the work of earlier thinkers such as Giambattista

---

[3] Mikhail Bakhtin, "Discourse in the Novel", in *Dialogic Imagination*, ed. Michael Holquist, Austin: University of Texas Press, 1981, 288.
[4] Cf. Christina Schäffner, "Metaphor and Translation: Some Implications of a Cognitive Approach", *Journal of Pragmatics*, XXXVI/7 (July 2004), 1253-69.

Vico in the eighteenth century,[5] however, in their own work, Lakoff and Johnson specifically emphasize metaphor as a means of linking and extending existing concepts. Thus, they propose, for example, that the concept ARGUE is mapped onto aspects of the concept WAR in a variety of expressions in English: "He *shot down* all of my arguments" or "Your claims are *indefensible*". Along with many other examples of this kind, metaphor is clearly shown to be a conceptual process used to describe the more abstract in terms of the concrete so that abstract experiences, ideas or feelings with no direct referent that may be particularly difficult to conceptualize are commonly articulated in terms of more concrete experiences deriving primarily from human beings' physical experience of their environment. This theory of metaphor again highlights the extent to which our conceptions of reality as expressed in language are inherently relative and culturally determined. Unless conventionalized, the comparisons occurring in metaphor are necessarily subjective – deriving from different viewpoints on the same experience, whether or not the experiences are common to more than one person.[6] Lakoff and Johnson make the point that our perception of argument in terms of war is in fact quite arbitrary.[7] Arguments might equally be perceived as a dance and one could imagine describing how people take steps forward and steps back in their arguments, at times moving in the same direction as others or even spinning round in circles.[8] Lakoff and Johnson emphasize that:

> Our values are not independent but must form a coherent system with the metaphorical concepts we live by. We are not claiming that all cultural values coherent with a metaphorical system actually exist, only that those that do exist and are deeply entrenched are consistent with the metaphorical system.[9]

---

[5] Hawkes, *Metaphor*, 38-39.
[6] It is still debatable to what extent certain concepts and corresponding conceptual metaphors may or may not be universal. See Schäffner, "Metaphor and Translation: Some Implications of a Cognitive Approach", 1264.
[7] George Lakoff and Mark Johnson, *Metaphors We Live By*, Chicago: University of Chicago Press, 1980, 4-5.
[8] Cf. Knowles and Moon, *Introducing Metaphor*, 88.
[9] Lakoff and Johnson, *Metaphors We Live By*, 23.

In moving to a new culture and adopting a foreign language, a person is obliged to adopt a discourse and with it the metaphors which characterize that discourse and shape the conceptualization of their environment. The foreign language discourse one encounters is likely to be founded on different conceptual mappings expressed in different linguistic metaphors. For example, in French, many linguistic metaphors are the same as in English, though concepts may be expressed in slightly different ways. The literal meaning of the English word "hollow" translates into French as *creux* but the metaphorical meaning of "hollow" is more likely to be translated as *faux* or *vain*.[10]

A real and personal awareness of linguistic arbitrariness is articulated by Eva Hoffmann in her own language memoir, where she describes herself as "a living avatar of structuralist wisdom". For Hoffman living in English has meant that her world and the words she uses to describe it have become disconnected; the world has become literally drained of its meaning, the life gone out of it.[11] However, in writing language learner narrative, the authors investigated here must find a way to resignify their experience and put words back onto the world. Part of this process involves developing their own metaphorical constructions of reality which may be done in a way that mediates between the conceptual and linguistic frameworks provided by the one or more languages within which they are operating. Later on in this chapter, the use of metaphor as mediator between languages will be explored in an analysis of one of the metaphors used in Nancy Huston's *Nord perdu* (1999). Firstly, however, the conceptual metaphors suggested to articulate the crisis of *Mündigkeit* engendered by the initial encounter with linguistic arbitrariness will be explored.

Metaphors of *Mündigkeit* as conventional metaphors

As discussed in the methodology section, for the purposes of this project, it is accepted that language has a large role to play in certain types of human thought. It is furthermore accepted that human beings are not limited in any absolute way by the conceptual structure developed through use of their early experienced language and that the possibility exists to extend the concepts developed in their early experienced language through the use of a later experienced language.

---

[10] Knowles and Moon, *Introducing Metaphor*, 81.
[11] Hoffman, *Lost in Translation*, 107.

The initial discussion that follows, however, rather than looking at metaphor as a mediator between one or more conceptual frameworks, examines how metaphors are used within one language to describe the experience of learning a foreign language. Thus the aim is to see how language learning, as a specific world experience, is conceptualized by means of metaphor. This metaphorical conceptualization of the experience is not necessarily innovative (involving a comparison between two items that are not usually connected in the language and culture in question) but may be conventional (the metaphor may be idiomatic in the later experienced language or may involve a comparison that is frequently made in the language). Following this initial discussion, consideration is taken of the possibility to extend the range of significance of metaphors through invoking concepts pertaining to more than one culture.

This chapter provides a comparison of the metaphors used across language learner narratives to discuss the themes of identity, language and social capital relating to the crisis of *Mündigkeit* as outlined in the introductory paragraphs of this chapter. It is also worth noting the possibility that the language learner narrative as a text type, reveals its own culture that overarches the cultures being discussed by the narrators and that it is this culture which informs the metaphorical description of the language learning situation. To give a brief example, one fundamental conceptual assumption underlying the production of these narratives in the first place is one highlighted by Lakoff as being rooted deep in Western Anglophone culture (if not others):

> Let us start with "Tell me the story of your life," which contains the conventional metaphor LIFE IS A STORY .... It is assumed that everyone's life is structured like a story, and the entire biographical and autobiographical tradition is based on this assumption. Suppose someone asks you to tell your life story. What do you do? You construct a coherent narrative that starts early in your life and continues up to the present.[12]

The metaphor of LIFE IS A STORY represents a crucial conceptual assumption that underpins the very act of writing a language learner narrative and furthermore supports arguments for a cross-cultural autobiography being written as a means to create a new life for oneself

---

[12] Lakoff and Johnson, *Metaphors We Live By*, 172.

in the foreign culture. One of the language learner narratives seems to play directly with this conceptual assumption. In Luc Sante's *The Factory of Facts* (1998) the beginning of the narrative is repeated nine times each with slight variations on the facts, thereby highlighting the constructed nature of autobiographical narrative and its status as story rather than reality. The reader is left wondering which of the more outrageous facts might actually be true.[13]

The first metaphor to be explored here in detail across a range of texts may be articulated as THE FOREIGN LANGUAGE IS A HUMAN BEING. As indicated above, two further conceptual metaphors that may be more directly related to the suggested loss of *Mündigkeit* or maturity in the unfamiliar or foreign context will also be considered. The first of these to be explored relates to the perception of infantilization in the foreign language and may be articulated as: THE NON-FLUENT SPEAKER IS A CHILD. The other of these sees the foreign culture as a threatening place of incarceration rather than as a welcoming guest-house. This metaphor may be articulated as THE FOREIGN LANGUAGE AND CULTURE ARE A TRAP. Following this, two metaphors relating to the destabilized sense of self and identity in the foreign culture are explored, these are THE FOREIGN LANGUAGE IS A COSTUME and THE FOREIGN CULTURE IS A PLAY.

The foreign language is a human being

Many language learners in language learner narratives describe the foreign language in some way as if it were a human being. This may occur through making the foreign language the agentive subject of a clause or through specific metaphorical descriptions of the foreign language that refer to the language as if it were a person. This conceptual metaphor widely underpins many of the statements in Ariel Dorfman's language learner narrative. In this autobiography, the author describes his changing allegiances to both languages and nations. Having moved from Argentina to the USA with his parents as a child, he falls in love with the English language. When his parents move with him to Chile at the age of twelve, Dorfman bides his time until he can return to the USA fourteen years later. Here, he finally comes to renounce English and to return to South America where he works in support of Salvador Allende's socialist movement in Chile. Reflective of these changing allegiances, for Dorfman it appears as if

---

[13] Sante, Luc, *The Factory of Facts*, London: Granta Books, 1998, 1-8.

Spanish and English were two different characters inside his head, engaged in a military struggle. Dorfman speaks of "surrender to English",[14] having Spanish as "an ally inside me"[15] or "crow[ing] victory" and not "cornering me".[16]

The cultural battle between his childhood enamoration with the US and his adult commitment to the Chilean nation, which forms an explicit theme of Dorfman's text, is reflected in the way in which the languages relating to these two nations are metaphorically described. The narrator appears as a geographical territory that two warring nations are attempting to conquer. As a child he has imprisoned the invading Spanish, only for it to be released at a later stage in his life. He talks of "smother[ing]" the language, "closing the door" to it and "throwing away the key".[17]

In anthropomorphizing the languages, authors have projected the various power struggles and human relationships of daily life onto them. For Özdamar, the script appears as a threatening teacher – the letters "wait" for her in the *Schriftzimmer* and Ibni Abdullah declares that the script will not "forgive" her for her lack of concentration.[18] Other writers interpret their bilingual situation in a similar way to Dorfman. Alexakis, for example, suggests that instead of French conquering him, perhaps he can conquer French:

> J'ai constaté depuis que le point de vue de ce linguiste est plus répandu que je ne le croyais. On se réjouit que le français conquière des étrangers, mais on n'est nullement convaincu que ceux-ci puissent à leur tour conquérir la langue. On les considère davantage comme des représentants d'une autre culture, des ambassadeurs d'un au-delà, que comme des créateurs originaux, des auteurs à part entière.[19]

---

[14] Ariel Dorfman, *Heading South, Looking North: A Bilingual Journey*, London: Hodder and Stoughton, 1998, 41.
[15] *Ibid.*, 48.
[16] *Ibid.*, 116.
[17] *Ibid.*, 60.
[18] Özdamar, *Mutter Zunge*, 32.
[19] Alexakis, *Paris-Athènes*, 16: "I have since noticed that this linguist's point of view is more widespread than I thought. People rejoice that French is conquering foreigners, but are not at all convinced that the foreigners can in turn conquer the language. People consider them more as representatives of another culture, ambassadors from beyond, than as original creators, authors in their own right" (my translation).

As "ambassador from beyond" Alexakis perceives his expected contribution to French society to be one of friendly exoticism, rather than one in which he takes active control of French cultural heritage through "conquering" its language.

Where the relationship to the language is more harmonious, this is expressed in metaphors that suggest the language to be a lover or a close friend, rather than an invader from another country: "But Spanish was there at the beginning of my body or perhaps where my body ended and the world began, coaxing that body into life as only a lover can, convincing me slowly, sound by sound, that life was worth living."[20]

The embodiment of the foreign language as a lover is also found in Alexakis' *Paris-Athènes* (2006) where he expresses a desire to "converser sereinement avec elle" meaning the French language.[21] In this case, the grammatical necessity in French of signalling the abstract concept "French language" with a gendered pronoun contributes significantly to the anthropomorphosis. The resolution of the self-betrayal that occurs on using the French language and engaging with this other comes through the marriage of the languages in an act of self-translation of his writing from Greek to French. With his languages closely married in this way, Alexakis feels that there is no risk of betraying either his languages or himself.

> On m'a parlé d'un écrivain étranger qui a fini par épouser sa traductrice française: "Eh bien, ai-je pensé, moi, je suis ma propre femme!" J'ai été assez heureux pendant un moment. Je n'avais le sentiment ni de me trahir, en utilisant deux langues, ni de les trahir.[22]

A sense of interpersonal familiarity and closeness to a language in abstraction from any person speaking it is also expressed by Richard Rodriguez writing in the following passage from his collection of autobiographical essays in *Hunger of Memory* (1982):

> Another day, a dark-faced old woman – her hand light on my shoulder – steadied herself against me as she boarded a bus. She murmured

---

[20] Dorfman, *Heading South, Looking North*, 12.
[21] Alexakis, *Paris-Athènes*, 45: "to converse serenely with her" (my translation).
[22] *Ibid.*, 15: "Someone told me of a foreign writer who ended up marrying his French translator. 'So', I thought, 'I am my own wife!' For a little while, I was quite happy. I didn't feel like I was betraying myself or my languages by using two of them."

something I couldn't quite comprehend. Her Spanish voice came near, like the face of a never-before-seen relative in the instant before I was kissed.[23]

Similarly, Elizabeth Dykman, in her essay "The Vagabond Years" (2000) describes moving away from Poland and speaking English as being like losing someone close to her:

> At the time I could not have foreseen that by departing Poland I would also forsake my closeness to the Polish language. It is a loss that I continue to mourn. Though I still speak Polish, time has irrevocably erased a particular sense of intimacy I shared with my native tongue, and the new languages I have since acquired, regardless of my efforts to "adopt" them, will never supplant the void created.[24]

The closeness to the Polish language that she feels, appears to be implicitly connected to its common origin with her as an individual, as if it were a blood relative rather than an unrelated stranger. She has attempted to "adopt" other languages, but she cannot relate to them in the way that she used to relate to Polish. This compares with Rodriguez' description of the Spanish voice that appeared to him as "the face of a never-before-seen relative". The earlier experienced language represents intimate connection even when the individual using the language is a complete stranger. A further example is found in Chang-Rae Lee's *Native Speaker* (1995) where the protagonist experiences familiarity with a person he has barely met that is evoked solely by language. On visiting his college friend Albert's house after his mother's death, he recounts the following experience:

> Then Albert's mother called happily to him in Korean, "Now you've come home!" and although her accent was different, too breathy, nearly Japanese, the inflection of the words was just that of my mother's, so much so that I nearly dropped my duffel and went to the strange-faced woman standing there in the busy kitchen .... And while sitting at dinner listening to her ..., a familiarity arose that should have been impossible but wasn't and made me feel a little sick inside. It wasn't that Albert and I were similar; we weren't, our parents weren't. It was something else.[25]

---

[23] Rodriguez, *Hunger of Memory*, 25.
[24] Dykman, "The Vagabond Years", 31.
[25] Lee, *Native Speaker*, 89.

From these examples, it can be seen that emotionally, the "familiarity" of the earlier experienced language appears frequently to be conceptualized in terms of a literal "family". The close relationship between these two concepts is also evident in their etymological connection through the Latin root *familia* meaning "household" or "family". In the connection between family and familiarity present in these language learner narratives, the metaphorical use of *familia* in the word "familiarity" appears unconsciously reliteralized and then in turn remetaphorized as a trope for evoking the familiarity of the early experienced language. In other words the term "familiarity" is reliteralized through its representation in the image of a "close relative", while this image concurrently works against this literalization through its evocation of the term "familiarity". A close reciprocal relationship between "familiar" and "family" is presented. The question of whether these, perhaps unconscious, conceptual associations are determined by the etymological connections present in the languages known by the writers, in, for example, the English "family"/"familiarity", the French *famille/familier*, the Spanish *familia/familiar*, or more universally embedded in the human psyche through the emotional experience of familiarity no matter whether or not these etymological connections exist in the writer's languages is one that must for the time being remain unanswered. Each of these writers is familiar with a language in which this etymological connection exists even if their mother-tongue does not reveal the same association.

The non-fluent speaker is a child
This second metaphor is articulated most directly by the Anglophone Canadian, Nancy Huston, who describes her experience of living in France as follows:

> A l'étranger, on est enfant à nouveau, et dans le pire sens du terme: infantilisé. Réduit à l'*infans*, c'est-à-dire au silence; privé de parole. Totalement idiot et impuissant![26]

---

[26] Huston, *Nord Perdu*, 78: "Living abroad, you are a child again, and in the worst sense of the term: infantilized. Reduced to *infans*, that is, to silence; deprived of speech. Completely stupid and powerless!"

Verena Stefan, who grew up in the German-speaking region of Switzerland describes her experience of North America as "Learning the world new, like a child".[27] In *Something to Declare* (1998), Julia Alvarez, who moved from the Dominican Republic to the USA, expresses frustration at being treated like a child on a return visit to her Aunt and Uncle in her homeland because of her poor command of the Spanish language which she has not spoken for many years: "But I can't help thinking that in part, Utcho and Betty treated me like a ten-year-old because I talked like a ten-year-old in my halting, childhood Spanish."[28]

The American, Karen Ogulnick writing in *Onna Rashiku* or *Like a Woman* (1998) about her experiences in Japan complains of being talked down to in "baby Japanese"[29] and wonders "if [she] was the same person who had left home at 17, financed her own college education, and traveled around the world alone at 19, or, an infantilized 24-year-old woman who needed to be helped and taken care of".[30]

Eva Hoffman moved from Poland to Canada as a young adolescent and in her later autobiography, *Lost in Translation* (1989) plays on the old English proverb "children should be seen and not heard" as a way to describe her sense of invisibility in the foreign culture:

> Because I'm not heard, I feel I'm not seen. My words often seem to baffle others. They are inappropriate, or forced, or just plain incomprehensible .... People look past me as we speak. What do I look like here? Imperceptible, I think; impalpable, neutral, faceless.[31]

Writing in *The Philosopher's Demise: Learning French* (1995), Richard Watson reverses the power relations suggested by the infantilization of the language learners in the narratives above and perhaps in return for his fellow students' perception of him "as a funny little old man with a white beard who was earnest and wanted to learn but who just wasn't very good or very bright" and his teacher

---

[27] Verena Stefan, "Here's Your Change 'N Enjoy the Show", in *Language Crossings: Negotiating the Self in a Multicultural World*, ed. Karen Ogulnick, New York: Teachers College Press, 2000, 25.
[28] Alvarez, *Something to Declare*, 66.
[29] Ogulnick, *Onna Rashiku (Like a Woman)*, 8.
[30] Ibid., 6.
[31] Hoffman, *Lost in Translation*, 147.

calling him an "imbecile"³² he makes French out to be an effeminate childish language:

> Notice the gutturals in the English and German. You can really curse with *g* and *d*. And you might think "Mon Dieu!" could be half saved with the *d*, but no chance, for you must emasculate it by sliding up into the French *u* sound, which requires you to purse your lips and point them up at a forty-five degree angle to make that high *ew* sound that exists in practically no other language but French. It is the *ew* of "ew, la, la" made by a little English girl with a twist in her body, the edge of her skirt held up between thumb and index finger, her head tilted, her eyes half closed and glazed, to represent someone (that's right, a French someone) who thinks herself most hoity-toity – which itself comes surely from the French for high roof... In plain English, it is embarrassing for an American to pronounce the French *u* because the mere sound of it suggests that the speaker thinks very highly of himself or herself, "ew...dew tell..."

> All right. All right. But remember, I'm not trying to be reasonable about it. I'm just giving you my unadulterated, stupid, automatic response. Real Men Don't Speak French.³³

In an unrelated context, Stefan appears to perceive for herself the emasculation expressed here by Watson in another male writer at a (coincidentally) Francophone meeting:

> At a francophone writers [*sic*] meeting I saw somebody without a voice, with a painful expression on his face for hours. It told of a far too stretched attention span, of emotional insecurity, of feeling awkward in his skin. He was one of the guest writers and he didn't speak French. I saw him shrinking into nobody by the hour, since he couldn't make proof of his existence, his thinking, by naming it. Therefore he found himself in a low feminine status. His posture and gestures spoke of confinement, of not-reaching-far-out, of not-taking-a-stand, of the stress of being excluded and wanting to belong. The tension between his very virile appearance and his weak social

---

³² Watson, *The Philosopher's Demise*, 61 and 40.
³³ *Ibid.*, 54: In another passage (53) Watson objects to the French word "l'oiseau" ("bird") on the basis that "It is a word that cannot be pronounced without simpering, a word whose use should be restricted to children under five."

position was striking. Apart from that, I saw a human being stripped of language and suffering torments.[34]

The concealed rage at the powerlessness engendered by having to speak French expressed in these two passages and the despair at the infantilized social position the language learner is forced to adopt is reflected in textual passages where metaphors suggest a feeling of being trapped, imprisoned or encased as will now be discussed.

The foreign language and culture are a trap

As in the case of infantilization, this conceptual metaphor describes the experience of loss of agency in the unfamiliar/foreign context and particularly lost linguistic agency. As shown below, it is bound up both with the loss of this linguistic capital as well as with a consequent loss of the sense of self.

The conceptual metaphor THE FOREIGN LANGUAGE AND CULTURE ARE A TRAP appears to transcend a wide variety of cultural contexts of text production even when the explicit terms in which it is conveyed might appear to be quite different. It is intimately bound up with a perceived loss of agency, including all kinds of physical and emotional restrictions on the language learner, such as varying forms of imprisonment or encasement. US-born Karen Ogulnick, who spent considerable time in Japan, expresses the conceptual sense of confinement, alteration of outward appearance and inauthenticity through referring to the Japanese art of *tsutsumu*, a special form of gift-wrapping:

> My desire to "fit into" and be accepted by the society in which I lived and worked ... made me a willing participant in my own process of compartmentalisation: a new public, outer self encased the inner. I became wrapped up in pretty packaging.[35]

This metaphor proves particularly satisfying since its expression of the sense of being confined makes use of a specific cultural practice from the later experienced context precisely concerned with reshaping authentic appearance and boxing things up. This contrasts with the arguably weaker metaphor used by Hoffman when she describes this

---

[34] Stefan, "Here's Your Change 'N Enjoy the Show", 28.
[35] Ogulnick, *Onna Rashiku (Like a Woman)*, 35.

inability to "fit in" in terms of a "clumsy and overblown" astronaut suit – a metaphor seemingly plucked out of the blue. However, what we see in both cases is the fact that the different perception of the self in the later experienced context is being conceptualized as a physical incongruity between the authentic body and the physical shape it must assume in the later experienced culture. To employ a few further metaphors, there is a Kafkaesque sense of having been uncomfortably metamorphosed while for everyone else the world is going on, for the most part, as normal.[36] There is a pervading sense of being trapped inside the wrong language and culture. It is as if life in the foreign language were a kind of "locked-in syndrome" where no one hears the speaker's real thoughts and all communication is a long arduous process, requiring patient concentration on blinks of the eye which slip the subject in and out of the surrounding world.[37]

In Özdamar's *Mutter Zunge* (1998) this entrapment takes the more allegorical form of the protagonist being kept for a month in a *Schriftzimmer* or writing room by her Arabic teacher. This voluntary imprisonment can be interpreted as a symbol for the narrator's sense of loss of agency, also represented in passages conveying the narrator's internal monologue with her lover where she describes her tongue being bound to his hair and where she describes herself as being "the slave of [his] countenance", as in the following quotation:

> Ich lernte die Schrift schlecht, weil ich immer mit dem Ibni Abdullah, der in meinem Körper war, mit anderen Wörtern sprach: "Du Seele in meiner Seele, keine ist dir ähnlich, ich opfere mich für deine Schritte. Mit deinen Blicken schautest du mich an, ich gebe mich zum Opfer deinem Blicke. Verwahrlost, Haar gelöst, fortwimmern will ich, mit einem Blick hast du meine Zunge an deine Haare gebunden. Ich bin die Sklavin deinen [*sic*] Antlitzes."[38]

---

[36] Cf. Franz Kafka, *Die Verwandlung*, Frankfurt am Main: Fischer Taschenbuch Verlag, 1999.
[37] Jean-Dominique Bauby, *The Diving Bell and the Butterfly*, London: Harper Perennial, 2008.
[38] Özdamar, *Mutter Zunge*, 31: "I learnt the script poorly because I always spoke to Ibni Abdullah, who was in my body, in other words: 'You soul of my soul, no one resembles you, I sacrifice myself to your steps. Your gaze fell upon me, I sacrifice myself to your gaze. Bedraggled, hair loose, I want to whimper away, with one look you have bound my tongue to your hair. I am the slave of your countenance'" (my translation).

Other writers experience the loss of agency, not in strict terms of being boxed-in, imprisoned or tied-up in a way that inhibits the self and the self's contact with the foreign culture but in terms of a kind of numbness and emotional disconnection between the self, the physical body and the foreign culture. It is as if the foreign language were a barrier to the electrification of a sense of self through the external world. This sense of being disconnected or literally out of touch is evoked in a passage by Verena Stefan through describing French as not being at her own body temperature.

> My being-in-progress doesn't have a body yet in the new language, maybe a bit of an English body, but almost no French textual body. No feet, no bones, no muscles. The words haven't reached body temperature yet as in writing, when every word of the text to come has to assume one's body temperature to become fully alive.[39]

Nancy Huston describes meeting a Scottish woman who has married a Corsican and relates the quite tragic despair that the woman feels at having no emotional connection to French:

> "J'ai épousé un Corse" me dit-elle, "et voici plus de vingt ans que j'habite ici .... Je parle le français constamment et couramment, sans problèmes .... Mais, comment dire ... elle ne me *touche* pas, cette langue, et ça me désespère." Elle en avait presque les larmes aus yeux. "Quand j'entends *bracken, leaves, fog,* je vois et je sens ce dont il s'agit, les couleurs de l'automne, l'humidité ... alors que si on me dit *fougère, feuilles, brouillard,* ça me laisse de glace."[40]

Huston identifies with this despair and attributes it to the woman not having integrated all the lullabies, jokes, whispers, rhymes, multiplication tables, names of departments, and books into her *chair* or flesh since she was a little girl. In *Mutterzunge* (1998), Emine Sevgi

---

[39] Stefan, "Here's Your Change 'N Enjoy the Show", 24.
[40] Huston, *Nord Perdu*, 62: "'I married a man from Corsica', she told me, 'and I've been living here for more than twenty years now .... I speak French constantly and fluently, without any problem ... but, how should I say it, the language doesn't *move* me, and that makes me sad.' She nearly had tears in her eyes. 'When I hear *bracken, leaves, fog,*' I can see and feel what they mean, the colours of autumn, the humidity ... but when someone says to me *fougère, feuilles, brouillard,* it just leaves me cold'" (my translation).

Özdamar appears to express something similar when she writes: "In der Fremdsprache haben Wörter keine Kindheit."[41]

The loss of a physical and emotional connection to language can create an acute sense of loss of self. In John David Morley's *Pictures from the Water Trade* (1985) the protagonist is disturbed by his now automatic use of Japanese body language. Like many Japanese people, he finds himself mechanically bowing at the end of a phone conversation before replacing the receiver, even though there is no one there to see him. He feels he is "beginning to lose touch with himself".[42]

The significant differences in body language in Anglophone and Japanese culture result in a similar experience for Karen Ogulnick, who, watching herself on videotape, notes how she has adopted new gestures of femininity, matching the body language of Japanese women. These movements are more controlled, soft and polite. She covers her mouth delicately when she laughs. It is an alienating discovery.[43]

These tropes of entrapment and disconnection, seem to suggest that the self experienced in the foreign context is conceived of as a surface phenomenon that covers and perhaps threatens to suffocate the authentic identity beneath it, restricting an authentic engagement with the foreign culture. This conception of identity in the later experienced culture as external to the speaker is something that can be seen in other textual passages conceptualizing the new identity as a kind of disguise, mask or other kind of clothing.

The foreign language is a costume and the foreign culture is a play
Reference has already been made to Eva Hoffman's perception that she has been stuffed into "some clumsy and overblown astronaut suit" that enrages the "light-footed dancer" she really feels herself to be.[44] Ilan Stavans, writing in *On Borrowed Words: A Memoir of Language* (2001) uses the metaphor more to convey the lack of ownership of the foreign language, as if he were "inhabiting a rented house" or

---

[41] Özdamar, *Mutter Zunge*, 44: "In the foreign language words have no childhood" (my translation).
[42] Morley, *Pictures from the Water Trade*, 247.
[43] Ogulnick, *Onna Rashiku (Like a Woman)*, 1.
[44] Hoffman, *Lost in Translation*, 119.

"borrowing another person's suit".[45] Greta Hofmann Nemiroff, writing in Karen Ogulnick's anthology of essays about language learning creates an extended metaphor on the basis of this conceptual representation:

> If German inhabits my body, English clothes me in a well-tailored and somewhat elegant costume .... If German resides within the marrow of my bones and English is a well-designed costume, French is the light outergarment that enhances my appearance and provides protection in inclement weather.[46]

In addition to the sense that the foreign language is a costume, many authors convey their experience of living in the foreign culture as acting or performance. In the later experienced cultural context they do not see themselves or indeed the foreign culture as authentic but rather as a play in which they enter onto the stage under a mask.

In Nancy Huston's text there is a widespread underlying conceptual metaphor which might be read as either THE FOREIGN CULTURE IS A PLAY or LIVING IN EXILE IS THEATRE:

> Eh oui. C'est comme ça. Personne n'est impressioné par ce que vous faites. Depuis toutes ces années, persuadé d'épater une galerie lointaine, vous vous livrez à vos acrobaties devant une salle déserte.[47]

> Choisir à l'âge adulte, de son propre chef, de façon individuelle pour ne pas dire capricieuse, de quitter son pays et de conduire le reste de son existence dans une culture et une langue jusque-là étrangères, c'est accepter de s'installer à tout jamais dans *l'imitation, le faire-semblant, le théâtre*.[48]

---

[45] Stavans, *On Borrowed Words*, 224.
[46] Greta Nemiroff, "No Language to Die in", in *Language Crossings: Negotiating the Self in a Multicultural World*, ed. Karen Ogulnick, New York: Teachers College Press, 2000, 17.
[47] Huston, *Nord Perdu*, 28: "Ah, yes. That's how it is. No one is impressed by what you are doing. For all these years, persuaded that you were amazing a distant crowd, you have been pursuing your acrobatics in front of an empty theatre."
[48] *Ibid.*, 30: "To choose, as an adult, on your own initiative, in an individual if not fickle way, to leave your own country and spend the rest of your life in a culture and a language which had been foreign up to that point, is to accept to live the rest of your life in imitation, make-believe and theatre" (my translation).

> On entraperçoit le *vrai vous* que recouvrait le masque et l'on saute dessus.[49]
>
> Si l'on arrache carrément le masque, à quoi ressemble le visage qu'il révèle?[50]

Huston describes her situation as the theatre of exile, where a person is constantly pretending. She feels as if she is playing at being a French-speaker. Every role she plays in life seems somehow distanced from her real self. Even as a mother the foreign language stops her from taking herself seriously: "Dès que je me mets en colère contre un de mes enfants, par exemple, mon accent empire et j'ai du mal à trouver mes mots: cela déclenche l'hilarité en face et, au bout d'un moment, je suis obligée de rire moi aussi."[51] The longer she wears the mask, the more distanced she becomes from the Anglophone child she once was. There is a geographical and psychological distance there which it is hard to overcome. She sees her geographic exile as instituting a break with childhood. There is no seamless continuity between her childhood and her adult exiled self: "L'exil géographique veut dire que l'enfance est loin: qu'entre l'avant et le maintenant, il y a rupture."[52]

The changes in herself that develop as she lives out her life in exile, including the development of a social distance that separates her from the original milieu of her family, these might all have been perceived as the natural course of things as she becomes an adult, had she stayed at home. But in exile, the social distance appears to be an issue of geographical distance. She returns home and revisits places and activities of her childhood. She speaks to her family as she always used to and, realizing that they have little understanding of her life abroad, it is as if suddenly her life in France is of no importance at all.

---

[49] *Ibid.*, 33: "People see the *real you* that the mask was hiding and they jump on it" (my translation).
[50] *Ibid.*, 39: "If you tear off the mask completely, what does the face underneath look like?" (My translation).
[51] *Ibid.*, 38-39: "As soon as I get angry with one of my children, for example, my accent gets worse and I struggle to find words. That causes the other person to laugh and after a while I can't help but laugh myself" (my translation).
[52] *Ibid.*, 20: "Geographic exile means that childhood is far away, that between the past and the present there is a break" (my translation).

In her exile she has been performing in front of an empty theatre, alone.

In Özdamar's *Mutter Zunge* (1998) the narrator also expresses dislocation from childhood. At the start of the narrative the narrator, who has moved to Berlin from Turkey, goes on a search for her lost origins having noted that words have no childhood in the foreign language. Eva Hoffman echoes this sentiment. For her, English words do not have the same emotional force as the Polish ones she grew up with.

> English words don't hook on to anything .... The words float in an uncertain space. They come up from a part of my brain in which labels may be manufactured but which has no connection to my instincts, quick reactions, knowledge.[53]

For Hoffman, formulating her words in a foreign language forces her speech to present itself as an unsatisfying "aural mask": "My speech, I sense, sounds monotonous, deliberate, heavy – an aural mask that doesn't become me or express me at all."[54]

Living in Lille, Alexakis expresses his sense of being an outsider as if he were a member of the audience at a play. Rather than getting involved with the foreign "play" as Huston does, Alexakis places himself as a passive spectator:

> D'une certaine manière, je n'ai jamais vécu à Lille. Je cultivais mon absence. J'étais surpris quand on m'adressait la parole, comme le serait un spectateur interpellé en pleine représentation par un comédien. Je ne faisais pas partie de la troupe.[55]

This passivity and lack of agency in the foreign culture is one that Alexakis appears to welcome and even "cultivate", but that is not the case for all the language learners.

Throughout Chang-Rae Lee's *Native Speaker* (1995) the "spy" is used as an extended, perhaps exaggerated, metaphor for the sense of

---

[53] Hoffman, *Lost in Translation*, 108.
[54] *Ibid.*, 118.
[55] Alexakis, *Paris-Athènes*, 161: "In some ways, I never lived in Lille. I cultivated my absence. I was surprised when someone spoke to me, just as a member of the audience would be if an actor called out to him in the middle of a play. I wasn't part of the troupe" (my translation).

inauthentic identity and not quite belonging to one's society that being a second-generation immigrant can provoke. Fitting into US culture would require, as it were, a defamiliarization of the family, and an uncomfortable alienation from the familial identity. Once, when his father is shouting at his mother with what is described as an "awful stream of nonsensical street talk", the young protagonist berates him with long English words, like "socioeconomic" and "intangible", he has learnt at school – the alternative authority for his identity. Eventually his mother hits him across the back of the head and shouts in Korean "*Who do you think you are?*".[56] This question reverberates throughout his adult identity as a spy. In this text, differences between languages are again metaphorized in terms of clothing and entrapment:

> I thought English would be simply a version of our Korean. Like another kind of coat you could wear. I didn't know what a difference in language meant then. Or how my tongue would tie in the initial attempts, stiffen so, struggle like an animal booby-trapped and dying inside my head.[57]

Within Western discourses of identity as a whole, the concept of identities as performance is perhaps not particularly unusual – the metaphor can be found in the well-known extract from Shakespeare's *As You Like It* (1623): "All the world's a stage", though it almost certainly dates back even before then. In 1963, William E. Miller discusses the origin of this extended metaphor, suggesting several sources.[58] These include Withal's 1584 *Dictionarie* which quotes a similar metaphor in Latin from Marcellus Palingenius Stellatus' *Zodiacus Vitae* (*c.* 1530), Alexander Fleming's *The Diamond of Deuotion* (1581) and a free translation of a letter from Cicero to Lucceius made by Alexander Fleming entitled *A Panoplie of Epistles* (1576). The age of the sources cited by Miller suggest that the comparison between the world and the stage is relatively deeply rooted in Western culture. It might indeed be more appropriate to view the metaphors THE FOREIGN LANGUAGE IS A COSTUME and THE FOREIGN CULTURE IS A PLAY as instances of a more general

---

[56] Lee, *Native Speaker*, 58.
[57] *Ibid.*, 217.
[58] William E. Miller, "All the World's A Stage", *Notes and Queries*, X/3 (March 1963), 99-101.

conceptual metaphor infusing Western discourse, stated as THE WORLD IS A STAGE.

It is certainly clear that the descriptions which conceive of the experience of being a language learner in terms of wearing a mask or being a spy rely on an underlying conception of identities as performances or sets of particular conventional acts and behaviours that in some way may be considered more authentic than the acts and behaviours carried out while "wearing a mask" or "being a spy". In order for these metaphors to be appropriate, there is an assumption that there is an original self which is disguised.[59] In Shakespeare's text, the metaphor of the world as a stage is used in order to describe the changed appearance and behaviour of man over the course of his lifetime. His linguistic dexterity and appealing expressiveness aside, the fact that Shakespeare's text is so appealing in its highlighting of the changing roles suggests that the default conception of "individuals" is one in which there is some form of socio-temporal homogeneity.

In a similar vein, but different style to Shakespeare, Jay Lemke also suggests in his discussion of the construction of the social semiotic subject that the concept of the individual is in fact a complex abstraction from a range of participant roles and an ever-changing physicality that looks very different at eight months to how it looks at eighty years.[60] The tropes of "wearing a mask" or "being a spy" that arise so frequently in language learner narratives are only valid within a discourse of the individual that assumes and expects a degree of continuity in participant roles and physical appearance over a span of time. Again, this raises questions as to whether this conception of consistency, and the consequent idea that THE WORLD IS A STAGE upon which a homogeneous self plays different parts, are ones that belong to a particular Western discourse, or potentially derive from

---

[59] Lemke, *Textual Politics*, 86ff.

[60] *Ibid.*, 88: "It is of course possible to specify sufficiently the detailed behaviour of a social-biographical individual so as to define a class with a unique member. This is close to the common sense practice; if it looks like (same semiotic body, with movement pattern, voice quality, etc.) the person, and behaves in context like the person (participant roles), it is taken to be the person. The classic problem of how to detect an impostor or 'double' demonstrates the relevant considerations in the construction of the social-biographical individual. The 'perfect impostor' *is* in principle the person she or he impersonates, except for a different *long term* biographical history that may in fact be entirely irrelevant to the person-of-the-moment in all their social interactions."

innate modes of conceptualization of the self and others that have more universal validity. This is a complex question that must be left for future consideration.

For the time being, the preliminary analysis shows a striking degree of resonance across texts that could be attributed to the common European culture against which each text has been produced, or alternatively could be suggested to imply universal underlying conceptions of how an individual experiences their social position in an unfamiliar culture. Metaphors of entrapment, infantilization and disguise are linked through notions of loss of agency and inauthentic identity that both link to the destabilization of a sense of self in the unfamiliar language and culture.

It is certainly striking that, at an underlying level, so many of the textual metaphors appear to transcend the cultural and linguistic backgrounds of a range of authors from diverse contexts. Despite their apparently lonely and individual struggles, these language learners seem all to be united in their common human experiences of coming to terms with life abroad. What might be described as if it were a novel event or episode is in many cases simply a novel metaphor. Perhaps it is simply that we feel compelled to resignify in metaphors of our own that mediate between the universal core of human experience and its particular sociohistorical manifestation in our own life worlds. What this exploration of language learner narratives seems to suggest is that metaphor might itself be metaphorized as a range of disguises that bedazzles us with rhinestones of style and detracts attention from the universality of our human experiences and the concepts that underlie their articulation.

Certainly, this exploration of metaphor shows that in a wide variety of language learner narratives hailing from diverse sociohistorical contexts the relationship between the later experienced culture and the language learner is conceptualized in highly similar ways, many of which centre around the unequal power relations between the speaker and the host culture. Many of these metaphors have been shown to lend themselves to interpretation within the framework of a struggle for *Mündigkeit* that is engendered by a loss of linguistic competence, a loss of linguistic capital and a loss of stable sense of self that would furnish a clear position from which to speak. The latter is continually challenged by the new orientations towards others and new conceptualizations of the self presented by the host culture.

As shown in the above analysis, the relations between the non-native speaker and the host culture are frequently interpreted in terms of relations between two people, where the later experienced culture represents the dominant Other, silencing the non-native speaker. In Dorfman's text, the relations involve a clear power struggle where one language seeks repeatedly to gain supremacy over him.

Carrying with them alternative conceptions of themselves and of others to those current in their new society, and lacking the linguistic and social competence appropriate to the new context, the narrators frequently find or feel themselves to be in a position of low social status, devoid of the linguistic capital that could enable articulation of *Mündigkeit*. This experience is articulated in the texts as a metaphorical entrapment or infantilization.

For the language learners attempting to regain *Mündigkeit* and recreate a new identity appropriate to the foreign context, a sense of inauthenticity develops where this new identity does not match the experiences of primary socialization. In these texts the newcoming speaker frequently feels him/herself to be only an actor in a play; wearing a disguise/costume; or working as a spy. These metaphors reiterate the perception that each language represents a different identity or persona. In contrast to the inauthentic nature of the foreign self, the early experienced language is frequently described as a close friend or lover. Thus, it would seem that one means to overcome the sense of loss and betrayal that living in the foreign culture provokes and to unite the dual or perhaps even duelling identities is to create a metaphorical love relationship between the foreign language and the early experienced language. In Özdamar this takes the form of the protagonist falling in love with her Arabic teacher, in Alexakis it is articulated as marrying together his French and Greek so that he becomes his own wife and no longer feels that he is constantly betraying himself or his languages.

As suggested above, if these recurrent conceptual metaphors are not attributed to universal experiences of language learning then, at the very least, the significant parallels across texts must be attributed to a common over-arching Western discourse that informs how these writers have conceptualized their experience, even allowing for – as one reasonably can in most cases – their ignorance of each other's precise texts. In examining this suggested discourse of language learner narrative, the framework of struggles with *Mündigkeit* appears to function to a high degree as a means to understand many of the qualitative experiences of language learning, as they have been represented in these cross-cultural autobiographies. If we accept the framework of *Mündigkeit* as one that underpins language learner narrative, then the conceptual metaphors described above can be viewed as the conventional metaphors of this discourse that frame how language learning in a non-native culture is experienced. In other words, language learner narrative can be suggested, implicitly, to construct the language learning situation in terms of a struggle for *Mündigkeit*.

In contrast to this, the following section considers some of the metaphors used in these texts that do not fall into the conventional articulation of struggles with *Mündigkeit* described above. These are the more novel and enigmatic uses of metaphor that conceptualize the language learning situation and the speaker's place within that situation in more ambiguous ways. The following discussion acts as a prelude to Chapter Nine that discusses the function of a wider spectrum of types of language play (metaphor included) in the encounter with a foreign language and what this suggests about *Mündigkeit*.

Creative metaphors in language learner narrative
As mentioned at the very beginning of this chapter, the assignment of the metaphors in language learner narratives to underlying conceptual metaphors and the interpretation of these conceptual metaphors in terms of a framework of *Mündigkeit* has itself involved a creative metaphorical process of subjective conceptual comparison that relies on the subjective discovery of a wealth of relevant metaphors for support. The following brief discussion touches on the ambiguity of reference that literary texts can rely on in their attempt to discover new meaning and to create new metaphors for describing human experience. This limited discussion, which would certainly be worth pursuing in further research, aims to suggest ways in which apparent complexity of reference and uniqueness of conceptualization nonetheless seem to make use of more universal underlying conceptualizations.

This discussion centres on two particularly interesting phrases taken from language learner narratives. The first of these is "in der Fremdsprache haben Wörter keine Kindheit" taken from Özdamar's

Mutter Zunge where it appears with very little immediate context. The second of these is Nancy Huston's use of the phrase "nord perdu".

Emine Sevgi Özdamar's phrase "in der Fremdsprache haben Wörter keine Kindheit" can be interpreted in one of several ways. Firstly, it can be seen as another example of the anthropomorphosis of the foreign language, suggesting that the foreign language is an adult figure in which there is no room for childish- or childlikeness. In this case the phrase would be used in a matter of fact way, almost as a command that informs the reader that there is no messing when it comes to using the foreign language. This might imply that using a foreign language, no matter how much the speaker might be infantilized by others, in fact involves the immediate adoption of fully mature non-native identity, since the childish stages of language acquisition that occur in the first language are socially circumscribed and unavailable to the adult newcoming speaker. However, interpreted in this way, the statement would seem to contradict the poetic playfulness of the text in which it is embedded, as well as the playfulness exhibited in other language learner narratives.

Secondly, the statement might be interpreted as a nostalgic statement of regret for the loss or devaluation of early childhood experience that occurs when using the foreign language, since the foreign words do not evoke memories of childhood experiences in which the words were first learnt, for the newcoming speaker. It is this loss described by the despair of the Scottish woman described by Nancy Huston at how little French words "touch" her. Childhood is not present in the foreign language.

Finally, to return to Özdamar, within the context of her whole text the phrase, "in der Fremdsprache haben Wörter keine Kindheit" could be seen as an expression of frustrated realization that it is impossible to be reborn into a foreign language. This is also symbolized by the protagonist throwing her writing in Arabic onto the motorway. As an extension of this, the phrase can perhaps also be interpreted as a refusal of the self-incurred infantilization that the protagonist has undergone in trying to be reborn into her earlier culture via the alien Arabic script. This latter interpretation imbues the statement with wishful thinking – if only it were possible to have a mature identity in the foreign language, if only it were possible to learn a foreign language without being forced into an infantilized position that attempts to reclaim the childhood connections that the foreign language does not possess. If only the foreign language had no childhood.

The ambiguities in this metaphor serve to demonstrate an instability as well as a richness of meaning. It leaves a gap in signification that entails a proliferation of meaning and possible experiences, leaving a trail of possible interpretations in its wake. It disperses and scatters meaning through oblique connotation of a range of cultural and personal experience that overlay the underlying more universal conceptualization of the foreign language or the words of the foreign language as human beings. This example suggests a possible layering of metaphor on three levels from the universal to the cultural collective in diverse forms and ultimately to the personal. It is at the level of the cultural and personal that the issues of interpretation and multiplicity of meaning seem to arise.

An alternative to this dispersal of meaning is the use of metaphor as a means to fuse significations deriving from different linguistic and cultural contexts in a way that harmonizes diverse modes of meaning into one clear articulable whole. One metaphor used by Nancy Huston seems to adequately express this harmonization. It forms the title of Huston's essay and it is that of "losing one's north".[61] Huston appropriates this French idiom and imbues it with a range of meaning that allows her to articulate her experience of moving from Canada to France. When she speaks of "nord perdu" it appears to mean several things. Firstly, in a figurative sense it contains within it its idiomatic French meaning of confusion that describes how the author feels in exile. Secondly, in a more concrete way the lost north represents the loss of her geographic homeland in Canada that is literally located in the north.[62] Aspects of her identity are tightly bound up with this lost north, so much so that she feels as if there must be a version of herself still living there.[63] Finally, the idiom resonates in English with the cries of a sailor all at sea who has lost his bearings and cannot find his course. This interpretation tallies with Huston's implications in other metaphors that she conceives of life as a linear journey in which you

---

[61] "The lost north" of the title is part of a French idiom meaning to get confused or lose one's reason.
[62] Huston, *Nord Perdu*, 15: "Mon pays c'était le Nord, le Grand Nord, le nord vrai, fort et libre. Je l'ai trahi, et je l'ai perdu" ("My country was the North, the Great North, the true, strong and free north. I betrayed it, and I lost it"; my translation).
[63] *Ibid.*, 109-11.

travel from childhood to adulthood. Her current situation abroad has broken this journey, leaving the author feeling both disoriented and confused.

Given the range of meaning possible in the short phrase "nord perdu" it is unsurprising that Huston uses it for the title of her essay. The phrase resonates with a sense of France, a sense of Canada and a sense of the oceans between them. The metaphor bobs in the Atlantic between Canada and France, searching for its place.

Even given the complexity of Huston and Özdamar's metaphors, however, both articulate at a fundamental level, a sense of loss or lack. In particular, a sense of lost homeland and childhood bound up with a rootlessness of identity experienced in the foreign culture. In the first case, the lost north partly represents the lost homeland in the north as well as lost orientation, and in the second a loss of childhood is articulated. The significance of this loss must then be interpreted culturally and personally. The difference between these and the other metaphors discussed in the main body of this discussion is the greater range of reference entailed by the metaphor of the lost north and by that of the foreign language having no childhood that appear to bind up several abstract ideas so as to evade direct description of the concrete physical experiences that underpins the metaphor. It is, perhaps, this skilled cloaking of information about the concrete conceptualization of life abroad that allows the reader to insert his or her own significations into the text and so to engage in dialogue with the narrator and perceive the text as a more satisfying literary product.

CHAPTER NINE

LANGUAGE PLAY AND *METAMÜNDIGKEIT*
IN LANGUAGE LEARNER NARRATIVE

> Like fiction, play is a kind of carnival reality ... , parallel to the real world but having its own meanings.[1]

Having to speak and use a foreign language is often thought of as a constraint on expression, but for some authors of language learner narratives writing in the foreign language presents an increased freedom and an opportunity to play with and reflect on style and language. This chapter examines the use of language play in two multilingual texts and argues that this language play is representative of a process of *Metamündigkeit* in which a movement towards an alternative kind of Enlightenment, subsuming both the rational and the irrational, the conscious and the unconscious, in which the linguistic is suffused with the non-linguistic, is exhibited in the integration and interplay of languages deriving from different cultures and linguistic communities. The distinction between *Mündigkeit* and *Metamündigkeit* will be developed in relation to Kristeva's ideas about the "semiotic" and "symbolic" that are expressed in *La Révolution du Langage Poétique* (1974).[2] *Metamündigkeit* is interpreted as a poetic counterpart to the project of rational Enlightenment. It is a form of Enlightenment that lies not in discovering one absolute truth, but is the end result of a process in which rather than seeking truth through the application of reason within the bias of language, the symbolic function of language is highlighted as the symbolic order is infused with the rhythmic

---

[1] Guy Cook, "Language Play, Language Learning", *ELT Journal*, LI/3 (July 1997), 227.
[2] Julia Kristeva, *La Révolution du Langage Poétique*, Paris: Editions du Seuil, 1974.

articulations that precede meaning, what Kristeva terms the "semiotic".³

The chapter begins by considering how Yoko Tawada and Zé Do Rock make use of German and suggests some effects of their, at times, radical defamiliarization of the language, before considering how this may be attributed to a process of *Metamündigkeit*. Some of the examples taken from these texts will appear silly, but the nature and function of this linguistic "silliness" is precisely one of the main points of interest of the following discussion.

Language play in multilingual texts

One of the authors who engages most keenly with the substance of language is the Japanese author Yoko Tawada who now lives and works in Germany. In much of her writing she presents a critical awareness of the German language that highlights the structure of the language both on semantic and formal levels. Some of the ways in which she engages with the German language are presented below. These features predominantly include:

- Play on concrete and metaphoric word meanings.
- Anthropomorphosis of language.
- Word association.
- Play with word forms e.g. letters, suffixes, prefixes, alliteration, assonance.

In her essay "Sprachpolizei und Spielpolyglotte" (2007) in the book of the same name, Tawada honours the poet Ernst Jandl (1925-2000) with prose passages alluding to particular poems he has created. As a concrete poet, Jandl emphasized linguistic form in his writing

---

[3] It must be noted, however, that no signifying system, such as language, can be exclusively symbolic. In Kristeva's words: "Le sujet étant toujours sémiotique *et* symbolique, tout système signifiant qu'il produit ne peut être 'exclusivement' symbolique, mais il est obligatoirement marqué par une dette vis-à-vis de l'autre" (Kristeva, *La Révolution du Langage Poétique*, 22). "Because the subject is always *both* semiotic *and* symbolic, no signifying system he produces can be either "exclusively" semiotic or "exclusively" symbolic, and is instead necessarily marked by an indebtedness to both" (Julia Kristeva, *Revolution in Poetic Language*, trans. Margaret Waller, New York: Columbia University Press, 1984, 24). While the multilingual play discussed here reflects aspects of the semiotic more than the symbolic, the semiotic chora that Kristeva is concerned with is in fact pre-linguistic.

and poetry performance, playing with sounds, orthography and the shape of words on the page. In her essay Tawada herself engages with the form of language and the relationship between the sign and the signified. This language play is not, however, restricted to the essay honouring Jandl but is a feature of Tawada's writing that occurs in many of her other texts.

The first example of language play to be investigated here and which is commonly found in Tawada is a play on the metaphoricity of words. Frequently, this play is represented by a shift from the expected abstract use of a term so that the concrete concept underlying a particular metaphor is brought to the fore. This foregrounding of the metaphoric process through reliteralization has the effect of both highlighting and undermining the German conceptual framework in a humorous way as expectations of conventional linguistic usage in German are subverted:[4]

> Du sagst, du möchtest eine Tafel Schokolade haben. Möchtest du eigentlich eine Tafel haben oder eine Schokolade? Gab es zuerst die Schokolade oder die Tafel, die noch nicht Schokolade geworden ist?[5]

In other instances, it is the abstract concept of "language" as a whole that is treated as if it were a concrete object. Tawada's style mimics that of a scientific investigation into the object, language. This scientific style is marked by generalized statements in the present simple and present perfect tense. The statements are, however, undermined by subjective associations that enter into the "objective" description and bring the discussion away from a supposed concrete reality of language into a bizarre fictional world where, for example, the opponents of noodle/pasta dishes have invented the separation of words:

---

[4] This represents a theory of humour as the gap between expectation and actuality. An overview of research into humour is presented in Simon Critchley, *On Humour*, London: Routledge, 2002.

[5] Yoko Tawada, *Sprachpolizei und Spielpolyglotte*, Tübingen: Konkursbuch Verlag Claudia Gehrke, 2007, 25: "You say you would like to have a bar [board] of chocolate. Do you actually want a bar [board] or chocolate? What came first – the chocolate or the bar [board] that has not yet become chocolate?" (This and all subsequent translations from Tawada's works are my own.)

> Wörter werden zählbar, wenn sie getrennt geschrieben werden. Wenn sie ohne Lücken dastehen würden, würde ein Text wie eine lange Nudel aussehen. Die Gegner der Nudelgerichte haben die Worttrennung erfunden.[6]

As a present perfect statement, this assertion is provided with the air of scientific validity and yet the preceding statement on which it relies is based on a subjective comparison between wordsrunningoneintotheotherandapieceofspaghetti. The tenuousness of this comparison only serves to re-emphasize the relative arbitrariness of the comparison implicit in the conventional metaphor "eine Tafel Schokolade". Instead of a "board of chocolate" why not speak of a "plank of chocolate" (*ein Brett Schokolade) or a "bar of chocolate" as is done in English? As Lakoff and Johnson's *Metaphors We Live By* (1980) also highlights, there is much in language that is a form of conventionalized subjective comparison. Tawada's linguistic play toys with the German language and creates humour through this child-like irreverence for the conventions of meaning and language use in German culture.

This play with concrete word form and the simultaneous shifting between concrete and metaphorical meanings is revealed again in the following passage:

> Ein Mus ist kein Muss. Das Mus ist eine süße Masse, grammatikalisch gesehen, unzählbar. Buchstäblich gesehen ist es aber zählbar: M und U und S: das sind drei Buchstaben. Was du zählen kannst, kannst du auch umstellen. Ums, Sum, Usm, Smu, Msu. Die Buchstaben sind bereit, durcheinandergewürfelt zu werden. Sie sind Würfel auf einem Spieltisch.[7]

---

[6] Tawada, *Sprachpolizei und Spielpolyglotte*, 26: "Words become countable when they are written separately. If they were to stand there without gaps between them, a text would look like a long piece of spaghetti. Pasta dish opponents invented the separation of words."

[7] *Ibid.*, 28: "Mush is no must. Mush is a sweet mass, from a grammatical perspective, uncountable. From a literal perspective it is, however, countable: M and U and S and H: that's four letters. Whatever you can count you can also reorganize. Umsh, Hsum, Ushm, Smuh, Msuh. The letters are happy to be thrown at random. They are dice on a gambling table."

This passage conveys to the reader a more explicit childlike delight in the form of language.[8] Firstly, the lack of semantic connection between the formally connected words *Mus*, *Muss* and *Masse* is highlighted. Following this, the word *buchstäblich* ("literally") is employed in a way that compounds and confounds its literal and metaphoric meanings. This word is most commonly employed with the abstract meaning of "literal" thereby taken to mean "in a concrete/formal or non-abstract way". However, Tawada uses the word *buchstäblich* itself "in a concrete/formal or non-abstract way", thus applying the abstract and concrete meanings of this word both at once, since to use the word *buchstäblich* in a concrete way means to invoke its derivation from the word *Buchstabe* meaning "letter". The concrete meaning of this word could therefore be translated as "in terms of the letters themselves". In this instance the word is punning on itself. By using *buchstäblich* in this way, Tawada draws attention to the concrete letter form of the word *Mus* rather than the concept of "puree" that the letter form signifies. As the reader's mind is forced to flip dizzyingly between the concrete and abstract meanings of the word *buchstäblich* it becomes clear that they both refer to the same thing, that is in a metaphoric sense to the concrete visual form of the word *Mus* (as opposed to its grammatical or semantic properties that cannot be seen), or in a literal sense to "the letters themselves". The letters of the word *Mus* are at issue both literally and "letterally".[9]

Following this, the letters of the word *Mus* are then compared to dice on a gambling table. This metaphor again suggests that language is perceived as an arbitrary agglomeration of sounds and letters and also perhaps that there is something fateful and random about its arrangement, rather than ordered and pre-determined.

Tawada not only re-literalizes or re-concretizes language through shifting between metaphoric and literal word meanings, but contrary to the usual rules of language in which it is understood that a word is a sign for a particular referent as Tawada indicates herself in the essay "Sprachpolizei und Spielpolyglotte" (2007),[10] she employs a word as

---

[8] This is perhaps heightened by the passage's focus on *Mus* ("puree"), a common baby-food.
[9] The English translation "literally" is also an abstraction from the Late Latin word *litteralis* meaning "of or belonging to letters or writing".
[10] Tawada, *Sprachpolizei und Spielpolyglotte*, 33: "'Die Wörter sollten nicht das sein, was sie meinen', sagt der Zollbeamte der Grammatik. 'Man darf aus dem Wort "Drogen" keine Drogen machen. Man darf nicht die Drogen aus dem Land der

if it *were* the referent it describes, thus disrupting the basis of signification at a fundamental level. More than representation, this tactic posits identity between signifier and signified. The word "bed" *is* a bed:

> Außerdem dürfe ein "b" nicht wie ein kriechender Frühlingswind schleichend hörbar werden, sondern müsse explosiv auftreten. Das "Bett" zum Beispiel, da müsse man mit einem Schwung hineinspringen und nicht heimlich hineinkriechen.[11]

Besides this example from *Überseezungen* we find the following more extreme example in "Sprachpolizei und Spielpolyglotte" in which Tawada plays with form and meaning as if the written form could directly change the meaning of a word:

> Wenn du "Rad fahren" getrennt schreiben willst, fahren wir mit zwei Fahrrädern durch die Gegend. Wenn du das Wort lieber zusammenschreiben willst, fahren wir mit einem Tandem.[12]

The way in which Tawada metaphorizes language as a concrete object is also reflected in her anthropomorphosis of language and positioning of elements of grammar as if they could be the agents within particular propositions. It is as if there is a desire to bind language more closely to the objects it represents so that it becomes itself an object and/or an agent, something tangible and corporeal and less an arbitrary representation of the environment. Ernst Jandl's poetry also insists on linguistic corporeality but in a slightly different way – many of his poems were written to be read aloud. The written versions of his poems do not exist as self-sufficient works of literature in the same way as other non-concrete poems.[13] Jandl used readings of his poetry

---

Wörtlichkeit einschmuggeln.'" "'The letters should not be what they mean', says the customs officer for grammar. 'You should not make drugs out of the word "drugs". You should not smuggle the drugs in from the land of literality'."

[11] Yoko Tawada, *Überseezungen*, Tübingen: Konkursbuch Verlag Claudia Gehrke, 2006, 12: "Besides a 'b' should not make itself heard in a sneaky way like a creeping spring breeze, but should arrive with a bang. 'Bed', for example, you should jump into it with a bounce and not stealthily crawl into it."

[12] Tawada, *Sprachpolizei und Spielpolyglotte*, 26: "If you want to write 'ride a bicycle' separately, let us ride around the place with two bicycles. If you would rather write the word together, let us ride a tandem."

[13] See http://www.ernstjandl.com/bio_lesungen.html.

as a means to gain interest in his publications, rather than using his publications as a means to gain interest in his readings. They are transcriptions of a spoken event. Tawada's imagination takes the importance of live language a step further. For Tawada, language does not require a speaking agent, instead, she bypasses the subject producing it and animistically invests words with independent life of their own:

> Auf meinem Schreibtisch gibt es eine Landstraße, auf der jedes Wort frei fahren kann. Dort fährt ein Kaffee ohne Tasse oder ein Nebensatz ohne Komma.[14]

> Im Vergleich zu den onomatopoetischen Obdachlosen haben die mittellosen Adjektive ein leichteres Leben. Dennoch leiden sie unter der Diskriminierung. Sie werden unterschätzt, weil viele glauben, die Adjektive seien nur Dekoration.[15]

> Die Schriftzeichen interessiert es vielleicht gar nicht, was sie in einem Land bedeuten. In Deutschland bedeuten sie das, in Frankreich jenes. Sie sind Reisende, sie werden unterwegs immer wieder anders verstanden, je nachdem, in welcher Sprache sie übernachten. Ihre Körper bleiben aber dieselben, nämlich ein "d", ein Halbkreis mit einer erhobenen Hand, und ein "u", ein leeres Gefäß.[16]

> Außerdem glaubte ich nicht, daß das Wort "es" keine Bedeutung hatte. In dem Moment, in dem man sagt, daß es regnet, entsteht ein Es, das das Wasser vom Himmel gießt. Wenn es einem gut geht, gibt es ein Es, das dazu beigetragen hat. Dennoch schenkte [sic] ihm keiner besondere Aufmerksamkeit. Es besaß nicht einmal einen Eigennamen.

---

[14] Tawada, *Sprachpolizei und Spielpolyglotte*, 27: "On my desk there is a road on which every word can travel freely. There goes coffee without a cup or a subordinate clause without a comma."
[15] *Ibid.*, 31: "In comparison to the homeless onomatopoeic words, the impecunious adjectives have an easier life. Nonetheless, they suffer discrimination. They are underestimated because many believe that adjectives are just decoration."
[16] Tawada, *Überseezungen*, 33: "The written characters are perhaps not at all interested in what they mean in a particular country. In Germany they mean this, in France that. They are travellers, on their travels there are understood differently again and again according to which language they are staying over in. But their bodies remain the same, namely a 'd', a semi-circle with a raised hand, and a 'u', an empty vessel." In commenting on Tawada's metalinguistic games, the validity of her claims is not at issue, only her formal play.

Aber es arbeitete immer fleißig und wirksam in vielen Bereichen und lebte bescheiden in einer grammatischen Lücke.[17]

In a similar anthropomorphizing vein, Tawada talks of separable and inseparable verbs, playing on the grammatical and the everyday meanings of the word "Paar": "Das getrennte Paar wieder zusammenzubringen und das untrennbare Paar zu trennen, sind weder Aufgaben eines Linguisten noch eines Therapeuten."[18] Allusions to psychoanalytic treatment for language and also for human relationships to language are found again in the following passage:

> "Laut und Luise" ruft der Sohn, wenn er an seine Mutter denkt. "Das ist nicht normal, du bist krank", sagen ihm seine Freunde. Der Sohn geht zu einem Analytiker. "Herr Patient, an der Stelle Ihres Vaters steht ein Adverb. Sie wollen ein Adverb töten, um mit Ihrer Mutter zu schlafen."[19]

The attribution of spirit to these signifiers, which Tawada's anthropomorphoses represent, is a move that dissociates the signifier from the signified in order to create a new object, a new life-form itself worthy of being subject to signification, but that also constitutes a potential intentional subject in a process of signification. The relations between subject, signifier, signified and object are all four simultaneously disrupted in a carnivalesque inversion. The foolish signifiers are elevated to the position of royal subjects of language for the day. Thus *es* is no longer an empty grammatical signifier

---

[17] Tawada, *Talisman*, 14: "Besides, I did not believe that the word 'it' had no meaning. At the precise moment one says that 'it' is raining, an 'it' appears who is pouring water from the sky. When 'it' is going well for you, there is an 'it' which has contributed to that. Nonetheless, paid him very little attention. It did not even have a proper name. But it worked industriously and effectively in many areas and lived modestly in a grammatical hole."

[18] Tawada, *Sprachpolizei und Spielpolyglotte*, 27: "Bringing the separated pair back together and separating the inseparable pair are jobs for neither the linguist nor the therapist."

[19] *Ibid.*, 32: "'Laut and Luise' calls the son when he thinks of his mother. 'That is not normal, you are sick', his friends tell him. The son goes to an analyst. 'Mr Patient, in place of your father there is an adverb. You want to kill an adverb in order to sleep with your mother.'" "Laut und Luise" is also an explicit reference to Ernst Jandl's poetry collection of the same name: Ernst Jandl, *Laut und Luise*, Neuwied: Luchterhand, 1971.

representing an indeterminate object, but is honoured with recognition as an active agent producing meaning in a variety of contexts.

This is a position that *es* cannot, however, authentically perform, just as to put on a doctor's white coat does not make one a doctor. In a carnival, where *es* moves from vehicle of signification to subject, the signifiers have been lost and an incapable subject has been gained. In such a carnival it is not a particular social hierarchy that is at stake, but a wider concept of symbolic order. To blur subject with signifier and signified is to challenge the very basis upon which meaning is possible and, in Kristevan terms, to enter the condition of the semiotic:

> Le sémiotique serait alors pré-thétique et antérieur à la signification, parce qu'il est antérieur à la position du sujet. Il n'y a pas de Sens préalable à l'ego cogitant dans une proposition, mais il y a des articulations hétérogènes à la signification et au signe: c'est la chora sémiotique ... [20]

The threat of the dissolution of meaning through the transgression of boundaries that maintain the symbolic order finds its release in the humour that Tawada's passage provokes.[21] We recognize Tawada's language play and gain reassurance from the writer's position as producer of meaning.

In other passages in "Sprachpolizei und Spielpolyglotte" (2007) the accepted relationship between signifier and signified is disrupted through the development of tenuous links between the meanings and forms of different words. The passage from one sentence to the next is not guided so much by logic as by conceptual and formal associations provoked by different words and phrases, as in the following passage:

> Eine Tafel Schokolade ist erlaubt, zwei Tafeln Schokolade könnten Karies verursachen, drei Tafeln Schokolade werden von manchen schon als Sünde angesehen. Dennoch kennt der Appetit kein Ende.

---

[20] Kristeva, *La Révolution du Langage Poétique*, 35: "The semiotic can thus be understood as pre-thetic, preceding the positing of the subject. Previous to the ego thinking within a proposition, no Meaning exists, but there *do* exist articulations heterogeneous to signification and to the sign: the semiotic *chora* ..." (Kristeva, *Revolution in Poetic Language*, 36).

[21] See for example, Sigmund Freud, *Der Witz und Seine Beziehung zum Unbewussten*, Frankfurt am Main: Fischer Taschenbuch Verlag, 2006, 160-66.

> Die meisten essbaren Dinge sind unzählbar: Honig, Nudeln, Gemüse.²²

The counting of bars of chocolate leads into the concept of an insatiable appetite – one with "no end" that leads to the thought that many foodstuffs in German, as in many other languages, are uncountable. There is an implied spurious logic between the two facts – (a) that appetite has no end (whose appetite? an appetite for what?) and (b) that many foodstuffs are uncountable and thus in some sense also have no end.

Tawada also frequently plays with the form of words irrespective of their meanings. In "Sprachpolizei und Spielpolyglotte" she plays with alliterative monosyllables such as *Mehl, Milch, Mus* ("flour, milk, puree"); and word series in which the phonetic form gradually lengthens *Mühe, Mut* and *Müdigkeit* ("effort, courage, fatigue"). The passage of prose is then written not on a basis of logical discussion but on the basis of the mental associations to which these word groups give rise. Similarly, in the following passage from *Überseezungen* (2006), it is a kind of "logic" by association that produces the following false etymology for the word *Maultasche* (a kind of "raviolo"):

> Eine Maultasche war eine Mischung aus einem Großmaul und einem Taschendieb. Eine Tasche, eine Flasche, eine Kappe. Diese Wörter kamen mir fast wie persönliche Beleidigungen vor.²³

In "Eine Tasche, eine Flasche, eine Kappe" the concern is with sound irrespective of meaning. It is the sound that implies verbal attack, not the word itself. In her much earlier writing in *Ein Gast* (1993) Tawada directly expresses this sense that the sounds of the foreign language appear disconnected from their meanings:

---

²² Tawada, *Sprachpolizei und Spielpolyglotte*, 26: "One bar of chocolate is allowed, two bars of chocolate could cause tooth decay, three bars of chocolate would be viewed by some as a sin. Yet the appetite knows no end. Most edible things are uncountable: honey, pasta, greens."
²³ Tawada, *Überseezungen*, 27: "A raviolo (mouth pocket) was a combination of a big mouth and a pickpocket. A pocket, a bottle, a cap. These words appeared to me almost like personal insults."

Language Play and Metamündigkeit   221

> Ein seltsames Gefühl: Ich spreche einen vollständigen Satz aus, wie zum Beispiel "Ich fahre morgen nach Zürich", und denke dabei, vielleicht bedeutet der Satz gar nichts. Vielleicht waren die Wörter nur eine zufällige Kombination der Abfälle von Tönen, die einfach durch Schwingungen zustande kamen. [24]

Tawada consistently problematizes how meaning is created in language and the rules by which language operates. This stance towards language is explicitly articulated in "Sprachpolizei und Spielpolyglotte" (2007):

> Was getrennt wird und was zusammenbleiben muss, wird durch bestimmte Regeln bestimmt. "Die Regeln müssen sein", sagen dir nicht die Polizisten, sondern deine Freunde. "Das ist eine Spielregel, daran musst du dich halten, sonst spielen wir nicht mi[t] dir." Demokratische Freunde verkaufen dir den Zwang als Spielregeln.[25]

Tawada tests this *Spielregel* metaphor by seeing how much language really can be played with and how much language exerts a prescriptive force on those using it. Again, language is anthropomorphized as Tawada evokes the effects of linguistic tyranny: "Die Grenzpolizei teilt die Partikel in drei Gruppen auf: Illegale Einwanderer, Minderjährige und die Lautpoesie." [26] Tawada's language play exerts pressure on linguistic tyranny, dissolving relationships between signifier and signified that are necessary for the stability of the symbolic order.

Language play in Zé Do Rock's *fom winde ferfeelt*

In *fom winde ferfeelt* (1995) Zé Do Rock, born in 1956 in Porto Alegre in Brazil, also exhibits quite dramatic language play that

---

[24] Yoko Tawada, *Ein Gast*, Tübingen: Konkursbuchverlag, 1993, 114-15: "A strange feeling: I pronounce a complete sentence such as, for example 'I am travelling to Zürich tomorrow' and think as I do so, perhaps the sentence does not mean anything at all. Perhaps the words were just a coincidental combination of dwindling tones, which only came about through vibrations."
[25] Tawada, *Sprachpolizei und Spielpolyglotte*, 28: "What is separate and what must stay together is fixed by specific rules. 'Rules are rules', say your friends rather than the police. 'That's a rule of the game, you have to obey it or we won't play with you.' Democratic friends sell you coercion as rules of the game."
[26] *Ibid.*, 31: "The border police divides the particles up into three groups: illegal immigrants, minors and sound poetry."

subverts the *Spielregel* of German. The narrative in *fom winde ferfeelt* (1995) is perhaps best described as a mixed genre text that incorporates features and themes from travel writing and autobiography as well as forming a critique or treatise on the German language and in particular German spelling. Spelling is one aspect of language in which the prescriptions of the *Spielregel* are most present to the consciousness of a reader or writer in any particular language, given not only their codification in dictionaries, but also the fact that spelling is one of the aspects of language bound up with the highest level of social conformity.

In *fom winde ferfeelt* one of the aims of the text is a critique of the German spelling system and the development of a reformed orthography that Zé Do Rock calls *Ultradeutsch*. Rock carries out this reform as a writer at play, rather than with the authority of a language academician. As the chapters progress, more and more rules are added to the spelling system:

- Die Abschaffung des Großschreibzwangs (11) ("Abolition of compulsory capitalization").[27]
- *ist, nicht, nichts* werden *is, nich, nix* (13) ("*ist, nicht, nichts* become *is, nich, nix*").
- die akkusativendung nach artikeln und pronomen, die mit *n* enden, wird weggelassen: ich hab dein hund gesehn (13) ("the accusative ending after articles and pronouns that end with *n* will be left off: ich hab dein hund gesehn").
- es gibt keine kommaregel mehr. sie werden gesetzt, wo man eine pause für nötig hält (15) ("there are no more comma rules. they are placed where a pause is considered necessary").
- der gebrauch von apostrophen is nich mehr zwingend: *ich hab s* oder *ich hab's* (15) ("the use of apostrophes is no longer compulsory").
- der flotte dreier is im schwerdeutschen nich erlaubt. *der papppolizist, das betttuch, das ballleder* sind verbotene formen (16) ("the saucy threesome is not permitted in difficult German. *der papppolizist, das betttuch, das ballleder* are forbidden forms").

---

[27] This and all subsequent translations from Zé Do Rock are my own.

Language Play and Metamündigkeit 223

- keine silbentrennungsregeln mehr. ma trennt dort, wo s nich mehr weitergeht (18) ("no rules for syllable division any more. you divide where't can't go on any longer").
- die regeln zum getrennt- oder zusammenschreiben werden abgeschafft. ma schreibt wie ma will. Wenneinerwillkanneralleszusammenschreibenaberniemandwirdihnverstehnodersich kaumdiemühegeben (22) ("the rules for writing separately or together are abolished. you write however you like. Ifyoulikeyoucanwriteeverythingtogetherbutnoonewillunderstandyouorhardlymaketheeffortto").
- das ß wird durch *ss* oder *sz* ersetzt. (27) ("ß is replaced by *ss* or *sz*").
- lange *e*'s in der letzten silbe bei mehrsilbigen wörtern werden – wenn dem *e* kein *h* folgt – verdoppelt: trotzdeem, phänomeen (41) ("long *e*'s in the last syllable of polysyllabic words will be doubled – if no *h* follows the *e* - : trotzdeem, phänomeen").
- *h*'s, di nich ausgesprochen werden und kein einfluss auf die aussprache ham, verschwinden: tema, teori, rytmus. das wort *katarrh* verliert genauso das *h*, auch wenn s ganz dick kommt (47) ("*h*'s which are not pronounced and have no influence on pronunciation will disappear: team, teori, rytmus. the word *katarrh* will also lose the *h*, even if it comes on very thick").
- die denung eines vokals wird nich mer angezeigt. *fülen* wi *spülen*, *tir* wi *dir* (47) ("the lengthening of a vowel will no longer be indicated. *fülen* like *spülen*, *tir* like *dir*").
- das *ph* wird *f* geschrieben. filosof, fase, falanx (55) ("*ph* is written *f*. filosof, fase, falanx").
- fremd- und lenwörter werden verdeutscht (56) ("foreign and loan words will be germanicized").
- doppelkonsonanten di nach eim unbetontem vokal sten, werden vereinfacht. alee, alein, milion (60) ("double consonants standing after an unstressed vowel will be simplified. alee, alein, milion").
- fremd-, lenwörter und abkürzungen krigen ein doppelkonsonanten, wenn der vokal davor kurz is und keine 2 konsonanten danach vorhanden sind. fitt, ass, popp-hitt. und: buss, katt, tittel (107) ("foreign words, loan words and abbreviations get a double consonant if the vowel before them

is short and no two consonants are present after it. fitt, ass, popp-hitt. und buss, katt, tittel").
- *chs* wird in den fällen wenn *x* gesprochen *x* geschriben. axe, dax, fux (137) ("*chs* in thoses cases where it is pronounced *x* will be written *x*. axe, dax, fux").

The rules continue on and on at frequent intervals throughout the text so that even as the reader grows closer to the text through increasing familiarity with Zé Do Rock's spelling system, the text moves away from the reader with its new rules and complications.[28] Each chapter poses a new potential difficulty of decipherment. An example from a later chapter reads:

> mit ultradoitsh wer was fyr di umwelt getan. wenn ma ultradoitsh sraibt, spart ma 10 prozent papir, da es 10 prozent kyrza is (di wörta an sic sind noc kyrza, aba di lerroime zwishen den wörtan blaiben glaic) ...
>
> es wird auc stendig argumentirt, das di sprace als kulturgut nic dauand geendat werden darf. aba si endat sic dauand. im doitshen gibt es fil, fil mer regeln als for 100 iaren. nur: solange sic di regeln fermeren, srait kaina auf. nur wenn ma ferainfacen will.[29]

The complexity involved in penetrating the text to uncover meaning is heightened in places through the spelling being changed to reflect the appearance of the spelling system of the country being described in the text. The paragraph about Finland is full of umlauts and double vowels:

---

[28] This works against any suggestion that the rather anarchic spelling system might function democratically to in fact make learning orthography easier for native speakers. For further discussion of this, see Andreas Schumann "Sprachspiel und Individualität: Neue Tendenzen einer Literatur der Migration" in *Literatur als Spiel: Evolutionsbiologische, Ästhetische und Pädagogische Konzepte*, eds Thomas Anz and Heinrich Kaulen, Berlin: Walter de Gruyter, 2009.

[29] Zé Do Rock, *fom winde ferfeelt*, Berlin: Edition Diá, 1995, 218-19: "with ultrajurman something will be done fe de environment. if yer rite ultrajurman you save 10 percent paper becoz it is 10 percent shorter (de wordz in demselves ar even shorter but de gaps bitween words stay de same) ... peepul constantly argu that langwidge az a cultural asset shud not be kontinuly chainjed. but it chainjes kontinuly. in jurman dair ar meny meny mor roolz dan 100 yeerz ago. ownly: az long az the roolz multipliy no won criyz out. ownly if yer wont te simplifiy."

ich untahalt mi ständi mit finän, di kainä andrä spraache könän. mit händän und füüssän, mund, naasä und augän. ich spräch schoon fliissänd gestisch. is ja kain wunda. en dutsänd spraaken in so kuaza zait.³⁰

The paragraph about Norway parodies the written character(s) of Norwegian by converting the *Ultradeutsch* as follows:

sch > *sk*
ck > *kk*
w > *v*
o > *å*
ch > *g*
ö > *ø*

> vir faren de norske kyste runter, entlang de herrlige fjords und besuken mein froind Bjarte in Oslo, de ig fån Cheyenne, USA, kenn. da bleib ig einige månate und arbeit in en umzugsfirma als møbelpakker. de normenn sind etvas nasjonalistiker eingestellt als mitteleuropeer. si vållen immer vissen, vas ma fån ir land helt und ham en bisschen lille-brors-kompleks, en kleiner-bruder-kompleks gegenüber de svenske.³¹

And so it continues with mimicry of *Berlinisch*:

> wenn ma disem stadtplan jlauben soll, fährt unsre s-ban durch Ostberlin. kann ja nich sein. wa können doch heute nich schon in eim andren land jewesen sein. ne s-ban kann doch nich durch 2 länder faren. und wenn, dann müssten wa et jemerkt ham.³²

---

³⁰ *Ibid.*, 131: "i constäntly göt into cönversation with finns who could speek no othä langwidge. with hands änd feet, mouth, nose and eyes. i alrädy spoke fluänt gesture. it's indeed nö wundä. a duzän langwidges in such a short tiym.
³¹ *Ibid*: "we travel doun the norske cowst, along de byutilige fjords and vizit miy frend Bjarte in Oslo, hu i no fråm Cheyenne, USA. i stay dair a fyu månds and wurk in a remuval cumpany az a furnicher pakker. de normen ar a bit mor nasyonalistik dan sentral yuropeeans. day alwayz wånt te no wåt yu tink ov dair kuntry and hav a bit ov a lille-brors-kompleks, a litel-bruver-kompleks towårdz de svenske."
³² *Ibid.*, 132: "if ya te bleev dis sity mep, our s-barn gowz tru Eestburlin. dat kawn be riy. we kanno av been in a difrent kuntry awredy todiy. an s-barn kanno travel tru 2 kuntreez. and if it kan, den we mus hav notist." See also Stephen Barbour and Patrick Stevenson, *Variation im Deutschen: Soziolinguistische Perspektiven*, Berlin: Walter de Gruyter, 1998, 124-27.

Dutch:

> hollands is een spraach twischen duits en englis, ma kan vele woorde uismaken. op de autobaan bit ik de een oder andre farer, ons in de naxte ausfaart ruistulassen.[33]

Here Zé Do Rock plays on the fact that many German words beginning with "z" are found with an initial "t" in Dutch,[34] so that *zwischen* ("*tussen*" in Dutch) becomes *twischen*. Long vowels in Dutch are also generally marked with a double vowel in closed syllables and where German has the diphthong "au" [aʊ] the diphthong [œy] spelt "ui" is frequently found in Dutch.

French:

> isch erraischté die tancstéllé und stieg in ain aouto mit offénér tur, ound vollté leausfaren, als ein mir ounbécanntér mensch doursch die bayfarêrtur ainstieg. isch béraitété misch vor, sainé frêssé zou zertrümmern ound ihn anschliessend raouszouschmaissen ...[35]

Here Zé Do Rock not only plays on the spellings of monophthongs in French many of which contain multiple vowels and the use of "e" but also on the common French mispronunciations of German such as use of "sh" [ʃ] for "ch" [ç].

There are many other examples as the narrator moves about the globe. The following are some brief samples:

---

[33] *Ibid.*, 133: "hollands iz a langwidge bitwissen jurman and inglis, yu kan mayk uit meny woordz. op de mowterbaan i ask won or de uder drijver te let us uit at de naakst egzit."

[34] This is a more or less systematic phenomenon. The northern lowlands of the Germanic speaking area did not undergo the Second or High German Sound Shift in c. 500 AD. As a consequence of this shift initial voiceless plosives developed into initial voiceless affricates in most of the dialects of German excepting some in the far north including those that became Dutch. The shift [k] to [kx] occurred only in the far South in what are now mostly Southern German, Southern Austrian and Swiss dialects of German.

[35] Rock, *fom winde ferfeelt*, 135: "i rricht zé pétrrol stayshoun and got intu a carr viz open dor and wonteed tu sét of vén a perrson i deed not no got in tru zé pasenjer dor. i preeperrt tu deestrouy eez fês and tu chok eem out."

Turkish:

> türken sind ser gastfröyndlich, ma könnte fast sagen tsü gastfröyndlich. di alte und verwurzelte tradizion schreibt es vor, und si ham spass daran. das trempen is schwirig, da alle wagen anhalten, auch di, in denen eine flige schwirigkeiten hätte platz tsü finden.[36]

Portuguese:

> einmal will isch eim prtgueisch ein witz erzäln. "nein", sagt er, "nein, nein und nein. isch hab dis prtgisnwitze dik. isch vill kein einzgn prtgisnwitz in meim lebn mer hörn!" "na gut", sag isch, "ich werd dir kein prtgisnwitz mer erzäln."[37]

Through altering the spelling in this way, in the absence of being able to hear the different languages the narrator is encountering, the written text is given a foreign "accent". Reading comprehension is slowed, just as listening comprehension would be slowed in a foreign language or in orally accented speech.[38] More generally, Zé Do Rock's changes to German spelling effectively defamiliarize the orthographic system at the same time as producing a new idiosyncratic system that at times risks degenerating into linguistic babble that no one, save the author, can understand. We now turn to consider in more depth the potential significance of the language play in Zé Do Rock's and Tawada's writing.

---

[36] *Ibid.*, 123: "türks ar very höspitabel, yu kud almowst say tü höspitabel. the old and rutid tradizion priscriybz it and day injöy it. hich-hiyking iz difikult bekoz evry kar stops, eeven dowz a fliy wüd hav problemz fiynding a seet in."

[37] *Ibid.*, 144: "one tiym i wont te tel a prtugeez jowk. 'no' he sez, 'no, no and no. i du not vont te heer anuver prtugeez jowk in miy liyf agayn!' 'good den', i say, 'i wownt tel yu eny mor prtugeez jowks.'"

[38] In addition to Tawada's direct allusion to Ernst Jandl's "Laut und Luise", a poet who maintained links with the Wiener Gruppe, this is a further way in which both the work of Tawada and Zé Do Rock lend themselves to comparison with this group of poets working in post-1945 Austria. As Butler notes, in their experiments with dialect poetry Artmann, Rühm and Achleitner were interested in the visual "alienation effect" of dialect literature when it was written phonetically. We can consider Zé Do Rock and Tawada either consciously or unconsciously to be following in the tradition of the Wiener Gruppe's "anarchic individualism" as a means to contest alienation by the German language, whereas the Wiener Gruppe saw themselves as contesting the suppression of artistic experimentation that had occurred under Nazism. See Michael Butler, "From the 'Wiener Gruppe' to Ernst Jandl", in *Modern Austrian Writing: Literature and Society after 1945*, eds Alan Best and Hans Wolfschütz, London: Oswald Wolff and New Jersey: Barnes and Noble Books, 1980, 236-51.

What is language play?

Language play is by no means restricted to texts written by newcoming speakers of the language used, or in which more than one language is used or represented, although the allusion to other languages vastly heightens the facility to pun. James Joyce's *Finnegans Wake* (1939) is a prime example. This text has been described as "the most thoroughgoing example of multilingual word play ever devised by man".[39] Terry Eagleton cites Joyce's work as exemplary of Julia Kristeva's theory of the semiotic.[40] In Eagleton's account, he describes the semiotic as follows:

> The child in the pre-Oedipal phase does not yet have access to language ("infant" means "speechless"), but we can imagine its body as criss-crossed by a flow of "pulsions" or drives which are at this point relatively unorganised. This rhythmic pattern can be seen as a form of language, though it is not yet meaningful. For language as such to happen, this heterogeneous flow must be as it were chopped up, articulated into stable terms, so that in entering the symbolic order this "semiotic" process is repressed. The repression, however, is not total: for the semiotic can still be discerned as a kind of pulsional pressure within language itself, in tone, rhythm, the bodily and material qualities of language, but also in contradiction, meaninglessness, disruption, silence and absence.[41]

Given the bodily, non-linguistic nature of the semiotic, we cannot expect true engagement with it through language, but there is much in language play, often in a much more highly conscious and cerebral way, that approximates to the meaningless, disorganized, non-linguistic rhythmic pattern described by Eagleton above. The language learner who does not yet have access to the symbolic order as it is presented by the later experienced language may experience a closer relationship to the semiotic, to the meaningless rhythm and flow of, as yet, unknown or barely known words. The learner is not aware of meaningful content, but of the rhythm of language itself. For Kristeva music is a non-verbal signifying system constructed "exclusivement à

---

[39] Vivian Mercier, *The Irish Comic Tradition*, London: Oxford University Press, 1962, cited in Walter Redfern, *Puns*, Oxford: Basil Blackwell, 1984, 166.
[40] Eagleton, *Literary Theory*, 164.
[41] *Ibid.*, 163.

partir du sémiotique"[42] and for an individual listening to an unknown foreign language, the sounds they hear might as well be music.

Explicit and metaphorical allusions to the musical qualities of different languages certainly occur in more than one language learner narrative, the two below among others:

> It's as important to me to speak well as to play a piece of music without mistakes. Hearing English distorted grates on me like chalk screeching on a blackboard, like all things botched and badly done, like all forms of gracelessness. The odd thing is that I know what is correct, fluent, good, long before I can execute it.[43]

> De manière fortuite, il se trouve que l'apprentissage de la langue française a coïncidé dans ma vie avec la découverte du clavecin (1971). Et que, deux ans plus tard (1973), l'abandon de ma language maternelle a été accompagné d'un abandon analogique du piano. Ce paradigme secret, aberrant peut-être, me forme et me déforme depuis un quart de siècle. L'anglais et le piano: instruments maternels, émotifs, romantiques, manipulatifs, sentimentaux, grossiers où les nuances sont soulignés, exagérées, imposées, exprimées de façon flagrante et incontournable. Le français et le clavecin: instruments neutres, intellectuels, liés au contrôle, à la retenue, à la maîtrise délicate, une forme d'expression plus subtile, plus monocorde, discrète et raffinée. Jamais d'explosion, jamais de surprise violente en français, ni au clavecin. Ce que je fuyais en fuyant l'anglais et le piano me semble clair.[44]

In moving away from the semiotic chora towards the symbolic order, the child learning its first language begins by playing with

---

[42] Kristeva, *La Révolution du Langage Poétique*, 22.
[43] Hoffman, *Lost in Translation*, 122.
[44] Huston, *Nord Perdu*, 65, "By coincidence, it turns out that learning the French language occurred at the same time in my life as discovering the harpsichord (1971). And that, two years later (1973), abandoning my mother tongue similarly accompanied giving up the piano. This secret, perhaps absurd, pattern, has been shaping and misshaping me for a quarter of a century. *English and the piano*: maternal instruments, emotive, romantic, manipulative, sentimental, crude, in which the subtleties are underlined, exaggerated, obvious, expressed in a blatant and incontrovertible way. *French and the harpisichord*: neutral, intellectual, linked to control, restraint, delicate mastery, a form of expression that is more subtle, more monotonous, discreet and refined. There is never any explosion or violent surprise in French, nor on the harpsichord. It seems clear to me what I was trying to escape in fleeing from English and the piano" (my translation).

language, babbling with the sounds that surround him/her, then trying out combinations of sounds and phrases as a means to express different discoveries, needs and feelings, but also, as it were, to flex their linguistic muscles and get a feel for the language on their tongue.[45] This semiotic play represents part of a linguistic evolution towards what is meaningful, acceptable and demanded by the symbolic order,[46] beginning with the narrowing of babbled phonemes down to those used within the language spoken by the parents – one of the first elements of transmitted culture. This babbling is a means to appropriate and understand the vehicles of symbolic meaning and how they are to be used within a particular social context. It is constrained by the elements of language available to the child in its environment but otherwise appears only to be limited by the whim of the child's pleasure in experimentation.

In *Numbers* (1973), Jakov Lind describes a reversal of this process in his relationship to German after the holocaust and his migration to London and to the English language:

> Madder than anything was to think I could ever unlearn sounds I knew by heart and kidneys and replace them with other and better sounds. To do that, I had to try to go back to a time before I knew any language, back into a near autistic state of mind that communicates on a level of la-la. In order not to get too deep into these diapers (and I was conscious it was regression), I had to switch my concern from basic needs for food and shelter – the political-economic bag – to a universal, essential state of existence that begins even before speech, before hearing.[47]

Lind finds himself in a position in which he feels he must reject the symbolic order as it was mediated to him in his earlier experienced language, a language that had been used to "yell and scream at people with venom and hatred, with threats and murderous slogans, since it became a language of decrees and curfews, inhuman laws and black-framed announcements, a language of lies and falsehood, of murder

---

[45] David Crystal describes aspects of early language play in *Language Play*, London: Penguin, 1998, 164-73.

[46] It can be seen as representing a developmental stage in communication. En route to developing their own communication systems dolphins and songbirds also go through a stage of "babbling" (Christine Kenneally, "So You Think Humans are Unique?" *New Scientist*, 24 May 2008, 30).

[47] Jakov Lind, *Numbers: A Further Autobiography*, London: Cape, 1973, 75-76.

and death".⁴⁸ This rejection of the social order leads to a regression to the pre-verbal semiotic of "la-la".

Lind is aware of his regression, and unless situated within a social context where language play is explicitly permitted, the newcoming adult learner of a foreign language is "not allowed" to babble. When this pre-verbal babble erupts as language play, though the babble may be available to all, language play itself may not be as egalitarian or democratic as various commentators on the pun might wish to suggest.⁴⁹ While it is true that anyone can engage in playing with language, the social situations and the social roles with which language play is associated are subject to specific pragmatic rules that restrict its performance. Anyone can play with language but how that language play is perceived by others is socially circumscribed.⁵⁰ Crystal himself cites the professions within which language play is more commonly found and accepted such as comedy, copywriting and writing in general. However, even in non-professional situations, language play in adulthood serves a specific social purpose and as Crystal also highlights, it is itself subject to specific social rules.⁵¹ This includes what Crystal terms "ping-pong punning",⁵² crosswords, imitating voices, jokes and children's rhymes and games among other

---

⁴⁸ *Ibid.*, 75. The diaries of Victor Klemperer are well-known accounts of how the ideology of Nazism came to re-shape and re-signify the German language. See, for example, Victor Klemperer, *The Language of the Third Reich*, London and New York: Continuum, 2000. James Underhill also provides a very interesting account of the construction of Nazi discourse, based on Klemperer's work and Goebbels' diaries in *Creating Worldviews: Metaphor, Ideology and Language*, Edinburgh: Edinburgh University Press, 2011.
⁴⁹ Cf. Redfern, *Puns*, 175.
⁵⁰ In a similar vein, Stuart Sim criticizes Geoffrey Hartman's suggestion in *Saving the Text* that punning is a value-free activity (both in terms of production and reception), since the prerequisite for punning is "knowledge of language and its codes on the part of both producer and receiver .... Where knowledge is concerned, value judgements of some description always *are* applicable and innocence is chimera." The punner is reliant, for example, on the receiver accepting their right to use and misuse particular linguistic codes. (Stuart Sim, "Deconstructing the Pun", *British Journal of Aesthetics*, XXVII/4 [Autumn 1987], 327.)
⁵¹ Crystal, *Language Play*, 5. Crystal considers language play to be a significant part of the maintenance of healthy social relationships.
⁵² *Ibid.*, 2. To give the flavour of this, here Crystal gives an example of a conversation kitty-littered with a *cat*alogue of "cat" puns.

things. Language play finds itself restricted and frowned upon in many circumstances for the sake of meaningful communication.[53]

In *Der Witz und Seine Beziehung zum Unbewussten* (2006) Sigmund Freud suggests that focusing on the sounds of words, as in language play, instead of upon their meanings, as in meaningful communication, may in fact require less psychical effort: "Wir dürfen wirklich vermuten, daß damit eine große Erleichterung der psychischen Arbeit gegeben ist und daß wir uns bei der ernsthaften Verwendung der Worte durch eine gewisse Anstrengung von diesem bequemen Verfahren abhalten müssen."[54] If language play were not restricted for the sake of meaningful communication, it could not take on its power to subvert and interrogate the symbolic order, since there would be no symbolic order to subject to question. It tugs at the hem of society, and is frequently assigned to the domain of childhood to keep it out of trouble:

> The pun remains an embarrassment to be marginalised or controlled by relegation to the realms of the infantile, the jocular, the literary. It survives, tenaciously, as freak or accident, hindering what is taken to be the function of language: the clean transmission of a pre-existing, self-sufficient, unequivocal meaning. It is a characteristic mode of the dream, the witticism, the slip of the tongue: those irruptions of the disorderly world of childhood pleasures and unconscious desires into the clear and linear processes of practical and rational thought, those challenges to what Johnson very precisely articulates as the domain of "reason, propriety and truth".[55]

---

[53] Cf. *Ibid.*, 183: "[School is where] language play has traditionally been frowned upon. For, if a child dared to play with language in the classroom – adopt a funny voice or say some of the silly things illustrated in earlier chapters – what would most teachers do? Would they welcome it, reinforce it, praise it? Or would they perhaps say (and I am now quoting from classroom observations) that such language is 'better off in the playground', that this is 'where we are sensible, not silly', that we 'don't use words like that in here'?"

[54] Freud, *Der Witz und Seine Beziehung zum Unbewussten*, 133: "It may really be suspected that in doing so we are bringing about a great relief in psychical work and that when we make serious use of words we are obliged to hold ourselves back with a certain effort from this comfortable procedure" (Sigmund Freud, *Jokes and Their Relation to the Unconscious*, trans. James Strachey, London: Penguin, 1991, 167-68).

[55] Derek Attridge, "Unpacking the Portmanteau, or Who's Afraid of *Finnegans Wake*?", in *On Puns: The Foundation of Letters*, ed. Jonathan Culler, Oxford: Basil Blackwell, 1988, 140.

At the further extreme, stepping, as it does, outside the bounds of conventional communication, in the wrong context language play risks taking on the appearance of "madness". Indeed, many of the ways in which Tawada uses language resemble aspects of schizophrenic discourse. The sequence *"Mühe, Mut* and *Müdigkeit"* could be interpreted as an example of "clanging" or the chaining together of similar-sounding words that can be found in the language of people experiencing schizophrenia.[56] The stringing together of sentences on the basis of word associations is another feature of such discourse.[57] Referring to "krankhafte Zustände der Denktätigkeit" Freud again attributes the prevalence of language play in these conditions to the decrease in psychical expenditure that such use of language requires.[58]

Naturally, a distinction must be made between this relatively uncontrolled use of language and the more controlled and at times what appear to be highly cerebral uses of language play, exemplified by, for example, Joyce's *Finnegans Wake* (1939). However, the parallel between language play and schizophrenia highlights a common fate of language play, namely, that it is frequently associated with the marginalized groups of society – the young, the mad, the artists and in the case of the texts cited here, the immigrants.

It is evident that "language play" as a phenomenon, when referred to in the literature, is extremely broad and full of contradictions. On the one hand, in terms of competence, it is a democratic phenomenon, since anyone who can use language can play with language, but on the other hand, in terms of performance, language play is not acceptable in all social situations. Furthermore, in terms of reception, language play can also act to exclude and ostracize people addressed who are unable to make out the play on words, or understand the joke. The appreciation of language play requires particular social and linguistic competence, particularly when it involves more than one language. As Nilsen points out in an article on bilingual language play:

> Bilingual humor is quite sophisticated – so sophisticated that it took a long time to figure out the score. So sophisticated that many people

---

[56] Michael Covington, Congzhou He, Cati Brown, Lorina Naçi, Jonathan McClain and Bess Sirmon Fjordbak, "Schizophrenia and the Structure of Language: The Linguist's View", *Schizophrenia Research*, LXXVII (April 2005), 86.
[57] *Ibid.*, 87.
[58] Freud, *Jokes and their Relation to the Unconscious*, 168.

don't realise that the number zero which is sometimes referred to as a "goose egg" is the monolingual equivalent of the bilingual (English-French) tennis metaphor "love", which is "l'oeuf", the French word for "the egg".[59]

In terms of the pun, Sim furthermore makes the point that "Punning ... is a highly complex mental activity requiring a considerable knowledge of language and its codes on the part of both producer and receiver".[60]

The linguistic manipulations that the label "language play" is used to describe are also extremely varied and embrace all kinds of linguistic creativity and rhetorical devices including the babbling of infants, jokes, puns, false etymologies, neologisms, litotes, hyperbole, ritual insults, irony, parody, zeugma, oxymoron, metaphor, rhyme, onomatopoeia, alliteration, consonance, assonance, funny voices, limericks, acrostics, lipograms, crosswords, poetry, nonsense, rhyming slang, anagrams, acrostics and baby talk or child-directed speech. There is furthermore, no consensus on which linguistic levels are involved in language play. Where for Freud "play upon words" consists of "focusing our psychical attitude upon the *sound* of the word instead of upon its *meaning*",[61] Walter Redfern is of the opinion that "Onomatopoeia, alliteration, consonance or assonance – all devices in which there is an echo-effect, a chiming or a clanging – *seem very close* to wordplay".[62] From a linguist's point of view, such as Crystal's, language play would encompass all levels of linguistic structure, that is sound, meaning, syntax, and even vocal quality as in "funny voices" and "baby talk".

---

[59] Don Nilsen, "Bilingual and Bidialectical Language Play", *Rocky Mountain Review of Language and Literature*, XXXV/2 (1981), 132. According to the Oxford dictionary's website, the connection between the shape of 0 and an egg also explains the cricketing expression "out for a duck", that can be traced back to the 1860s (http://www.askoxford.com/asktheexperts/faq/aboutwordorigins/outforaduck).
[60] Sim, "Deconstructing the Pun", 327.
[61] Freud, *Jokes and their Relation to the Unconscious*, 167: "unsere psychische Einstellung auf den Wortklang anstatt auf den Sinn des Wortes zu richten" (Freud, *Der Witz und Seine Beziehung zum Unbewussten*, 133).
[62] Redfern, *Puns*, 99 (my emphasis): one could argue, however, that Redfern's use of the word "wordplay" is distinct from "language play" in that it refers only to play with meaning.

The linguist Guy Cook defines language play as language focused on "form and fiction" rather than on "meaning and reality",[63] which revives a now long-disputed dream of purely mimetic language. This dichotomy is therefore neat but unfortunately somewhat suspect. How are we truly to draw the line between language play and the "rest" of language, presumed to be "serious" and meaningful, particularly when much of language play is for the most part an act of linguistic creativity, features of which – such as metaphor, alliteration or neologism, among others – we inevitably find within even the most "serious" of texts? And yet, despite its apparent ubiquity, we still feel that language play, particularly play on meaning, lies at the margins of language, something to be repressed and expunged from the serious task of uncovering true meanings:

> Jokes, like puns, are philosophically puny. Or worse. The air of crime clings to puns. In some contexts the use of a pun is enough to convict one of the fallacy of equivocation, and even where "simply" fun, we refuse to laugh. By groaning, we punish the punster. Apparently we take puns more seriously than we consistently insist.[64]

Not only then, does language play, according to Freud, require less "psychic effort", occuring as it does in "pathological state[s] of thought-activity" such as schizophrenia, it has also, particularly in the case of puns that play with meaning, the "air of crime", going as it does, against the usual law or logocentrism of language. In Giles and Oxford's "Multidimensional theory of laughter causation", cited by Sim, "Puns are placed in the first category of 'humorous laughter', regarded as 'an overt expression of "rebellion" to social pressures, codes and institutions'".[65] As Bates furthermore explains, the ambiguity of meaning inherent in the pun undermines the communication upon which any society depends:

> That is why the pun has traditionally been treated as an anarchist, as a traitor who breaks rank with meaning. Since the mind "naturally discards all associations likely to impede understanding", as Saussure suggested in the Course in General Linguistics (1916), he had nothing

---

[63] Cook, "Language Play, Language Learning", 224.
[64] Gordon C.F. Bearn, "The Possibility of Puns: A Defense of Derrida", *Philosophy and Literature*, XVIII/2 (October 1995), 329.
[65] Sim, "Deconstructing the Pun", 328.

but contempt for "feeble puns based upon ridiculous confusions which may result from homonymy pure and simple".[66]

Language play is mad, criminal or childish. It is uncontrolled and/or uncontrollable. It represents minority and marginalization, not mastery. It appears as the antithesis of rational Enlightenment proclaimed by Kant, since by undoing language, it also undoes a solid foundation for reason. And yet, this would be to forget that it can also be highly deliberate and sophisticated. Furthermore, far from being marginal, in Anglophone postmodern society, language play such as punning, at the very least within the hands of the copywriters, is increasingly visible: "Children should be seen and not hurt";[67] "I brake for coffee."[68] To paraphrase Brock Haussamen, the pun has gone public. It would seem that decades of the deconstruction of truth and language, in part reflected in and arising out of stories of migration, as well as the development of increasingly sophisticated marketing and advertising techniques that use aesthetics to sell goods, have led to a widespread celebration of structural critique in the form of language play, irony and humour, all of which no longer find themselves at the margins of our culture's consciousness. To groans of despair, one might say that there's something punny going on.

How then, are the babblings of an infant, the incoherence of schizophrenia and the linguistic play of a writer or copywriter to be distinguished? All of these linguistic productions could be viewed as lying on a continuum ranging between sense and nonsense. The child's highly asocial babbling has limited symbolic value, the schizophrenic's involves confused symbolic values and the play of the writer highlights symbolic values by changing the shape of the vehicles of meaning. For the most part, there is a degree of intent behind what the writer does with language, whereas the baby represents a state in which control over language and meaning is still neophyte and the schizophrenic a state in which control over language

---

[66] Catherine Bates, "The Point of Puns", *Modern Philology: A Journal Devoted to Research in Medieval and Modern Literature*, XCVI/4 (May 1999), 424.
[67] Brock Haussamen, "Puns, Public Discourse and Postmodernism", *Visible Language*, XXXI/1 (January 1997), 53.
[68] *Ibid.*, 58. A quick flick through any local business index will reveal a plethora of "punny" names for hairdressing salons – among some of the punnier from the Irish *Golden Pages*, 2008: "Cut Above", "Hair Matters", "Hairobics" and "Curl Up and Dye". A pun at any price.

and meaning has been lost. However, without entering into a debate about authorial intent and constructing a psychological profile of writers, it is more difficult to uncover the extent to which the irrational irrupting into a text is rationally manipulated and within the author's control, or if, alternatively, s/he is giving free reign to formal association between different linguistic structures.

It is certainly interesting that multilingual writers sometimes engage in multilingual play to the extent that they may alienate potential readers and create nonsense of their own writing. We see later in this chapter how Todorov compares his own situation as a migrant between cultures to a state of schizophrenia. The wilful disruption of linguistic norms again reveals parallels with the marginal and hyperreflexive state of the schizophrenic. In an essay that compares cultural disembedding in the modern age to the situation of schizophrenia and suggests that the former may exacerbate the latter, Louis Sass provides the following picture of the schizophrenic situation that is worth quoting in full:

> People with schizophrenia have a particularly fraught relationship to marginal play. Their alienation and hyperreflexivity can sometimes give them a kind of special insight into the arbitrariness and consequent absurdity of social conventions, and they often have a natural affinity for the marginalized and self-marginalizing edges of society. Often they seem to adopt what seems, in any particular society, to be the "path of most resistance" (Schooler and Caudill 1964: 177), and they may adopt a stance of hyperautonomy and contrarianism that may be experienced as the epitome of willful defiance (Sass 1992: 108-15). This contrarianism may involve, at least in part, an active identification with an outsider role that is also being imposed upon them by an ostracizing society. There is also a sense in which their cognitive eccentricities are more affliction than act – less a matter of being motivated to hear the beat of a different drummer than of a simple inability to stay in step. Further, the meta-moves and frame breaking in which they so readily engage may also be rather beyond their control – not so much a game at which they play as a kind of uncontrolled slippage that plagues them.[69]

---

[69] Louis Sass, "'Negative Symptoms', Commensense, and Cultural Disembedding in the Modern Age", in *Schizophrenia, Culture and Subjectivity: The Edge of Experience*, eds Janis H. Jenkins and Robert Barrett, Cambridge: Cambridge University Press, 2004, 317.

The hyperreflexivity of schizophrenia finds parallels in the metalinguistic awareness required for language play and in the defamiliarizing effect of being a newcoming writer in a foreign culture, though in the case of schizophrenia the language play is involuntary. Postmodernity also frequently demands this kind of hyperreflexivity in the adoption and performance of identity whether or not one is in one's own culture. Are these writers simply performing a kind of schizophrenic discourse that suits an age questioning faith in language and reason, or are they literally being driven mad by their outsider position? Should we view this writing not as an end statement, but as a search within and around meaning that explores not the truth of the world, but the truth of language? The following section explores the possible significance and function of language play in language learner narratives and multilingual texts in relation to Kristeva's ideas in *La Révolution du Langage Poétique* (1974).

From the beginnings of the *Sprachkrise* in the nineteenth century the relationship between the speaking subject and language as well as between language and reality has been increasingly subject to question.[70] In her study of a variety of multilingual authors Simone Hein-Khatib situates these authors as descendants of the *SprachkritikerInnen*. Picking up on Eva Hoffman's description of her experience of writing in English, Hein-Khatib describes the relationship between writers and their texts in a foreign language as one of *doppelte Distanz* or double distance. As Hein-Khatib argues, this double distance provides the writers with a sense of freedom in regard to the foreign language. Writers play with language as a means to appropriate as well as to subvert new linguistic norms:

> Die Aneignung der fremden Sprache wird für die Literaturschaffenden möglich durch ihre Veränderung, ihre Verfremdung, durch ihre Anpassung an das individuell Gemeinte. Die Verfremdung einer Sprache bedeutet, daß bestehende sprachliche Normen überschritten und gebrochen werden. Gerade die Fremdheit einer Sprache ist es aber nun, das "Unvertrautsein" mit ihr, die Distanz zwischen den innersten Empfindungen und den fremden Wörtern, die durch eine Sprachgrenzüberschreitung so offensichtlich werdende Arbitrarität von signifié und signifiant, die den Bruch mit der Norm erleich[t]ert.[71]

---

[70] Hein-Khatib, *Sprachmigration und Literarische Kreativität*, 42-43.
[71] *Ibid.*, 100: "The adoption of the foreign language is made possible for writers of literature through its transformation, its alienation, its assimilation to individual

Hein-Khatib's concept of appropriation through defamiliarization is highly pertinent to the language learner narratives and multilingual texts discussed above; however, there is another aspect to this defamiliarization that makes Hein-Khatib's interpretation somewhat questionable. On one level, we all defamiliarize the language(s) we use since we use in them in our own unique way, producing sounds with a unique voice-box configuration and writing letters with unique handwriting, however, this language will be recognized as mostly conforming to the constraints of one particular language. The defamiliarization that occurs in multilingual texts frequently involves more than one language and in the most extreme cases, raises the question as to which pre-existing language is being used. What certain multilingual authors seem to be involved in is not so much the diligent appropriation of an existing foreign language as the radical use and abuse of that language in the creation of highly individualized speech that manipulates and abuses the linguistic and cultural order upon which it is based. It can be highly political. A highly similar process is found, for example, in the antilanguages of criminal groups. As an example, Bryan Reynolds provides an analysis of the use of cant in Early Modern England and how it was positioned in relation to the official culture of the times in a relationship of both dependence and difference as a means to distinguish criminal groups from the rest of society. It is interesting to note that one Early Modern English chronicler, William Harrison, described cant as being "without all order or reason". As Reynolds comments:

> To Harrison, this language was reasonless simply because it was spoken by people who led alternative lives, without conventional "reason". Moreover, it was spoken by people who blatantly violated the official "order" of things.[72]

In fact, the relationship between language play and reason is somewhat more complex than either Harrison or Reynolds suggest. To

---

meaning. The alienation of a language means that existing language norms are transgressed and broken. It is, however, precisely the foreignness of a language, the 'not-being-familiar' with it, the distance between innermost feelings and foreign words, the arbitrariness of signifié and signifiant made so obvious by the transgression of a language boundary, which facilitates a break with the norm" (my translation).

[72] Bryan Reynolds, "Criminal Cant: Linguistic Innovation and Cultural Dissidence in Early Modern England", *LIT: Literature Interpretation Theory*, IX/4 (1999), 380.

extend Stuart Sim's interpretation of the pun as a "manoeuvre" rather than as a physiological reflex, language play, as shown above, may be understood as an attempt to undermine the authority of an existing discourse in a manner that is far from innocent. The conceptual metaphor of military/revolutionary strategy that seems to underpin the description of the pun as a "manoeuvre", adequately reflects the hidden power struggle in which this form of language is involved:

> Hartman does not pun as he sneezes, he puns as he manoeuvres; with wit, guile, and all the rhetoric that the learned critic has at his command: "I must pun as I must manoeuvre". The reflex of wit is consciously striven for, and only comes to the highly motivated rebel carrying out his operations inside the framework of language, according to a pre-arranged plan of action.[73]

This kind of language play can therefore be interpreted as the process of deconstructing existing linguistic and cultural structures in order to produce new linguistic capital. This deconstruction can only proceed through a judicious manipulation of language that requires a high level of understanding and in Sim's words "wit, guile, and all the rhetoric that the learned critic has at his command". It is through demonstrating this wit and guile that the language learner reveals that his linguistic competence is worthy of social recognition as linguistic capital. In employing this machinery, that is, the technology of language play, the writer renegotiates symbolic power and his/her position within the foreign society. The foreign language no longer represents a cultural order that threatens the newcoming speaker with silence, but is bent to the will of the writer and becomes a tool in the potential creation of a new cultural and linguistic order arising out of the co-mingling of those that preceded it. This renegotiation may involve the eruption of the rhythmic pattern described by Kristeva as the chora into the existing symbolic order as represented by a particular culture, but it is frequently a controlled eruption conducted under scientific conditions.

For Kristeva, this process, that results in poetic language, involves the codification of primary processes, rhythms and alliterations closer to the unconscious, that she calls the semiotic, within "the language of signs constructed in grammar and logic":

---

[73] Sim, "Deconstructing the Pun", 332.

> This is for me an instance of both a subjective crisis and an amplification of the register of expression, since repression is overcome and the individual is exposed to his passions, while, at the same time, he becomes able to formulate them and to communicate with others. This is what I call "text". It resembles the "poetic" in the Jakobsonian sense, but my formulation includes the psychoanalytic aspect of the phenomenon, that is, the unconscious and the drives.[74]

In this exposition of her theory, the poetic appears to mediate between unconscious drives and a logical language of signs as a semiotized symbolic. This is problematic for the argument developed here, since it is evident that we can make distinctions between playful and non-playful language only with difficulty, so that aspects of what Kristeva describes as the semiotic may be found in any text, not just the poetic. The symbolic order cannot be entirely symbolic, unless it forms some kind of ideal symbolic logic.

Similary, from the discussion above, we might imagine that different linguistic and cultural orders can be interpreted as a multiplicity of symbolic orders that represent diverse instances of the Kristevan concept of universal symbolic order. However, it quickly becomes clear that the symbolic order that a text is assumed to belong to can only ever be hypothetical – an ideal of order that is never in fact realized in actual culture, but which is a useful hook on which to pin a generalized cultural image. In fact, each culture is better seen not as representing a symbolic order, but a particular pattern of symbolic play. The symbolic can never be absolutely ordered: it can only exhibit certain recurrent recognisable tendencies and patterns. In view of this fluidity, it is perhaps better conceived of as a hypothesized group of clusters of symbols, rather than as an order. This would rather suggest the inherent fluidity in the groupings of symbols and in the arrangement of groups over spans of time. "Symbolic order" suggests a fixed abstract totality that cannot exist. The rest of this discussion will therefore emphasize the process of "symbolic ordering" in which the drive towards order is in continual tension with a process of semiosis that both serves to create as well as to destroy order and which may affect the idealized presence of order to differing

---

[74] Julia Kristeva and Ross Guberman, *Julia Kristeva, Interviews*, New York: Columbia University Press, 212.

degrees at different times.[75] The rhythms of the semiotic are always present in the play of the symbolic which is never completely ordered, but at times steadied through repetition of particular patterns of symbolic linkage and interaction. The migrant, the artist and the writer are all implicated in challenging those repetitions.

In questioning the patterns and tendencies of a perceived cultural and linguistic order the intercultural writers discussed here have found a means to overcome the potential silence imposed upon them. The semiotic process of language play with which they are engaged echoes an evolution towards linguistic mastery through which all human beings progress, as well as processes of linguistic creativity that all recurrent patterns of symbolic play require in order to maintain and renew themselves. The writers shift symbolic orderings towards the semiotic in a primarily conscious way.

The reader is witness to the gestation of meaning and a process of *Metamündigkeit* in which the subject seeks to dissolve not just the idealized, metaphorical boundary between two different symbolic orderings but also the split between mind and body that language suggests and largely inaugurates. The increased suffusion of symbolic ordering through the semiotic by these authors can also be interpreted as an appeal to a grounding for meaning and sense of self in a pre-linguistic corporeality, such as that described by Todorov in his essay "Dialogisme et Schizophrénie" (1984). For Todorov physical work is a means to overcome the split sense of self that comes from different performances of identity in one culture and then in the other in which there appears no prospect of integrating the two:

> L'une des deux vies devait évincer alors entièrement l'autre. Pour éviter cette sensation, à Sofia, je me refugiais chaque fois que c'était possible dans le travail physique, en dehors du contact social: je fauchais l'herbe du jardin, taillais les arbres, enlevais la terre; un peu comme, lorsqu'on se sent mal à l'aise dans une situation nouvelle, on propose volontiers ses services pour éplucher les pommes de terre ou on accepte avec empressement de faire une partie de ping-pong, heureux de retrouver au moins l'intégrité de son corps.[76]

---

[75] This does not obviate the continued human tendency to perceive "symbolic order" as an idealized abstraction of cultural and linguistic phenomena in a particular location, thus where necessary, reference will be made to "perceived symbolic order".

[76] Tzvetan Todorov, "Dialogisme et Schizophrénie", in *Language and Literary Theory: In Honor of Ladislav Matejka*, eds Benjamin Stolz, I.R. Titunik and Lubomír

The turn to the physical substance of language, the play with its sounds and letters found in the work of Tawada and Zé Do Rock can be interpreted not just as intentional subversion of predominating perceived symbolic orders, but perhaps also as an attempt to discover security and familiarity in the physical substance of language, in a similar way to that in which Todorov gains comfort from physical work. Just as Chinese characters are used in the West as works of art, the formal components of language are available for all to play with irrespective of first language and culture. The level of comprehension of the language and the culture it is associated with are in some respects irrelevant in terms of formal play. Emphasizing the formal components of German allows Tawada to disregard usual structures of meaning and make the language her own. Zé Do Rock achieves this by disregarding the cultural values attached to standard orthography. Even if he may never be considered a native speaker of German, he has appropriated and remodelled the written language.

The suggestion here is not so much that the poetic and defamiliarizing devices encountered in these multilingual texts represent a revolution that threatens a particular pattern of symbolic ordering in actuality, but rather that the authors exert pressure on that symbolic ordering through creative language play. Allowing the semiotic to hold sway in greater measure within a particular symbolic order is however not merely a paratelic activity engaged in for its own sake, rather it represents a specific relation to a perceived symbolic order and to symbolic ordering as a whole. It is an individualistic postmodern statement in which rather than conforming to the language, writers seek to make the language perform a new identity, one that they have invented for it. In Zé Do Rock's use of German, German maintains its genetic core – read out loud the words would still be German – but read on the page, German wears different national costumes, performing a variety of identities.

These semiotic performances exert their own kind of symbolic power, one which paradoxically threatens to alienate the person

---

Doležel, Ann Arbor: University of Michigan Press, 1984, 574: "One of the two lives was then to oust the other completely. In Sofia, in order to avoid this feeling, I took refuge in physical work whenever I could, beyond human contact: I mowed the lawn, pruned the trees, removed soil; almost like when you feel uncomfortable in a new situation and you volunteer your services to peel potatoes, or you eagerly accept a game of table tennis, happy to at least recover the integrity of your body" (my translation).

addressed and create a nonsense of the whole process, but in which, to a certain extent, the writers show greater symbolic might. Language dances to the tune of the semiotic and spins towards the universal drives and rhythmic articulations in the unconscious of every language. Language play highlights the universal processes of semiosis that underpin any perceived symbolic order and in doing so it simultaneously subjects that order to threat. Unlike child's play, the language play of these writers is not wholly innocent, but a bid for power over the language that threatens to dominate them and condemn them to silence. Engaging universal processes of semiosis can be seen as part of a quest to claim validity for oneself as a human being within a perceived foreign symbolic order. The pre-Oedipal realm of Kristeva's semiotic (*le sémiotique*) invoked in these texts, echoes a non-verbal, corporeal homeland. Yet, its codification with the symbolic, can be interpreted as a deliberate manoeuvre that undermines a perceived symbolic order and exposes its fluidity.

Mündigkeit as we have seen, is about the ability to reason for oneself without the aid of another, the conditions for which are precluded by the linguistic and thereby social nature of reason. Engaging with the structure of language as in language play, suggests the possibility of laying bare the illusions of language, as well as uncovering the universal corporeal and concrete foundations of meaning that are posited in Lakoff and Johnson's theory of metaphor. *Metamündigkeit*, then, would not be "das Vermögen sich seines eigenen Verstandes zu bedienen" ("the ability to make use of one's own reason"), expressed in logical argumentation, but instead would involve the expression of the cultural construction of understanding and language. It highlights the fluidity of the boundaries between perceived symbolic orders as well as those between mind and body, rational and irrational. The inherent ambiguity in the Greek prefix "meta" meaning variously "with", "after", "between" and "among" suggests this straddling, as well as the movement to a plane from which we implicitly critique *Mündigkeit* itself, just as "metalinguistics" looks at language instead of simply using it. However, *Metamündigkeit* is not a field of study, but a subject position, and it does not take place from a position superior to *Mündigkeit* but is involved with and makes use of it. *Metamündigkeit* can only occur within, after, between and among a condition of

Mündigkeit. It plays with *Mündigkeit* and in so doing questions it and threatens its dissolution.

The fortuitous alliteration in the word furthermore emphasizes the word play that forms the expression of *Metamündigkeit*. This word play reveals particular concern with the melding and interaction of one or more different linguistic and cultural frameworks. It can also be seen as a sophisticated linguistic manoeuvre and a bid for symbolic power that has been denied or limited in the foreign culture.

CHAPTER TEN

CONCLUDING THOUGHTS

This book has set out to consider how a partially revised concept of *Mündigkeit*, as implicitly defined in Kant's essay "Beantwortung der Frage: Was ist Aufklärung?" (1784), proves productive in the analysis of texts that describe the process of second language acquisition. As a conceptual tool for the analysis of these texts, *Mündigkeit* is relevant for several reasons. In particular it picks up on the challenge to the Enlightenment discourse and resituates a key concept from that discourse at the centre of the discourse of this research project. However, within this positioning of a transcendental signified for the limited discourse of this book that apparently reconfirms poststructuralist arguments, it is precisely the discovery of commonalities of human experience that cut across human interactions with language from diverse sociocultural and historical circumstances that has been at issue. In examining the representation of *Mündigkeit* this research has attempted to draw out how individuals engage in the process of "putting words on the world" and what this means for the individual, the words and our conception of the world. In so doing, the project has been working on the boundary between language and reality, partially unpicking this relationship and showing how it can affect us (in a physiological/emotional sense) and what it can mean for us (in a linguistic/mental sense).

As indicated above, the term *Mündigkeit* has acted as a centrifugal point around which spin many of the key issues engendered by our acquisition and use of language, such as: the power relations inscribed in language, the construction of identity through language, the pursuit of reason within language and the communicative and expressive tension between the individual and society generated by language. In this concluding chapter, the arguments for using *Mündigkeit* in this centrifugal way will be reviewed and expanded, emphasizing how the cross-cultural texts discussed here have been shown to engage with issues of *Mündigkeit*, albeit using diverse means of expression that are shaped, among others, by linguistic, cultural, historic, social and individual creative factors.

In Chapter Five *Mündigkeit* was defined as the ability to reason without the aid of another. In using the concept within this book, the focus has been on the possession of the linguistic competence that develops that reason. The actual performance or expression of *Mündigkeit* is facilitated by the possession of linguistic capital. It is this facilitating effect of linguistic capital that partially constrains the expression of reason voiced from a position of relative autonomy. Both the reason and the autonomy that Kant describes as necessary to *Mündigkeit* rely on the socially determined factors of linguistic competence and linguistic capital that constrain autonomy.

It must be noted that *Mündigkeit* has not been conceived of here as an end state. There is no such thing as absolute *Mündigkeit*, which in itself would entail absolute rationality, power, authority and autonomy, etc. Instead, it is conceived of as a factor negotiated in all of our interactions with language and which both informs and is achieved through linguistic expression. As suggested by the many issues linked to it in the paragraph above and here also by its position as a transcendental signified, it is a complex somewhat elusive concept that represents many of the key concepts relevant to human interaction with each other and with our environment, namely linguistic competence, rationality, identity, autonomy, power and authority. To be *mündig* in any given situation is to possess these qualities and abilities and to express those qualities and abilities is an act of *Mündigkeit*.

All of the authors of language learner narratives described in this book are to varying degrees in possession of *Mündigkeit* that they have partially exhibited through the act of producing a unique text that demonstrates linguistic competence and through the linguistic capital demonstrated by the fact of having that text published, thereby giving the originator of that text additional socially sanctioned authority. However, this does not vouch for the autonomy or rationality of the ideas presented in these texts. Chapters Six to Nine of this book have shown how a lack of *Mündigkeit* is perceived and/or performed in these texts in a variety of ways. The analysis of *Mutter Zunge* (1998) in Chapters Six and Seven shows how a lack of *Mündigkeit* is enacted in the text both thematically and stylistically. The narrator of the text is shown to lose *Mündigkeit* through a perceived loss of identity and lack of authority as a rootless lovelorn migrant in Germany subject to the authority of her teacher. The text also performs a loss or lack of *Mündigkeit* through its repetitive syntactic structures, juxtaposition of verb phrases and more general ambiguity of meaning.

Chapter Eight also demonstrates a perceived lack of *Mündigkeit* as a textual theme expressed by the metaphors used in the texts. It is shown that many of the metaphors used for describing the experience of learning a foreign language in these texts may be grouped according to a more limited number of underlying conceptual metaphors that in turn can be associated with issues surrounding *Mündigkeit*. The key underlying conceptual metaphors that appear to reoccur in these texts are The Foreign Language is a Human Being; The Foreign Language and Culture are a Trap; The Non-Fluent Speaker is a Child; The Foreign Language is a Costume and The Foreign Culture is a Play. These metaphors, which describe perceptions of loss of agency and inauthenticity in the foreign language, suggest a destabilization of identity and a loss of autonomy that has implications for *Mündigkeit*. The fact that underlying metaphors can be found that appear to accord with the perceptions articulated in a range of texts, concurrently supports a possible universality of the negotiation of *Mündigkeit*, though further research into other Western and non-Western texts would need to be conducted before this could be confirmed. However, in linking issues of *Mündigkeit* with conceptual metaphors grounded in human embodiment (that is, the smallness of the child, the containment of the body, the change in appearance of an actor in a play) the concept of *Mündigkeit* is given a concrete basis relating to a reality external to language, which suggests the possibility that the concept does indeed contain more truth than simply acting as a discursive centrepiece around which the arguments of this book flow.

Chapter Nine moves away from issues surrounding the lack of *Mündigkeit* and considers the process of creatively constructing and restructuring *Mündigkeit* that occurs through making use of devices of language play. It is argued that this language play engages with the power structures that determine linguistic capital in the foreign culture, dismantling these and attempting to reproduce this in a novel form. This language play is a confrontation with the social power structures that surround the acceptance of linguistic competence in the foreign culture and that threaten the language learner with infantilization, imprisonment and even "mutilation".[1] The production of the text can be viewed as an attempt to acquire the authority denied to these authors in the foreign culture, the language play as an attempt to claim an identity within the foreign language through reconfiguring patterns of symbolic order in the foreign language by infusing the language with the rhythmic articulations of a universal Kristevan semiotic. As Tawada makes a play-object of the German language it is no longer the culture that infantilizes her, but she who infantilizes the German language, deflating its significance. This textual renegotiation of the linguistic competence that constitutes linguistic capital within a particular culture is construed as *Metamündigkeit* and it involves, either consciously or unconsciously, an awareness of the many ways in which different cultural and historical contexts form and deform social and material truth in language.

Future directions

The issue of the relevance of *Mündigkeit* to the analysis of language learner narratives has raised a huge number of research questions and areas for consideration, not all of which this brief treatment has been able to engage with. Just some of the key topics touched on in this book, such as language learning, Enlightenment and culture, are in themselves vast. The arguments presented here have naturally had to be selective in which aspects of these broader topics are engaged with, so as to find the key points of contact and relevance that drive the argument forward, by providing evidence for the relevance of *Mündigkeit* to language learner narratives in a variety of ways. In addition to the use of these rich concepts, the project has introduced several new concepts that could be further developed through application to the analysis of other texts. These include the redefinition of *Mündigkeit*, as well as the introduction of the terms *Untermündigkeit*, *Metamündigkeit*, "interscription" and, naturally, "language learner narrative". Furthermore, the multidisciplinary appeal of issues of language, migration and *Mündigkeit* could lead to investigation of these topics from a diverse range of approaches, as will be indicated below. These suggestions are intended as a very

---

[1] This vivid metaphor was spontaneously used in a conversation I had with an Italian Graduate Teaching Assistant describing his experiences of writing and teaching in English.

small subsection of the possibilities for research into this area, some aspects of which researchers are already pursuing. As Steven Kellman notes in the introduction to *The Translingual Imagination* (2000), with reference to the study of literary texts of all kinds written in languages learnt later in life by their authors:

> The ideal student of translingualism would be a polyglot polymath, a monster of erudition who would know far more than I about Chinese who compose poetry in Korean, or Finns who render fiction in Swedish. If translingualism advances to its limits in the utopia of panlingualism, a scholar can merely long for omniscience and bite his tongue.[2]

To begin with language learner narrative, there are many ways in which research into this topic could be furthered. As outlined in Chapter Two, the label of language learner narrative is intended to be applied quite broadly – in this project it has been used to refer predominantly to extracts from (semi-)autobiographical prose texts written by authors who have lived abroad for an extended period of time post-1950. There is plenty of room here for the discovery of texts in different eras of history, in different locations describing a more diverse range of language learning experiences, including the development of literacy.

Helga Ramsey-Kurz has already devoted considerable attention to representations of characters who cannot read in *The Non-Literate Other: Portrayals of Illiteracy in Twentieth-Century Novels in English* (2007), but this could be extended to other languages and contexts. From a sociolinguistic, rather than a literary point of view, another potentially enlightening area for research could involve gathering, transcribing and analysing narratives of language learning from recent non-literate migrants who are learning a foreign language at the same time as learning to read for the first time.

Texts from other eras of history might also be of interest for research in sociolinguistics. An example of language learner narrative that might be of particular interest for an historic study of language attitudes and metalinguistic commentary or for purposes of

---

[2] Kellman, *The Translingual Imagination*, xii.

comparison with more recent language learner narratives comes from the preface of *Der Welsche Gast* (1216) by Thomasin von Zerklaere:[3]

dâ von sult ir mir merken niht,	Deshalb sollt ihr es mir nicht ankreiden,
ob mir lîhte geschiht,	wenn es mir vielleicht passiert, den
etlîchen rîm *ze über*heben,	einen oder anderen Reim zu verfehlen,
daz er nien werde reht gegeben.	so daß er nicht korrekt erscheint. Es muß
mir muoz ouch werren vil dar an,	mir ja arg zu schaffen machen, daß ich
daz ich die sprâche niht wol *k*an.	die Sprache nicht völlig beherrsche.
dâ von sô bite ich elliu kint,	Deshalb bitte ich alle jungen Leute,
des wîse liute gebeten sint	worum weise Leute, weil sie
stun*t* von ir gewizzen muote	unterrichtet,
und von ir sinne und von ir guote,	verständig und wohlmeinend sind,
daz siz lâzen âne râche,	seit eh und je gebeten worden sind,
swes mir gebreste an der sprâche.	daß sie ungestraft lassen,
ob ich an der tiusche	was ich an sprachlichen Mängeln habe.
missespriche,	Wenn ich falsches Deutsch spreche,
ez ensol niht dunken	braucht das nicht merkwürdig zu
wunderliche,	erscheinen,
wan ich vil gar ein walich bin;	denn ich bin nun einmal durch und durch
man wirtes an mîner tiusche inn.	Italiener,
Ich bin von Frîûle geborn	das merkt man an meinem Deutsch.
Und lâze gar âne zorn,	Ich bin im Friaul geboren
swer âne spot mîn getiht	und lasse es ungekränkt zu,
und mîne tiusche bezzert iht...	wenn einer ohne Spott mein Werk
Tiusche lant, enphâhe wol,	und mein Deutsch verbessert...
als ein guot hûsvrouwe sol,	Deutsches Land, empfange freundlich
disen dînen welhschen gast	wie es sich für eine gute Hausherrin
	schickt, diesen deinen welschen Gast ...

---

[3] Thomasin von Zerklaere, *Der Welsche Gast*, Berlin: Walter de Gruyter, 2004, 24, ll.55-74: "Thus you should not blame me, when it so happens that one or the other of my rhymes is off and does not appear correctly. The fact that I do not have complete mastery of the language makes things difficult. And so I ask of all young people what has long since been asked of all wise people, because they are educated, intelligent and well-intentioned that they do not chastise me for my linguistic deficiencies. If I speak incorrect German, that need not appear odd, since I am after all an Italian through and through, you can tell by my German. I was born in Friuli and will welcome without being offended anyone who corrects my work and my German without derision...German Land, receive kindly, as befits a good hostess, this your foreign guest ..." (my translation with Cordula Politis). With thanks to Tim Jackson for bringing this text to my attention.

Other possible examples can be found in Kellman, as for example, the following more ancient short text of language learner narrative that suggests a very different attitude to the language learning situation than the portrayal of crisis represented in many more recent texts:

> Apuleius begins *The Golden Ass* by recounting how he studied Greek and then, "Mox in urbe Latia advena studiorum, Quiritium indigenam sermonem aerumnabili labore, nullo magistro praeeunte, aggressus excolui" .... [Soon after (as a stranger) I arrived at Rome, where by great industry, and without instruction of any schoolmaster, I arrived at the full perfection of the Latin tongue].[4]

As already mentioned, the focus in this book has predominantly been on autobiographical representations of language learning, including both the more prosaic and the more literary, but attention might also be paid to the textual construction of language learning in poetry and in further, more definitely, fictional literary texts, in which the protagonist and the author are not so closely identified. Subsets of language learner narratives might also be identified in which are described experiences of first language acquisition and bi- or multilingualism.

Besides the analysis of a wider range of language learner narratives, another aspect of this project that merits further consideration is the application of Lakoff and Johnson's theory of conceptual metaphor to the analysis of language learner narratives. Constructions of the language learning situation by way of conceptual metaphors could be compared across a greater number of languages and texts. In this vein, it might also be very useful, firstly, to determine if any language learner narratives can be found that do not derive from Western culture and more especially to discover how experiences of language learning might (or might not) be articulated in non-Indo-European languages. It is not necessarily to be expected that language learner narratives are common to all cultural contexts, particularly since language learner narrative as a discourse appears to have its most certain exponents in texts deriving from contemporary Anglophone culture, particularly from Australia, the US and Canada. Again, any linguistic analysis of such texts would need to be conducted on the basis that the texts may represent a (semi-)fictional construction of

---

[4] Kellman, *The Translingual Imagination*, 8.

experience, though how the experience is constructed in metaphor is nonetheless interesting and might offer simultaneous insights to the fields of literature, sociology and psychology.

A particularly fruitful area for research could be an analysis of literary texts in terms of the relation between metaphor and migration. Migration can itself be viewed as a metaphor of metaphor, in which conceptual shifts and translations take place. Such a project might also build on the work of Mark Turner presented in *The Literary Mind: The Origins of Thought and Language* (1996) to examine the metaphorical portrayals of migration in texts by translingual authors at an allegorical level.[5] Such a project might also involve scope to redeploy the proposed concepts of *Metamündigkeit*, *Untermündigkeit* and *Mündigkeit* as they have been defined here.

The critical approach suggested in the definition of interscription also warrants further development in application to other texts. Ideally, this very large project would involve detailed single studies of particular authors that take into account the sociohistorical context of textual production, the author's own relation to that context, the conditions of textual production and the historical, if not the social, context of reception. This understanding would inform a close analysis of the language of the text. As a project, it would serve to inform our understanding of the complex relations between the individual and society in both our construction and reception of meaning (including the interscription itself), as well as more modestly providing a thorough-going approach to the interpretation of texts by particular authors.

The suggestions for further research presented here provide just a minimal hint of the scope for research raised by the key concepts and themes presented in this book. Each of the above suggestions might also be approached from a variety of disciplinary angles including linguistics, corpus linguistics, cognitive linguistics, sociology, psychology, literary and cultural studies. Exploration of issues of linguistic and cultural migration may itself require disciplinary migrations of concepts and assumptions that will serve all the better to make sense of the complex fields of interacting conceptual frameworks that arise in contexts of vast migration and cultural contact. Travelling this road of research is likely to be long, but varied,

---

[5] Mark Turner, *The Literary Mind: The Origins of Thought and Language*, New York and Oxford: Oxford University Press, 1998.

and who knows whence we might ultimately migrate in our understanding of what language means to us.

In spite of the vast potential for research into similar questions, the more limited discussion of narratives of language learning presented in this book has aimed to discover some of the universal aspects of this process embedded in this smaller corpus of texts, through considering the validity of applying the concept of *Mündigkeit* to the analysis of these texts of language acquisition. There has been an attempt to discover some of the fundamental thematic issues that reoccur in narrative engagement with the process of language learning, which, I would suggest, may equally well apply to a variety of contexts of language acquisition, even despite the narrowed focus here on (semi-)autobiographical narratives of later language acquisition.

In applying *Mündigkeit* to the analysis of these texts, the aim has not been to use the texts as sociological data that might refute or support the actual possibility of discovering universal truths, however, the issue of the relationship between language and truth has been highlighted in the analysis. The act of autobiography, can be interpreted as an act of self-construction, whether or not the construction accords with the original thoughts, feelings and experiences of the author. In a sense, the narrative creates its own reality.

Rather than pursuing a debate that opposes realist and poststructuralist views of language, the aim has been to illuminate how language might be both universally grounded and yet culturally, socially and individually refined in order to represent that universe. To go back to Searle's arguments, much of our reality is indeed social and linguistic, and yet underpinning the complexities of this social reality, as hinted at in Chapter Eight, there may be universal components to those social realities that provide certain limits of conceptualization and engagement. The negotiation of *Mündigkeit* might well indeed be one such universal component. At the very least, within the analysis of literary constructions of language learning and multilingualism presented in this book, *Mündigkeit* has proven to be a valuable tool in unpicking and unpacking the complex issues of language, identity and reality presented by these texts. It has also permitted the shedding of light on both the affective and cognitive implications of living in a foreign culture and how these might be textually constructed and mediated. In this way, it is hoped that the arguments presented here also make a more concrete contribution to further understanding of some of the more elusive qualitative aspects of language acquisition. Through the dialogue and discourse of language learner narrative engendered by these texts, these culturally and individually shaped acts of *Mündigkeit* offer a contribution to understanding how we construe our own engagements with language in the everyday reality of our lives.

APPENDICES

Appendix I: Defining language memoir

Cross-cultural autobiography (as used by Pavlenko, 2001): Immigrant autobiographies, ethnic autobiographies and any other narrative which explores transition to a foreign culture whether permanent or temporary. Stylistic variants: Cross-cultural lifewriting; cross-cultural memoirs.

Ethnic autobiographies (as used by Pavlenko, 2001): Immigrant autobiographies as well as narratives of those who came to the New World as children or who grew up in ethnic neighbourhoods. Stylistic variants: Cross-cultural lifewriting; cross-cultural memoirs.

Immigrant autobiographies (as used by Pavlenko, 2001): Memoirs written by first generation immigrants who arrived as teenagers or adults and who write about both cultures. Stylistic variants: Immigrant memoirs; immigrant narratives; immigrant lifewriting.

Language learner diaries (as used by Benson and Nunan, 2004): A diary made by language learners which is used to facilitate their second language acquisition.

Language memoir (as used by Kaplan, 1994): Twentieth-century autobiographical writing about learning a second language or another discourse of the mother tongue, French and English examples given.

Language memoir (as used by Kramsch, 2005): As per Kaplan, 1994.

Language memoir (as used by Pavlenko, 2001): Twentieth-century (American) cross-cultural autobiography about the acquisition of a second language. Stylistic variants: Language learning memoirs autobiographies of second language learners; language learning autobiographies; language learning narratives; language learning stories.

Memoirs of language migration (as used by Besemeres, 2005): A text describing a permanent move to the foreign culture such as Eva Hoffman's *Lost in Translation*. Stylistic variant: Language memoir.

Narratives of language immersion (as used by Besemeres, 2005): A subgenre of travel writing which describes a temporary period of stay abroad. Stylistic variants: Memoirs of language immersion; memoirs of cultural and linguistic immersion; narratives of language travel.

Reflective accounts of multiple language use (as used by Kramsch, 2005): A type of language memoir which reflects on the use of multiple languages.

Translingual texts (as used by Kellman, 2000): Literary and philosophical texts of any kind which have been written in a language which is not the author's mother tongue.

Appendix II: Selected sources of language learner narrative

The following texts are listed chronologically with text type in brackets.

Antin, Mary, *The Promised Land*, 1912 (migrant autobiography).
Rudkowski, Fannia Goldberg, "Mastering the English Language", in *Pomegranates: A Century of Jewish Australian Writing*, 1941 (essay).
Kazin, Alfred, *A Walker in the City*, 1951 (ethnic autobiography).
Nabokov, Vladimir, *Speak, Memory*, 1951 (autobiography).
Nabokov, Vladimir, *Pnin*, 1957 (novel).
Sartre, Jean-Paul, *Les Mots*, 1964 (autobiography of literary discourse acquisition).
Handke, Peter, *Kaspar*, 1967 (fictional play).
Brooke-Rose, Christine, *Between*, 1968 (autobiographical novel of multilingualism).
Hélias, Paul Jakez, *Le Cheval D'Orgueil*, 1975 (autobiography of second language acquisition).
Kingston, Maxine Hong, *The Woman Warrior: Memoirs of a Girlhood Among Ghosts*, 1975 (semi-fictional autobiography).
Liverani, Mary Rose, *The Winter Sparrows: A Glasgow Childhood*, 1976 (autobiography of monolingual migration).
Canetti, Elias, *Die Gerettete Zunge*, 1977 (autobiography of multilingualism).
Ackermann, Irmgard, ed., *Als Fremder in Deutschland*, 1982 (anthology).
Ackermann, Irmgard, ed., *In Zwei Sprachen Leben*, 1983 (anthology).
Charef, Medi, *Le Thé au Harem d'Archi Ahmed*, 1983 (novel).
Ernaux, Annie, *La Place*, 1983 (autobiography of literary discourse acquisition).
Sarraute, Nathalie, *Enfance*, 1983 (autobiography of multilingualism).
Zongren, Liu, *Two Years in the Melting Pot*, 1984 (personal essays).
Djébar, Assia, *L'Amour, la Fantasia*, 1985 (autobiography).
Morley, John David, *Pictures from the Water Trade*, 1985 (semi-autobiographical novel).
Todorov, Tzvetan, *Bilinguisme, Dialogisme et Schizophrénie*, 1985 (personal essay).

Ishiguro, Kazuo, *An Artist of the Floating World*, 1986 (novel).
Green, Julien, *Le Langage et son Double*, 1987 (dual language autobiography).
Shammas, Anton, *Arabesques*, 1988 (novel).
Alexakis, Vassilis, *Paris-Athènes*, 1989 (autobiography of language migration).
Hoffmann, Eva, *Lost in Translation*, 1989 (autobiography of language migration).
Young, Cathy, *Growing up in Moscow: Memories of a Soviet Childhood*, 1989 (autobiography).
Codrescu, Andrei, *The Disappearance of the Outside*, 1990 (essays).
Cofer, Judith Ortiz, *Silent Dancing: A Partial Remembrance of a Puerto Rican Childhood*, 1990 (autobiography of bilingualism).
Mura, David, *Turning Japanese*, 1991 (autobiography).
Davidson, Cathy, *36 Views of Mount Fuji: On Finding Myself in Japan*, 1993 (personal essays on language travel).
Gahse, Zsuzsanna, *Übersetzt: Eine Entzweiung*, 1993 (personal essay).
Kaplan, Alice, *French Lessons*, 1993 (autobiography).
Tawada, Yoko, *Ein Gast*, 1993 (personal essays).
Hirsch, Marianne, "Pictures of a Displaced Girlhood", in *Displacements*, 1994 (personal essay).
Novak, Jan, "My Typewriter Made Me Do It", in *Altogether Elsewhere*, 1994 (personal essay).
Alexakis, Vladimir, *La Langue Maternelle*, 1995 (novel).
Lee, Chang-Rae, *Native Speaker*, 1995 (semi-fictional autobiography).
Rock, Zé Do, *fom winde ferfeelt*, 1995 (autobiographical travel writing).
Rodriguez, Richard, *Hunger of Memory*, 1995 (autobiography).
Watson, Richard, *The Philosopher's Demise: Learning French*, 1995 (language biography).
Ayim, May, *Blues in Schwarz und Weiss*, 1996 (poems).
Chamoiseau, Patrick, *Une Enfance Créole*, 1996 (novel).
Derrida, Jacques, *Le Monolinguisme de l'Autre ou la Prothèse d'Origine*, 1996 (autobiographical reflections).
Tawada, Yoko, *Talisman*, 1996 (essays).
Ayim, May, *Nachtgesang*, 1997 (poems).

Bond, Michael, *Working at the Interface of Cultures: Eighteen Lives in Social Science*, 1997 (anthology of autobiographical essays).
Hegi, Ursula, *Tearing the Silence: Being German in America*, 1997 (anthology of autobiographical essays).
Lvovich, Natasha, *The Multilingual Self*, 1997 (language biography).
Makine, Andreï, *Le Testament Français*, 1997 (semi-autobiographical novel).
Mori, Kyoko, *Polite Lies: On Being a Woman Caught between Cultures*, 1997 (autobiographical essays).
Sebbar, Leïla, *Une Enfance Algérienne*, 1997 (anthology of Algerian writers).
Steiner, George, *Errata: an Examined Life*, 1997 (autobiography).
Wierzbicka, Anna, "The Double Life of a Bilingual", in *Working at the Interface of Cultures*, 1997 (autobiography).
Alvarez, Julia, *Something to Declare*, 1998 (autobiography).
Dorfman, Ariel, *Heading South, Looking North: A Bilingual Journey*, 1998 (autobiographical essays).
Fitzherbert, Katrin, *True to Both my Selves*, 1998 (autobiography).
Ogulnick, Karen, *Onna Rashiku (Like a Woman): The Diary of a Language Learner in Japan*, 1998 (language biography).
Özdamar, Emine Sevgi, *Mutterzunge*, 1998 (semi-fictional autobiography).
Saalfeld, Lerke von, *Ich habe eine Fremde Sprache gewählt*, 1998 (anthology of autobiographical essays).
Sante, Luc, *The Factory of Facts*, 1998 (autobiography).
Schami, Rafik, *Damals Dort und Heute Hier*, 1998 (interview).
Taufiq, Suleman, *Das Schweigen der Sprache*, 1998 (poems).
Anzaldúa, Gloria, *Borderlands/La Frontera*, 1999 (autobiography).
Djébar, Assia, *Ces Voix qui m'Assiègent*, 1999 (autobiography).
Huston, Nancy, *Nord Perdu suivi de Douze France*, 1999 (autobiographical essays).
Mar, Elaine, *Paper Daughter: A Memoir*, 1999 (ethnic autobiography).
Said, Edward, *Out of Place*, 1999 (autobiography).
Agosin, Marjorie, *The Alphabet in My Hands: A Writing Life*, 2000 (autobiography).
Aguilera, Luis Gabriel, *Gabriel's Fire*, 2000 (autobiography).
Benyoëtz, Elzar, *Die Zukunft sitzt uns im Nacken*, 2000 (collection of aphorisms).

Brintrup, Lilianet, "Turbulent Times", in *Becoming American*, 2000 (personal essay).
Danquah, Meri Nana-Ama, *Becoming American: Personal Essays by First Generation Immigrant Women*, 2000 (anthology of autobiographical essays).
Ha, Jin, *Waiting*, 2000 (novel).
Kim, Helen, "Beyond Boundaries", in *Becoming American*, 2000 (personal essay).
Lee, Helie, "Dissassembling Helie", in *Becoming American*, 2000 (personal essay).
Mori, Kyoko, "Becoming Midwestern", in *Becoming American*, 2000 (personal essay).
Ogulnick, Karen, ed., *Language Crossings: Negotiating the Self in a Multicultural World*, 2000 (anthology of language biography).
Saine, Ute Margaret, "Now Is the Time to Try Something – But Have I Got Nine Lives", in *Becoming American*, 2000 (personal essay).
Trojanow, Ilija, *Döner in Walhalla: Texte aus der anderen deutschen Literatur*, 2000 (anthology).
Belcher, Diane *et al.*, *Reflections on Multiliterate Lives*, 2001 (anthology of essays by academics).
Lefèvre, Kim, *Métisse Blanche*, 2001 (semi-autobiographical novel).
Stavans, Ilan, *On Borrowed Words: A Memoir of Language*, 2001 (autobiography).
Alexakis, Vladimir, *Les Mots Etrangers*, 2002 (autobiography).
Banciu, Carmen-Francesca, *Berlin ist mein Paris: Geschichte aus der Hauptstadt*, 2002 (autobiography).
Chiellino, Gino, *In Sprachen Leben: Meine Ankunft in der Deutschen Sprache*, 2003 (prose, poetry and essays).
De Courtivron, Isabelle, *Lives in Translation: Bilingual Writers on Identity and Creativity*, 2003 (anthology of autobiographical essays).
Hamilton, Hugo, *The Speckled People: Memoir of a Half-Irish Childhood*, 2003 (autobiography of bilingualism).
Kellman, Steven, *Switching Languages: Translingual Writers Reflect on Their Craft*, 2003 (anthology of autobiographical essays).
Sebbar, Leïla, *Je ne Parle pas la Langue de mon Père*, 2003 (autobiography).

Cellier-Gelly, Micheline *et al.*, *Entre Deux Langues: Autobiographie et Bilinguisme*, 2004 (anthology of excerpts).
Lesser, Wendy, *The Genius of Language: Fifteen Writers Reflect on Their Mother Tongues*, 2004 (anthology of autobiographical essays).
Abu-Jaber, Diana, *The Language of Baklava: A Memoir*, 2005 (ethnic autobiography).
Turnbull, Sarah, *Almost French*, 2005 (autobiography).
Tawada, Yoko, *Überseezungen*, 2006 (essays).
Besemeres, Mary and Anna Wierzbicka, *Translating Lives: Living with Two Languages and Cultures*, 2007 (anthology of autobiographical essays).
Guo, Xiaolu, *A Concise Chinese-English Dictionary for Lovers*, 2007 (semi-fictional autobiography).
Tawada, Yoko, *Sprachpolizei und Spielpolyglotte*, 2007 (essays).

Appendix III: All verb forms in *Mutter Zunge* categorized by tense

Tense	#Verbs	Verb Forms
Preterite	79	*ankam, arbeitete, dachte, fiel, flog, fragte (x4), hatte (x5), hing, kam (x5), kamen (x3), konnte (x3), lächelte, lief, legten, lag, machte (x3), meinten, reinkam, sagte (x10), schaute, schickten, sah (x5), sah...an, sahen, war (x13), waren, saß (x2), sprach, sprachen, stand, wartete, wusch, wurde, wickelten, wußte (x2)*
Present simple	69	*arbeitest, atme, bellen, denke, denkst, dreht (x2), druckt, erinnere (x5), erzähle, erzählen, erzählst (x2), erzählt, fährt, fotografiert, gebe, gibt, hab, hast (x2), hat, hält, heißt (x2), knirschen, komme, kommen, kann, lacht, läßt, laufen (x2), liest (x2), rauchen, reden, redet, sagte, schneiden, bin (x3), ist (x4), sind (x3), war, saß, sitzt, spreche, sprichst, springe, springst, steh(e), steht, überlege, verbietet, vorstelle, wackeln, warten*
Present perfect	40	*geblieben, gebracht, gefragt, gegangen (x3), gewöhnt, gehört, gekommen, gelassen, geholt, gekommen, gesagt (x8), geschnappt (x2), geseh(e)n (x3), gesessen, gesprungen (x2), gestanden (x2), getrunken, vergossen, verloren (x5), geweint (x2), geworden*
Infinitive	27	*angucken, aufhängen, ausweisen, erinnern, erleben, erzählen (x3), fallen, fangen, fassen, finden, fühlen,*

		hören, machen, pflücken, rausspucken, sagen, schämen, sehen (x4), suchen, verfluchen, verstecken, wiedererkennen
Future tense	6	zurückgehen (x2), waschen, sprechen, lernen, abholen
Past subjunctive	6	wüßte (x2), wären, könnten (x2)
2nd person imperative/1st person singular present tense	5	geh (x3), steh(e) auf (x2)
Imperative	3	such, gehe, zieh...an
Pluperfect	3	hatte geweint, hatte getötet, hatte erzählt
Unconjugated verbs in infinitive form	2	sitzen (x2)
Present subjunctive	1	Gebe
Pluperfect subjunctive	1	hätte gesagt
Preterite passive with "sein"	1	war bekannt gemacht
Past participle as adjective	1	Verboten

Appendix IV: Recurrent motifs of *Mutter Zunge* in context

Hand

(15) seine **Hand** roch nach Rosen .... "... die **Hand** der schlagenden Meister stammt aus dem Paradies, wo Sie schlagen, werden dort die Rosen blühen."
(18-19) Manche sind dünne Waisen mit bleichen Gesichtern, manche Allahs Vogel, sie wandern **Hand** in **Hand** .... Ibni Abdullah hat meine **Hand** aufgemacht und einen neugeborenen Paradiesvogel da reingetan.
(19) Als ich zum Schreiben mein Hemdärmel hochzog, sah ich, daß Herr Ibni Abdullah auf meine **Hand**gelenke schaute, als ich die Schrift zuende geschrieben hatte, sah ich ihn noch immer auf meine **Hand**gelenke gucken ....
(20) Ibni Abdullah nahm die leere Kaffeetasse aus meiner **Hand** ....
(30) "... Ich soll meine **Hand** über meinen Mund gehauen haben in diesem Moment."
(32) keine **Hand** habe ich gefunden, die sie ihm abwischt ....
(38) Zeliha gab allen Frauen Messer in die **Hand**.
(43) Ibni Abdullah nahm meine **Hand** ....
(43) "Deine traurige **Hand** über mein Herz haltend, lege ich das Licht deines Gesichts in den Himmel."
(45) Ich ging mit Ibni Abdullah, der in meinem Körper ist, Zeitung in der **Hand**, in die Nähe der Autobahn.
(47) Das war ein Mädchen, sie saß auf einer Parkbank, sie hatte in der **Hand** Möhrensalat mit Senf, sie weinte.

Mund

(12) er lacht nicht, ich erzähle ihm von jemandem, der die Geschichten mit seinem **Mundwinkel** erzählt, oberflächlich.
(13-14) In den Tagen hatten sie Mahir mit Kugeln getötet. Mahirs Bruder saß da, als ob er in seinem **Mund** was Bitteres hatte und es nicht rausspucken konnte ....
(18) Es kamen aus meinem **Mund** die Buchstaben raus.
(23) Ibni Abdullah kam, legte seinen **Mund** zwischen meine Wange und **Mund**, ich bin ruhig.
(27) Ich sah, wie das Meer aus dem **Mund** dieses Tieres rauskam.

(27) "Du feine Rose meiner Gedanken,
Du lustige Nachtigall meines Herzens.
Ich habe dich gesehn.
Dein feuriger **Mund**,
deine Grübchen in deinen Wangen.
Du hast mich verbrannt ...."
(28) dein **Mund**, wenn er was sagt, das bringt die Toten ins Leben zurück.
(29) Ich suchte arabische Wörter, die es noch in türkischer Sprache gibt. Ich fragte Ibni Abdullah: "Kennst du sie?"
Leb – **Mund**
Ducar – Befallen
Mazi – Vergangenheit
Medyun – verbunden
Meytap – Feuerwerkskörper
Yetim – Waise
(30) Ich soll meine Hand über meinen **Mund** gehauen haben in diesem Moment.
(31) "Gib mir deine Spucke in meinen **Mund**."
(39) Ich sah, als er kam, daß er seine Hände über seinen **Mund** schlug, wie bei dem toten israelischen Soldaten, was er mir erzählt hatte, daß er den Toten sah, und schlug seine Hände plötzlich über seinen **Mund**.
(39) "... Was für eine Gewandtheit, dein **Mund** mein **Mund**,
das macht die Sehnsucht größer,
laß mich, laß diese Liebende,
ich will Trümmer werden."
(40) Mit welcher Sprache soll mein **Mund** sprechen, daß mein Geliebter es sieht ....
(41) "**Mund**, das hast du schon mal gefragt", sagte Ibni Abdullah ....

BIBLIOGRAPHY

Primary sources
Alexakis, Vassilis, *Paris-Athènes*, Paris: Stock, 2006.
Alvarez, Julia, *Something to Declare*, New York: Penguin, 1998.
Anzaldúa, Gloria, *Borderlands/La Frontera*, San Francisco: Aunt Lute Books, 1999.
Banciu, Carmen-Francesca, *Berlin ist mein Paris: Geschichte aus der Hauptstadt*, Berlin: Ullstein, 2002.
Bauby, Jean-Dominique, *The Diving Bell and the Butterfly*, London: Harper Perennial, 2008.
Belcher, Diane Dewhurst and Ulla Connor, *Reflections on Multiliterate lives*, Clevedon: Multilingual Matters, 2001.
Belfellah, Abdellatif, "Deutsche Sprache. Gnade, Erfahrung und Prüfung in einem fremden Idiom", *Lettre International*, XX (Spring, 1993), 60-61.
Biondi, Franco, "Deutsche Sprache, Schwergemachte Sprache", *Sehnsucht im Koffer*, eds Franco Biondi, Barbara Rieder and Michael Tonfeld, Frankfurt am Main: Fischer-Taschenbuch-Verlag, 1981, 44-46.
Brooke-Rose, Christine, *Between*, London: Joseph, 1968.
Canetti, Elias, *Die Gerettete Zunge: Geschichte einer Jugend*, Munich: Carl Hanser Verlag, 1989.
Cellier-Gelly, Micheline, Claire Torreilles and Marie-Jeanne Verny, eds, *Entre Deux Langues: Autobiographie et Bilinguisme*, Paris: Adapt Editions, 2004.
Chamoiseau, Patrick, *School Days*, London: Granta, 1998.
Chamoiseau, Patrick, *Une Enfance Créole: Chemin-d'Ecole*, Barcelona: Editions Gallimard, 1996.
Charef, Mehdi, *Le Thé au Harem d'Archi Ahmed*, Paris: Mercure de France, 1983.
Çirak, Zehra, *Leibesübungen: Gedichte*, Cologne: Kiepenheuer and Witsch: 2000.

Codrescu, Andrei, *The Disappearance of the Outside: A Manifesto for Escape*, St Paul, MN: Ruminator Books, 1990.

Cofer, Judith Ortiz, *Silent Dancing: A Partial Remembrance of a Puerto Rican Childhood*, Houston, TX: Arte Publico Press, 1990.

Danquah, Meri Nana-Ama, ed., *Becoming American: Personal Essays by First Generation Immigrant Women*, New York: Hyperion, 2000.

De Courtivron, Isabelle, ed., *Lives in Translation: Bilingual Writers on Identity and Creativity*, New York: Palgrave MacMillan, 2003.

Déguignet, Jean-Marie, *Mémoires d'un Paysan Bas-Breton*, Ergué-Gabéric: An Here, 1998.

Derrida, Jacques, *Le Monolinguisme de l'Autre ou la Prothèse d'Origine*, Paris: Editions Galilée, 1996.

Djébar, Assia, *Ces Voix Qui m'Assiègent*, Paris: Editions Albin Michel, 1999.

Dorfman, Ariel, *Heading South, Looking North: A Bilingual Journey*, London: Hodder and Stoughton, 1998.

Dykman, Elizabeth, "The Vagabond Years", in *Language Crossings: Negotiating the Self in a Multicultural World*, ed. Karen Ogulnick, New York: Teachers College Press, 2000, 30-34.

Ernaux, Annie, *La Place*, Paris: Gallimard, 1983.

Everett, Daniel, *Don't Sleep, There are Snakes: Life and Language in the Amazonian Jungle*, London: Profile Books, 2008.

Fitzherbert, Katrin, *True to Both My Selves*, London: Virago, 1998.

Goldsworthy, Vesna, *Chernobyl Strawberries: A Memoir*, London: Atlantic Books, 2006.

Green, Julien, *Le Langage et son Double*, Paris: Editions du Seuil, 1987.

Goethe, Johann Wolfgang von, *Wilhelm Meisters Lehrjahre* (1796), Munich: Deutscher Taschenbuch Verlag, 1999.

Guo, Xiaolu, *A Concise Chinese-English Dictionary for Lovers*, London: Random House, 2007.

Handke, Peter, *Kaspar*, Frankfurt am Main: Suhrkamp, 1968.

Hélias, Pierre-Jakez, *Le Cheval d'Orgueil*, Paris: Plon, 1975.

Hessler, Peter, *River Town: Two Years on the Yangtze*, New York: HarperCollins, 2001.

Hoffman, Eva, *Lost in Translation*, London: Vintage, 1989.

Huston, Nancy, *Nord Perdu: Suivi de Douze France*, Montréal Leméac: Actes Sud, 1999.

Ishiguro, Kazuo, *An Artist of the Floating World*, London: Faber, 1986.
Jandl, Ernst, *Laut und Luise*, Neuwied: Luchterhand, 1971.
Kafka, Franz, *Die Verwandlung*, Frankfurt am Main: Fischer Taschenbuch Verlag, 1999.
Kafka, Franz, "Ein Bericht für eine Akademie", in *Franz Kafka: Sämtliche Erzählungen*, ed. Paul Raabe, Frankfurt am Main: S. Fischer, 1969, 166-74.
Kaminer, Wladimir, *Schönhauser Allee*, Munich: Wilhelm Goldmann Verlag, 2001.
Kaplan, Alice, *French Lessons*, Chicago and London: University of Chicago Press, 1993.
Kingston, Maxine Hong, *The Woman Warrior: Memoirs of a Girlhood Among Ghosts*, New York: Random House, 1975.
Lee, Chang-Rae, *Native Speaker*, London: Granta in association with Penguin, 1995.
Lesser, Wendy, ed., *The Genius of Language: Fifteen Writers Reflect on their Mother Tongues*, New York: Anchor Books, 2004.
Lee, Helie, "Disassembling Helie", in *Becoming American: Personal Essays by First Generation Immigrant Women*, ed. Meri Nana-Ama Danquah, New York: Hyperion, 2000, 126-37.
Lind, Jakov, *Numbers: A Further Autobiography*, London: Cape, 1973.
Liverani, Mary Rose, *The Winter Sparrows: Growing Up in Scotland and Australia*, Melbourne: Sphere, 1980.
Lvovich, Natasha, *The Multilingual Self*, Mahwah, NJ: Lawrence Erlbaum Associates, 1997.
Makine, Andreï, *Le Testament Français*, London: Sceptre, 1997.
Mori, Kyoko, *Polite Lies: On Being a Woman Caught between Cultures*, New York: Henry Holt and Company, 1997.
—, "Becoming Midwestern", in *Becoming American: Personal Essays by First Generation Immigrant Women*, ed. Meri Nana-Ama Danquah, New York: Hyperion, 2000, 138-45.
Morley, John David, *Pictures from the Water Trade: an Englishman in Japan*, London: Deutsch, 1985.
Mura, David, *Turning Japanese*, New York: Anchor Books, 1991.
Nemiroff, Greta Hofmann, "No Language to Die in", in *Language Crossings: Negotiating the Self in a Multicultural World*, ed. Karen Ogulnick, New York: Teachers College Press, 2000, 13-20.

Niele, Irmina van, "Wandering Words", conference paper presented at Royal Irish Academy Conference: *In/Difference: Current and Historical Perspectives on Cultural Contact*, University of Limerick, 9-10 November 2007.

Novak, Jan, "The Typewriter Made Me Do it", in *Altogether Elsewhere: Writers on Exile*, ed. Marc Robinson, Boston and London: Faber and Faber, 1994, 261-66.

Ogulnick, Karen, *Onna Rashiku (Like a Woman): The Diary of a Language Learner in Japan*, Albany, NY: SUNY Press, 1998.

—, ed., *Language Crossings: Negotiating the Self in a Multicultural World*, New York: Teachers College Press, 2000.

Özdamar, Emine Sevgi, *Das Leben ist eine Karawanserei: Hat Zwei Türen, Aus einer Kam ich Rein, Aus der Anderen Ging ich Raus*, Cologne: Kiepenheuer and Witsch, 1994.

Özdamar, Emine Sevgi, *Mutter Zunge*, Cologne: Kiepenheuer and Witsch, 1998.

Pamuk, Kerim, *Sprich Langsam, Türke*, Hamburg: Lutz Schulenburg, 2002.

Rock, Zé Do, *fom winde ferfeelt*, Berlin: Edition Diá, 1995.

Rodriguez, Richard, *Hunger of Memory*, New York: Bantam Dell, 1982.

Rudkowski, Fannia Goldberg, "Starting School and Mastering the English Language", in *Pomegranates: A Century of Jewish Australian Writing*, ed. Gael Hammer, Newtown: Millenium Books, 1988, 111-13.

Said, Edward, *Out of Place: A Memoir*, London: Granta Books, 1999.

Sante, Luc, *The Factory of Facts*, London: Granta Books, 1998.

Sarraute, Nathalie, *Enfance*, Paris: Gallimard, 1983.

Saine, Ute Margaret, "Now Is the Time to Try Something – But Have I Got Nine Lives?", in *Becoming American: Personal Essays by First Generation Immigrant Women*, ed. Meri Nana-Ama Danquah, New York: Hyperion, 2000, 165-75.

Sartre, Jean-Paul, *Les Mots*, Paris: Gallimard, 1964.

Stavans, Ilan, *On Borrowed Words: A Memoir of Language*, New York: Penguin, 2001.

Stefan, Verena, "Here's Your Change 'N Enjoy the Show", in *Language Crossings: Negotiating the Self in a Multicultural World*, ed. Karen Ogulnick, New York: Teachers College Press, 2000, 21-29.

Tawada, Yoko, *Ein Gast*, Tübingen: Konkursbuchverlag, 1993.
—, *Sprachpolizei und Spielpolyglotte*, Tübingen: Konkursbuch Verlag, Claudia Gehrke, 2007.
—, *Talisman*, Tübingen: Konkursbuchverlag, 1996.
—, *Überseezungen*, Tübingen: Konkursbuch Verlag Claudia Gehrke, 2006.
Turnbull, Sarah, *Almost French: A New Life in Paris*, London and Boston: Nicholas Brealey Publishing, 2005.
Watson, Richard, *The Philosopher's Demise: Learning French*, Columbia, MO and London: University of Missouri Press, 1995.
Zerklaere, Thomasin von, *Der Welsche Gast*, Berlin: Walter de Gruyter, 2004.
Zongren, Liu, *Two Years in the Melting Pot*, San Francisco: China Books and Periodicals, 1984.

Secondary sources
Ackermann, Irmgard, ed., *Als Fremder in Deutschland: Berichte Erzählungen, Gedichte von Ausländern*, Munich: Deutscher Taschenbuch Verlag, 1982.
Adelson, Leslie, *The Turkish Turn in Contemporary German Literature*, New York: Palgrave Macmillan, 2005.
—, "The Turkish Turn in Contemporary German Literature and Memory Work", *Germanic Review*, LXXVII/4 (Winter 2002), 326-38.
Adjahi, Christine, "Femmes Africaines en Immigration: Quels Parcours et Quelles Pratiques? L'exemple de Christine Adjahi", *Mots Pluriels*, XXIII (March 2003): http://www.arts.uwa.edu.au/Mots Pluriels/MP2303ca.html
Adorno, Theodor, *Erziehung zur Mündigkeit*, Frankfurt: Suhrkamp Verlag, 1970.
Álvarez, Inma, "Foreign Language Education at the Crossroads: Whose Model of Competence?", *Language, Culture and Curriculum*, XX/2 (2007), 126-39.
Andrews, Walter, *Poetry's Voice, Society's Song: Ottoman Lyric Poetry*, Washington: University of Washington Press, 1985.
Anz, Thomas and Heinrich Kaulen, eds, *Literatur als Spiel: Evolutionsbiologische, Ästhetische und Pädagogische Konzepte*, Berlin: Walter de Gruyter, 2009.

Appel, René, "Language, Concepts and Culture: Old Wine in New Bottles?", *Bilingualism: Language and Cognition*, III/1 (September 2000), 5.

Attridge, Derek, "Unpacking the Portmanteau, or Who's Afraid of *Finnegans Wake?*", in *On Puns: The Foundation of Letters*, ed. Jonathan Culler, Oxford: Basil Blackwell, 1988, 140-55.

Austin, Timothy, "Review of *Style and Structure in Literature: Essays in the New Stylistics*, ed. Roger Fowler", *Journal of Aesthetics and Art Criticism*, XXXVI/1(Autumn 1977), 107-109.

Aytaç, Gürsel, "Sprache als Spiegel der Kultur: Zu Emine Sevgi Özdamar's Roman *Das Leben ist eine Karawanserei*", in *Interkulturelle Konfigurationen: Zur deutschsprachigen Erzählliteratur von Autoren nichtdeutscher Herkunft*, ed. Mary Howard, Munich: Iudicium, 1997, 171-78.

Bakhtin, Mikhail, "Discourse in the Novel", in *Dialogic Imagination*, ed. Michael Holquist, Austin: University of Texas Press, 1981, 259-422.

—, "The Problem of Speech Genres", in *The Discourse Reader*, eds Adam Jaworski and Nikolas Coupland, London and New York: Routledge, 1999, 121-32.

Barbour, Stephen and Patrick Stevenson, *Variation im Deutschen: Soziolinguistische Perspektiven*, Berlin and New York: Walter de Gruyter, 1998.

Barnard, Frederick, "Aufklärung und Mündigkeit – Thomasius, Kant, Herder and The Enlightenment", *Deutsche Vierteljahrsschrift für Literaturwissenschaft und Geistesgeschichte*, LVII/2 (1983), 278-93.

Barthes, Roland, "The Death of the Author", in *Image-Music-Text*, ed. and trans. Stephen Heath, London: Fontana, 1977, 142-48.

Bates, Catherine, "The Point of Puns", *Modern Philology: A Journal Devoted to Research in Medieval and Modern Literature*, LXXXXVI/4 (May 1999), 421-30.

Bearn, Gordon, "The Possibility of Puns: A Defense of Derrida", *Philosophy and Literature*, XVIII/2 (October 1995), 330-35.

Beaugrande, Robert-Alain de and Wolfgang Dressler, *Introduction to Text Linguistics*, London: Longman, 1981.

Bedient, Calvin, "Kristeva and Poetry as Shattered Signification", *Critical Inquiry*, XVI/4 (Summer 1990), 807-29.

Begemann, Christian, "'Kanakensprache'. Schwellenphänomene in der Deutschsprachigen Literatur Ausländischer AutorInnen der Gegenwart", in *Schwellen: Germanistische Erkundungen einer Metapher*, eds Nicholas Saul, Daniel Steuer, Frank Möbus and Birgit Illner, Würzburg: Königshausen and Neumann, 1999.

Beiser, Frederick, "The Context and Problematic of Post-Kantian Philosophy", in *A Companion to Continental Philosophy*, eds Simon Critchley and William R. Schroeder, Oxford and Malden, MA: Blackwell, 1999, 21-34.

Bell, Nancy, "Exploring L2 Language Play as an Aid to SLL: A Case Study of Humour in NS-NSS Interaction", *Applied Linguistics*, XXVI/2 (June 2005), 192-218.

Belz, Julie, "The Myth of the Deficient Communicator", *Language Teaching Research*, VI/1 (January 2002), 59-82.

— and Jonathon Reinhardt, "Aspects of Advanced Foreign Language Proficiency: Internet-Mediated German Language Play", *International Journal of Applied Linguistics*, XIV/3 (2004), 324-62.

Benson, Phil and David Nunan, eds, *Learners' Stories: Difference and Diversity in Language Learning*, Cambridge: Cambridge University Press, 2004.

Berger, Peter L. and Thomas Luckmann, *The Social Construction of Reality: A Treatise in the Sociology of Knowledge*, London: Penguin, 1966.

Besemeres, Mary, *Translating One's Self: Language and Selfhood in Cross-Cultural Autobiography*, Oxford: Peter Lang, 2002.

—, "Anglos Abroad: Memoirs of Immersion in a Foreign Language", *Biography*, XXVIII/1 (Winter 2005), 27-42.

— and Maureen Perkins, "Translated Lives", *Mots Pluriels*, XXIII (March 2003): http://www.arts.uwa.edu.au/MotsPluriels/ MP2303edito1.html

— and Anna Wierzbicka, *Translating Lives: Living with Two Languages and Cultures*, Queensland: University of Queensland Press, 2007.

Best, Alan and Hans Wolfschütz, eds, *Modern Austrian Writing: Literature and Society after 1945*, London: Oswald Wolff, 1980.

Bird, Stephanie, *Women Writers and National Identity: Bachmann, Duden, Özdamar*, Cambridge: Cambridge University Press, 2003.

Blackall, Eric, ed. and trans. in collaboration with Victor Lange, *Goethe: The Collected Works – Wilhelm Meister's Apprenticeship*, Princeton, NJ: Princeton University Press, 1995.

Boa, Elizabeth, "Sprachenverkehr: Hybrides Schreiben in Werken von Özdamar, Özakin und Demirkan", in *Interkulturelle Konfigurationen: Zur deutschsprachigen Erzählliteratur von Autoren Nichtdeutscher Herkunft*, ed. Mary Howard, Munich: Iudicium, 1997, 115-18.

Bond, Michael, ed., *Working at the Interface of Cultures: Eighteen Lives in Social Science*, London and New York: Routledge, 1997.

Booth, Wayne, "Book Review: *Metaphors We Live By*", *Ethics*, XCIII/3 (April 1983), 619-21.

Bordwell, David, *Making Meaning: Inference and Rhetoric on the Interpretation of Cinema*, Cambridge, MA: Harvard University Press, 1989.

Bourdieu, Pierre and John B. Thompson, *Language and Symbolic Power: The Economy of Linguistic Exchanges*, Cambridge: Polity in association with Basil Blackwell, 1991.

Bradford, Richard, *Roman Jakobson: Life, Language, Art*, London: Routledge, 1994.

Brandt, Bettina, "Collecting Childhood Memories of the Future: Arabic as Mediator Between Turkish and German in Emine Sevgi Özdamar's Mutterzunge", *Germanic Review*, LXXIX/4 (Fall 2004), 295-316.

Brintrup, Lilianet, "Turbulent Times" in *Becoming American: Personal Essays by First Generation Immigrant Women*, ed. Meri Nana-Ama Danquah, New York: Hyperion, 2000, 12-20.

Brose, Karl, "Erziehung zu Frieden und Mündigkeit", *Wissenschaft und Frieden*, II (1989): http://www.wissenschaft-und-frieden.de/seite.php?artikelID=0814.

Bruner, Jerome, *Acts of Meaning*, Cambridge, MA: Harvard University Press, 1990.

Burke, Lucy and Tony Crowley, eds, *The Routledge Language and Cultural Theory Reader*, London and New York: Routledge, 2000.

Burrows, John, *Computation into Criticism: A Study of Jane Austen's Novels and an Experiment in Method*, Oxford: Clarendon Press, 1987.

Butler, Michael, "From the 'Wiener Gruppe' to Ernst Jandl", in *Modern Austrian Writing: Literature and Society after 1945*, eds Alan Best and Hans Wolfschütz, London: Oswald Wolff, 1980.

Byram, Michael, *Teaching and Assessing Intercultural Communicative Competence*, Clevedon: Multilingual Matters, 1997.

— and Michael Fleming, *Language Learning in Intercultural Perspective: Approaches through Drama and Ethnography*, Cambridge: Cambridge University Press, 1998.

Cameron, Deborah, "Evolution, Science and the Study of Literature: A Critical Response", *Language and Literature*, XX/1 (February 2011), 59-72.

Carruthers, Peter and Jill Boucher, *Language and Thought: Interdisciplinary Themes*, Cambridge: Cambridge University Press, 1998.

Chandler, Daniel, *Semiotics: The Basics*, London: Routledge, 2002.

Chatzidimitriou, Ioanna, "'I have no History': Negotiating Language in Vassilis Alexakis's *The Mother Tongue*", *The Comparatist*, XXX (May 2006), 101-12.

—, "Language(s) of Dispossession: Silent Geographies in Vassilis Alexakis's *Paris-Athènes*", *Dalhousie French Studies*, LXXVI (Fall 2006), 113-19.

Cook, Guy, "Language Play, Language Learning", *ELT Journal*, LI/3 (July 1997), 224-31.

Cook, Guy, *Language Play, Language Learning*, Oxford: Oxford University Press, 2000.

—, "Language Play, Language Learning", *ELT Journal*, LI/3 (July 1997), 224-31.

Covington, Michael, Congzhou He, Cati Brown, Lorina Naçi, Jonathan McClain and Bess Sirmon Fjordbak, "Schizophrenia and the Structure of Language: The Linguist's View", *Schizophrenia Research*, LXXVII (April 2005), 85-98.

Cowley, Peter, "Lost and Found – the Language of Exile", *Mots Pluriels*, XXIII (March 2003): http://www.arts.uwa.edu.au/Mots Pluriels/MP2303pc.html.

Critchley, Simon, *On Humour*, London: Routledge, 2002.

Crystal, David, *A Dictionary of Linguistics and Phonetics*, Oxford: Blackwell, 1997.

—, *Language Play*, London: Penguin, 1998.

Culler, Jonathan, ed., *On Puns: the Foundation of Letters*, Oxford: Basil Blackwell, 1988.
Curtiss, Susan, *Genie: A Psycholinguistic Study of a Modern-Day "Wild Child"*, New York: Academic Press, 1977.
Cyrus, Norbert and Dita Vogel, "Germany", in *European Immigration: A Sourcebook*, eds Anna Triandafyllidou and Ruby Gropas, Aldershot and Burlington, VT: Ashgate, 2007, 127-40.
Davies, Alan, *The Native Speaker: Myth and Reality*, Clevedon: Multilingual Matters, 2003.
De Groot, Annette, "On the Source and Nature of Semantic and Conceptual Knowledge", *Bilingualism: Language and Cognition*, III/1 (April 2000), 7-9.
Deleuze, Gilles and Félix Guattari, *Kafka: Pour une Littérature Mineure*, Paris: Éditions de Minuit, 1975.
Derrida, Jacques, *L'Ecriture et la Différence*, Paris: Editions du Seuil, 1967.
—, *Writing and Difference*, London: Routledge, 2001.
—, "Die Struktur, das Zeichen und das Spiel im Diskurs der Wissenschaften vom Menschen", in *Texte zur Literaturtheorie der Gegenwart*, eds Dorothee Kimmich, Rolf G. Renner and Bernd Stiegler, Stuttgart: Philipp Reclam jun., 1996, 301-13.
—, "Structure, Sign and Play in the Discourse of the Human Sciences", in *Writing and Difference*, trans. Alan Bass, London: Routledge, 1978, 278-94: http://hydra.humanities.uci.edu/derrida/sign-play.html.
— and Avital Ronell, "The Law of Genre", *Critical Enquiry*, VII/1 (Autumn 1980), 55-81.
Eagleton, Terry, *Literary Theory: An Introduction*, Malden, Oxford, and Victoria: Blackwell, 1996.
Engelmann, Hugo, "The Non-Literate, the Psychotic, and the Child: A Reconsideration", *Anthropological Quarterly*, XXXVI/1 (January 1963), 27-33.
Fabb, Nigel, *Linguistics and Literature: Language in the Verbal Arts of the World*, Oxford: Blackwell, 1997.
Fachinger, Petra, "Lost in Nostalgia: The Autobiographies of Eva Hoffman and Richard Rodriguez", *MELUS (Journal of the Society for the Study of the Multi-Ethnic Literature of the United States)*, XXVI/2 (Summer 2001), 111-27.

Fanetti, Susan, "Translating Self into Liminal Space: Eva Hoffman's Acculturation in/to a Postmodern World", *Women's Studies*, XXXIV/5 (July/August 2005), 405-19.

Fischer, Sabine and Moray McGowan, *Denn du Tanzt auf einem Seil: Positionen Deutschsprachiger MigrantInnenliteratur*, Tübingen: Stauffenburg, 1997.

—, "From *Pappkoffer* to Pluralism", in *Turkish Culture in German Society Today*, eds David Horrocks and Eva Kolinsky, Oxford: Berghahn Books, 1996, 1-22.

Fjellestad, Danuta Zadworna, "The Insertion of the Self into the Space of Borderless Possibility: Eva Hoffman's Exiled Body", *MELUS (Journal of the Society for the Study of the Multi-Ethnic Literature of the United States)* XX/2 (Summer 1995), 133-47.

Forster, Leonard, *The Poet's Tongues: Multilingualism in Literature*, London: Cambridge University Press in Association with the University of Otago Press, 1970.

Fowler, Roger, *Linguistic Criticism*, Oxford: Oxford University Press, 1986.

—, *Linguistics and the Novel*, London: Methuen, 1977.

—, *Literature as Social Discourse: The Practice of Linguistic Criticism*, London: Batsford Academic and Educational, 1981.

Fox, Frampton, "Reducing Intercultural Friction through Fiction", *International Journal of Intercultural Relations*, XXVII/1 (February 2003), 99-123.

Franceschini, Rita and Johanna Miecznikowski, eds, *Leben mit Mehreren Sprachen – Vivre avec Plusieurs Langues: Sprachbiographien – Biographies Langagières*, Bern: Peter Lang, 2004.

Francis, Wendy, "Clarifying the Cognitive Experimental Approach to Bilingual Research", *Bilingualism: Language and Cognition*, III/1 (April 2000), 13-15.

Freud, Sigmund, *Der Witz und Seine Beziehung zum Unbewussten*, Frankfurt am Main: Fischer Taschenbuch Verlag, 2006.

—, *Jokes and Their Relation to the Unconscious*, London: Penguin, 1991.

Fritz, Daniela Regina, "Language Socialisation, Communicative Competence and Identity: Literary Representations of the Language Learner in Twentieth-Century German Literature", University of California, Berkeley, 2001 (unpublished dissertation).

Genette, Gérard, "Genres, 'Types', Modes", *Poétique*, XXXII (1977), 389-421.

Ghaussy, Sohelia, "Das Vaterland Verlassen: Nomadic Language and 'Feminine Writing' in Emine Sevgi Özdamar's *Das Leben ist Eine Karawanserei*", *The German Quarterly*, LXXII/1 (Winter 1999), 1-16.

Goddard, Cliff, "The Search for the Shared Semantic Core of all Languages", in *Meaning and Universal Grammar – Theory and Empirical Findings, Volume I*, eds Cliff Goddard and Anna Wierzbicka, Amsterdam: John Benjamins, 2002, 5-40.

Grimm, Jacob and Wilhelm Grimm, *Deutsches Wörterbuch Bd. 1. Lief 1.* (1885), Leipzig: Verlag von S. Hirzel, 1962.

Grosjean, François, *Life with Two Languages: An Introduction to Bilingualism*, Cambridge, MA and London: Harvard University Press, 1982.

Haines, Brigid and Margaret Littler, *Contemporary Women's Writing in German: Changing the Subject*, Oxford, New York: Oxford University Press, 2004.

Halliday, Michael A.K., *Language, Context, and Text: Aspects of Language in a Social-Semiotic Perspective*, Oxford: Oxford University Press, 1989.

—, "The Linguistic Study of Literary Texts", in *Proceedings of the Ninth International Congress of Linguists*, Cambridge, MA, August 27-31, 1962, London, The Hague, Paris: Mouton, 1964, 302-307.

— and Ruqaiya Hasan, *Cohesion in English*, London: Longman, 1976.

—, *Language, Context, and Text: Aspects of Language in a Social-Semiotic Perspective*, Oxford: Oxford University Press, 1989.

Haussamen, Brock, "Puns, Public Discourse and Postmodernism", *Visible Language*, XXXI/1 (January 1997), 53-61.

Haverkamp, Anselm, *Metapher: Die Ästhetik in der Rhetorik: Bilanz eines Exemplarischen Begriffs*, Munich: Wilhelm Fink Verlag, 2007.

Hawkes, Terence, *Metaphor*, London: Methuen, 1972.

—, *Structuralism and Semiotics*, London: Routledge, 2003.

Hein-Khatib, Simone, *Sprachmigration und Literarische Kreativität: Erfahrungen Mehrsprachiger Schriftstellerinnen und Schriftsteller bei ihren Sprachlichen Grenzüberschreitungen*, Frankfurt am Main: Peter Lang Verlag, 1998.

Helgerson, Richard, "Review of *Language as Ideology* by Gunther Kress and Robert Hodge; *Language and Control* by Roger Fowler and *Literature, Language and Society in England, 1580-1680*", by David Aers, Bob Hodge and Gunther Kress, *Comparative Literature*, XXXV/4 (September 1983), 362-73.

Hirsch, Marianne, "Pictures of a Displaced Girlhood", in *Displacements: Cultural Identities in Question*, ed. Angelika Bammer, Bloomington: Indiana UP, 1994, 71-89.

Hockey, Susan, *Electronic Texts in the Humanities: Principles and Practice*, Oxford: Oxford University Press, 2000.

Hodge, Robert and Gunther Kress, *Social Semiotics*, Cambridge: Polity, 1988.

Hodgson, Marshall, *The Venture of Islam: Conscience and History in a World Civilization*, Chicago and London, 1974.

Hoggart, Richard, *The Uses of Literacy: Aspects of Working-Class Life, with Special References to Publications and Entertainments*, London: Chatto and Windus, 1971.

Holquist, Michael, ed., *Dialogic Imagination*, Austin: University of Texas Press, 1981, 259-422.

Horrocks, David and Eva Kolinsky, *Turkish Culture in German Society Today*, New York and Oxford: Berghahn, 1996.

Howard, Mary, ed., *Interkulturelle Konfigurationen: Zur deutschsprachigen Erzählliteratur von Autoren nichtdeutscher Herkunft*, Munich: Iudicium, 1997, 171-78.

Iser, Wolfgang, *The Act of Reading: A Theory of Aesthetic Response*, Baltimore and London: John Hopkins University Press, 1980.

Jackson, Frank and Michael Smith, eds, *Oxford Handbook of Contemporary Philosophy*, Oxford: Oxford University Press, 2005.

Jakobson, Roman, "Closing Statement: Linguistics and Poetics", in *Style in Language*, ed. Thomas A. Sebeok, Cambridge, MA: MIT Press, 1971, 350-77.

Jankowsky, Karen, "German Literature Contested: The 1991 Ingeborg-Bachmann-Prize Debate, 'Cultural Diversity,' and Emine Sevgi Özdamar", *The German Quarterly*, LXX/3 (Summer 1997), 261-76.

Jaworski, Adam and Nikolas Coupland, *The Discourse Reader*, London and New York: Routledge, 1999.

Jenkins, Janis H. and Robert Barrett, eds, *Schizophrenia, Culture and Subjectivity: The Edge of Experience*, Cambridge: Cambridge University Press, 2004.

Jones, Randall, Erwin Tschirner, Isabel Buchwald and Antina Ittner, *A Frequency Dictionary of German: Core Vocabulary for Learners*, London: Routledge, 2006.

Joyce, James, *Finnegans Wake* (1939), London: Penguin, 2000.

Kant, Immanuel, "Beantwortung der Frage: Was ist Aufklärung?" (1784), in *Was ist Aufklärung?*, ed. Ehrhard Bahr, Stuttgart: Philipp Reclam, 1974, 9-17.

Kaplan, Alice, "On Language Memoir" in *Displacements. Cultural Identities in Question*, ed. Angelika Bammer, Bloomington: Indiana University Press, 1994, 59-70.

Kellman, Steven, *The Translingual Imagination*, Lincoln, NB and London: University of Nebraska Press, 2000.

Kenneally, Christine, "So You Think Humans are Unique?", *New Scientist*, 24 May 2008, 30.

Kim, Helen, "Beyond Boundaries", in *Becoming American: Personal Essays by First Generation Immigrant Women*, ed. Meri Nana-Ama Danquah, New York: Hyperion, 2000, 113-25.

Kinast, Eva, "Interkulturelles Training", in *Handbuch Interkulturelle Kommunikation und Kooperation*, eds Eva Kinast, Alexander Thomas and Sylvia Schroll-Machl, Göttingen: Vandenhoeck and Ruprecht, 2003, 181-216.

Kinginger, Celeste, "Bilingualism and Emotion in the Autobiographical Works of Nancy Huston", *Journal of Multilingual and Multicultural Development*, XXV/2-3 (2004), 159-76.

Klemperer, Victor, *The Language of the Third Reich*, London and New York: Continuum, 2000.

Kluge, Friedrich, *Etymologisches Wörterbuch der Deutschen Sprache*, Berlin: Walter de Gruyter, 1934.

Knowles, Murray and Rosamund Moon, *Introducing Metaphor*, London: Routledge, 2006.

Kolenda, Konstantin, "On Human Emotions", *American Anthropologist*, New Series, LXXXIX/4 (December 1987), 946-47.

König, Werner and Hans-Joachim Paul, *Dtv-Atlas zur Deutschen Sprache*, Munich: Deutscher Taschenbuch Verlag GmbH, 1978.

Konuk, Kader, *Identitäten im Prozess: Literatur von Autorinnen aus und in der Türkei in Deutscher, Englischer und Türkischer Sprache*, Essen: Blaue Eule, 2001.

Korth, Britta, "Analyzing Language Biographies: Concepts of Language and Language Learning", 2001: http://www.eric.ed.gov/ERICWebPortal/detail?accno=ED462000

Kramsch, Claire, *The Multilingual Subject: What Foreign Language Learners Say about their Experience and Why it Matters*, Oxford: Oxford University Press, 2009.

—, "Beyond the Second vs. Foreign Language Dichotomy: The Subjective Dimensions of Language Learning" in *Unity and Diversity in Language Use*, eds Miller Kristyan S. and Paul Thompson, London: Continuum, 2002, 1-21.

—, "The Multilingual Experience: Insights from Language Memoirs", *Transit*, I/1, 2005, Article 50905: http://escholarship.org/uc/item/9h79g172.

—, "Preview of *The Multilingual Subject* by Claire Kramsch", *International Journal of Applied Linguistics*, XVI/1 (March 2006), 97-110.

—, "The Privilege of the Intercultural Speaker", in *Language Learning in Intercultural Perspective: Approaches through Drama and Ethnography*, eds Michael Byram and Michael Fleming, Cambridge: Cambridge University Press, 1998.

—, "Social Discursive Construction of Self in L2 Learning" in *Sociocultural Theory and Second Language Learning*, ed. James Lantolf, Oxford: Oxford University Press, 2000, 133-54.

Kristeva, Julia, *La Révolution du Langage Poétique*, Paris: Editions du Seuil, 1974.

—, *Revolution in Poetic Language*, trans. Margaret Waller, New York: Columbia University Press, 1984.

— and Ross Guberman, *Julia Kristeva, Interviews*, New York: Columbia University Press, 1996.

Kumar, Anant, *Kasseler Texte*, Schweinfurt: Wiesenburg Verlag, 1998.

Kuruyazici, Nilüfer, "Emine Sevgi Özdamars *Das Leben ist eine Karawanserei* im Prozeß der Interkulturellen Kommunikation" in *Interkulturelle Konfigurationen: Zur Deutschsprachigen Erzählliteratur von Autoren Nichtdeutscher Herkunft*, ed. Mary Howard, Munich: Iudicium, 1997.

Lakoff, George and Mark Johnson, *Metaphors We Live By*, Chicago; London: University of Chicago Press, 1980.
Lantolf, James, ed., *Sociocultural Theory and Second Language Learning*, Oxford: Oxford University Press, 2000.
Larkin, Nora, *Changing Ethnic Identities in Post-National Germany: A Study of Turkish-German Literature, Politics and Society*, University of New Hampshire, 2006 (unpublished article): http://www.unh.edu/urc/sites/unh.edu.urc/files/media/pdfs2011/award_pdfs/2006/paper_larkin.pdf
Lawson, Richard H., *Understanding Elias Canetti*, Columbia: University of South Carolina, 1991.
Lejeune, Philippe, *Le Pacte Autobiographique*, Paris: Editions du Seuil, 1996.
Lemke, Jay L., *Textual Politics: Discourse and Social Dynamics*, London: Taylor and Francis, 1995.
Levine, Glenn, "*The Multilingual Subject* by Claire Kramsch", *The Modern Language Journal*, XCV/2 (June 2011), 324-26.
Lévi-Strauss, Claude, *Structural Anthropology*, Harmondsworth: Penguin, 1972.
Levinson, Stephen, *Pragmatics*, Cambridge: Cambridge University Press, 1983.
Li, Houxiang, "Claire Kramsch: The Multilingual Subject", Oxford: Oxford University Press, 2009", *Applied Linguistics*, XXXII/1 (February 2011), 113-26.
Lippman, Walter, *Public Opinion*, 1922: http://www.gutenberg.org/ebooks/6456.
Little, David and Radka Perclová, *European Language Portfolio Guide for Teachers and Teacher Trainers*, Strasbourg: Council of Europe, 2001.
Littler, Margaret, "Diasporic Identity in Emine Sevgi Özdamar's *Mutterzunge*", in *Recasting German Identity: Culture, Politics, and Literature in the Berlin Republic*, eds Stuart Taberner and Frank Finlay, Rochester, NY: Camden House, 2002, 219-34.
Lodge, David, *The Language of Fiction*, London: Routledge, 2002.
Lyotard, Jean-François, *The Postmodern Condition: A Report on Knowledge*, Manchester: Manchester University Press, 1979.
Macey, David, *The Penguin Dictionary of Critical Theory*, London: Penguin Books, 2000.

McGowan, Moray, "Turkish-German Fiction Since the Mid 1990s", in *Contemporary German Fiction: Writing in the Berlin Republic*, ed. Stuart Taberner, Cambridge: Cambridge University Press, 2007.

Margaroni, Maria "'The Lost Foundation': Kristeva's Semiotic *Chora* and its Ambiguous Legacy", *Hypatia*, XX/1 (Winter 2005), 78-98.

Matthes, Frauke, "Beyond Boundaries? V.S. Naipaul's *The Enigma of Arrival* and Emine Sevgi Özdamar's *Mutter Zunge* as Creative Processes of Arrival", *eSharp: Electronic Social Sciences, Humanities, and Arts Review for Postgraduates*, V (Summer 2005): http://www.gla.ac.uk/media/media_41169_en.pdf

Mautner, Thomas, *Dictionary of Philosophy*, London: Penguin, 2005.

Meizoz, Jérôme, *Le Droit de "Mal Ecrire" Quand les Auteurs Romands Déjouent le "Français de Paris"*, Carouge-Genève: Editions Zoé, 1998.

Mercier, Vivian, *The Irish Comic Tradition*, London: Oxford University Press, 1962.

Meyer, Jim, "What Is Literature? A Definition Based on Prototypes", *Work Papers of the Summer Institute of Linguistics, University of North Dakota Session*, 1997, Vol. 41: http://www.und.edu/dept/linguistics/wp/1997Meyer.PDF

Miller, Robert, "Beyond Postmodernism? Toward a Philosophy of Play", December 2001: http://home.vicnet.net.au/~exist/pdf/2001_December.pdf.

Miller, William E. "All the World's A Stage", *Notes and Queries*, X/3 (March 1963), 99-101.

Milz, Sabine, "Ethnicity and/or Nationality Writing in Contemporary Canada and Germany: A Comparative Study of Marlene Nourbese Philip's and Emine Sevgi Özdamar's Writing of Hybridity and its Public and Critical Reception", *Zeitschrift für Anglistik und Amerikanistik: A Quarterly of Language, Literature and Culture*, XLVIII/3 (2000): http://docs.lib.purdue.edu/clcweb/vol2/iss2/4/

Moi, Toril, "Reading Kristeva: A Response to Calvin Bedient", *Critical Inquiry*, XVII/3 (Spring 1991), 639-43.

Moretti, Franco, *The Way of the World: The Bildungsroman in European Culture*, London: Verso, 1987.

Mukařovsky, Jan, "Standard and Poetic Language", in *The Routledge Language and Cultural Theory Reader*, eds Lucy Burke and Tony Crowley, London and New York: Routledge, 2000, 225-30.

Murray, D.W. and Gregory Button, "Some Problems of Wierzbicka's 'Simples'", *American Anthropologist*, New Series, XC/3 (September 1988), 684-86.

Nekvapil, Jiří, "Language Biographies and the Analysis of Language Situations: On the Life of the German Community in the Czech Republic", *International Journal of the Sociology of Language*, CLXII (2003), 63-83.

Neubert, Isolde, "Searching for Intercultural Communication: Emine Sevgi Özdamar – A Turkish Woman Writer in Germany", in *Postwar Women's Writing in German: Feminist Critical Approaches*, ed. Chris Weedon, New York and Oxford: Berghahn Books, 1997, 153-68.

Nilsen, Don, "Bilingual and Bidialectical Language Play", *Rocky Mountain Review of Language and Literature*, XXXV/2 (1981), 128-37.

Ong, Walter J., *Orality and Literacy: The Technologizing of the World*, London and New York: Routledge, 1996.

Outram, Dorinda, *The Enlightenment*, Cambridge: Cambridge University Press, 2005.

Owen, Ursula, "Apprenticeship in Assimilation", *Index on Censorship*, XXXI/3 (2002), 179-82.

Ozil, Şeyda, "Einige Bemerkungen über den Roman, *Das Leben ist eine Karawanserei* von Emine Sevgi Özdamar", *Diyalog*, I (1994), 125-31.

Pavlenko, Aneta, *Emotions and Multilingualism*, Cambridge: Cambridge University Press, 2005.

—, "Language Learning Memoirs as a Gendered Genre", *Applied Linguistics*, XX/2 (June 2001), 213-40.

—, "The Making of an American: Negotiation of Identities at the Turn of the Twentieth Century", in *Negotiation of Identities in Multilingual Contexts*, eds Aneta Pavlenko and Adrian Blackledge, Clevedon: Multilingual Matters, 2004, 34-67.

—, "New Approaches to Concepts in Bilingual Memory", *Bilingualism: Language and Cognition*, III/1 (September 2000), 1-4.

—, "Second Language Acquisition by Adults: Testimonies of Bilingual Writers", *Issues in Applied Linguistics*, IX/1 (1998), 3-19.

— and Adrian Blackledge, *Negotiation of Identities in Multilingual Contexts*, Clevedon: Multilingual Matters, 2004.

Pennycook, Alastair, "'The Rotation Gets Thick: The Constraints Get Thin': Creativity, Recontextualisation, and Difference", *Applied Linguistics*, XXVIII/4 (December 2007), 579-96.

Phipps, Alison, *Learning the Arts of Linguistic Survival*, Clevedon: Channel View Publications, 2007.

— and Mike Gonzalez, *Modern Languages: Learning and Teaching in an Intercultural Field*, London: SAGE, 2004.

Piaget, Jean, *Language and Thought of the Child*, London: Routledge, 1959.

Pinker, Steven, *How the Mind Works*, New York and London: W.W. Norton, 1997.

Ramsdell, Lea, "Language and Identity Politics: The Linguistic Autobiographies of Latinos in the United States", *Journal of Modern Literature*, XXVIII/1 (Autumn 2004), 166-76.

Ramsey-Kurz, Helga, *The Non-Literate Other: Readings of Illiteracy in Twentieth-Century Novels in English*, Amsterdam: Rodopi, 2007.

Rankin, Walter, "Subverting Literary Allusions in Eliot and Özdamar", *Comparative Literature and Culture: A WWWeb Journal*, VIII/3 (2006): http://docs.lib.purdue.edu/clcweb/vol8/iss 3/6.

Redfern, Walter, *Puns*, Oxford: Basil Blackwell, 1984.

Reynolds, Bryan, "Criminal Cant: Linguistic Innovation and Cultural Dissidence in Early Modern England", *LIT: Literature Interpretation Theory*, IX/4 (1999), 369-95.

Richards, Ivor A., *Practical Criticism*, London: Routledge and Kegan Paul, 1966.

Rivkin, Julie and Michael Ryan, eds, *Literary Theory: An Anthology*, Malden, MA, and Oxford: Blackwell, 2004.

Robbins, Robin, ed., *The Complete Poems of John Donne*, Harlow: Pearson, 2010.

Robins, Robert H., *A Short History of Linguistics*, London: Longman, 1997.

Roudiez, Leon S., "Introduction", in *Revolution in Poetic Language* by Julia Kristeva, New York: Columbia University Press, 1974.

Sanders, I., "An Obsession with Words", *The Nation*, CCXLVIII/23 (12 June 1989), 821-22.

Sass, Louis, "'Negative Symptoms', Commensense, and Cultural Disembedding in the Modern Age", in *Schizophrenia, Culture and Subjectivity: The Edge of Experience*, eds Janis H. Jenkins and

Robert Barrett, Cambridge: Cambridge University Press, 2004, 303-25.

Saul, Nicholas, Daniel Steuer, Frank Möbus and Birgit Illner, eds, *Schwellen: Germanistische Erkundungen einer Metapher*, Würzburg: Königshausen and Neumann, 1999.

Saussure, Ferdinand de, *Cours de Linguistique Générale* (1916), Paris: Payot, 2005.

Schäffner, Christina, "Metaphor and Translation: Some Implications of a Cognitive Approach", *Journal of Pragmatics*, XXXVI/7 (July 2004), 1253-69.

Schestokat, Karin, "Bemerkungen zur Hybridität und zum Sprachgebrauch in Ausgewählten Texten von May Ayim und Yoko Tawada", *Glossen*, VIII (1999): http://dickinson.edu/glossen/heft8/schestokat.html.

Schmidt, James, "What Enlightenment Was: How Moses Mendelssohn and Immanuel Kant Answered the *Berlinische Monatsschrift*", *Journal of the History of Philosophy*, XXX/1 (January 1992), 77-101.

Schumann, Andreas, "Sprachspiel und Individualität: Neue Tendenzen einer Literatur der Migration", in *Literatur als Spiel: Evolutionsbiologische, Ästhetische und Pädagogische Konzepte*, eds Thomas Anz and Heinrich Kaulen, Berlin: Walter de Gruyter, 2009.

Searle, John R., *The Construction of Social Reality*, London: Penguin, 1995.

Sebeok, Thomas A., ed., *Style in Language*, Cambridge, MA: MIT Press, 1971.

Selinker, Larry, "Interlanguage", *International Review of Applied Linguistics in Language Teaching*, X/3 (1972), 209-31.

Seyhan, Azade, *Writing Outside the Nation*, Princeton, NJ and Oxford: Princeton University Press, 2001.

Shakespeare, William, *Romeo and Juliet*" (1595-96), in *The Portable Shakespeare*, New York: Penguin, 1977, 211-311.

Shklovsky, Viktor, "Art as Technique", in *Literary Theory: An Anthology*, eds Julie Rivkin and Michael Ryan, Malden, MA and Oxford: Blackwell, 2004, 15-21.

Sim, Stuart, "Deconstructing the Pun", *British Journal of Aesthetics*, XXVII/4 (Autumn 1987), 326-34.

Smith, Lee and Raymond Klein, "Evidence for Semantic Satiation: Repeating a Category Slows Subsequent Semantic Processing", *Journal of Experimental Psychology*, XVI/5 (September 1990), 852-61.
Sokel, Walter H., "The Love Affair with the Mother Tongue: On the Relation between Autobiography and Novel in Elias Canetti", *Germanic Review*, LXXVIII/1 (Winter 2003), 39-48.
Song, Min Hyoung, "A Diasporic Future? *Native Speaker* and Historical Trauma", *LIT: Literature Interpretation Theory*, XXII/1 (2001), 79-96.
Sperber, Daniel and Deirdre Wilson, "Pragmatics", in *Oxford Handbook of Contemporary Philosophy*, eds Frank Jackson and Michael Smith, Oxford: Oxford University Press, 2005.
Steinman, Linda, *Language Learner Narratives: Bridges to SLA Literature and SLA Pedagogy*, University of Toronto, 2004 (unpublished doctoral dissertation).
Stolz, Benjamin, I.R. Titunik and Lubomír Doležel, eds, *Language and Literary Theory: In Honor of Ladislav Matejka*, Ann Arbor: University of Michigan Press, 1984f.
Sundquist, John, "The Mapping Problem and Missing Surface Inflection in Turkish-German Interlanguage", *Proceedings of the 7th Generative Approaches to Second Language Acquisition Conference* (GASLA 2004), ed. Laurent Dekydtspotter *et al.*, Somerville, MA: Cascadilla Proceedings Project, 2005, 238-50: http://www.lingref.com/cpp/gasla/7/paper1170.pdf.
Swift, Jonathan, *Gulliver's Travels*, London: Penguin, 2001.
Taberner, Stuart and Frank Finlay, eds, *Recasting German Identity: Culture, Politics, and Literature in the Berlin Republic*, Rochester, NY: Camden House, 2002.
Thompson, John B., "Translator's Introduction", in Pierre Bourdieu, *Language and Symbolic Power: The Economics of Linguistic Exchanges*, Cambridge: Polity, 1991.
Thomson, Anne, *Critical Reasoning: A Practical Introduction*, London: Routledge, 2002.
Ting-Toomey, Stella, "An Intercultural Journey: The Four Seasons", in *Working at the Interface of Cultures: Eighteen Lives in Social Science*, ed. Michael Bond, London and New York: Routledge, 1997, 202-15.

Todorov, Tzvetan, "Dialogisme et Schizophrénie", in *Language and Literary Theory: In Honor of Ladislav Matejka*, eds Benjamin Stolz, I.R. Titunik and Lubomír Doležel, Ann Arbor: University of Michigan Press, 1984, 565-75.
Tomashevsky, Boris, "Literary Genres", *Russian Poetics in Translation*, V, 1978, 52-93.
Turner, Mark, *The Literary Mind: The Origins of Thought and Language*, New York and Oxford: Oxford University Press, 1998.
Underhill, James, *Creating Worldviews: Metaphor, Ideology and Language*, Edinburgh: Edinburgh University Press, 2011.
Van Dijk, Teun, "Critical Discourse Studies: A Sociocognitive Approach", in *Methods of Critical Discourse Analysis*, eds Ruth Wodak and Michael Meyer, London: SAGE Publications, 2009, 62-86.
Veteto-Conrad, Marilya, *Finding a Voice: Identity and the Works of German-Language Turkish Writers in the Federal Republic of Germany to 1990*, New York: Peter Lang, 1996.
—, "German Minority Literature: Tongues Set Free and Pointed Tongues", *The International Fiction Review*, XXVIII/1 and 2 (2001), 81-82: http://journals.hil.unb.ca/index.php/IFR/article/view/7693/8750
Vygotsky, Lev, *Thought and Language* (1934), Cambridge, MA, and London: MIT Press, 1986.
Wales, Katie, "In Memory of Roger Fowler (1938-99)", *Language and Literature*, IX/1 (February 2000), 5-6.
Wardhaugh, Ronald, *An Introduction to Sociolinguistics*, Oxford: Blackwell, 1998.
Watzinger-Tharp, Johanna, "Turkish-German Language: An Innovative Style of Communication and its Implications for Citizenship and Identity", *Journal of Muslim and Minority Affairs*, XXIV/2 (October 2004), 285-94.
Wellek, René and Austin Warren, *Theory of Literature* (1949), Harmondsworth: Penguin Books, 1978.
Wierschke, Annette, "Auf den Schnittstellen Kultureller Grenzen Tanzend: Aysel Özakin und Emine Sevgi Özdamar", in *Denn du Tanzt auf einem Seil: Positionen Deutschsprachiger MigrantInnenliteratur*, eds Sabine Fischer and Moray McGowan, Tübingen: Stauffenburg, 1997, 179-94.

Wierschke, Anette, *Schreiben als Selbstbehauptung: Kulturkonflikt und Identität in den Werken von Aysel Özakin, Alev Tekinay und Emine Sevgi Özdamar, mit Interviews*, Frankfurt am Main: IKO, 1996.

Wierzbicka, Anna, *Understanding Cultures through Their Key Words: English, Russian, Polish, German and Japanese*, Oxford: Oxford University Press, 1997.

—, "In Defense of 'Culture'", *Theory and Psychology*, XV/4 (August 2005), 575-97.

—, "The Double Life of a Bilingual: A Cross-cultural Perspective", in *Working at the Interface of Cultures: Eighteen Lives in Social Science*, ed. Michael Bond, London and New York: Routledge, 1997, 108-19.

—, "Emotions across Cultures: Similarities and Differences", *American Anthropologist*, New Series, XC/4 (December 1988), 982-83.

—, "Human Emotions: Universal or Culture-Specific?" *American Anthropologist*, New Series, LXXXVIII/3 (September 1986), 584-94.

—, "Semantic Primitives: A Rejoinder to Murray and Button", *American Anthropologist*, New Series, XC/3 (September 1988), 686-89.

Wietholter, Waltraud, "Sprechen-Lesen-Schreiben. Zur Funktion von Sprache und Schrift in Canettis Autobiographie", *Deutsche Vierteljahrsschrift für Literaturwissenschaft und Geistesgeschichte*, LXIV/1 (March 1990), 149-71.

Wittgenstein, Ludwig, *Tractatus Logico-Philosophicus/Logisch-philosophische Abhandlung*, Frankfurt am Main: Suhrkamp, 2003.

Wodak, Ruth and Michael Meyer, eds, *Methods of Critical Discourse Analysis*, London: SAGE Publications, 2009.

Zhengdao Ye, Veronica, "'La Double Vie de Veronica': Reflections on My Life as a Chinese Migrant in Australia", *Mots Pluriels*, XXIII (March 2003): http://www.arts.uwa.edu.au/MotsPluriels/MP2303vzy.html

INDEX

Ackermann, Irmgard, 45
actualisace (*see* foregrounding)
Adelson, Leslie: Özdamar, 142, 157; touching tales, 15; *The Turkish Turn*, 15, 139 n.1;
Adorno, Theodor, *Erziehung zur Mündigkeit*, 121
Alexakis, Vassilis, 47; *Paris-Athènes*, 52, 54, 97, 190-91, 202, 206
alienation, 148, 182, 203; "alienation effect", 227 n.38; in schizophrenia, 237; of language, 238
alphabetamorphosis, 147
alterity, 15 (*see also* otherness)
Alvarez, Julia, 45; *Something to Declare*, 8-9, 45, 194
amae, 79
ambiguity, 83, 168, 173, 207; in puns, 235; tolerance for, 21
Andrews, Walter, *Poetry's Voice, Society's Song*, 168, 175-78
anthropocentrism, 76, 148
Appel, René, 79
applied linguistics, 65-66

Arabic, 19, 41; in Özdamar, 20, 141-43, 145-48, 153-54, 179, 181-82, 208
Atatürk, 141
Aufklärung (*see* Enlightenment)
Ausländer, Rosa, 25 n.4
author intention, 108
authority, 11, 32, 43 n.51, 118, 127, 142, 203, 222, 248; claim to, 250; in Ottoman Divan poetry, 177; in Özdamar, 144-45, 148, 150-54; undermining of, 240
autobiography, 24; cross-cultural, 13, 26, 29-30, 57, 255; immigrant, 16
auto-ethnography, 28
Aytaç, Gürsel, 134

baby talk, 121, 234
Bakhtin, Mikhail, "Discourse in the Novel", 185
Banciu, Carmen-Francesca, *Berlin ist mein Paris*, 116
Barnard, Frederick, 113
Barthes, Roland, "Death of the Author", 108
Beaugrande, Robert-Alain de, 93 n.26, 171

Beckett, Samuel, 25 n.4
Begemann, Christian, 139
Belfellah, Abdellatif, 111
Benson, Phil, 25-27
Berger, Peter, *The Social Construction of Reality*, 74-77
Besemeres, Mary, 24, 29, 30-35, 42; identity, 124
Bildungsroman, 33, 135-37; classification principle, 136-37; transformation principle, 136
bilingualism, 79-80, 83 n.55
binary oppositions, 142, 145
biographie langagière (*see* language biography)
Blanchot, Maurice, 51
Boa, Elizabeth, 139 n.1
body language, 153, 199
body, the, 68, 75; and language, 228, 242-44; metaphors of, 184, 191, 197-98, 200, 204 n.60; in Özdamar, 145, 148, 151-54, 167, 176
Bordwell, David, 38 n.44
Boucher, Jill, 114-16
boundaries, 51, 66, 239 n.71, 242, 247
Bourdieu, Pierre, 127-28; habitus, 67; linguistic capital, 19, 21, 33, 59, 62, 64, 126-29, 196, 205-206, 240, 248-50; symbolic power, 101, 122, 126-29, 146, 240, 244-45; *Language and Symbolic Power*, 111, 126-27

Brandt, Bettina, 139 n.1
Brooke-Rose, Christine, *Between*, 38
Brooks, Cleanth, 91
Bruner, Jerome, 124
Burrows, John, 102, 103 n.44
Butler, Michael, 227 n.38
Buxton, David, 105
Byram, Michael, 60-64

Canetti, Elias, *Die Gerettete Zunge*, 38, 48-49
canon, 47
cant, 239
capital: cultural, 142; linguistic (*see* Bourdieu, Pierre); social, 21, 184, 188; symbolic, 21, 184
Carruthers, Peter, 114-16
Catherine the Great, 25
censorship, 128
Chamoiseau, Patrick, *Une Enfance Créole*, 9, 11, 42
Chandler, Daniel, 50, 99, 100-105
Chinese culture, 15, 35-37
chirographic culture, 8-11
Chomsky, Noam, 93
Christianity, 81, 146
Çirak, Zehra, *Leibesübungen*, 174 n.21
code-switching, 132, 145, 169
codes, 70-71, 128, 231 n.50, 234-35; social, 67-68
cohesion, 95-98, 168
collectivism, 14, 124; collectivity, 66-68, 95 n.32
collocation, 97-98
colonialism, 42-44

competence: intercultural, 27, 62-63; linguistic, 2, 4, 19-21, 60-64, 111, 114, 115, 118, 120-23, 125-32, 141-42, 144, 147, 154, 162, 164, 205, 233, 240, 248-50
concept-association model (*see* shared-concept model)
conceptual framework, 3, 19, 70, 79, 81-82, 107, 182, 188, 213, 254
concordance programme, 102
concrete poetry, 133
condensation (*see* dreams)
conjunction, 96, 98, 158, 172; additive, 98; adversative, 98; causal, 99
Conrad, Joseph, 25 n.4
consciousness, 67, 75, 105, 107, 124; postmodern, 4-5
constitution thesis, 114, 116
constructivism, 74, 76
context of production, 160; of reception, 47, 254
corpus linguistics, 102
Council of Europe, 27
creole, 9; creolization, 169
Critical Discourse Analysis (CDA), 61-62, 93 n.29, 94
critical incidents, 35; reasoning, 7, 113-14, 120, 123, 127
critic, the, 18, 51, 85, 90, 92, 99, 104, 106-109
cultural homogeneity, 141; relativism, 7 n.13
Curtiss, Susan, 49 n.76

Darwinist perspective, 81

Davies, Alan, 60
De Groot, Annette, 83 n.54
deconstruction, 137, 236, 240
defamiliarization, 36, 89, 134, 140-41, 158, 169, 182, 203, 212, 239
Déguignet, Jean-Marie, 44
Derrida, Jacques; **Works:** *Le Monolinguisme de l'Autre*, 38, 42-43; "The Law of Genre", 17, 23, 30 n.24, 38, 51; "Structure, Sign and Play/*La Structure, Le Signe et le Jeu*", 3, 6
determinism: cultural, 32; linguistic, 32
Deutsches Rechtswörterbuch, 119
diachronic analysis, 87, 100
dialogue, 32-33, 56, 82, 97, 101, 102, 131, 152, 171, 182, 210, 256
difference, 4, 5, 15, 16, 61, 63, 100, 106, 124, 154, 185, 203, 239
discursive system, 6
disfluency phenomena, 173
displacement, 4-6 (*see also* dreams)
Donne, John, "The Sun Rising", 149-50
doppelte Distanz (*see* Hein-Khatib)
Dorfman, Ariel, *Heading South, Looking North*, 48, 189-91, 206
dreams, 131; condensation, 131; displacement, 131
Dressler, Wolfgang, 171

Durkheim, Emile, 87
Dijk, Teun van, 62, 95 n.32
Dykman, Elizabeth, "The Vagabond Years", 53, 192

Eagleton, Terry, 85, 89, 91, 99 n.40, 228
early experienced language, 64, 83, 123, 124, 169, 185, 187, 193, 206
ego, 66, 219
egocentric logic, 131, 133
Eikhenbaum, Boris, 85
ellipsis, 96, 97, 172
Enlightenment, the, 1-2, 4, 17, 112-13, 211, 236, 247, 250
Entfremdung (*see* alienation)
entrapment, 21, 185, 197, 199, 203, 205-206
epistemology, 4, 73
Ernaux, Annie, *La Place*, 49
ethnocentrism, 34, 35, 37, 81
ethnographic data, 26, 28
European Language Portfolio, 27
Everett, Daniel, *Don't Sleep There Are Snakes*, 81-82
exile, 4, 23, 200-202, 209
exoticization, 47

Fairclough, Norman, 61-62
Feminist theorists, 100, 143, 146
feral children, 124
first experienced language, 42
foregrounding, 89-90, 213
foreign language pedagogy, 26, 59, 66
Foreigner Talk, 121

formal logic, 9
Forster, Leonard, 132-33
Fowler, Roger, 18, 36, 69, 86, 90 n.18, 92-95, 97, 98, 101-102, 104-105
Fox, Frampton, 82 n.53
Francis, Wendy, 83 n.55
French novel, 136; speakers, 61; structuralism, 86, 88
Freud, Sigmund, 3, 131; *Der Witz und seine Beziehung zum Unbewussten/Jokes and their Relation to the Unconscious*, 232-34
Fritz, Daniela, 25-26
Fuling, 35, 37

Gastarbeiter, 47, 48 n.69; *Gastarbeiterliteratur*, 47-48
gazel, 175,
genealogies, 8
Genette, Gérard, 29-30 n.24
Genie, 49 n.76
genre, 17, 23-58, 222
Goethe, Johann Wolfgang von, *Wilhelm Meisters Lehrjahre*, 135-36, 138
Goldsworthy, Vesna, 131 n.39
grammaticality, 60-61, 64, 128
grand narratives, 5-6
Greeks, 9, 15
Grice, Paul, 93
Grimm brothers, 118-19
Grosjean, François, 80 n.47, 83-84 n.55

habitual perception, 89; habitualization, 89

habitus (*see* Bourdieu, Pierre)
Haines, Brigid, 19, 170, 172
Halliday, M.A.K., 18, 73-75, 92, 96-98
Handke, Peter, *Kaspar*, 25, 123
Hasan, Ruquaiya, 96, 98
Hegi, Ursula, 25 n.4
Heidegger, Martin, 3
Hein-Khatib, Simone, 238-39; *doppelte Distanz*/double distance, 238
Helias, Pierre-Jakez, *Le Cheval d'Orgueil*, 44
Hessler, Peter, *River Town*, 32, 33, 35-37
Hockey, Susan, 102-103
Hodge, Robert, 70-75, 93 n.29
Hoffman, Eva, *Lost in Translation*, 4, 25 n.4, 26 n.9, 28, 30, 31, 38, 40, 45, 53, 117, 187, 194, 196, 199, 202, 229, 238
humour, 213 n.4, 214, 219, 236
Huston, Nancy, *Nord Perdu*, 38, 47, 53, 187, 193, 198, 200-202, 208-10, 229
hybridity, 140
hyperlinking, 52, 57; hyper-literariness, 182; *Hypermündigkeit*, 21, 123; hyper-textuality, 51

identity: crisis of, 184, 241; cultural, 16, 61, 145, 148; language and, 15, 185; linguistic, 16, 61; national, 61, 142, 157

ideological critique, 95
ideology, 4, 105, 231 n.48
idiolect, 131
immigration, 47
implicature, 93
Indians, 15
individual, 12-13, 16, 61, 62, 66, 67-68, 74, 75, 78, 82, 87, 94, 95 n.32, 113, 123-28, 139, 204, 247, 254; individualism, 227 n.38; individuality, 129, 133, 137
infantilization, 21, 185, 189, 194, 196, 205, 206, 208, 250
integration: of people, 32, 40; of languages/cultures, 182, 211
cultural communication, 35, 61-62; (communicative) competence (*see* competence); mediator, 107; speaker, 59-64; training, 82
interlanguage, 169; interlingual, 169, 171; interscription, 106-109, 250, 254; interscriptor, 107-108; intertextuality, 51, 109
intracultural communication, 61
irony, 234, 236

Jakobson, Roman, 85, 88-90, 133, 241
Jandl, Ernst, 212-13, 216, 218 n.19, 227 n.38
Japanese, 31, 45, 46, 79, 194, 196, 199
jargon, 101

Johns Hopkins' Conference, 3
Johnson, Mark, 20, 78, 183, 185-86, 188, 214, 244, 253
Jones, Randall, 162
Joyce, James, 51 n.77, 228, 233

Kafka, Franz, 25, 197
Kaminer, Wladimir, 46
Kant, Immanuel, 1-2, 4, 111-13, 117-18, 120, 127, 236, 247-48
Kaplan, Alice, 17, 23-24, 26 n.9, 28-33, 39-41, 45
Kellman, Steven, 25, 41, 251, 253
Kemal, Mustafa (*see* Atatürk)
Kinast, Eva, 82 n.52
Kluge, Friedrich, 118
Konuk, Kader, 140 n.3, 144-145
Koranic texts, 143, 144
Kramsch, Claire, 26 n.6, 38, 40, 41, 60, 61, 65-68
Kress, Gunther, 18, 70-75, 93 n.29
Kristeva, Julia, the semiotic, 68, 211, 212 n.3, 219, 228-29, 238, 241, 244, 250; the symbolic, 211, 212 n.3, 241, 244
Kumar, Anant, 122 n.27

Labov, William, 93, 129
Ladino, 48
Lakoff, George, 20, 21 n.29, 78, 183, 185-86, 188, 214, 244, 253

language biography, 17, 24, 27, 28
language learner narratives, 2-4, 7-9, 13-14, 16-20, 22, 24, 28, 40, 42, 48-50, 52, 54, 56-57, 59, 63, 83, 94, 183-84, 187-89, 204-208, 229, 238-39, 250-53, 256; authors of, 14, 63, 82, 129, 132, 184, 187, 211, 248; definition of, 50-57 70-71, 98, 134, 137; sources of, 40-50; language learning, 54, 56, 162, 250, 253; affective aspects, 25, 65, 207; process of, 25, 26-27, 41, 57, 59; representation of, 2-3, 13, 23, 25-26, 28-29, 42, 50, 52, 65, 69, 84, 184, 188, 200, 207, 253, 255
language play, 21, 131, 207, 211-245, 249-50
languaging, 28 n.15, 65
langue, 87-88, 100
Larsson, Hans, 131
later experienced language, 2 n.3, 13, 45, 50, 53, 64, 70, 83, 169, 185, 187, 188, 228
Latin script, 141
Law of Islam, 143
Lawson, Richard, 38 n.43
learner diaries, 25, 31
learning histories, 26-27
Lee, Chang-Rae, *Native Speaker*, 7-8, 192, 202-203
legal responsibility, 118-19
Lemke, Jay, 18, 76-77, 204
Lesser, Wendy, 41-42

Lessing, Gotthold Ephraim, 119
Lévi-Strauss, Claude, 8, 71, 88
lexical cohesion, 96-98; reiteration, 97-98
Li, Houxiang, 68
life histories, 28; narratives, 28
Lind, Jakov, 230-31
linguacentrism, 76
linguistic capital (*see* Bourdieu)
Linguistic Criticism, 18, 69, 86, 92-93, 95, 99, 101, 104 n.47
linguistic performance, 59, 64; relativity hypothesis, 115-16; sign, 3, 5, 12, 72, 79, 88, 104, 107, 123, 170, 213, 219 n.20, 241; sign system, 104
Lippman, Walter, 68 n.19
literacy, 8 n.16, 9, 10, 14, 15, 251
literariness, 50, 89, 90 n.18, 134, 135, 171
literary criticism, 50, 86, 92, 99 n.40, 103, 104; linguistics, 69
literaturnost (*see* literariness)
Littler, Margaret, 19, 133 n.42, 139 n.1, 142-43, 145, 147-48, 170, 172
Liverani, Mary Rose, 49
Lodge, David, 92 n.25
logocentrism, 7, 235
Luckmann, Thomas, 74-76, 77 n.41
Luria, Alexander Romanovich, 10, 14

Luther, Martin, 119
Lyotard, Jean-François, 5, 8

Macey, David, 3, 86, 88, 124 n.30
McGowan, Moray, 139 n.1, 48 n.69
Makine, Andreï, 47
Mannheim, Karl, 135
Matthes, Frauke, 139 n.1
maturity, 111, 135-36, 189
meaning-making, 5, 13, 20, 71, 108
Meister Eckhart, 146,
Meizoz, Jérôme, 43-44
melting-pot, 45
memoir: language (learning) memoir, 17, 23-58, 65, 187; of language immersion, 30-31, 33; of language migration, 30-33
metalinguistic reflection, 52-53
Metamündigkeit, 21-22, 63 n.10, 68, 135, 211-12, 242, 244-45, 250, 254
metaphor, 13, 20-21, 54, 62, 65, 73, 74, 78, 84, 91, 111, 120, 132, 183-210, 212-16, 221, 229, 234-35, 240, 242, 244, 249, 250 n.1, 253, 254; in Özdamar, 145, 148, 151, 154, 157 n.2, 174, 175
metaphysics, 6, 73
migrants, 5, 15, 16, 29, 47, 121, 125, 139, 140-41, 144, 154, 169, 182, 203, 221, 233, 237, 242, 249, 251; migrant literature, 47

Migrantenliteratur (*see* migrant literature)
Milz, Sabine, 140 n.2
mimetic plane, 72-73
modernity, 137-38
monolingual, 5, 32
Moretti, Franco, 135-37
Mori, Kyoko, *Polite Lies*, 45
Morley, John David, 52, 199
morpheme, 94; morphology, 94, 105
Mukařovsky, Jan, 89-90; foregrounding (*see* foregrounding)
Mund, der, 120, 160, 175,
Mund, die, 118
Mündel, 21, 118
Mündigkeit, 1-7, 17, 19-22, 59-62, 64, 69, 71, 84, 106, 111-37, 247-50, 254-56; and *Metamündigkeit*, 211, 244-45; metaphors of, 183-84, 187-89, 205-207; in *Mutter Zunge*, 139, 141-43, 148
Mündlein, das, 118
Mündligkeit, 21
Mura, David, 46
mysticism, 76, 142, 144 n.13, 145, 146, 177, 182
myth, 8, 60, 63, 100, 105

Nabokov, Vladmir, 41
nationhood, 15-16
native competence, 60; speaker, 56, 59-61, 63-64, 161, 224 n.28, 243
Nemiroff, Greta Hoffman, "No Language to Die in", 200

New Criticism, 86, 91
newcoming speaker, 27, 160-61, 206, 208, 228, 238, 240
Nietzsche, Friedrich, 3
non-literate, 10, 251
non-native speaker, 59-61, 63 n.10, 64, 206
nonsense, 68, 234, 236, 237, 244
Nunan, David, 25-27

Ogulnick, Karen, 196, 199; **Works:** *Language Crossings*, 28, 31, 200; *Onna Rashiku*, 31, 45-46, 194, 196, 199
Ong, Walter J., 8-10, 12, 15
ostranenie (*see* defamiliarization)
Other, the, 3, 37, 43 n.51, 67, 95 n.32, 148
otherness, 15, 17, 61, 147, 148, 150
Ottoman Divan poetry, 141, 160, 168, 175-77, 182
Ottoman literature (*see* Ottoman Divan poetry)
Özdamar, Emine Sevgi, 47-48; *Mutter Zunge*, 139-156, 157-182; cohesion, 160-61; imagery, 174-81; linguistic analysis, 157-182; repetition, 166-68, 182; use of tenses, 164-66; verb frequency, 163-64

parataxis, 98
parody, 37, 234
parole, 87, 88, 100

patriarchalism, 100, 106, 143, 146
Pavlenko, Aneta, 3 n.4, 15 n.27, 16, 26, 29, 30 n.25, 40, 41, 78-79
Phipps, Alison, 28 n.15, 65
phonology, 94, 95, 105
phrasal repetends, 102
Piaget, Jean, 131-32, 134
pidginization, 169
Pinker, Steven, 78
Pirahã tribe, 81-82
Platen, 119
pluriculturalism, 27; plurilingualism, 27
poetic function, 90, 133; language, 89-90, 133, 241; style, 141, 180
postmodernism, 2, 4-8, 17, 29 n.21, 40, 138; identity, 238, 243; and language play, 236, 238
poststructuralism, 3-4
power, 23, 59, 95 n.32, 118 n.21, 244; in *Mutter Zunge*, 147, 151, 152, 177; symbolic (*see* Bourdieu)
power relations, 61, 64, 94, 95 n.32, 100, 106, 129, 141, 190, 194, 205, 206, 240, 247-49
powerlessness, 61, 62, 179, 193 n.26, 196
Practical Criticism, 86, 90-91
pragmatics, 88, 93, 94
pre-verbal, 231
progression, 95
proposition, 72-74, 95, 216, 219 n.20

prosody, 105
puns, 131, 215, 228, 231-32, 234-36, 240

qualitative analysis, 40

Ramsey-Kurz, Helga, 251
Ramuz, Charles-Ferdinand, 43
Ransom, John Crowe, 91
rational communication, 133, 173 n.19
rationality, 3, 117, 130, 248
reality, 2, 11, 12-13, 16, 18, 30 n.24, 69, 71-78, 80, 89, 114, 185-87, 189, 211, 213, 235, 238, 247, 249, 255
reason, 7, 19, 81, 112-17, 119-20, 122, 124, 125, 127-30, 133, 134, 211, 232, 239, 244, 247, 248; and emotion, 142, 144, ; loss of, 19, 151-52, 153-54, 209 n.61, 236; in *Mutter Zunge*, 139, 142, 148, 151
reference, 96; anaphoric, 96; cataphoric, 96; endophoric, 96; exophoric, 96
regional varieties, 49, 87
regionalisms, 43
requirement thesis, 114-15
resocialization, 21, 138
Reynolds, Brian, 239
rhetoric, 15, 94; devices, 91, 234
Richards, I.A., 86, 90-91
Rilke, Rainer Maria, 132
Robins, Robert, 87
Rock, Zé Do, 212, 221-27, 243

Rodriguez, Richard, *Hunger of Memory*, 25 n.4, 26 n.9, 38, 48, 191-92
rose, the, 19, 69, 77 n.41, 141, 142, 144-45, 151, 160, 175-76, 178, 180
Rousseau, Jean-Jacques, 43
Russian Formalism, 85, 88; novels, 135

Said, Edward, 40-41
Sante, Luc, 189
Sartre, Jean-Paul, 49
Sass, Louis, 237
Saussure, Ferdinand de, 85-88, 100, 235
savoirs, 62-63
schizophrenic discourse, 233, 236-38
Schumann, Andreas, 224 n.28
scientificity, 101
Searle, John, 77 n.41, 255
Second Language Acquisition (SLA), 23, 24, 28, 29, 31, 65, 66
selfhood, 15, 62, 66, 67, 124, 125, 145, 148, 154, 184, 189
Selinker, Larry, 169 n.10
semantic satiation, 161; semantics, 94
semiosic plane, 72; semiosis, 21, 70, 73, 241, 244; semiotic, the (*see* Kristeva, Julia); semiotic criticism, 99, 101
Seneca, 25 n.4
sentence, the, 92-94, 96

separate-concept model, 83 n.55
Sercu, Lies, 63
Seyhan, Azade, 4-5, 14-15
Shakespeare, William, 69, 77 n.41, 203, 204; **Works:** *As You Like It*, 203; *Romeo and Juliet*, 69, 77 n.41
Shammas, Anton, 25 n.4
shared-concept model, 83 n.55
Sheldon, Steve, 81
Shklovsky, Victor, 86, 89, 134
signified, 21, 72, 105, 123, 147, 213, 216, 218, 219, 221; transcendental, 3, 247-48; signifier, 17, 19, 21, 52, 54, 57, 68, 71, 72, 105, 147, 174, 182, 216, 218, 219, 221
Sim, Stuart, 231 n.50, 234, 235, 240
social control, 76; role, 125, 231; semiotics, 18, 69-72, 75, 99, 105
sociolinguistics, 87, 93-94, 251; psychology, 94
Sokel, Walter, 38 n.43
Specific Language Impairment, 115
Sperber, Dan, 93
Sprachbiographie (*see* language biography)
Sprachkrise, 238
Stavans, Ilan, *On Borrowed Words*, 45, 199
Stefan, Verena, "Here's Your Change 'N Enjoy the Show", 194, 195, 198
Steiner, George, 25 n.4, 41

Index

Steinman, Linda, 28, 39
stereotypes, 34, 68 n.19, 89
structuralism (*see* French structuralism)
stylistics, 86, 92; computational, 103 n.44
subject, 4, 13, 38, 51, 65-67, 109, 184, 204, 212 n.3, 218, 219 n.20, 238, 242, 244; construction of, 120, 122-24, 130
subjective response, 104; subjectivity, 4, 16, 40, 66, 68, 73
substitution, 96, 97, 166, 169
Swift, Jonathan, *Gulliver's Travels*, 36
syllogism, 10
symbolic [1], 68; symbolic [2], 68; ordering, 69, 241-43; power (*see* Bourdieu, Pierre); system, 143; symbolic, the (*see* Kristeva, Julia)
synchronic analysis, 87
synonyms, 98
syntagmatic relations, 88
syntax, 94, 105, 168, 172, 173, 234

Tate, Allen, 91
Tawada, Yoko, 38, 46, 117, 212-21, 227, 233, 243, 250
testimonios, 28
text linguistics, 93, 94, 171 n.14
textual analysis, 10, 18, 58, 85, 99; textuality, 51, 171

thematic analysis, 103; thematization, 95
third geography, 14-15
Third Space, the, 140
Thomson, Anne, 113-14, 117
Todorov, Tzvetan, 237, 242, 243
Tomashevsky, Boris, 38 n.44
Töpffer, Rodolphe, 43
transcendental signified (*see* signified)
translingualism, 25, 48, 49, 78, 251, 254
travel writing, 24, 30, 32, 33, 35, 222
truth, 2-4, 7-14, 66, 73, 74, 81, 211, 232, 236, 238, 249, 250, 255; absolute, 7-11, 211; contingent, 9; instability of, 10; universal, 2, 7, 255
Tschirner, Erwin, 162-63
Turnbull, Sarah, *Almost French*, 32-35, 45
Turner, Mark, 254
Tynanov, Yury, 86

Ultradeutsch, 222, 225
unio mystica, 146
Unmündigkeit, 111, 112, 119-21, 143-44
unreason, 12, 124, 131, 145, 148, 238-39
Untermündigkeit, 21, 250, 254

Veteto-Conrad, Marilya, 122 n.27
Vico, Giambattista, 185-86
Vormund, 19, 21, 119

Warren, Austin, 91
Warren, Robert Penn, 91
Watson, Richard, *The Philosopher's Demise*, 45, 194, 195
Wellek, René, 91
Whorfian Hypothesis (*see* linguistic relativity hypothesis)
Wierschke, Annette, 139 n.1, 157
Wierzbicka, Anna, 42, 63 n.10, 81 n.48
Wietholter, Waltraud, 38 n.43
Williams Syndrome, 115
Wilson, Deirdre, 93
Wittgenstein, Ludwig, 71, 114-15
Wodak, Ruth, 62
Wolf, Christa, 25-26
word, 10-11, 78-79, 83, 87, 132, 146; formation, 94; frequency, 102; meaning, 94, 212, 215
world view, 185, 231 n.48
written characters, 52, 217, 225

youth, 135-38

Zerklaere, Thomasîn von, *Der Welsche Gast*, 252

www.ingramcontent.com/pod-product-compliance
Lightning Source LLC
Chambersburg PA
CBHW070750020526
44115CB00032B/1611